Robert Bruce Mullin is Associate Professor of Religion at North Carolina State University. Russell E. Richey is Professor of Church History and Associate Dean at Duke University Divinity School.

D0801861

REIMAGINING
DENOMINATIONALISM

RELIGION IN AMERICA SERIES
Harry S. Stout, General Editor

Reimagining Denominationalism

Interpretive Essays

Edited by
ROBERT BRUCE MULLIN
RUSSELL E. RICHEY

New York   Oxford
OXFORD UNIVERSITY PRESS
1994

Oxford University Press

Oxford   New York   Toronto
Delhi   Bombay   Calcutta   Madras   Karachi
Kuala Lumpur   Singapore   Hong Kong   Tokyo
Nairobi   Dar es Salaam   Cape Town
Melbourne   Auckland   Madrid

and associated companies in
Berlin   Ibadan

Library of Congress Cataloging-in-Publication Data
Reimagining denominationalism : interpretive essays /
edited by Robert Bruce Mullin, Russell E. Richey.
p.   cm.—(Religion in America series [Oxford University Press])
Includes bibliographical references.
ISBN 0-19-508778-X
1. Christian sects—United States.
2. United States—Church history.
3. United States—Religion.
I. Mullin, Robert Bruce.
II. Richey, Russell E.   III. Series.
BR515.R39   1994   280'.0973—dc20   93-31858

2 4 6 8 9 7 5 3 1

Printed in the United States of America
on acid-free paper

Acknowledgments

This volume began as a series of conversations, continued as a conference under sponsorship of the Lilly Endowment, and eventuates now as a volume, which we hope in turn will prompt more conversations. Along the way the project has acquired many debts. We extend thanks especially to Craig Dykstra, program director at Lilly for his interest and support; to the Divinity School, Duke University, and Dean Dennis Campbell and the National Humanities Center and Executive Associate Richard R. Schramm, who served as hosts and sponsors for the conference; to the Department of Philosophy and Religion at North Carolina State University, and the Department of Religious Studies at the University of North Carolina–Chapel Hill and the Divinity School for sponsorship; to Grant Wacker, who teamed with us in building the conference; to Ann Rives and Mary Deasey Collins, who handled much of the detail in communications; to Ann Rives for compiling the index and Kelly Jarrett for checking bibliographical references; to many individuals who gave us helpful counsel, including W. Clark Gilpin, E. Brooks Holifield, Daniel W. Howe, George Marsden, Harry Stout, and Peter W. Williams; to the Southeast Colloquium on American Religious Studies (SCARS), for its critique of the collection of essays; and to our families, who gave us time to devote to the project.

Contents

II MODELS, 107

III CASE STUDIES, 199

Contributors

Nancy T. Ammerman, Associate Professor of Sociology of Religion, Candler School of Theology, is the author of *Baptist Battles: Social Change and Religious Conflict in the Southern Baptist Convention.*

Henry Warner Bowden, Professor of Religion, Douglass College (Rutgers University), is the author of *Church History in an Age of Uncertainty: Historiographical Patterns in the United States, 1906–1990.*

Jay P. Dolan, Professor of History, University of Notre Dame, is the author of *The American Catholic Experience: A History from Colonial Times to the Present.*

Will B. Gravely, Professor of Religious Studies, University of Denver, is the author of *Gilbert Haven, Methodist Abolitionist: A Study in Race, Religion and Reform, 1850–1880.*

William R. Hutchison, Charles Warren Professor of Religion in America, Harvard University, is the author of *Errand to the World: American Protestant Thought and Foreign Missions.*

Christa R. Klein, Project Director on Seminary Trusteeship Programs and Consultant on Evaluation of Research in Religion, Lilly Endowment, Inc., is the author of *Politics and Policy: The Genesis and Theology of Social Statements in the Lutheran Church in America.*

Charles H. Long, Professor of the History of Religions, University of California, Santa Barbara, is the author of *Significations: Signs, Symbols, and Images in the Interpretation of Religion.*

Bradley J. Longfield, Assistant Professor of Church History, University of Dubuque Theological Seminary, is the author of *The Presbyterian Controversy: Fundamentalists, Modernists, and Moderates.*

Laurie F. Maffly-Kipp, Assistant Professor of Religious Studies, the University of North Carolina–Chapel Hill, is the author of *Religion and Society in Frontier California.*

James H. Moorhead, Mary McIntosh Bridge Professor of American Church History, Princeton Theological Seminary, is the author of *American Apocalypse: Yankee Protestants and the Civil War, 1860–1869.*

Robert Bruce Mullin, Associate Professor of Religion, North Carolina State University, is the author of *Episcopal Vision/American Reality: High Church Theology and Social Thought in Evangelical America.*

Robert A. Orsi, Professor of Religious Studies, Indiana University, is the author of *The Madonna of 115th Street: Faith and Community in Italian Harlem, 1880–1950.*

Marc Lee Raphael, Sophia and Nathan S. Gumenick Professor of Judaic Studies, The College of William and Mary, is the author of *Profiles in American Judaism: The Reform, Conservative, Orthodox and Reconstructionist Traditions in Historical Perspective.*

Russell E. Richey, Associate Dean and Professor of Church History, The Divinity School, Duke University, is the author of *Early American Methodism.*

Jan Shipps, Professor of History and Religious Studies, Indiana University–Purdue University at Indianapolis, is the author of *Mormonism: The Story of a New Religious Tradition.*

Jean Miller Schmidt, Professor of Modern Church History, The Iliff School of Theology, is the author of *Souls or the Social Order: The Two Party System in American Protestantism.*

REIMAGINING
DENOMINATIONALISM

Introduction

RUSSELL E. RICHEY
ROBERT BRUCE MULLIN

A distinctive mark of North American religious life is its luxuriant denominational composition, long a fascination of both foreign visitors and native commentators. Indeed, observers in most periods of U.S history have thought the denomination the obvious and fundamental unit of the American religious landscape. Just as the state was composed of competing political parties and the economy of diverse business enterprises, so too religious life was made up of the various denominations. It was usually argued, however, that the denomination was more than merely a religious organization; it constituted a distinctively American contribution to religious taxonomy, a religious form that successfully accommodated traditional religious claims and affirmations to the voluntarism and free association of a free society. In making such observations, commentators typically conceded that denominationalism was not unique to the United States, indeed derived from seventeenth-century British Protestantism;[1] however, here denominations became the predominant form, the foundational element in the country's religious life. It is little wonder that many interpreters chose to tell the story of religion in America as the stories of the individual denominations.[2]

At least since the Second World War, however, this approach and these popular assumptions have fallen from favor among professional scholars. Preferring more synoptic or analytical approaches to North American religion, scholars questioned the importance, and indeed even the relevance, of denominations. Increasingly, historians viewed denomination-centered history as quaint, parochial, and evocative of the long-standing but now passé Protestant hegemony. Indeed, the much-lauded renaissance of American religious historiography has been stimulated by a movement away from denominationalism. For a historian such as Sydney Ahlstrom, the only

3

rubric broad enough to encompass the entire sweep of the American story was a religious history that sought to include all types of movements, from agnosticism to astrology, and that by implication demoted denominationalism to merely a part of a larger story.[3]

Recent historical trends have either continued the criticism of denominations or deemed the topic beneath attention. An implicit part of the great scholarly interest in pandenominational phenomena (such as evangelicalism and gender studies, to name but two of the most prominent that have flowered in recent decades) is the belief that such phenomena make up the true core of religion in America and that institutions such as denominations were at best epiphenomena, or distinctions without real differences. This tendency has been furthered by recent work in sociology, typified by the writings of Robert Wuthnow, Wade Clark Roof, and William McKinney,[4] that finds ideology rather than traditional denominational issues (theology, polity, liturgy, praxis) now dividing American religion. Denominational distinctions, they argue, pale by contrast to the great issues separating American believers. They are distinctions without differences. Hence the easy assumption that such distinctions were also irrelevant in the past or that denominationalism is to be explained by recourse to other dynamics, perhaps simply to the factor of competition.[5]

Finally, even certain theological developments within the denominational communities themselves have contributed to the eclipse of interest in denominationalism. The great interest in the ecumenical vision, with its protest against a divided Christendom, that emerged after the First World War and reached its crescendo during the 1960s led many of the communities themselves to de-emphasize points of division and particularity in favor of a greater unity. Neo-orthodoxy reinforced the ecumenical critique, demanding a recovery of "true" ecclesiology and repudiating denominational self-conceptions and divisions, which it viewed as founded in merely human factors.[6] All these dynamics have helped nudge denominational studies into eclipse.

Yet ambivalence over denominationalism is nothing new. A case in point is the course traveled by Philip Schaff, often called the patriarch of the discipline of church history in America. As a relative newcomer to America, he attempted in 1854 to explain his new homeland and its institutions in *America: A Sketch of its Political, Social and Religious Character,*[7] in which he was largely critical of the American denominational system. It reflected for him the subjective and individualizing tendency of American religion, as well as its willingnesss to divide that which should be united, "the beautiful body of Jesus." As such, the denominational spirit was seen as fundamentally anti-Christian. So at first glance. Yet forty years later, at the end of his life in America, he came to a very different appreciation of denominationalism. His experience with American denominations convinced him that these divisions expressed not the failure of the Christian impulse but the vitality of religion in

America: "The historic denominations are permanent forces and represent various aspects of the Christian religion which supplement each other."[8]

Denominational Studies

Reasons for the eclipse and the ambiguity of denominationalism are not just extrinsic. Denominational studies themselves bear some responsibility for their own marginalization and do so because of the way they have traditionally chosen to focus the story.

Denominational studies ideally comprise a rich literary and artifactual array—including items of two types: first, what might be termed internal materials, those things generated by the movement for its use and self-perpetuation, and, second, the more external efforts to depict or describe the denomination, often for an outside audience. The former include material designed for liturgical and catechetical use, dogmatic treatises, apologetical pieces, biographies and spiritual narratives, judicatory proceedings, constitutions, commentaries, creeds, magazines, tracts, and various physical objects (from paintings to buildings that speak in their own way to those who can hear). These internal materials convey the vitality of the movement without worrying about their intelligibility to outsiders.

Relying on these expressions of the faith community, the second, external accounts reach for intelligibility, accent points of distinction, defend the denomination from its critics, and draw on the rich array of "internal" vitalities only in so far as they serve apologetic purposes. These productions aim to portray and picture the movement. Among the earliest efforts at denominational study of this second, more external variety were denominational histories. Histories of individual American denominations[9] began to appear around the turn of the nineteenth century, initially with two different audiences in view, serving two different purposes, and in two forms. Clergy members produced narratives documenting their own individual movements, written for their own members and with apologetical ends, sometimes to respond to external critics,[10] sometimes to settle internal scores.[11] Another type of narrative came from observers of the American scene—some clergy, some not, some European, some not—who wrote of the several, curious, voluntary American bodies, endeavoring to explain the phenomenon to the uncomprehending (especially Europeans). Although they covered the many churches, these collective accounts attempted little in the way of comparisons.[12] They simply juxtaposed denominational narratives. Indeed, one formula, continued to the present, permits adherents of each faith to tell its story. The juxtaposition of the accounts serves to mute triumphalism, focus on the essential narrative, and render distinctiveness in terms of the items of polity, belief, practice, ethic, or ethos that are most peculiar or unique.

The two "external" approaches to denominationalism conspired to

obscure the relation of the denomination to American society, to overlook the common characteristics of denominational style, to minimize
what denominations shared, to ignore their common purposes, and thus,
in a sense, to miss the whole point. The apologetical histories did so by
rendering narratives in a distinctive denominational idiom that domesti-
cated whatever was shared. The collective accounts did so by diverting
attention from the shared to the idiosyncratic. Neither captured the place
of the denomination in American life or did justice to the rich texture of
denominational life. Together these initial presentations created an impression of denominationalism from which it has never fully recovered.

Synthetic and discerning accounts in the nineteenth century by
Alexis de Tocqueville, Robert Baird, Philip Schaff, and others could never
undo those impressions.[13] As these and later analysts appreciated, American denominations, at least by the nineteenth century,[14] functioned very
much like public institutions, knitting persons into society, providing
order, disseminating culture, mediating between the diverse American
peoples and their union. Operating as voluntary institutions, under the
American game rules of freedom and toleration and with only the constituency and support they could garner, they increasingly pressed different (largely European) traditions into common denominational forms.
While competing fiercely and parading their distinctiveness, the denominations (at least some of them) nevertheless, for the most part, shared an
evangelical orthodoxy.[15] On that platform they joined, particularly in the
nineteenth century, in common enterprise, namely the creation of a Christian nation.

Denominations need, therefore, to be studied in relation to American
society, in terms of which they defined and define themselves. They also
deserve "external" or interpretive analyses that reflect the richer literary
and artifactual texture of internal life. Unfortunately, denominational studies have had difficulty capitalizing on these potentialities. They remain
imaged by the two nineteenth-century "external" approaches, despite a
century and half of corrective effort. That image, in fact, gave us the
subtitle of the conference from which these essays emerge—"The Scholarly Writing of Denominational History: An Oxymoron?" The subtitle
expressed the disdain that those involved in denominational studies had
experienced from university colleagues, who conveyed in one way or
another the impression that the denomination was not worth intellectual
attention. The image, then, still haunts denominational studies, a point
effectively made by several of the papers, most notably those by Henry
Bowden and Charles Long.[16]

Perspectives on denominations and denominationalism have varied
over time and according to the historiographical, social, and theological
presuppositions that have been brought to them. It is the belief of the
editors of and the contributors to this volume that changes in both historiography and religious life portend a reevaluation of denominationalism.
The postmodernist movement away from overarching universals and to-

ward a renewed interest in particularity and individual story may serve to refocus attention on the rich inner life of specific denominational communities. If, as a number of the essays suggest, denominations have provided alternative cultural worldviews for their members, then they should prove of interest to students of the multicultural dimensions of American society. Conversely, the role of denominations in shaping a comparatively tolerant religious ethos might again become a focus for American cultural historians intent on analyzing the development of democratic institutions.

Finally, we sense that the religious communities themselves are beginning to show a new interest in their histories, as they strive to integrate their recent (and sometimes troubled) experiences into their longer story. Nor is it merely coincidental that this task is taking place as the twentieth century comes to a close and the implications of the arrival of the twenty-first century are beginning to be considered. Religious communities are much like other types of communities in that new challenges often lead to a reexamination of the past. And just as the challenge of the twentieth century led Philip Schaff and the authors of the American Church History Series to undertake their great series of denominational studies, so too one begins to see a new generation of denominational studies emerging to explain the past and to point the communities into the future. All augurs well for the future of denominational studies.

Although this collection had its origins in a conference entitled "The Scholarly Writing of Denominational History: An Oxymoron?", we discovered—and the reader of these essays mainly deriving from that conference[17] will discover—that the conference title no longer applies. Denominational studies actually have recovered much of the richness of the internal self-presentation of the movement, employing the tension between insider and outsider to interpretive advantage.[18] They now capitalize on the recent decades of suggestive interpretations of religion in American culture and of the social history of religions.[19] Analysts have begun to reflect self-consciously on the interaction between denomination and culture.[20] A new methodological awareness seems to be appearing,[21] one that, as we have noted, draws more deliberately and explicitly on a variety of disciplinary perspectives, including congregational studies, anthropology, sociology, history of religions, literary studies, and various historical methodologies. The new richness of denominational studies owes much to the investment that the Lilly Endowment has made in scholarship on American religious institutions.[22] Ironically, Lilly-inspired scholarship made the scholarly writing of denominational history no longer an oxymoron, but Lilly still had the grace to underwrite a conference that employed that title.[23]

The essays in this volume are designed both to inspire a new appreciation of the fruitfulness of denominational studies among the wider scholarly community and to offer a variety of models and approaches for those interested in taking up the task. Accordingly, the essays represent a number of methodologies that not only take different historical approaches but also make use of the disciplines of sociology, anthropology, and the history of religions. These differing methodologies in part reflect two distinct questions. The first is fundamentally historical: Have denominations played a significant role in the history of the nation? If so, what was their part and how did they exercise it? A second question concerns the present status of denominations: Do they now have an important part in American life and are they critical to an understanding of religion today?

The essays are intended as models in another sense. One of the results of the conference out of which many of these papers came was the conviction that denominational studies ought to be seen as a genre; common problems and issues can be found to one degree or another in the study of any denominational community. We have striven in these essays to raise these larger themes. Hence, even the essays in the third section, each of which focuses on a single religious tradition, are meant as case studies in how a denomination can be productively analyzed.

For this reason, we are unapologetic that the volume is weighted toward the Judeo-Christian tradition and particularly toward what have been called the "mainline" or "oldline" Protestant denominations, since it is among the students of these communities that one sees the new reexamination of denominationalism. This reality stems from two facts. First, it was in these communities that the understanding of denominationalism first appeared and was most readily adopted as adherents attempted to adapt their traditional religious claims to the contours of a free society. Second, these communities are crucially in need of new and innovative approaches of study. Our hope, however, is that the insights offered in these essays may help students of other religious communities better to conceptualize their work.

How are denominations to be studied? That question remains a threshold one for equally vital matters of definition, analysis, interpretation, and comparison. Getting beyond a truncated idiosyncratic image, scholars then must move on to give denominational studies richer content and sophistication. These essays start that process. The reader should not be surprised to discover that the authors do not agree. Fairly basic issues remain open. Denominations are a characteristic American religious institution. But are they to be so defined and understood? Or, should denominationalism be viewed in its larger Western context? Or, as Long suggests, should denominationalism be studied in comparison with similar phenomena in non-Western contexts?[24] And how, presuming that one does stay with a Western or an American context, should scholars take account of the Protestant, indeed the Puritan or Reformed, imprint on denominational character and development?[25] Denominationalism is not a Protestant exclusive; Judaism also is typically portrayed as denominationally divided.[26] And Roman Catholicism is, at least, considered in the same universe. But how can denominations and denominationalism be represented in such a way as to recognize both their Protestant hegemonic and their ecumenical character?[27] And does the phenomenon look very different if one takes a Catholic or Jewish or Lutheran or African-American point of departure?[28] Indeed, can the various differences in perspective, including that between the insider and the outsider, be rendered in a fresh way, one that has interpretive significance?[29] Might even the topics least appreciated in academe, those that seem preeminently "insider"— polity, structure, officialdom, organization, institutions—turn out to be intellectually interesting?[30]

The Volume

The essays in this book are grouped into three major sections: Overviews, Models, and Case Studies. We preface each section with a short introduction, providing a pithy characterization of each essay. The reader should find those three introductions to be a useful map to the volume. In general, essays in Section I concern themselves with the nature, value, and perspective of denominational studies. Examining the genre, they paint with broad strokes. Those of Section II focus particularly on methodology, each modeling a new approach to denominational studies. In Section III the authors put a fresh set of questions to specific denominations or denominational families, elicit interesting data, and gain thereby a new angle on familiar stories. Denominations are indeed reimagined.

NOTES

1. Winthrop S. Hudson, "Denominationalism as a Basis for Ecumenicity: A Seventeenth-Century Conception," *Church History* 24 (1955): 32–50; reprinted in Russell E. Richey, ed., *Denominationalism* (Nashville, Tenn.: Abingdon, 1977), pp. 19–42, as the lead essay.

2. An early representative of the genre is Thomas Branagan, *Concise View of the Principal Religious Denominations in the United States of America* (Philadelphia, 1811). The formula continues to be used to this day.

3. Sydney E. Ahlstrom, *A Religious History of the American People* (New Haven: Yale University Press, 1972).

4. See Wade Clark Roof and William McKinney, *American Mainline Religion* (New Brunswick, N.J.: Rutgers University Press, 1987); Robert Wuthnow, *The Struggle for America's Soul* (Grand Rapids, Mich.: William B. Eerdmans Publishing Co., 1989) and *The Restructuring of American Religion* (Princeton: Princeton University Press, 1988).

5. See, for example, Roger Finke and Rodney Stark, *The Churching of America, 1776–1990: Winners and Losers in Our Religious Economy* (New Brunswick, N.J.: Rutgers University Press, 1992).

6. Forceful in making such assertions was H. Richard Niebuhr. See his *Christ and Culture* (New York: Harper, 1951) and *The Social Sources of Denominationalism* (New York: H. Holt and Co., 1929).

7. Trans. from the German, ed. Perry Miller (Cambridge, Mass.: Harvard University Press, Belknap Press, 1961; first published in 1854 in German and in 1855 in English).

8. Both quotations are taken from excerpts in Klaus Penzel, ed., *Philip Schaff: Historian and Ambassador of the Universal Church, Selected Writings* (Macon, Ga.: Mercer University Press, 1991), pp. 169–176, 308–310.

9. British denominational history surfaced earlier, as for instance, Thomas Crosby's *The History of the English Baptists,* 4 vols. (London, 1738–40).

10. Isaac Backus, *A History of New England, with Particular Reference to . . . Baptists,* 3 vols. (Boston, 1777–96). The apologetical note was clear. In another respect, Backus provides an early counterexample to the generalization being pressed here, namely, that denominational history tended to ignore its context. To the contrary, Backus set the Baptist story against the evolution of religion in New England. Another early Baptist example of sensitivity to context is Morgan Edwards, *Materials toward a history of the Baptists,* a multivolume effort, partially published, partially left in manuscript. For description and location, see *A Baptist Bibliography,* ed. Edward C. Starr, 25 vols. (Rochester: American Baptist Historical Society, 1947–76), 7:42–43. That attention to context and larger view of its purposes would not remain the norm of denominational historiography.

11. Jesse Lee, *A Short History of the Methodists* (Baltimore, 1810).

12. One of the earliest of these was Thomas Branagan, *A Concise View.*

13. Alexis de Tocqueville, *Democracy in America,* ed. Phillips Bradley, 2 vols. (New York: Vintage Books, 1954; translated from French editions of 1835, 1840); Robert Baird, *Religion in America,* abr. and ed. Henry Warner Bowden (1856; repr. New York: Harper & Row, 1970); Philip Schaff, *America.*

14. For an effort to portray a sequence of distinct stages of denominational relation to the social order, see the essay in this volume by Russell E. Richey, "Denominations and Denominationalism: An American Morphology."

15. This point is made explicitly by Baird, who notes that American movements are to be divided into evangelical and nonevangelical.

16. Bowden, "The Death and Rebirth of Denominational History"; Long, "The Question of Denominational Histories in the United States: Dead End or Creative Beginning?"

17. A number of the essays were presented at the conference; others were invited from participants. The sole exception is that by Will B. Gravely, "African Methodisms and the Rise of Black Denominationalism," which was solicited so as to round out the volume and had been previously published in *Rethinking Methodist History: A Bicentennial Historical Consultation,* ed. Russell E. Richey and Kenneth E. Rowe (Nashville, Tenn.: Kingswood Books of The United Methodist Publishing House, 1985).

18. The reader should note especially the papers by Robert A. Orsi, " 'Have You Ever Prayed to Saint Jude?': Reflections on Fieldwork in Catholic Chicago"; Robert Bruce Mullin, "Denominations as Bilingual Communities"; and Jan Shipps, "Remembering, Recovering, and Inventing What Being the People of God Means: Reflections on Method in the Scholarly Writing of Denominational History."

19. See especially Jay P. Dolan, "The People as Well as the Prelates: A Social History of a Denomination," and Jean Miller Schmidt, "Denominational History When Gender Is the Focus: Women in American Methodism."

20. See Mullin, "Denominations as Bilingual Communities," and James H.

Moorhead, "Presbyterians and the Mystique of Organizational Efficiency, 1870–1936."

21. William R. Hutchison, "Denominational Studies in the Reshaping of American Religious History"; Nancy T. Ammerman, "Denominations: Who and What Are We Studying?"; Marc Lee Raphael, "Reform, Conservative, and Orthodox Judaism in America: Is There an Alternative to Denominationalism?"; Shipps, "Remembering, Recovering, and Inventing What Being the People of God Means"; and Orsi, "Have You Ever Prayed to Saint Jude?"

22. See particularly the fruits of two studies of mainline denominations. One, actually a multivolume series entitled *The Presbyterian Presence,* is edited by Milton J Coalter, John M. Mulder, and Louis B. Weeks (Louisville, Ky.: Westminster/John Knox, 1990–92). The last volume, a synthetic essay by the editors that pulls together the findings from the previous seven, is entitled *The Reforming Tradition: Presbyterians and Mainstream Protestantism in the Twentieth Century* (Louisville, Ky: Westminster/John Knox, 1992). The other project is *A Case Study of Mainstream Protestantism: The Disciples' Relation to American Culture,* ed. D. Newell Williams (Grand Rapids, Mich.: William B. Eerdmans Publishing Co., 1991).

23. The conference itself was jointly sponsored by the National Humanities Center, where much of it transpired, The Divinity School of Duke University, and the religion programs of North Carolina State University, the University of North Carolina at Chapel Hill, and Duke University. The editors reiterate their appreciation to these several institutions for support that elicited the creativity herein represented.

24. Long, "The Question of Denominational Histories in the United States."

25. On this point, see Joseph L. Blau, *Judaism in America. From Curiosity to Third Faith* (Chicago: University of Chicago Press, 1976), and Alan Silverstein, "Serving the Jews in the Pews: Megatrends Shaping the Reform Movement in American Judaism: 1840–1930" (Ph.D. diss., Jewish Theological Seminary, 1992). The latter reviews the literature on this issue. On the particularly Reformed dimension of denominationalism, see Christa R. Klein, "Denominational History as Public History: The Lutheran Case."

26. But see the essay herein by Raphael, "Reform, Conservative, and Orthodox Judaism in America."

27. This point is wrestled with by Richey in "Denominations and Denominationalism."

28. On this point, see Laurie F. Maffly-Kipp, "Denominationalism and the Black Church," and Christa R. Klein, "Denominational History as Public History: The Lutheran Case," as well as the essays already mentioned covering Catholicism and Judaism.

29. This point is suggestively explored by Orsi.

30. As indeed they do in the hands of James H. Moorhead, "Presbyterians and the Mystique of Organizational Efficiency, 1870–1936," and Bradley J. Longfield, " 'Denominational' Colleges in Antebellum America?: A Case Study of Presbyterians and Methodists in the South."

I

OVERVIEWS

The essays in this section all consider where denominational studies have come from and where they might be heading. All the essays recognize that the American religious landscape has changed dramatically, after what some have called the Second Disestablishment, from the way it was during the earlier periods both of the flourishing of denominational studies and of their waning. The writers in different ways attempt to suggest a new place for denominational studies within this changed environment.

Henry Warner Bowden offers a historical survey of the rise of denominational history from the early nineteenth century to the present and analyzes why it has not flourished as a genre during much of the twentieth century. He argues that denominational studies have advanced when they have been in step with the trends of the larger historical guild and have suffered when they have been conceived of in narrow institutional terms.

William Hutchison addresses the question of the value of denominational studies and contrasts confessional "insider" histories (which he likens to autobiographies) and external case-study histories, which he likens to critical biographies. For him, meaningful denominational histories should be guided by the same rules that govern serious biographies and must involve a concern to show the interrelationship between the particular community and the larger social milieu. When they accomplish this, they offer a crucial insight into American religious life.

Jay R. Dolan traces trends in Catholic historiography from Peter Guilday to the present. He notes the movement away from prelate-centered, apologetical history and toward a larger encompassing of the role of the laity and a greater openness to new methodological approaches.

Laurie F. Maffly-Kipp examines the historiography of the African-American religious communities. As she suggests, concerns about setting forth a racial and cultural unity have long led scholars to downplay denominational differences in favor of a common "Negro church." This perspective, however, flattens and distorts the religious heritage of the black religious community, which has been marked by differentiation and conflict as well as by consensus and unity. A study of denominationalism within the African-American community can help correct this misconception.

Part of the crisis in denominational studies, argues Russell E. Richey, is an inadequate appreciation of the dynamism of the phenomenon. Denominationalism is not one thing but a changing entity. Thus, Richey offers a series of typologies to explain the nature of denominationalism at various points of American history to identify its inner dynamic.

Finally, Charles Long, a noted scholar of the history of religions, raises a number of questions about the larger meaning of denominational studies. What, he asks, have denominational studies to do with the broader study of religion, and how does a renewed interest in denominationalism relate to the role of "civil religion" in America? For Long, the changed nature of religion in American society forbids any return to traditional denominational studies, and he offers instead a broader cross-cultural understanding.

The Death and Rebirth of Denominational History

HENRY WARNER BOWDEN

The title of this essay derives from a rather whimsical appropriation of words used by A. F. C. Wallace. In his study of Seneca Indians, westernmost of the five tribes constituting the Iroquois League, Wallace traced the cultural decline of those proud people and then their partial recovery thanks to the ministrations of a native prophet named Handsome Lake. The general concept he used to depict this reclamation process was "revitalization." In this essay I borrow the concept and apply it to the broad field of denominational history. But there is one proviso. Wallace defined revitalization as a deliberate, self-conscious movement, a process pursued over time with great determination.[1] The Senecas came back from the edge of oblivion because they tried hard to do so. This was revitalization in the classic sense, but in my view the revitalization of denominational history does not quite fit the standard definition because, thus far, change does not seem to have been deliberate or self-conscious. Denominational history drifted toward the edge of historiographical oblivion, true enough, but current signs of improvement do not indicate that this recovery has been very carefully thought out at all.

It is important that readers of this brief survey notice from the outset that its concentration is on denominational *histories,* not on the more inclusive field of denominational studies that contains discrete, usually monographic, works. Generations of students have produced studies of both mainstream and marginal denominations. These afford interesting fields of comparative analysis, both across time periods regarding a single group and within the same time period regarding several contemporaneous groups. But the essay at hand eschews those studies, many of which are still pertinent and admirable, and adheres instead to historical works

17

that cover particular denominations from their origins down to the time
of historical composition.

I

Another arbitrary bracket imposed on this essay is to take *denomination*
in a specific way—to consider denominations a product of events originally set in motion in eighteenth-century America. Before the Revolution
and the separation of church and state at the federal level, most religious
groups considered themselves to be transplanted representatives of true
churches in their homeland that in turn were proper descendants of
original Christianity. Histories of such groups, such as Cotton Mather's
Magnalia Christi Americana, focused on segments of ecclesiastical reality but treated them as embodiments of the whole—or all that really
counted. Denominations emerged after the national government refused
to support one group over others as the true embodiment of ancient
orthodoxy. The legal, sociological, and psychological origins of denominations lie in the 1790s, and so histories of their experience can begin no
earlier than that date.

The intellectually laggard quality of denominational histories is apparent almost at once. Despite the fact that religious groups had assumed
different relationships with federal (and most state) government and
with each other, early denominational historians continued to view their
subjects in the same old perspective. Early denominational histories in
America were thus noteworthy in two respects. They usually spanned
quite an inclusive chronology (some began with Creation and the Garden
of Eden), placing American churches at the most recent stage of the
continuum, and they harbored a distinctly apologetic tone. The second
characteristic accounts for the first. Since most historians of this first
generation assumed that the denomination was either the only true embodiment of divine economy or at least its best current representative,
they demonstrated such claims by tracing the survival of ancient teachings to present vindication in their own particular church. Denominational rivalry spawned many such works, and their ulterior motives led to
long disquisitions on authentic baptism, ordination, polity, and creeds,
and on the proper theological perspective on evangelism.[2]

A variation on this triumphalism smacked a little more of a characteristically "American" trait—an emphasis on pragmatic success in substan-
tiation of a denomination's claimed superiority. Only growing churches
could utilize this theme, of course, but those benefiting most from the
Second Great Awakening could point to rapidly increasing membership
as proof of their correct beliefs and behavior. Less dynamic groups had to
fall back on orthodoxy and orthopraxy, taking what solace they could find
in the thought that truth is not necessarily popular. But this equation of
success with propriety exists in the literature, fully a century before

William Warren Sweet stressed the idea in his studies of religion on the frontier.[3]

These histories of denominations written from a defensive frame of mind show that their authors had not yet really accepted denominationalism. When churches in post-Revolutionary America found themselves on an equal basis with each other, regarded without favor or hostility by a neutral government, the situation pointed to an eventual acceptance of parity among them. As long as champions of specific groups asserted that some organizational structure or doctrinal emphasis was superior to others, however, they were still arguing particularistic issues that went back as far as the sixteenth century. Denominational histories that exalted one church at the expense of others did not reflect the new context in which American churches existed.

By the late 1840s, however, some historians began treating denominations as equal partners in the larger task of evangelizing America. Some were more equal than others in these works, with evangelical Protestants, such as Methodists, Baptists, Disciples, and Presbyterians, leading the way. Then came Lutherans and Episcopalians, who preferred traditional confessions and liturgies to revivals, with Catholics barely acknowledged as legitimately Christian or even welcome in the country. Others, such as Mormons, represented beliefs just too ludicrous to consider seriously.[4] This kind of denominational overview denied parity among all churches, but at least it moved toward a more latitudinarian acceptance of major Protestant bodies.

Treatments of this sort continued through the 1880s,[5] and it is worth noting that, technically speaking, they were not denominational histories at all. The change from apologetics to a more leveling perspective first appeared in general overviews of religion in America. Surveys of religious influences in national culture treated denominations as components of a larger picture. Much of their individuality was lost and their unique features disregarded in order to discuss collective effect. While this new viewpoint developed over several decades, histories of specific denominations nevertheless continued to perpetuate exclusivist attitudes, perhaps employing a less strident tone than was typical of their predecessors but still espousing a viewpoint that was parochial and isolated.[6]

Most nineteenth-century histories of denominations followed standard patterns and barely deviated from accepted formulae. If there was any adaptation to new ideas and circumstances, it was manifested in muted criticisms of other churches and in less assertive claims about the worth of a single group. The single exception to this tedious state of affairs appeared in the last decade of the century, when the thirteen-volume American Church History Series was published between 1893 and 1897, providing historical data on a total of nineteen denominations. Although a joint effort involving three editors and twenty-two authors, the project stemmed from the genius of Philip Schaff, whose original concept and steady encouragement helped ensure its successful completion. As counterbalance to the polemics of earlier works, this series of denominational histories was irenic and openly ecumenical. Schaff and the historians he recruited accepted denominationalism as a fact of American ecclesiastical life. That allowed writers to consider their respective churches as parts of a larger whole, all of which were legitimate embodiments of variegated Christianity.[7] Even Catholics were included in this remarkably inclusive series.[8]

Like most other Americans, Schaff accepted denominationalism as a basic reality, but he looked to the future as well. The multiplicity of American churches was for him a transitional step, a preliminary circumstance before the eventual reunion of Christendom. Denominational histories that were uncomfortable with the notion of parity invariably stressed their own virtues at the expense of others. By contrast, denominational histories written from a Schaffian vantage point accepted parity and eschewed invidious comparisons. They anticipated the rise of a new church, not the perpetuation of old ones. The ecumenical perspective undergirding the American Church History Series placed denominational history in a new context. The resulting volumes were refreshingly innovative and stimulating. They did not set a trend, though, or inaugurate a new era in denominational historiography. Most products in the field continued to follow the familiar, somewhat hackneyed, schematics well into the twentieth century.

The basic problem with standard denominational histories at the beginning of this century was that they resembled dinosaurs. By not adapting to a changing world, they became increasingly out of place in the modern context. Satisfied with presenting materials according to parochial formulae, they remained insensitive to new historiographical trends and slowly became an endangered species. The genre reached stasis. All variations on the basic themes had been produced, all changes rung, and there was nothing more to do with such studies but insert current data. Professional historians found them not so much incorrect as uninteresting. They were living fossils, curiosities stemming from a bygone era, out of step with the accelerating changes taking place in the historians' world of ideas and researches.

The larger world of early-twentieth-century American historiography pulsed with a new dynamism. People studied new topics from new perspectives; in addition, they were fired with an overall revisionist motivation, deliberately emending the work of previous generations. Historians such as Charles A. Beard, for example, took a traditional topic like constitutional history and turned it upside down with an economic interpretation.[9] Frederick Jackson Turner, to name another, introduced the importance of frontiers in American experience and stimulated research along those lines for several decades.[10] James Harvey Robinson represented an additional departure by concentrating on ordinary lives rather than those of the elite and on social history instead of politics and wars.[11] This "New History" was as appropriate to its context as was Schaff's set of denominational histories. Just as the American Church History Series stood on a complete acceptance of denominationalism, so Robinson's New History and its focus on the everyday concerns of common people was the logical outgrowth of the modern acceptance of social democracy.

These samples of new writing evinced a dynamism among American historians, who also embodied strains of the revisionist, progressivist thought current in their day. Denominational histories appearing at the same time displayed little evidence of such attitudes. They still contained standard accounts of institutional expansion, the bricks-and-mortar emphasis familiar to generations of readers. They still concentrated on ruling bodies, hierarchies, and administrative machinery, the ecclesiastical equivalent of the earlier obsession with political history in America. They still included arcane topics of interest to no one outside the denomination in question and, as time passed, to fewer people inside it as well.[12] Outdated, unaware of or unconcerned about the basic shifts in the historiographical world, the writings of this period were about as close to death as denominational history came. It almost died of intellectual starvation, deserving such a fate not because its subject matter was questionable but because its monotonous presentation had become irrelevant.

II

Looking on the brighter side of things, there were several valuable qualities to be found in the denominational histories that had accumulated up to the 1930s. They preserved basic information about personnel, dates, the sites of razed buildings, the composition and task of committees, and other such phenomena currently retrievable only because recorded in those old volumes. They also furnish us with a general understanding of how these denominations began and grew, including the geographical areas in which they flourished best. Sometimes there are statistics as well, and even though we cannot trust them completely, they are nevertheless helpful. Once church historians began adopting the canons of scientific history, they tended to include more quantifiable evidence in their works. Denominational historians acknowledged the importance of objective observation and detached reporting, too, and because of that their data contain great quantities of useful particulars.

It is significant that church historians shifted from apologetics to scientific history at the turn of the twentieth century. Much more important than that, however, was a historiographical event that occurred a few years later, namely, the collapse of scientific history as an ideal for everyone. However slowly denominational historians were affected by such a trend, and they inevitably were, the gradual revitalization of denominational studies is a result of the many options that emerged when historians in general turned their backs on the scientific ideal. These options appeared after the paradigm of absolute objectivity and presuppositionless reporting of events-as-they-actually-happened was finally put to rest.[13] Once historians again admitted that they worked with some set of preconceived ideas and values, it was permissible to proceed after making one's perspective explicit.

Among those who chose to study religious phenomena from an historical perspective, four basic positions appeared in the modern—post-1930—historiographical period. One point of view harked back to the previous era with what at first glance seemed to be a revival of the old apologetics. During the rise of neo-orthodox theology and the decline of Social Gospel emphases, various historians began to call for a "high-church" perspective that stressed the unique and edifying character of ecclesiastical bodies. Influential voices at Union Seminary in New York and at the Chicago Divinity School argued that churches were the locus of salvation experience and that their histories should claim first place as the linchpin of western civilization. Cyril C. Richardson and James H. Nichols best articulated the viewpoint that assumed there was something supernatural in churches. Because there was an intangible presence, they urged that historical studies of tangible institutions locate the presence of God therein and thus identify signs of providential guidance.[14]

This assertion of Christianity's uniqueness called for pliant methods to accommodate the topic's special nature. All of it was reminiscent of the old denominational histories that bristled with defensive appeals for special consideration. The general historiographical situation had changed so much since the 1930s, however, that few denominational historians took up this resurgent high-church theory. Ironically enough, even those who plumped for a neo-orthodox definition of the church were unable to fulfill their own mandate and produce a different kind of history in support of their theologically inspired priorities. Subjective insights might be considered legitimate once again, but the influence of factual reporting and naturalistic explanation remained strong enough to keep theologically dominated history to a minimum.

A second option appealed to many of those interested in chronicling American denominational experience, whether focusing on the collective experience or on individual groups. This broad and variegated perspective stressed the interaction between churches and their cultural environments and comprised two ways of thinking. One approach looked for the manner in which cultural factors had influenced aspects of religion in particular contexts. Discussions of historical or environmental conditioning had grown to some strength during the twentieth century, with notable works by Peter G. Mode and Shirley Jackson Case as leading examples.[15] These works continued to serve as powerful models for authors throughout the modern historiographical period.

Another way of looking at things in this same perspective, supported by many more practitioners, concentrated on the influence that churches had exerted on cultural conditions, rather than the other way around. This emphasis on social effectiveness became one of the most widely utilized perspectives in modern times. Kenneth Scott Latourette employed this theme on a global scale in surveys that covered two millennia, while William Warren Sweet applied the same viewpoint to American phenomena during the few centuries of expansion and activism here.[16] In the previous century historians had touted social significance to enhance their churches' religious worth; in the modern period social effectiveness was cited to promote churches as culturally significant human institutions. Those who no longer had any interest in discussing proper modes of baptism, credentials for ordination, or the superiority of a given theological preference could still discuss their churches' relevance as important components of social life. They could point to religiously generated reforms as a means of showing how churches served practical human needs and contributed to progressive change through gradual social improvement.

By the middle of the twentieth century, a third perspective had become noticeable within the general guild of American historians. Partly as a result of the competition between ideologies that developed during World War II and the ensuing cold war, possibly also because of harsh challenges from Third World countries, many historians began to search for core values embedded in America's past. This search was the fundamental motivation behind consensus history, and many valuable studies were produced on the course of democratic thought, the preservation of civil liberties, the gradual recognition of minority rights, and the other basic principles that undergirded American life. Roland H. Bainton and Sidney E. Mead produced outstanding writings on the religious aspects of this perspective, discussing separation of church and state as the backbone of American freedoms, together with an appreciation of the nation's traditional commitment to free speech and the consequent toleration of confessional differences.[17] Denominational historians were free to blend this consensus point of view into their surveys, showing how their particular group had retained both the central values of western Christianity and the moral principles that had helped make American society a stable and beneficial one. One proponent of this perspective went so far as to label these religious strong points as "The Great Tradition of the American Churches."[18]

A fourth historiographical pattern emerged to new respectability in modern times, one that argued for the importance of ideas as a topic of scholarly inquiry. Adherents of this perspective were divided into two groups, with the majority classified as intellectual historians, or those who valued ideas because they were a key factor in explaining human behavior. Believing that thought led to action, these historians focused on the first part of the equation in order to grasp the entire sequence. One of those who studied religious ideas on a broad canvas was John T. McNeill, whose pioneering efforts at portraying the intellectual roots of social reform movements stimulated many similar studies.[19] H. Shelton Smith worked primarily with American thought, following the evolution of Calvinist doctrine into liberal activism and demonstrating the ways in which racist conceptions had blighted America's civil rights record for hundreds of years.[20] Denominational historians eagerly seconded this emphasis, perhaps because they had been accustomed to giving theology high priority in their work all along. But the resurgence of intellectual history in twentieth-century historical circles was unquestionably a tonic for this traditional and familiar aspect of religious studies.

Some preferred to study the history of ideas, instead of intellectual history, giving attention to ideas in and of themselves rather than prizing their utility in explaining something else. Fascinated with the beauty of a system's architectonics or admiring an idea's pertinence and duration, these historians did not much care whether thought led to action; ideas themselves were worth study, and their existence alone justified close scrutiny and analysis. Perry Miller surged to the forefront of the history of ideas with his studies of Puritanism.[21] His heroic efforts finally made the subfield respectable, and other historians of religious ideas, such as Herbert W. Schneider, expanded it to cover all major intellectual emphases in the American past.[22]

To summarize, four perspectival clusters rose from the ashes of scientific history: a renewed emphasis on theological presuppositions, an interest in the interaction between religious and cultural forces, a search for consensus, and a reinvigorated appreciation of ideas, either for their discrete value or for their role as animating factors in behavioral patterns. Students of religious phenomena benefited from the end of the rule of science as much as did their colleagues in other parts of the guild. Each of the four categories had its adherents, but the distribution was uneven. Most historians were inclined to operate from the second or fourth points of view, whereas only a few chose the first or the third. Most religious studies in the modern period have discussed ideas as keys to action and have studied the effects of that action on social patterns.

In addition to those major strands, another modern historiographical event has made possible the revitalization of denominational history. Between 1960 and 1972 six comprehensive narratives of religion in America appeared, synthesizing the best findings available through decades of monographic researches.[23] These surveys provided a general format within which denominational historians could chart their own church's particular experience in light of larger trends and interdenominational activities. These overviews were the true inheritors of Schaff's American Church History Series, accepting plural denominations as axiomatic and discussing their interaction against the backdrop, not of anticipated reunions, but of general American cultural life. These surveys were exemplary in their sensitive appreciation of specialized research projects. Each of them discussed events with perspectives that combined social impact, intellectual underpinning, and consensus. More important, they summarized current findings on a host of different subthemes and represented the state of the art in scholarship.

In the last quarter of the twentieth century few new comprehensive narratives have appeared. Most historians of American religion are now exploring new questions in new ways, building up a treasure of new monographs with new ideas and fresh information. This accumulated knowledge will eventually serve as data for another set of overviews to be written in the twenty-first century; in the meantime they provide additional hope for the revitalization of denominational studies.

To augment the increase in topical diversity, methodological experimentation is now expanding. Today's scholars are putting questions together and applying them to heretofore neglected subject matter, appreciably enlarging the scope of learning. Voices from minority groups have made all Americans more acutely aware of the roles that blacks, Hispanics, and Native Americans have played in religious history. Another neglected theme has been the spiritual experience of the various practical roles performed by women from every ethnic group. The need to understand and appreciate these previously unstudied Americans as integral parts of the whole demands much more inquiry into their only partly known activities. New hypotheses drawn from interdisciplinary vantage points, including psychology and anthropology, have produced evocative interpretations of familiar information.[24] All this potential bodes well for denominational historians—if they avail themselves of it.

Cultural change has affected the present climate of opinion enough to make historians aware that many new and different questions need answering and that neglected aspects of the American past need rescuing from obscurity. Religious historiography reached a synthesizing plateau by 1975 and at this writing is in another period of monographic experimentation, the benefits of which will be proportional to its ingenuity and to the willingness of researchers to uncover new material. Denominational studies will be revitalized to the degree that their authors absorb these new perspectives; the writings will become interesting again if they incorporate new materials and concepts to expand their subject matter and produce more comprehensive coverage of the many types of people who have been part of denominations.

III

Denominational history came perilously close to death because it did not adapt rapidly enough to changing historiographical patterns. It drifted toward extinction by remaining too much the same old thing. The significant changes that occurred in the historical profession in the twentieth century have indirectly contributed to a potential revitalization of denominational studies. This "trickle-down" process reveals little self-conscious leadership that has set out to reform denominational history with new perspectives. It seems that denominations, like the poor, will always be with us, and so the best face we can put on the situation is to make sure that inquiries into their existence are as sophisticated as possible by keeping up with modern historiographical options. Individual historians have undoubtedly made their own choices about methods, materials, and interpretive themes, but there is no discernible pattern to recent adjustment or much explanation to why they occurred. Still, there is reason to hope that denominational histories will continue to benefit from greater acquaintance with the larger field of historical professionalism,[25] for denominational history will thrive insofar as it conforms to the standards maintained by professional historians.

Denominational history will not thrive insofar as it conforms to standards laid down by those in charge of ecclesiastical administration; any orientation of this sort ties the historian to theological agendas and bureaucratic priorities that divert scholars from their primary loyalty. The highest priority among critical historians is to have their work reflect criteria shared within professional circles regarding factual accuracy, balanced interpretations, and cultural relevance. Of those three areas, I suggest that the really crucial choices have to be made in the third category. Denominational historians pass muster fairly well these days when it comes to using evidence and interpreting it fairly. However, excellence is determined by the criteria used to decide what topics are relevant enough to include in one's work.

When church leaders define relevance, they consult little more than official blueprints or their personal hopes for their organization's future development. The standards involved are necessarily parochial, and historians who submit to such an imposition have forfeited one of their most important responsibilities.[26] The challenge to professional historians who are interested in denominational matters is to decide among themselves what is worth studying in the ecclesiastical past, rather than letting an outsider use alien criteria to decide for them.

There is an old saw that says people cannot serve two masters; they must serve either God or mammon. I suggest that respectable historians should do neither. Previously, religious historians tried to serve God by tracing providential guidance in human events, and their tools proved inadequate to the task. All history, including religious history, is a humanistic discipline, a point that few dispute any longer. Religious historians are too modest to think that their limited methods can descry God's presence on earth. But at the same time they should also be too proud to allow nonhistorians to do their thinking for them. The professional guild is flexible and full of options regarding procedure and relevant subject matter. Anyone who accepts criteria and expectations generated by those outside the guild begins with second-rate standards and produces work of marginal value. People who are subjects of a study should not control those who conduct the investigation.

Denominational history, if it is to be truly reenergized, should now try to qualify for all of Wallace's definition of revitalization. That is to say, today's historians of particular churches should decide deliberately and self-consciously that they will improve their work by adhering to the highest professional standards. They should strive constantly to define relevance by means of criteria developed within the historical guild, not according to the limited perceptions and self-serving needs of a single religious institution.

N O T E S

1. Anthony F. C. Wallace, *The Death and Rebirth of the Seneca* (New York: Knopf, 1969).

2. Sample works include John Henry Hobart, *An Apology for Apostolic Order and its Advocates* (New York: T. and J. Swords, 1807) and *The Principles of the Churchman Stated and Explained, in Distinction from the Corruptions of the Church of Rome, and from the Errors of Certain Protestant Sects* (New York: T. and J. Swords, 1819), and Samuel Howard Ford, *The Origins of the Baptists, traced back by Milestones on the Track of Time* (Nashville, Tenn.: South-West Publishing House, 1860). See also Charles Hodge, *The Constitutional History of the Presbyterian Church in the United States of America* (Philadelphia: Presbyterian Board of Publication, 1851); for evidence of a similar point of view taught to Presbyterian divinity students for decades at Princeton Theological Seminary, see manuscript lecture notes by Samuel Miller, housed in Speer Library at that educational institution.

3. See, for example, Nathan Bangs, *History of the Methodist Episcopal Church from its Origin in 1776, to the General Conference in 1840,* 4 vols. (New York: Methodist Book Concern, 1838–40); David Benedict, *A General History of the Baptist Denomination in America and Other Parts of the World,* 2 vols. (Boston: Lincoln and Edmunds, 1813); and Richard M'Nemar, *The Kentucky Revival* (Albany: E. and E. Hosford, 1808).

4. Robert Baird, *Religion in America: or, An Account of the Origin, Progress, Relation to the State, and Present Condition of the Evangelical Churches in the United States, with Notices of the Unevangelical Denominations* (New York: Harper and Brothers, 1844).

5. Daniel Dorchester, *Christianity in the United States from the First Settlement down to the Present Time,* rev. ed. (New York: Phillips and Hunt, 1895); John Fletcher Hurst, *Short History of the Church in the United States,* A.D. *1492–1890* (New York: Harper and Brothers, 1890); Leonard Woolsey Bacon, *A History of American Christianity* (New York: The Christian Literature Co., 1897).

6. A brief sampling should include John G. Shea, *A History of the Catholic Church within the Limits of the United States: From the First Attempted Colonization to the Present Time,* 4 vols. (New York: J. G. Shea, 1886–92); J. M. Cramp, *Baptist History: From the Foundation of the Christian Church to the Close of the Eighteenth Century* (Philadelphia: American Baptist Publication Society, 1869); J. H. Allen, *Our Liberal Movement in Theology, . . . Shown in . . . the History of Unitarianism in New England* (Boston: Roberts Brothers, 1892); A. M. Barnes, *Pioneers in Methodism* (Nashville: Southern Methodist Publishing House, 1890); Thomas Armitage, *A History of the Baptists; traced by their Vital Principles and Practices, from the Time of Our Lord and Saviour Jesus Christ to the Year 1886* (New York: Bryan, Taylor, and Co., 1887); Albert E. Dunning, *Congregationalists*

in America (New York: J. A. Hill and Co., 1894); James M. Buckley, *A History of Methodism in the United States,* 2 vols. (New York: The Christian Literature Co., 1897).

7. Philip Schaff, Henry C. Potter, and Samuel M. Jackson, eds., *The American Church History Series, Consisting of a Series of Denominational Histories Published under the Auspices of the American Society of Church History,* 13 vols. (New York: The Christian Literature Co., 1893–97).

8. It is instructive to compare the more pugnacious attitudes of John G. Shea with the treatment given Catholicism by Schaff's picked author. See Thomas O'Gorman, *A History of the Roman Catholic Church in the United States,* vol. 9 (New York: The Christian Literature Co., 1895).

9. Charles A. Beard, *An Economic Interpretation of the Constitution* (New York: Macmillan, 1913) and *Economic Origins of Jeffersonian Democracy* (New York: Macmillan, 1915).

10. Frederick Jackson Turner, "The Significance of the Frontier in American History," *Annual Report of the American Historical Association for the Year 1893* (Washington, D.C.: U.S. Government Printing Office, 1894); *The Rise of the New West, 1818–1829* (New York: Harper and Brothers, 1906); and *The Frontier in American History* (New York: Henry Holt and Co., 1920).

11. James Harvey Robinson, *The New History: Essays Illustrating the Modern Historical Outlook* (New York: Macmillan, 1912).

12. A. H. Newman, *A Century of Baptist Achievement* (Philadelphia: American Baptist Publication Society, 1901); C. H. Forney, *History of the Churches of God in the United States of North America* (Harrisburg, Penn.: Publishing House of the Churches of God, 1914); Gaius G. Atkins and Frederick L. Fagley, *History of American Congregationalism* (Boston: Pilgrim Press, 1942); William T. Moore, *A Comprehensive History of the Disciples of Christ: Being an Account of a Century's Effort to Restore Primitive Christianity in its Faith, Doctrine, and Life* (New York: Fleming H. Revell, 1909); Thomas B. Neely, *American Methodism: Its Divisions and Unification* (New York: Fleming H. Revell, 1915); Edwin H. Rian, *The Presbyterian Conflict* (Grand Rapids, Mich.: William B. Eerdmans Publishing Co., 1940). As evidence of unthinking repetition, it is interesting to note that S. H. Ford's dated work on Baptists (originally published in 1860) was still being reprinted in 1950, issued at that time in Texarkana, Arkansas, by the Baptist Sunday School Committee.

13. For the best of the critics of scientific history, see Carl L. Becker, "Everyman His Own Historian," *American Historical Review* 37 (January 1932); "Detachment and Writing of History," *Atlantic Monthly* 106 (October 1910); and "What Are Historical Facts?" *Western Political Quarterly* 8 (September 1955). See also Charles A. Beard, "That Noble Dream," *American Historical Review* 41 (October 1935), and "Written History as an Act of Faith," *American Historical Review* 39 (January 1934).

14. Cyril C. Richardson, "Church History Past and Present," *Union Seminary Quarterly Review* 5 (November 1949); James H. Nichols, "Church History and Secular History," *Church History* 13 (June 1944), and "The Art of Church History," *Church History* 20 (March 1951).

15. Peter G. Mode, *The Frontier Spirit in American Christianity* (New York: Macmillan, 1923); Shirley Jackson Case, *The Evolution of Early Christianity: A Genetic Study of First-Century Christianity in Relation to Its Religious Environment* (Chicago: University of Chicago Press, 1914), *The Social Origins of Chris-*

tianity (Chicago: University of Chicago Press, 1923), and *Christianity in a Changing World* (New York: Harper and Brothers, 1949).

16. Kenneth Scott Latourette, *Christianity in a Revolutionary Age: A History of Christianity in the Nineteenth and Twentieth Centuries,* 5 vols. (New York: Harper and Brothers, 1959–62), and *A History of the Expansion of Christianity,* 7 vols. (New York: Harper and Brothers, 1937–45); William Warren Sweet, *The Story of Religion in America,* 6th ed. (New York: Harper and Brothers, 1950), and *American Culture and Religion: Six Essays* (Dallas, Tex.: Southern Methodist University Press, 1951).

17. Roland H. Bainton, *The Travail of Religious Liberty: Nine Biographical Studies* (Philadelphia: Westminster Press, 1951) and *Christian Unity and Religion in New England* (Boston: Beacon Press, 1964); Sidney E. Mead, *The Lively Experiment: The Shaping of Christianity in America* (New York: Harper and Row, 1963) and *The Nation With the Soul of a Church* (New York: Harper and Row, 1975).

18. Winthrop S. Hudson, *The Great Tradition of the American Churches* (New York: Harper and Brothers, 1953); see also his *Nationalism and Religion in America: Concepts of American Identity and Mission* (New York: Harper and Row, 1970) and his *Religion in America: An Historical Account of the Development of American Religious Life,* 3rd ed. (New York: Charles Scribner's Sons, 1981).

19. John T. McNeill, *Christian Hope for World Society* (New York: Willet, Clark and Co., 1937), *Modern Christian Movements* (Philadelphia: Westminster Press, 1954), and *The History and Character of Calvinism* (New York: Oxford University Press, 1954).

20. H. Shelton Smith, *Changing Conceptions of Original Sin: A Study in American Theology Since 1750* (New York: Charles Scribner's Sons, 1955) and *In His Image, But... Racism in Southern Religion, 1780–1910* (Durham, N.C.: Duke University Press, 1972).

21. Perry Miller, *Orthodoxy in Massachusetts, 1630–1650* (Cambridge, Mass.: Harvard University Press, 1933), *The New England Mind: The Seventeenth Century* (New York: Macmillan, 1939), and *The New England Mind: From Colony to Province (Cambridge, Mass.: Harvard University Press, 1953).*

22. Herbert W. Schneider, *The Puritan Mind* (New York: Henry Holt and Co., 1939) and *A History of American Philosophy* (New York: Columbia University Press, 1946).

23. Clifton E. Olmstead, *History of Religion in the United States* (Englewood Cliffs, N.J.: Prentice-Hall, 1969); H. Shelton Smith, Robert T. Handy, and Lefferts A. Loetscher, eds., *American Christianity: An Historical Interpretation With Representative Documents,* 2 vols. (New York: Charles Scribner's Sons, 1960–63); Winthrop S. Hudson, *Religion in America: An Historical Account of the Development of American Religious Life* (New York: Charles Scribner's Sons, 1965); Edwin S. Gaustad, *A Religious History of America* (New York: Harper and Row, 1966); Martin E. Marty, *Righteous Empire: The Protestant Experience in America* (New York: Dial, 1970); Sydney E. Ahlstrom, *A Religious History of the American People* (New Haven: Yale University Press, 1972).

24. A slight sampling of this rich and growing body of material would have to include Gayraud S. Wilmore, *Black Religion and Black Radicalism: An Examination of the Black Religious Experience* (Garden City, N.Y.: Doubleday, 1972), and Albert J. Raboteau, *Slave Religion: The "Invisible Institution" in the Antebellum South* (New York: Oxford University Press, 1978); Barbara L. Epstein, *The*

Politics of Domesticity: Women, Evangelism, and Temperance in Nineteenth-Century America (Middletown, Conn.: Wesleyan University Press, 1981), and Lois Boyd and R. Douglas Brackenridge, *Presbyterian Women in America: Two Centuries of a Quest for Status* (Westport, Conn.: Greenwood Press, 1983); Sacvan Bercovitch, *The Puritan Origins of the American Self* (New Haven: Yale University Press, 1975), and Philip Greven, *The Protestant Temperament: Patterns of Childrearing, Religious Experience, and the Self in Early America* (New York: Knopf, 1977); James H. Moorhead, *American Apocalypse: Yankee Protestants and the Civil War, 1860–1869* (New Haven: Yale University Press, 1978), and Joan Jacobs Brumberg, *Mission for Life: The Story of the Family of Adonirum Judson . . . and the Course of Evangelical Religion in the Nineteenth Century* (New York: Free Press, 1980); Stephen Gottschalk, *The Emergence of Christian Science in American Religious Life* (Berkeley, Calif.: University of California Press, 1973), and James A. Beckford, *The Trumpet of Prophecy: A Sociological Study of Jehovah's Witnesses* (New York: Wiley, 1975); Robert Mapes Anderson, *Vision of the Disinherited: The Making of American Pentecostalism* (New York: Oxford University Press, 1979), and Timothy P. Weber, *Living in the Shadow of the Second Coming: American Premillennialism, 1875–1982* (New York: Oxford University Press, 1979).

25. A striking example of such critical awareness applied to denominational studies is Russell E. Richey and Kenneth E. Rowe, eds., *Rethinking Methodist History: A Bicentennial Historical Consultation* (Nashville, Tenn.: Kingswood Books of The United Methodist Publishing House, 1985). A new series that also tries to put renewed sophistication into denominational studies has been launched by Greenwood Press of Westport, Conn. Volumes already appearing are David Robinson, *The Unitarians and the Universalists* (1985); William H. Brackney, *The Baptists* (1988); J. William Frost and Hugh Barbour, *The Quakers* (1988); and J. William T. Youngs, *The Congregationalists* (1990).

26. To mention just one example, Lester G. McAllister and William E. Tucker, *Journey in Faith: A History of the Christian Church (Disciples of Christ)* (St. Louis, Mo.: Bethany Presss, 1975), subordinated interpretive freedom to administrative concerns regarding provisional designs for ecclesiastical restructuring. History was appropriated to achieve cooperation among the membership for purposes of institutional harmony and strength.

Denominational Studies in
the Reshaping of
American Religious History

WILLIAM R. HUTCHISON

The conference for which this essay was first written carried a puckish yet deadly serious title: "The Scholarly Writing of Denominational History: An Oxymoron?" My first reaction to that query was a fairly simple negative: No, we are not in the discouraging position of struggling with an oxymoron. Thoroughgoing denominational interest is not automatically at odds with good scholarship—by which, I assume, we mean work that is critical, honest, and probing and that is not beholden to the promotional interests of a given group. In principle, at least, we should be able to treat a religious denomination with as much care and relative objectivity as historians are able to apply to anything else.

This, as I have said, was my initial reaction, but I did have second thoughts, at least to the extent of recognizing that other legitimate ways of defining denominational history can lead to a different answer. Russell Richey had offered one such definition in an encyclopedia article that, while it discussed several ways of studying religious organizations, had called only one of those ways "denominational history." Richey had reserved the term for "inside" interpretations that are meant to promote the cohesiveness and other genuine, deeply felt interests of the denomination. Such historical writing, he said, "assumes as appropriate, true, and defensible the distinctive aspects of ethos, belief, ethic, ritual, and structure defining the movement." He suggested that even today, when this kind of account "respects standards of historical objectivity, aims at impartiality, and often bends over backward to be self-critical . . . the parochial perspective remains."[1]

If we agree to constrict the terminology in that way, our answer to the oxymoron question indeed changes, or at least becomes more problematic. This sort of institutional history, while it may be enormously useful, is useful after the manner and in the style of autobiography. Richey in fact cited autobiographical work as the appropriate analogy.[2]

One could add that denominational history defined in this narrower way is also similar to literally scores of other types of narrative and analysis that are essential to historical writing: company histories, family histories, and commissioned studies of many kinds. Such histories are not written under the influence simply of a general point of view or a broad set of presuppositions. While no brand of historical writing yet devised is free of presuppositions, these histories are shaped additionally by the responsibility, rather consciously assumed, to further the aims of particular institutions. They are group autobiographies that perform an inspirational or cheerleading function.

As such, they may indeed be highly valuable, since they can reveal and express the ethos of the institution as no disinterested presentation could, but critical studies they are not. Unless their authors understand "group interest" very broadly—in fact, nearly *sub specie aeternitatis*—such historical work is quite unlikely to adhere to strict canons of scholarly research and writing.

It may be understood at this point why I keep referring to the more restricted definitions as someone else's idea—to avoid the brickbats and tomatoes hurled by people who think of themselves as denominational historians and who do not welcome the news that what they toil over is not really history. Our gratitude for the self-revelations of group autobiography will not blunt this response. One must in fact be ready for further complaints about condescension—about damning with faint praise, about being in general a nasty person.

Let me suggest, however, that the appropriate course of action for offended denominational historians is not to throw tomatoes but to claim the wider definition. In brief, if the term *denominational history* can be allowed to stand for all or most ways of studying religious institutions, then it will embrace scholarship undertaken with varying purposes and directed to a variety of readerships. It will become an umbrella term that encompasses both advocacy and disinterested study.

As may be obvious by now, I am inclined to adopt this broader definition and then to honor the necessary distinctions among forms of denominational study that serve different purposes and different constituencies. I shall nonetheless argue that the need *of the moment* is exactly what the title of the Lilly-sponsored North Carolina conference—however despairingly—implied. What we need just now is a kind of investigation that takes denominations seriously but that also submits them to the scrutiny of a rigorous scholarship and relates them to the concerns of extradenominational readers and scholars.

Given the various perplexities already mentioned, however, I think we have to consider a previous question: whether the denominational rubric is any longer useful—at all, and whatever the definition. No one, I suppose, would want to rule out any attempt whatever to chart the histories of these institutions. Yet the question whether denominationally configured studies should once again become a major preoccupation for religious and cultural historians is not an idle one.

Historians of American religion, if they have seemed to enter a negative response to that question, have done so not by denouncing or deriding denominational history but simply by placing almost everything else ahead of it. Yet there can be little doubt that some real and long-standing reservations undergird this habit of not-so-benign neglect. Not only have denominational chronicles seemed the very model of insider historiography; for not unrelated reasons they have been read, or left unread, with some of the feelings one might have about an annual report from American Tool and Die. As Henry W. Bowden remarks elsewhere in this volume, the genre has acquired a reputation for being uncommonly boring: monotonous in its preoccupation with self-congratulatory details, certainly irrelevant to the concerns of nonadherents.[3]

One might suppose that interest in denominational studies has waxed and waned with the changing fortunes of the ecumenical movement, but, in fact, denominational history has mostly waned. Frequently cast as villains in early ecumenical advocacy, denominations have scarcely fared better when unifying movements have themselves received a bad press, when, for example, ecumenical efforts have been discounted as attempts to circle the wagons of a beleaguered Protestant establishment.[4]

I think the two seemingly contradictory objections just mentioned are both worthy of respect. They are effective, however, principally as objections to denominational*ism*—to the spirit of separateness—or, in the second instance, as objections to the undue attention given to mainline institutional religion in past historiography. They are not effective as rationales for avoiding the study of denominations. To insist that chronicles of denominational experience be more accessible and more widely relevant is entirely in order, and I wish to be counted as enlisting in that effort. To decide, on the other hand, that we shall no longer give serious and extended attention to these organizations makes about as much sense as to decide that, for analogous reasons, economic historians should pay little or no attention to dominant industries or to decide that no political party should now gain historical attention if it has actually won presidential elections.

From that angle, a decision to dispense with denominational history would produce not merely gaps and silences—regrettable omissions. It would produce distortions just as serious as those of the denomination-ridden past. The better course, it appears, is to get past our sensitivities about possible invidious distinctions among different kinds of denominational study and try to see how to stimulate useful work—"good history"—within all those categories.

The purposes of the two principal types of denominational history—
confessional and critical—converge at various points; even when not
convergent, they strengthen each other. I have suggested already that
deeply committed group autobiography provides valuable materials for
the more disinterested kind of scholarship. I am now saying that the
process also works the other way. I argue, in fact, that even the more
negative or unfairly critical studies of religious denominations can enhance the quality of confessional histories, and certainly can benefit the
kind of self-critical history, written by adherents, that one might hesitate
to call confessional.

Examples of that phenomenon abound, enough so that it is probably
not necessary to dwell upon them. Two that spring to mind are the work
of Francis Jennings on missions to the Indians and that of Fawn Brodie on
Joseph Smith and the Mormons. I realize that Jennings, in his trashing of
Puritans and their motives in *The Invasion of America* (1975), was not
centering his attention on denominational history; yet it is a book that
does castigate the early New England congregational order—a reminder
that gleeful flagellation of that proto-denomination did not end with
Professors Parrington and Wertenbaker.[5] The point is that Jennings's very
negative interpretation of his own well-researched data has had to be
taken seriously. I believe that Jennings's characterizations, unfair as they
may be, have done nearly as much as the more favorable treatments, such
as Alden Vaughan's, to stimulate serious, more balanced, work on Puritan-
Indian relations.[6]

A better example for our purposes is the effect on Mormon historiography of Fawn Brodie's study of early Mormonism, *No Man Knows My
History*. It seems to me that the remarkable development of Mormon
historical studies from Brodie in 1971 to Philip Barlow's *Mormons and
the Bible* exactly twenty years later (Barlow is very much a Mormon)
provides eloquent testimony to the beneficial effects of outsider denominational studies that may be less than fair but that are also more than
merely flippant or dismissive.[7]

I shall not, however, spend time urging that we find more Brodies
who can provoke denominations into opening their archives and goad
other chroniclers into writing balanced accounts. It is more important, I
think, to consider some less dramatic, less ulcer-producing ways of stimulating good denominational history.

To me, at least, the path to be followed seems fairly clear. Its starting
point is an acknowledgment that denominations deserve historical inquiry because of their salience within very large-scaled issues in American cultural and religious history. Does this mean that the denominations
need not be studied for their own sake? Not necessarily. I am talking
about a two-track or multitrack system and assuming that the trains will
still be running on that other track, that we will still have more than
enough confessional studies, both good and not so good. I am indeed
arguing, however, that what we especially need for the reinvigoration of

denominational history are works whose presenting problems are those of the larger culture.

The analogy that may be most useful when we talk about this track is that of biography, as distinguished from autobiography. How are particular persons chosen for biographical study? What conditions the choice? Is it the need of descendants for ego enhancement or for vindication of the family name? Not often, fortunately. Is it a desire to promote the causes the person espoused? Frequently, but the result in such cases is quite likely not to be authoritative biography. Do we choose biographical subjects because of personal affinity? Yes, that is surely a factor, but that does not say much about why we choose one soulmate rather than any of a hundred others.

I think that, overwhelmingly, we choose a particular biographical subject because of a belief or a guess about that person's importance to broader historical developments whose significance is generally agreed upon. Thus, although we may not ordinarily use this terminology, a biography is quite likely to be a case study. I am suggesting, with respect to denominational history, that what we most need to elicit from our students and from ourselves are studies that chronicle the whole of a denomination's history, or a large segment of it, for the purpose of illustrating or questioning particular generalizations about American religion and American culture.

This may sound obvious, and perhaps it should, since there are precedents within the historiography of American religion. The study of denominational*ism,* if not of denominations, has been of interest less for its own sake than as a massive illustration of the glories and the faults in American modalities of church-state separation. Particular denominations, too, have attracted work that is only secondarily about those denominations, work that is primarily about, say, immigration, or revivalism, or racism.

My point, in other words, is not that denominational history as case study would be something new. It is that we do not have nearly enough of it. I think that, despite the kind of precedents I have just mentioned, roughly 80 percent of the history that is focused on denominations—and I mean to include some of the best examples—is simply not of this kind. A case study model dictates, and should ensure, that the relations between a religious phenomenon—a movement, a denomination—and the larger cultural scene receive attention that is central, integral, and sustained. Most dissertations and other works, if they analyze cultural relationships at all, do not accord them that sort of attention.

If we hope to resuscitate this subject that so many have considered moribund, we should try to shift the balance. If it is true that, up to now, about 20 percent of the historical work on denominations has been cast in something like a case study form, then perhaps 40 or 50 percent should be shaped that way in the immediate future. So this is a modest enough proposal. But I contend that, until such an approach does become more common, scholars of American religion—established or fledgling—are not going to be excited, any more than they are now, by the idea of writing something called denominational history.

To cite an example that for me is literally close to home, I believe that the late history of Unitarianism, or of what is now Unitarian Universalism, will not attract much scholarly attention until, like the pre-1860 history of the Unitarian denomination, it becomes part of conversations about American cultural, social, intellectual, and general history.

One might respond immediately that Unitarianism since the Civil War has simply not been as important culturally as was the Unitarianism of William Ellery Channing, Andrews Norton, Ralph Waldo Emerson, and Theodore Parker. That is true enough, just as it might be with respect to the later history of the Quakers, the Disciples, and several other denominations. Yet the story of Unitarian development after 1860 contains illustrative possibilities in relation to at least three kinds of broader issue— some that have been on the agenda for a long time yet never adequately explored, others that have only recently reached the forefront of historical interest and still others that have scarcely been formulated.

In the first category is, for example, the matter of American cultural and religious influence abroad. That Channing and Parker, as well as Emerson, enjoyed an extraordinary readership in Europe has been noted routinely, almost tiresomely, in most histories of Unitarianism from the late nineteenth century to the present. To that extent, the matter of overseas influence has long been on the agenda. But we can say what Mark Twain said about the weather: Everybody talks about it, and nobody does anything about it. Despite the frequent allusions to what should be a rich field for research, we have had precious little exploration of the nature and the extent of American Unitarian influence on the European liberalism of the late nineteenth century. That cross-cultural story needs to be told for its own sake and then incorporated in the historiography of the denomination.

In the second category, involving issues newly current in religious history, are questions such as the place of Unitarians and Unitarianism in the persisting cultural hegemony of the Protestant establishment. I shall return to this subject at the end of this essay.

The third category, the arena within which new questions about American religion are just beginning to be raised and treated, includes such rubrics as local history, regional history, prosopography, and what is now being called lived religion. Under this last heading, for example, we should be promoting studies to explore how a particular religious ideology, in this case covering a range from liberal Christian to humanist, was lived out in worship, preaching, praying, spirituality, social action, and daily lives.

Indeed, in connection with the study of a whole range of "liberal" denominations, the questions of what ordinary parishioners thought and did and of how they worshiped have not yet gained a place on the agenda. But they deserve to be there and would constitute one more way of approaching and stimulating denominational history from the outside.

One can, of course, approach the research-designing task from the opposite direction, that is, by identifying especially compelling topics, traditional and nontraditional, in American general and religious history and then discerning just where denominational case studies have been, or could be, especially helpful. We would find, I think, that topics such as racism, the immigrant experience, and church-state relations call for (and to some extent have already been accorded) close analysis in particular denominational crucibles. We might also find, however, that certain historiographic themes can provide stimuli and starting points for the study of virtually any of the denominations. Let me, in the balance of this essay, offer two examples of what I have in mind.

International comparative history, especially for the postcolonial era, is still one of the significantly unmet obligations facing those of us who study American religious history. We are inclined to think we already know the answer to Winthrop Hudson's question, "How American is Religion in America?"[8] And perhaps we do, but, as one of my proposals about Unitarian history has hinted, I think that until we run more comparisons between American denominations and their British or European counterparts, our generalizations about so-called American religion will be built on traditional and largely untested suppositions.

Even with respect to the immigrant churches, much remains to be done in the way of comparative analysis. We have a number of targeted comparative studies, such as those of Gillian Gollin and Timothy Smith, and work like James Bratt's on the Dutch Calvinists provides a leg up on full longitudinal comparison.[9] On the whole, however, the scholarship on immigrant churches has concentrated on patterns of assimilation and resistance in America, rather than on issues growing out of the relations between American and non-American experience. And here, I think, denominational or sectarian movements, as well as ethnic configurations, are appropriate units for close analysis.

Another topic that would be highly amenable to treatment in full denominational histories is the much-discussed subject of American religious pluralism. If we look hard at the question of how the chronicling of a denominational experience can get outside itself, how it can be related usefully to larger cultural issues, I suspect we will find that a number of the answers lie within this large and complex field of investigation that used to seem large but quite simple.

Time was when the story of American religious pluralism could be presented (or so we imagined) as a trajectory of increasing church-state separation, with religious freedom broadening down, like the English common law, from precedent to precedent. By the time when Sydney Ahlstrom was composing his massive account, however, the story was beginning to seem more somber than that, and less wholly edifying. For many or most historians, the word pluralism had by then come to signify—to borrow Stephen Vincent Benet's memorable phrase—"the America we have not been." Ahlstrom, whose view of the 1960s was almost apocalyptic, thought that until that decade the story of American religion had been one of a pluralism "struggling to be born."[10]

By the 1990s, twenty years after the publication of Ahlstrom's history, pluralism as a subject for investigation had become at least four subjects: (1) the implanting and persistence of pluralist ideals; (2) the fact of growing diversity, ethnic and religious; (3) the equally potent fact of a religious-cultural establishment—overwhelmingly white, male, and Protestant—that resisted the acceptance of diversity; and (4) the torturous yet noteworthy development, over the whole course of colonial and national history, of a realized pluralism.

How might this formidable, multifaceted subject on one hand and denominational studies on the other be brought together in mutually supportive and informing ways? We can begin to answer that question by recognizing that the newer thinking about the varied fortunes of pluralism in America throws traditional ideas about denominations into the proverbial cocked hat. To put this in a current scholarly patois, a sophisticated approach to pluralism "problematizes" many of our past assumptions about the functioning and contributions of denominations.

Until quite recently, observers and historians of American religion were unlikely to view the relationship between denominationalism and pluralism as even faintly problematic. From about the time of Crèvecoeur, the French observer of the 1780s, through that of Sidney Mead in the mid-twentieth century, the denominations or their predecessors stood for what Mead called "the shape of Protestantism in America." Denominationalism in fact functioned as the very linchpin of a lively and on the whole triumphant experimentation with religious liberty.[11]

While religious liberty had meant, most directly, the right of religious groups to operate without state control or supervision, it had also entailed, or was supposed to entail, the freedom of individuals to believe as they might wish, or even to disbelieve entirely. Especially through the nineteenth century, those observers who most admired the American way in religion repeated over and over the dithyrambic praise that Crèvecoeur had lavished on a social system that could make happy next-door neighbors of "a Catholic . . . a good honest plodding German Lutheran . . . a Seceder . . . [and] a Low Dutchman."[12] The institutionalization of religious liberty had guaranteed toleration and at least implied tolerance. Denominations, as institutions made possible by the first, were generally understood as committed in principle to the second.

Even later, when denominations once young and saucy were striking some critics as ossified or worse, the leading criticism was that they stood for inappropriate and unnecessary divisions in Christ's body and in that sense were guilty, not of a denial of pluralism, but of an excess or misapplication of pluralist ideals. While errant denominations in particular times and places—or, more often, their erring subdivisions—might be castigated as obstacles to the growth of pluralism, this was not the burden of most complaints about the denominational form itself. However criticized in other ways, the denomination held its own as the prime embodiment, in America, of an ordered, nondivisive religious freedom.

Admittedly, though, these assumptions constituted a conventional wisdom, and as usual there was a counterwisdom. From about the 1830s on, some foreign observers raised questions about the Americans' celebrated disestablishment of religion. Thanks to the more recent insights of Edward Norman, Robert Handy, and others, we are by now quite familiar with nineteenth-century allegations—not much noticed at the time, but highly credible in retrospect—that Protestant Americans had managed to construct an ersatz establishment more potent than the real thing. This substitute form, moreover, seems to have become stronger, or at least more visible and definable, as the actual diversity of the American population and American religion grew more pronounced.[13]

Just what one calls this American functional equivalent of European arrangements is not the overriding question. If *Protestant establishment,* for example, is a term that inescapably connotes constitutional preferment rather than just cultural authority, then we should avoid that term and agree on another one. Something existed that walked like a duck and quacked like a duck; but if we can achieve greater clarity by calling it a goose or chicken, I have no objection to our doing so.

Whatever the language, a major task still ahead for religious and cultural historians is the fashioning of a multidimensional account— replacing the older two-dimensional ones—of the adventures of pluralism on the American scene. This is clearly a project to which a renewed denominational history should be related and to which it could make enormously important contributions.

In this essay, I have urged that we not try to jettison denominational history or even, necessarily, to seek new names for the various ways of doing it. We should instead define more clearly the different purposes and readerships for denominational studies. We should then, in my opinion, agree to give special encouragement, at least for the foreseeable future, to the sort of account that is directed to those whose principal interest is American cultural history.

It may be objected (as the old didactic sermons used to put it) that while such schemes may work well for the study of Mormonism and pentecostal denominations and the black churches, they are not likely to stir up much activity in relation to what is usually called mainline religion. Why? Because so many of us are concerned to "de-center" American religion and culture and because (one may think) this de-centering propensity is not compatible with even mildly empathetic interest in the denominational history of Methodists or Unitarians.

I believe, however, that if we dig behind this kind of objection, what we usually find is a conflating of descriptive and normative considerations that is neither necessary nor tenable and that, ironically, harbors some of the very assumptions the objector wants to correct or transcend.

The older—really older—church historiography did conflate descriptive intentions and normative ones; surely there can be little question about that. It is not too much to say that, had those old boys (and they were old boys) not seen European and Protestant realities and the values attached to them as utterly central to the value system of American society, they would not have bothered to describe them at all.

Concerning more recent historiography, we find critical judgments more divided. R. Laurence Moore, for example, sees some quite recent descriptive history of the so-called religious mainline as still heavily freighted with the older intentions.[14] In the absence of explicit teleologies (and these are now usually absent), however, how can we know about those deeper motivations—about the "real" reasons why a particular historian has chosen to record a particular history? Even more to the point, how can we know exactly why a Hudson or an Ahlstrom has kept denominational Protestantism central to the interpretation of American religion? What I see, and am inclined to criticize, in the recent writing of religious history is not a persistence of the old intentions so much as a lack of clarity about intentions.

However that may be, past tendentiousness—in whatever historiographic era—does not force us to suppose that future descriptions of Protestant or other dominant structures must also be tendentious. Indeed, I would take this a step further: The delineation of what Catherine Albanese calls the "one religion" of Americans not only leaves room for an equivalent emphasis on the "many religions"; it is also abundantly clear that each kind of description is essential to the other. In other words, the implied choice between a de-centered history and one that continues to give prominence to Protestant and other dominant structures should not be a choice at all. Individual historians may well look intently in one direction and seem oblivious to the other as they carry out their own research topics, but for the field as a whole, neither sort of interest can prosper without the other.[15]

Even with respect to individual historians, I hope that most can manage both preoccupations. The need for "de-centering," descriptive as well as normative, is not going to go away. But that very fact means that, in the work of a given historian, the analysis of traditionally emphasized power structures will continue to be essential. It follows, I think, that while denominational studies, however purged and redirected, are not going to reclaim the status they enjoyed in earlier historiographic eras, they can and must assume a place of importance in the present radical re-visioning of American religious history.

NOTES

1. Russell E. Richey, "Institutional Forms of Religion," in *Encyclopedia of the American Religious Experience: Studies of Traditions and Movements,* ed. Charles H. Lippy and Peter W. Williams, 3 vols. (New York: Charles Scribner's Sons, 1988), 1:32–33. For valuable criticisms of earlier drafts of this paper, I am indebted not only to participants in the Lilly-sponsored conference held at Duke and the National Humanities Center but also to the members of the Harvard Colloquium in American Religious History, especially to Theodore Trost and Craig Townsend, who were the designated hitters for the session at which it was presented.

2. Ibid., p 34.

3. See the essay by Henry Warner Bowden, "The Death and Rebirth of Denominational History," pp. 20–21, in this volume.

4. For a summary of the reasons why denominational study has been suspect or unattractive, see Russell E. Richey's foreward to Richey, ed., *Denominationalism* (Nashville, Tenn.: Abingdon, 1977).

5. Francis Jennings, *The Invasion of America: Indians, Colonialism, and the Cant of Conquest* (Chapel Hill: University of North Carolina Press, 1975); Vernon L. Parrington, *Main Currents in American Thought,* 3 vols. (New York: Harcourt, Brace and Co., 1927–30), vol. 1: Thomas J. Wertenbaker, *The Puritan Oligarchy: The Founding of American Civilization* (New York: Charles Scribner's Sons, 1947).

6. Alden T. Vaughan, *New England Frontier: Puritans and Indians, 1620–1675* (Boston: Little, Brown, 1965).

7. Fawn Brodie, *No Man Knows My History: The Life of Joseph Smith, The Mormon Prophet,* 2d ed., rev. and enl. (New York: Knopf, 1945); Philip L. Barlow, *Mormons and the Bible: The Place of the Latter-day Saints in American Religion* (New York: Oxford University Press, 1991).

8. Winthrop Hudson, "How American is Religion In America?" in *Reinterpretation in American Church History,* ed. Jerald C. Brauer (Chicago: University of Chicago Press, 1968), pp. 153–167.

9. Gillian Lindt Gollin, *Moravians in Two Worlds: A Study of Changing Communities* (New York: Columbia University Press, 1967); Timothy L. Smith, "Lay Initiative in the Religious Life of American Immigrants, 1880–1950," in *Anonymous Americans: Explorations in Nineteenth-Century Social History,* ed. Tamara K. Hareven (Englewood Cliffs, N.J.: Prentice-Hall, 1971); James D. Bratt, *Dutch Calvinism in Modern America* (Grand Rapids, Mich.: William B. Eerdmans Publishing Co., 1984).

10. Stephen Vincent Benet, *John Brown's Body* (Garden City, N.Y.: Doubleday, Doran, 1928), p. 374; Sydney E. Ahlstrom, *A Religious History of the American People* (New Haven: Yale University Press, 1972), p. 12.

11. Sidney E. Mead, *The Lively Experiment: The Shaping of Christianity in America* (New York: Harper and Row, 1963), ch. 7.

12. J. Hector St. John de Crèvecoeur, *Letters from an American Farmer* (New York: E. P. Dutton, 1957), p. 45.

13. Edward R. Norman, *The Conscience of the State in North America* (London: Cambridge University Press, 1968); Robert T. Handy, *A Christian America: Protestant Hopes and Historical Realities* (New York: Oxford University Press,

1971). See also William R. Hutchison, "Innocence Abroad: The 'American Religion' in Europe," *Church History* 51 (March 1982): 71–84.

14. R. Laurence Moore, *Religious Outsiders and the Making of Americans* (New York: Oxford University Press, 1986), pp. 3–21.

15. Catherine L. Albanese, *America: Religions and Religion.* (Belmont, Calif.: Wadsworth, 1981).

The People as Well as the Prelates:
A Social History of a Denomination

JAY P. DOLAN

Denominational history has come a long way since the time of Philip Schaff. This is as true for historians of American Protestantism as it is for historians of American Catholicism. To understand the present style of writing denominational history, it is necessary to return to the past and to examine how historians, in this case historians of American Catholicism, have written denominational history.

Peter Guilday (1884–1947) was the most significant historian of American Catholicism in the first half of the twentieth century. The author of several books, he is best remembered for his two major biographical studies, *The Life and Times of John Carroll, Archbishop of Baltimore, 1735–1815* (1922) and *The Life and Times of John England, First Bishop of Charleston 1786–1842* (1927). Trained as an historian at Louvain University in Belgium, Guilday wanted to professionalize the study of American Catholic history. For this reason he became the driving force behind the founding of the *Catholic Historical Review* in 1915 and four years later founded the American Catholic Historical Association. In addition, he taught at Catholic University, where in 1914 he inaugurated a seminar in church history to train students in the study of American Catholicism. More than anyone else, Peter Guilday was responsible for the revival of interest in American Catholic history in the twentieth century, a field of study that had become moribund after the death of John Gilmary Shea in 1892. Through his teaching and writing he influenced a generation of historians, most notably John Tracy Ellis, who would eventually succeed Guilday as the premier historian of American Catholicism. Because of his influence and prominence, an understanding of Guilday's view of history and his ideas on how denominational history can best be written are essential for an understanding of the writing of American Catholic history in the twentieth century.

In the appendix to his biography of Bishop John England, Guilday wrote that "for many years to come, historians of the Catholic Church in the United States must content themselves with a biographical presentation of its past." He reasoned that, "owing to the scattered and unorganized condition of our archival sources, the more prudent method is to center around the great figures in our Church the story of their times; with the hope that, as the years pass, our documentary knowledge will be increased and the institutional factors of our Catholic life become more salient and tangible." Guilday went on to state that the life and times of John England "may well be taken as the history of the Church in the United States during the twenty-two years he presided over the See of Charleston."[1] In this statement Guilday made two important points: first, that historical biography was the key to unlocking the past, and second, that the goal of opening up the past was to understand more fully the history of the institution, or, as he put it, "the institutional factors of our Catholic life."

Guilday also followed two other key principles in his writing. He viewed his historical work as a form of apologetics. In other words, Guilday maintained, history rightly written would prove that Roman Catholicism was the true church, providing an important defense against the critics of Catholicism. In endorsing this principle Guilday showed himself to be a true representative of the Counter-Reformation mentality that had been developing among Catholics since the sixteenth century. The other principle that guided Guilday was the solicitation of episcopal approval for what he wrote; for this reason he was very cautious about what he wrote and would, as he put it, "quietly overlook" anything that was detrimental to the history of the church and to its leaders.[2] Such caution was indicative of the atmosphere that prevailed in the years following the condemnation of modernism when church leaders looked upon scholars with suspicion.

For Guilday, then, and his generation of historians, four principles guided their work. First, they would concentrate on biographical studies; second, these studies would form the foundation for an institutional history of Catholicism; third, the goal of their work was to defend the truth of Catholicism; and fourth, church history was to be selective, presenting what could be called "history without the warts." Institutional, biographical, apologetical, and promotional—these four terms characterized American Catholic history in the first half of the twentieth century.

John Tracy Ellis, whom Guilday described as his "providential successor," became the personification of American Catholic history for the post-World War II generation of scholars.[3] Ellis completed his doctoral studies in medieval history at Catholic University in 1930 and subsequently published his dissertation, *Anti-Papal Legislation in Medieval England (1066–1377)*. Shortly afterwards he entered the seminary to prepare for the priesthood. After ordination to the priesthood in 1938, he joined the faculty at Catholic University; in 1942 he published his second book, *Cardinal Consalvi and Anglo-Papal Relations, 1814–1824.* Trained as a medievalist and exhibiting a keen interest in modern European history, Ellis did not seem a likely heir to Guilday. But when Guilday's health failed, the rector of Catholic University asked Ellis to take over Guilday's courses in American Catholic history. Ellis's reply was typically very straightforward: "I do not know anything about the field." The rector's reply was equally blunt: "You can learn, can't you?" That brief exchange in 1941 launched the career of John Tracy Ellis as an historian of American Catholicism.[4]

Ellis's writings were of two types. The first type, which resembled the work of Guilday, was most apparent during the 1940s and early 1950s. It emphasized a biographical approach to religious history, as well as a focus on the institution. The best example of this phase of Ellis's work is his two-volume study of Cardinal Gibbons, *The Life of James Cardinal Gibbons, Archbishop of Baltimore, 1834–1921.* Published in 1952, it followed in the tradition of Guilday; more than a biography, it was a history of the life and times of Gibbons. The second type of historical writing reflected Ellis's interest in social and cultural history, an interest most likely kindled when Ellis studied with Arthur Schlesinger, Sr., at Harvard University in the spring of 1942. The one book that best exemplified this style of history was *American Catholicism,* part of the series *The Chicago History of American Civilization,* edited by Daniel J. Boorstin. Ellis's book grew out of a series of four lectures he gave at the University of Chicago in 1955. In this study, social movements, issues, and organizations occupied center stage.

By the 1950s the essay had become Ellis's chief form of publication. In numerous articles, which often originated as lectures, he charted a new direction in American Catholic historical studies. The most memorable of these essays was the paper he read at the 1955 meeting of the Catholic Commission on Intellectual and Cultural Affairs on the topic of "American Catholics and the Intellectual Life." Later that year the essay appeared in *Thought,* a Catholic journal, and was subsequently published as a pamphlet. In this phase of his career Ellis wrote about issues such as the intellectual life, higher education, religious freedom, and the education of priests.

Unlike Guilday, Ellis did not view church history as a branch of apologetics. He did not believe that church history "was meant to edify . . . and unpleasant episodes . . . were simply to be kept out of sight." Moreover, he continually urged truthfulness in the writing of history, and he himself could be very critical of the church and its leaders if he thought it necessary.[5] Nonetheless, he was writing in the 1940s and 1950s, and he manifested a defensive attitude that was common among Catholics at that time. In his best-seller, *American Catholicism,* he frequently pointed out the contributions that Catholics had made to the

United States and made statements that were gratuitous and misleading. One such statement pertained to the issue of racism in the twentieth century. After mentioning a few examples of church actions that opposed segregation, Ellis concluded that the "Church often has anticipated the most enlightened public sentiment on matters of this kind." What he failed to mention were the many actions of church leaders that defended the status quo of segregation.[6] In speaking about the bishops and politics, he claimed that the hierarchy left "complete freedom of political action" to individual church members. That was not entirely accurate either; bishops have at times tried to influence the politics of the people.[7]

In making these and similar statements, it seems clear that Ellis was trying to paint the best possible picture of American Catholic history. Even though he did not hesitate to criticize the church and its leaders, he often slipped into an apologetic style of writing, as is clear from a comparison of his 1956 history of American Catholicism and the 1958 study *The Emergence of Liberal Catholicism in America,* written by Robert Cross, a Protestant layman. Cross's book manifests none of the defensive and apologetic tone of Ellis's study.[8]

Unlike many historians of Catholicism in the Counterreform era, Ellis did not evidence prejudice and suspicion toward other religions; rather, he urged toleration and understanding. In many other respects, however, Ellis's approach to writing history was similar to that of Guilday.

Like Guilday, Ellis endorsed the idea of "scientific history"; in other words, history must be based on documentary evidence. As he put it, "no documents, no history." In his study of Gibbons he stated that he wanted "to allow the documents to speak for themselves so that the reader might have all the evidence before him."[9] The historical biography was also central to Ellis's writing; like Guilday, Ellis chose as the subjects of his biographies distinguished bishops. His other writings were also very institutionally oriented. Ellis was clearly an historian of the institutional church, and the dissertations he directed at Catholic University provide rather conclusive evidence of this propensity, for the vast majority were either episcopal biographies or institutional histories.[10] In his book *American Catholicism,* Ellis made a telling statement in this regard when he wrote that "[t]he question of nationalist feeling among the American Catholics, often so closely related to lay trusteeism, can be studied within the Church's hierarchy of these years more closely than they can be studied within the numerous and widespread clergy and laity." In other words, Ellis suggested, the best way to understand the people was to study the bishops—a very clerical view of church history. Subsequent historical studies have demonstrated how narrow this point of view was.[11]

Despite the fundamental parallels between the work of Ellis and that of Guilday, Ellis did offer something new and unique to American Catholic history. He became a publicist for reform in the American Catholic church and "used history as an instrument to promote changes he believed necessary to American Catholicism." Like the progressive historians of an earlier generation, "he possessed a present-mindedness that related events and developments of the past to questions of contemporary interest, and he used his addresses and publications to initiate change as well as to describe and explain it."[12] Some of the issues that he addressed include the use of the vernacular in worship, the selection of bishops, religious liberty, higher education, and the intellectual life. No other historian of American Catholicism, living or dead, has matched Ellis in this regard, and it is this aspect of Ellis's writing that has gained him the most fame.

In 1957 Henry J. Browne, a student of Ellis, wrote a progress report on the writing of American Catholic history in the period 1947–1957 and pointed out the main characteristics of American Catholic history during those years. After noting the emphasis on episcopal biography and Ellis's influence in this regard, he concluded that "[t]his zeal for episcopal biography has been an outstanding characteristic of the period coming to a close."[13] Other popular genres during the decade that were noted by Browne were histories of religious communities, histories of dioceses, and studies of lay organizations.

A decade later David J. O'Brien wrote a similar essay and concluded that "the dominant characteristics" of American Catholic historiography were "the same today as noted by Henry J. Browne a decade ago: heavy emphasis upon episcopal biography; intense concern with the internal controversies of the late nineteenth century; lack of interest in non-Irish Catholic groups and in the supposedly conservative nineteenth-century bishops; and an almost total neglect of Catholic thought and of the period since World War I. Of equal significance, O'Brien asserted, many works were unoriginal, avoiding all but the most cautious and judicious interpretations."[14] The reason for this, according to O'Brien, was the historians' view of the church; they had a very institutional understanding of the church, and for this reason "the history of the Church has been told in terms of the hierarchy with episcopal biography the typical mode of study."[15] But O'Brien pointed out that the winds of change were blowing across the landscape of American Catholic historiography and that a new understanding of the church had emerged as a result of the Second Vatican Council. In addition, social changes in the 1960s had radically altered the historical environment in the United States. A new day had dawned for both the church and the nation.

Awareness of these changes on the part of historians "might," in the opinion of O'Brien, "suggest alternative modes of analysis of the history of the Catholic Church in this country."[16] That is in fact just what has happened in the twenty-five years since O'Brien made his prediction. A new understanding of the church has emerged "at a time when American Catholics themselves" were "experiencing rapid social and intellectual transformation," and this twofold revolution has transformed the writing of American Catholic history.[17]

In 1968 two historians who in time would become major interpreters of the American Catholic past published their first books. The historians were Philip Gleason and David O'Brien, and their books, based on their doctoral dissertation research, were *American Catholics and Social Reform: The New Deal Years* by O'Brien and *The Conservative Reformers: German-American Catholics and the Social Order,* by Gleason. These publications were the first indications that American Catholic history was moving in a new direction. O'Brien and Gleason were laymen, and both were trained as American historians, not as church historians. Furthermore, neither of them was interested in writing the traditional episcopal, institutional history that had been in vogue for so long.

Gleason had studied with Thomas T. McAvoy at the University of Notre Dame, but his interests were quite different from McAvoy's. Gleason would describe himself as an intellectual historian who studies the history of immigration, specifically, the theme of Americanization. One of his principal concerns has been the role of religion in the process of Americanization, and he has argued that an understanding of the historical development of the American identity cannot be achieved without considering the role of religion. Catholicism enters his work as a force that has helped to shape the American identity in both the nineteenth and the twentieth centuries. Because of his interest in both intellectual history and the history of American Catholicism, Gleason has devoted much of his career to studying Catholic higher education. Rather than concentrate on the institutional history of Catholic higher education, he has directed his energies toward understanding the cultural and intellectual forces that shaped this educational enterprise.[18]

O'Brien did his doctoral work at the University of Rochester and taught at Loyola College in Montreal, Canada, in the mid-1960s. During these years he became concerned with the renewal of the church and society, and before long he had become an activist scholar in the tradition of the progressive historians who sought to integrate their scholarly work with political and social reform. His several books and numerous essays reflect his interest in the relationship between Catholicism and American society, especially his desire for the renewal of American society by the application of Catholic social teachings on justice and peace.[19]

What was new and different about Gleason and O'Brien was that they broke away from the type of history that was previously dominant among historians of American Catholicism. Gleason offered new ideas and categories with which to interpret the past; O'Brien brought a new perspective to the past, what he would eventually call the perspective of a "public Catholicism," and he consciously used history in his attempt to reform the church and the world. Neither writer evidenced the apologetical concern of earlier historians; both were writing in the post-Vatican II era, when Catholics were more at home in the United States than ever before and less self-conscious and defensive about their place in American society. Nor were Gleason and O'Brien writing for the approval of the hierarchy. Even though they offered new insights into American Catholic history, they represented only the first stage of a new age in the writing of this history. A new generation of historians would go beyond Gleason and O'Brien by asking new questions of the past and by seeking out new sources and new methodologies in their search to answer these questions.

The new social history that developed in the 1960s and 1970s favored the intensive study of individual communities. Such studies represented the first wave of the new social history. One of the first community studies of American Catholicism was my own dissertation, done at the University of Chicago. Published in 1975 under the title *The Immigrant Church: New York's Irish and German Catholics, 1815–1865,* it touched on several themes that were prominent in historical writing in the 1970s. These included the immigrants, the parish, and the religion of the people, all studied in the context of a single community. Another community study of this type was Charles Shanabruch's *Chicago's Catholics: The Evolution of an American Identity.* Published in 1981, it examined the ethnic diversity of Chicago Catholicism during the era of immigration. June Granatir Alexander's book *The Immigrant Church and Community: Pittsburgh's Slovak Catholics and Lutherans, 1880–1915* (1987) was an excellent study of Pittsburgh's Catholic and Lutheran Slovak communities, with the parish the focal point in this study of an immigrant community.

This focus on the parish was something new in American Catholic history. Writing the history of a parish was traditionally something done as part of a parish's celebration of a special anniversary, such as the fiftieth or one-hundredth anniversary of its founding. Such histories tended to celebrate the glories of the parish and its clerical leaders in a very uncritical manner. With the new emphasis on community studies, the parish now became a more viable institution to study; it provided a window to the history of a neighborhood and its people. The study of the parish also made sense theologically. The new theology of the Vatican II era stressed the local church, the people of God; the parish community best represented the incarnation of this idea. Historians of American Judaism and Protestantism also began to study the local congregation, and before long congregational studies became a buzzword among historians.

One ambitious American Catholic parish history study, *The American Catholic Parish: A History From 1850 to the Present* (1987), was a two-volume collection of six lengthy essays. Its uniqueness was that it sought to write a history of American Catholicism using the parish, rather than the bishop, as a key organizing principle. The essays were organized on a regional basis so that comparisons could be made about the development of the church in various regions of the country.[20]

The new social history stressed the study of groups, not just of individuals, and it sought to recover the history of the inarticulate lower classes. Known as bottom-up history, it fired the imagination of many historians and persuaded them to study groups such as slaves, laborers, and immigrants. Immigration history was also undergoing substantial development in these years, blending nicely with the emphasis on bottom-up history. Also part of the changing social picture was the civil rights movement and the stress on the history of blacks and of other minority groups. Later came the emergence of the new ethnicity, with renewed attention to white ethnic groups such as Italians and Poles.

All of these developments in the late 1960s and early 1970s resulted in an explosion in the number of studies focusing on immigrant communities. Many of these studies gave some peripheral attention to religion, most often Catholicism, given the heavy immigrant quality of nineteenth-century Catholicism. Others were more explicitly centered on the theme of religion; two such works were Silvano Tomasi's *Piety and Power: The Role of Italian Parishes in the New York Metropolitan Area* (1975) and Joseph John Parot's *Polish Catholics in Chicago, 1850–1920.* Both of these studies used the parish as the key organizing principle for their research. The history of black Catholics has also attracted the attention of scholars; in 1990 Cyprian Davis published the first comprehensive history of the black Catholic community, *The History of Black Catholics in the United States.*

An important development in the post-1970 era was the emergence of women's history, which transformed the study of American history and which had a significant impact on religious history as well. In her study of the emergence of the women's movement within contemporary American Catholicism, *New Catholic Women* (1985), Mary Jo Weaver wrote a detailed essay on the exclusion of women from American Catholic history, an omission that is less common today. The area that first attracted the attention of historians was the history of women religious. Mary Ewen's book *The Role of the Nun in Nineteenth-Century America,* published in 1979, was a pioneer study of this topic; since its publication, many other studies on the subject have appeared.

In recent years historians of American women religious, most of them members of religious orders, have formed their own organization and regularly publish a newsletter and convene conferences. Margaret S. Thompson, a laywoman and an historian at Syracuse University, has written numerous essays on the history of women religious from the perspective of a women's historian;[21] Patricia Byrne has written a major essay on the changing role of women religious in the twentieth century. Debra Campbell has also written an important essay that emphasizes the role of women in the history of twentieth-century American Catholicism,[22] and Karen Kennelly has edited a collection of essays, *American Catholic Women: A Historical Exploration* (1989), by scholars in this area; the essays in Kennelly's book clearly suggest that the history of American Catholic women is still in its early stages of development. James J. Kenneally has written a one-volume history, *The History of American Catholic Women* (1990), that chronicles the contributions that women have made to American Catholic history.

Another area of inquiry, virtually unmined by historians of American

Catholicism until the 1970s, is the religion of the people. The use of new types of sources, such as prayer books and sermons, and the methodological influence of anthropologists such as Clifford Geertz and Victor Turner have influenced this genre of history. My own study *Catholic Revivalism: The American Experience, 1830–1900* (1977) sought to uncover the religion of the people by examining the parish mission—its sermons, rituals, and structure. Joseph Chinnici has written extensively on the theme of piety and published a book on this topic, *Living Stones: The History and Structure of Catholic Spiritual Life in the United States* (1989), a comprehensive synthesis that is most original in its interpretation and that offers an entirely new perspective on the history of American Catholicism from the late eighteenth century to the present. Ann Taves's study *The Household of Faith: Roman Catholic Devotions in Mid-Nineteenth Century America* (1986) is another important study of Catholic piety. By focusing on the devotional literature of Catholicism, Taves is able to explore the rise of devotionalism in the nineteenth century and its role in shaping the Catholic mind of that era. In his study of Italian devotional practices, *The Madonna of 115th Street: Faith and Community in Italian Harlem, 1880–1950* (1985), and in his more recent work on devotion to St. Jude, Robert Orsi has demonstrated how an historian with imagination and new methodological tools can mine the riches of popular devotions.[23]

Another area of inquiry is the historical development of theology. Gerald P. Fogarty's study *American Catholic Biblical Scholarship: A History From the Early Republic to Vatican II* (1989) is a fine example of the insights an historian can bring to the intellectual heritage of Catholics. Joseph M. White's history of the seminary in the United States, *The Diocesan Seminary in the United States: A History from the 1780s to the Present* (1989), examines the education of priests and the place of theology in that education. R. Scott Appleby's study *Church and Age Unite: The Modernist Impulse in American Catholicism* (1992) examines the rise and fall of theological modernism.

In addition to these new areas of inquiries, historians have also turned their attention to more traditional themes. Diocesan histories have been a staple of American Catholic historiography for many years, but historians are now writing these histories with a new perspective, thus giving a fresh look to a traditional topic. Leslie Woodcock Tentler's history of the archdiocese of Detroit, *Seasons of Grace* (1990), is a fine example of this new style of diocesan history. In the introduction to her book, Tentler explains her approach to the subject, writing that she "was able to explore questions of particular interest to a new generation of Church historians—questions having to do with religious belief and practice, with the social dimension of parish life, with the impact of ethnic and racial and class divisions on the Church, with the relationship between Catholics and non-Catholics in politics and community life." She says that she has "tried, as far as my sources will allow, to create a portrait of the people who built the institutions that we call the Church in the Archdiocese of Detroit, and to place them, and the institutions that they built, in the context of one of the nation's most turbulent industrial cities and its developing hinterland."[24] Her study is a local history, but to give it a larger focus Tentler follows certain organizing themes that "shed light on the Church as a national, even occasionally as an international, institution." Her themes are the following: the Americanization of a polyglot immigrant institution, changing patterns of religious practice, the relationship of the priest to the people, the democratic tradition of lay involvement, the role and status of women in the church, and, finally, the relationship of Catholics to the non-Catholic world around them.[25] Tentler's study is the most successful effort thus far to write a new type of institutional history. Another fine effort is Thomas W. Spalding's history of the archdiocese of Baltimore, *The Premier See: A History of the Archdiocese of Baltimore, 1789–1989* (1989).

Writing histories of religious orders has seldom appealed to anyone outside those orders, but some studies challenge this pattern. In *Desegregating the Altar: The Josephites and the Struggle for Black Priests, 1871–1960* (1990), Stephen J. Ochs studied the Josephite order and their struggle to ordain black priests. More than a history of the Josephites, the book offers a compelling explanation of why there are so few black Catholic priests in the United States. Christopher Kaufmann's history of the Sulpicians, *Tradition and Transformation in Catholic Culture: The Priests of Saint Sulpice in the United States From 1791 to the Present* (1988), is much more than an institutional study.

Although the "zeal for episcopal biography" has greatly diminished, bishops can still claim historians among their admirers. Marvin R. O'Connell has written a magisterial biography of Archbishop John Ireland, *John Ireland and the American Catholic Church* (1988); Edward Kantowicz has authored a perceptive study of Cardinal Mundelein of Chicago, *Corporation Sole: Cardinal Mundelein and Chicago Catholicism* (1983); and James M. O'Toole thoroughly destroyed the myth surrounding Cardinal O'Connell of Boston in his impressive work *Militant and Triumphant: William Henry O'Connell and the Catholic Church in Boston, 1859–1944* (1992).

Gerald Fogarty is one of the best of the new generation of church historians; his study *The Vatican and the American Hierarchy From 1870 to 1965* (1982) is an excellent reminder that traditional church history, when done well, can be as revealing and as engaging as the new religious history that has developed since the 1970s. Another example of this genre is James Hennesey's general history, *American Catholics: A History of the Roman Catholic Community in the United States* (1981).

This brief survey of the new directions taken by American Catholic historiography since the 1970s indicates that the writing of American Catholic history has made a radical departure from the 1950s, when its chief characteristic was its "zeal for episcopal biography." Even more telling than these new themes, sources, and methodologies is a comparison between the background of the new breed of historian, and that of those who wrote in the Guilday era. In 1920 the membership of the American Catholic Historical Association was 90 percent male; of the 172 individuals who belonged to the association, 64 percent were priests. At a 1990 conference at the University of Notre Dame on the history of twentieth-century American Catholicism, fifty papers were presented. About half the people who presented papers were female (46 percent), and 84 percent of the presenters were laymen or laywomen; only 16 percent were clergy-men. These figures certainly represent a dramatic shift from the Guilday era. Equally telling is the educational background of the new historians. In the Guilday-Ellis era, anyone who wanted to become an historian of Ameri-can Catholicism would most likely have studied at Catholic University. That is no longer true. The new generation of historians has studied at a variety of universities, both private and public, Catholic and secular. Hav-ing left the Catholic ghetto, these writers have been influenced by histori-ans working in various American universities and by the changes that influenced these academies in the 1960s and 1970s. As a result of these changes, historians began to ask new questions of the past and to seek out new sources for their answers. Before long the "consensus" that had domi-nated historical writing disintegrated, and the new generation of historians remade American history. They also remade American Catholic history.

The new Catholic history that has emerged since the 1960s has many features that set it apart from the historical writing of the Guilday-Ellis era. First, no one model of history is dominant. Even though the "zeal for episcopal biography" that characterized the earlier era is gone, episcopal biographies still attract the attention of historians. Institutional studies also continue to be written, but many of them, like Tentler's work, have acquired a new look as they ask new questions of the past. Second, the new social history that has emerged in the academy since the 1960s has had a noticeable influence on the writing of American Catholic history and has turned the attention of historians to themes such as the history of African-Americans, women, and various immigrant groups. Third, the will-ingness of historians to cross disciplinary boundaries and to incorporate concepts and methodologies drawn from other disciplines has opened up a new area of inquiry—the study of popular belief. Finally, the new Catho-lic history lacks coherence and unity. In the 1940s and 1950s American Catholic history was distinguishable by its institutional focus and its en-dorsement of the concept of the progressive Americanization of the church and its people. There was a consensus about the history of the American Catholic experience. That is no longer true. The variety of topics that historians now study, the differences in methodologies, and the variety of perspectives and beliefs that historians bring to their work have shattered that consensus. This change is not peculiar to American Catholic history but is symptomatic of American history in general. Al-though many historians have lamented this lack of synthesis, the new social history of the United States in general and of Catholics in particular has demonstrated that history is never as simple as historians would like it to be. History is complex and never yields to the simple interpretation.

Replacing the consensus view of the past is a rich diversity in historical studies generated by the use of new types of sources and new methodologies, as well as by the asking of new questions about the past. In the case of American Catholic history, this diversity has revealed the richness of the American Catholic past and has nurtured a vision of the past that is much broader than that of the Guilday-Ellis era. The diversity of the new American Catholic history does not mean that coherence and synthesis are something of the past. There is sufficient coherence in the new history that a new and fresh interpretation of the past can be attempted, as I have tried to do in my own work *The American Catholic Experience: A History from Colonial Times to the Present* (1985).

Because it is so diverse and multifaceted, American Catholic history is now more easily integrated into the general history of the United States, especially in the areas of immigration history, intellectual and cultural history, and women's history. Historians of American Catholicism are also depicting this history on a larger canvas. They are taking into consideration external, cultural reasons for change, as well as reasons internal to Catholicism alone. The increasing significance of the middle class in the late nineteenth century is one example of such an external force; another is the influence of economic and cultural forces on American Catholics in the post-World War II era. As American Catholic history has become more integrated into American history, it has gained more recognition and respect from the historical academy. The more it has shed its narrow, apologetical perspective, the more this respect has increased.[26]

Denominational history is still a valuable enterprise, but it has taken on a new look as far as American Catholicism is concerned. The traditional style of history, with its focus on prelates and institutions, has receded into the background, and in its place is a new Catholic history. A very valuable aspect of this new style of history is its emphasis on themes or issues, which makes possible comparative analysis across denominational lines. Such analysis can only serve to enrich the study of American religious history. Unfortunately, not enough of this comparative analysis is being done. The parochial tendencies of denominational history have slowed such attempts, but the possibilities are very great.

The emphasis on community studies and the importance of the congregation in these studies is an obvious area for comparative studies of Protestant congregations, Catholic parishes, and Jewish synagogues. The late nineteenth and the early twentieth centuries are excellent places to begin, since all-encompassing, institutional congregations emerged in all three religious traditions during these years. The increase in clerical control in the nineteenth century is another common theme in American religious history. The democratization of religion in the early national period was not limited to Protestant denominations; Catholics as well as

Jews experienced a similar surge of democracy within their churches. The theme of modernist thought has attracted much attention in recent years, especially as it forced the realignment of American Protestantism in the early twentieth century with the emergence of fundamentalism; a similar realignment took place at this time among American Catholics and forced church authorities to speak out against theological modernism, and the emergence of conservative Judaism took place as a result of a similar aversion to modernist thought.

The role of women is a topic that many denominational historians are examining, and the opportunities for analysis across denominational boundaries are unlimited. Another area of comparison is the immigrant experiences of Protestants, Catholics, and Jews. Immigration was common to all three denominations, and the ways in which it influenced the churches and transformed the religious traditions of the people are just two possible areas of comparative analysis.[27] Finally, the various styles of leadership, as well as the formation of leadership within each tradition, could be another area of profitable comparative study.

Developments in the historical discipline over the past quarter century have not diminished the value of denominational history. What they have suggested is that denominational history must avoid the narrow, parochial view of the past and instead seek to incorporate the history of each denomination into the history of the culture in which it is situated. Denominational history also must avoid an apologetical and patronizing tone and must seek to be truthful. The writing of American Catholic history has achieved this stage of development; for this reason it has gained greater attention and respect from the historical academy.

A viable model for writing denominational history is the social history of religion. This is a style of history that seeks to emphasize the people, not just the prelates. For too long church history has meant the history of the clergy; the people were nowhere to be found. The developments of the past quarter century have shown how limited is this view. To continue to write denominational history and to leave out the people is no longer acceptable. Historians must realize this new reality and not be threatened by the new history. Change in the writing of history takes place in every generation, and such change in our own time should not be regarded negatively. As Peter Guilday noted many years ago, "Ecclesiastical history never stays written, either because each generation asks for a restatement of the past in terms of its own conditions, or because the constant discovery of fresh material brings new viewpoints and new problems."[28]

NOTES

1. Peter Guilday, *The Life and Times of John England, First Bishop of Charleston (1786–1842)* vol. 2 (New York: America Press, 1927).

2. Quoted in David O'Brien, "Peter Guilday: The Catholic Intellectual in the Post-Modernist Church," in *Studies in Catholic History in Honor of John Tracy Ellis,* ed. Nelson H. Minnich, Robert B. Eno, and Robert F. Trisco (Wilmington, Del.: Michael Glazier, 1985), p. 270; this is an excellent essay on Guilday. Henry Warner Bowden has also examined the writings of Guilday and of John Tracy Ellis in *Church History in an Age of Uncertainty: Historiographical Patterns in the United States, 1906–1990* (Carbondale, Ill.: Southern Illinois University Press, 1991).

3. O'Brien, "Peter Guilday," p. 261.

4. John Tracy Ellis, *Faith and Learning: A Church Historian's Story* (Lanham, Md.: University Press of America, 1989), p. 31.

5. John Tracy Ellis, "The Ecclesiastical Historian in the Service of Clio," *Church History* 38 (March 1969): 110; this essay is a good example of Ellis's endorsement of truth in historical writing.

6. John Tracy Ellis, *American Catholicism* (Chicago: University of Chicago Press, 1956), p. 146; see Stephen J. Ochs, *The Desegregated Altar: The Josephites and the Struggle for Black Priests 1871–1960* (Baton Rouge: Louisiana State University Press, 1990), for another view of the hierarchy's attitudes on race in the twentieth century.

7. Ellis, *American Catholicism,* p. 92; the best example of this is the 1886 mayoral election in New York City.

8. Robert D. Cross, *The Emergence of Liberal Catholicism in America* (Cambridge, Mass.: Harvard University Press, 1958).

9. Quoted in Jack Douglas Thomas, Jr., "Interpretations of American Catholic Church History: A Comparative Analysis of Representative Catholic Historians, 1875–1975" (Ph.D. diss., Baylor University, 1976), pp. 169–170.

10. See Ellis, *Faith and Learning,* pp. 45–51, where he writes about his students and their work.

11. See the work of Patrick W. Carey on trusteeism, *People, Priests, and Prelates: Ecclesiastical Democracy and the Tensions of Trusteeism* (Notre Dame, Ind.: University of Notre Dame Press, 1987).

12. J. Douglas Thomas, "A Century of American Catholic History," *U.S. Catholic Historian* 6, no. 1 (Winter 1987): 41, 44.

13. Henry J. Browne, "American Catholic History: A Progress Report on Research and Study," *Church History* 26, no. 4 (December 1957): 372.

14. David J. O'Brien, "American Catholic Historiography: A Post-Conciliar Evaluation," *Church History* 37, no. 1 (March 1968): 82.

15. Ibid., p. 87.

16. Ibid., p. 88.

17. Ibid., p. 80.

18. Gleason's major publications were published in two collections, *Keeping the Faith: American Catholicism Past and Present* (Notre Dame, Ind.: University of Notre Dame Press, 1987) and *Speaking of Diversity: Language and Ethnicity in Twentieth-Century America* (Baltimore: Johns Hopkins University Press, 1992); he also wrote a major essay, "American Identity and Americanization," for the *Harvard Encyclopedia of American Ethnic Groups* (Cambridge, Mass.: Harvard University Press, 1980), pp. 31–58.

19. O'Brien's publications include *The Renewal of American Catholicism* (New York: Oxford University Press, 1974), *Faith and Friendship: Catholicism in the Diocese of Syracuse, 1886–1986* (Syracuse: Diocese of Syracuse, 1987),

and *Public Catholicism: American Catholics and Public Life* (New York: Macmillan, 1988).

20. Jay P. Dolan, ed. *The American Catholic Parish: A History from 1850 to the Present* (New York: Paulist Press, 1987). The authors of these essays were Joseph J. Casino for the parish in the Northeast, Michael J. McNally for the Southeast, Charles E. Nolan for the South Central region, Jeffrey M. Burns for the Pacific states, Carol L. Jensen for the Intermountain West, and Stephen J. Shaw for the Midwest.

21. Two examples are Margaret S. Thompson, "Women, Feminism, and the New Religious History: Catholic Sisters as a Case Study," in *Belief and Behavior: Essays in the New Religious History,* ed. Philip VanderMeer and Robert Swierenga (New Brunswick, N.J.: Rutgers University Press, 1991), pp. 136–163; "Sisterhood and Power: Class, Culture, and Ethnicity in the American Convent," *Colby Library Quarterly* 25 (September 1989): 149–175.

22. Patricia Byrne, "In the Parish But Not of It: Sisters," and Debra Campbell, "The Struggle to Serve: From the Lay Apostolate to the Ministry Explosion," in *Transforming Parish Ministry: The Changing Roles of Catholic Clergy, Laity, and Women Religious,* ed. Jay P. Dolan, R. Scott Appleby, Patricia Byrne, and Debra Campbell (New York: Crossroad, 1990), pp. 109–200, 201–280.

23. Robert A. Orsi," 'He Keeps Me Going': Women's Devotion to Saint Jude and the Dialectics of Gender in American Catholicism, 1929–1965," in *Belief in History: Innovative Approaches to European and American Religion,* ed. Thomas Kselman (Notre Dame, Ind.: University of Notre Dame Press, 1991), pp. 137–172.

24. Leslie Woodcock Tentler, *Seasons of Grace: A History of the Catholic Archdiocese of Detroit* (Detroit, Mich.: Wayne State University, 1990), p. 2.

25. Ibid., pp. 3–6.

26. Paul Gerard Robichaud has examined the theme of class among Catholics in "The Resident Church: Middle-Class Catholics and the Shaping of American Catholic Identity, 1889–1899" (Ph.D. diss., University of California at Los Angeles, 1989); I have written on the social and cultural influences on post-World War II Catholicism in "American Catholics in a Changing Society: Parish and Ministry, 1930 to the Present," in Dolan et al., *Transforming Parish Ministry,* pp. 281–320.

27. For suggestions about the comparative study of immigrant Christianity, see Jay P. Dolan, "The Immigrants and Their Gods," *Church History* 57, no. 1 (March 1988): 61–72.

28. Guilday, *The Life and Times of John England,* vol. 2, p. 555.

Denominationalism and
the Black Church

LAURIE F. MAFFLY-KIPP

Given the many pressing social, economic, and political concerns within the contemporary African-American community, one need not search far for explanations as to why denominationalism and its implications for mainline black churches have not been "front-burner" subjects of debate in recent years. Yet this apparent neglect has a much longer history. With the important exception of Carter G. Woodson, scholars of the twentieth century have, in general, demonstrated significantly less interest in black denominations than did their nineteenth-century counterparts.[1] But the significance of denominationalism is a topic that bears reexamination in light of the current resurgence of interest in African-American religious history. Understanding the twentieth-century neglect of black denominations both provides important insights into their historical relevance and suggests new avenues for studying these religious institutions.

Several late-twentieth-century trends in the field of religious studies have shifted attention away from the study of black denominations. Most obviously, the widespread movement since the 1960s away from church history and toward the study of religious phenomena from a wider range of disciplinary perspectives has rendered institutional studies decidedly unfashionable. While this development has breathed new life into American religious history and specifically into the study of African-American religions, Albert Raboteau and David Wills have indicated its somewhat ironic consequences for black church history. If it is true that changes in the study of American religion were catalyzed by the cultural and intellectual changes of the 1960s, including the newly heightened awareness of African-American religious history, it is also the case that the ensuing movement away from church history was dictated by the well-trodden paths of denominational studies in Euro-American Protestantism. Yet the lengthy shelves of dusty and dog-eared institutional tomes largely rejected by contemporary scholars have no counterpart in the black denominations; "no comparable body of modern literature" exists against which scholars of African-American religion could react.[2]

This is not to suggest that scholarship in African-American religion is moribund. On the contrary, anthropological and sociological scholarship on black sects and cults, on the relationship between religion and politics, and on non-Christian religious groups has flourished since the 1970s. Adding substantially to the discipline as well is the current interest in literary criticism and its applicability to African-American narrative forms, advanced most notably by Henry Louis Gates, Jr.[3] Indeed, the latter approach might lend itself well to the use of denominational histories as primary source material, but scholars by and large have limited their discussions of narrative to the study of individual religious experiences, conversion accounts, and other sorts of religious testimonies, rendering even less visible the institutional contexts in which these accounts often appear.

All of these developments provide some insight into the dearth of twentieth-century black denominational studies, but a more intrinsic explanation lies in rhetorical and scholarly paradigms that have shaped the historiography of black denominational life over the past two centuries. It is here that we can begin to uncover the premises that have most forcefully moved African-American religious history away from a focus on denominations and that, in turn, suggest fruitful starting points for their reassessment.

The Birth of the Black Church

It is not an accident of history that the term *Negro church,* displaced a generation later by the phrase *black church,* came into common parlance in the twentieth century as a shorthand means of describing mainline black Protestant denominations. Indeed, this phrase is so widely used now that we hardly stop to think about the intellectual and cultural assumptions that its use connotes—or the differences and variations that it simultaneously obscures. Lawrence N. Jones provides an important reminder in his assertion that "there is no 'black church' in the conventional understanding of that term. There are denominations, composed of congregations of black persons and under their control, and there are countless free-standing congregations, but there is no one entity that can be called the black church."[4]

My purpose here is not to argue for or against the use of this term but instead to suggest that its rhetorical employment, and the concomitant reification of the notion of a monolithic institution called the black church, has a history and a current political significance that bear upon the study of black denominationalism. From the perspective of whites, the notion of a black church has often indicated a failure to see beyond racial difference as an explanatory vehicle. In its current form, tacit and possibly anachronistic understandings of race have shaped the puzzled queries of my white students when they first begin to learn about the rise of independent African churches in the early years of the nineteenth century. These students, for example, are hard-pressed to understand why the African Methodist Episcopal Church (AME), founded in 1816, and the African Methodist Episcopal Zion Church (AMEZ), established in 1821, did not simply join forces in one African-American denomination. The assumption underlying the question, of course, is that race must always have been the most salient reality for these Methodists; other issues, be they doctrinal, political, or cultural, surely were experienced as secondary loyalties.

Implicit in this kind of reasoning are a host of theoretical supposi-tions about the primacy of a racial identity that effectively obscures other sorts of loyalties. These assumptions, far from being limited to the inqui-ries of undergraduates, have a long history among white observers of African-American religious life. For example, in the years following the Civil War, a committee of the General Conference of the Methodist Epis-copal Church, South, tried to resolve the "problem" of black membership in its church by forging an agreement with AME missionaries—a move that prompted several delegates to remind the General Conference that the AME was not the only African Methodist denomination and that per-haps the AMEZ should also be consulted.[5] These instances, one in the 1860s and the other quite modern, reflect a long-standing and prevalent failure on the part of whites to see beyond the commonality of race to other sorts of religious issues that may separate, or at least distinguish among, African-American religious groups. One simply cannot assume that we know what racial identity meant for blacks at given points in time, nor can we take for granted that race consciousness determined other kinds of loyalties, including ecclesiastical and doctrinal identities. These sorts of blind spots have certainly affected the ways in which scholars traditionally have looked at—and have overlooked—the signifi-cance of denominationalism in black churches.

But if Euro-Americans rely on unspoken assumptions about the mean-ing of race in the black religious experience, the use of the term *black church* by African-American scholars often has more intentionally con-veyed normative suppositions about the connections between race and religion. Since the turn of the century, black scholars have self-consciously employed this phrase to symbolize racial, cultural, and religious unity, often in ways that have worked to obscure denominational boundaries.

Although the idea of a racial church appeared sporadically in nineteenth-century accounts of black Protestantism,[6] W. E. B. Du Bois first popularized the plight of a race living behind the "veil of color" in his classic *The Souls of Black Folk* (1903). In that study, the "Negro church" emerged as a social and cultural meeting point allowing for profound expressions of hope, sorrow, despair, and joy. Despite the many differences Du Bois noted between southern black folk religion and its northern, more "civilized" counterpart, the commonalities of the "more important inner ethical life" of blacks largely eclipsed distinctions based on region, doctrine, or confession. "The churches are differentiating," he acknowledged at the conclusion of his chapter on religion, "but back of this still broods silently the deep religious feeling of the real Negro heart, the stirring, unguided might of powerful human souls who have lost the guiding star of the past and seek in the great night a new religious ideal."[7] Du Bois had little use for denominational identity as such, but he realized the power that religious life exercised among African-Americans, particularly in the rural South.[8] He characterized "Negro religion" as a continuous and organic development, beginning in "pagan" Africa and culminating in the rational and orderly worship patterns of northern institutional black churches.

Widely recognized as one of the most eloquent statements of African-American spiritual striving, Du Bois's depiction of a unified entity called the Negro church caught on quickly. Especially notable is the fact that his most famous intellectual opponent, Booker T. Washington, also adopted this terminology (and capitalized the *C* in church) six years later when he agreed that "the Negro Church represents the masses of the Negro people. It was the first institution to develope [*sic*] out of the life of the Negro masses and it still retains the strongest hold upon them."[9] Using the term to serve significantly different ends, Washington placed more emphasis on the populist nature of the southern black religion and on the significance of the Negro church as an organization controlled exclusively by blacks. But he, too, underscored the essential unity of the race by downplaying confessional or doctrinal differences. In Washington's conception, the Negro church was historically significant because it articulated a vision of cultural cohesion and independence.

If the era of Du Bois and Washington gave birth to the notion of a unified organism called the Negro church, it was Carter G. Woodson's monumental *History of the Negro Church* (1921) that marked its coming of age as a scholarly paradigm. Ironically, Woodson's sprawling narrative of African-American religious history devoted the largest share of time to a decidedly traditional discussion of the specifics of denominational life in the nineteenth century; the account moves quickly from early efforts to evangelize the slaves to a study of the rise of independent African Baptist and Methodist churches, schisms within religious organizations, prominent preachers, the growth of religious education, and the relationship of politics to church life. Yet in the final fifty pages, as the story drew nearer to the time of writing, Woodson's language shifted into a broader discussion of the Negro church. It was here that his personal passion was most apparent as he outlined tensions between progressives and conservatives, the importance of the Social Gospel, and contemporary challenges facing the church. Despite nearly two centuries of institutional separation and differentiation, the concluding chapters depict a Negro

church fundamentally united in its common theological and racial struggle to carry the true banner of Christianity through an oppressive historical situation.[10] Racial and spiritual destiny had become intertwined and
were mutually reinforcing elements of African-American culture. "The
Negro Church," wrote Woodson elsewhere, "whether rural or urban, is
the only institution which the race controls. The whites being Occidental
in contradistinction to the Negroes who are Oriental, do not understand
this Oriental faith called Christianity and consequently fail to appreciate
the Negroes' conception of it."[11]

For Woodson as for Du Bois and Washington, therefore, the concept
of the Negro church functioned as much more than a sociological shorthand for a collection of independent religious organizations. In somewhat different ways, the notion of a single church reflected all three
writers' assumptions about—and aspirations for—the cultural and racial
unity of a people. Although the works of Du Bois and Woodson, in particular, were well grounded in nineteenth-century documentary sources and
demonstrated a remarkable degree of historical specificity about the formation of black churches, they also promulgated normative assumptions
about the organic and monolithic nature of the African-American religious community. For Du Bois, the Negro church was one step toward a
morally enlightened, educated African-American community, one born in
the polygamous clan life of Africa and gradually raised through evangelical frenzy to a "civilized" form in the African Methodist churches of the
northern states.[12] Washington extolled the virtues of an organization that
sprang from the initiative of the black masses and symbolized their ability
to function as an independent cultural force. Woodson's Negro church
reflected his theological commitment to African-American Christianity as
the "saving remnant" in an otherwise racist and unjust society.

Despite divergent racial aspirations, then, the functional reification of
the Negro church in the first decades of the twentieth century set the
terms for subsequent scholarly discussions of African-American Protestantism and greatly influenced the types of questions that later generations asked about black churches. Works by Benjamin E. Mays and Joseph
W. Nicholson in the 1930s and by St. Clair Drake and Horace R. Cayton in
the 1950s extended some of the metaphors of Du Bois's sociological
work by searching for the "soul" or "genius" of the Negro church, by
emphasizing its role as a means of racial advance, and by elaborating on
the importance of the church as one of the few social and cultural institutions controlled and owned by blacks.[13] None of these writers ignored
denominational distinctions; on the contrary, they provided some of the
most valuable statistical information that we possess about individual
black churches in the interwar period. But their ultimate concern, be-
trayed most evidently by their choice of terminology, was to paint a
portrait of overarching racial commonality. Indeed, Mays's and Nicholson's conclusions came close to the theological formulations of Woodson
a decade earlier: "This fellowship and freedom inherent in the Negro

church should be conducive to spiritual growth of a unique kind. . . . The Negro church has the potentialities to become possibly the greatest spiritual force in the United States."[14]

Prior to the 1960s, then, scholarly discourse about African-American religion deliberately turned away from discussion of denominational distinctions within African-American Protestantism to a form of consensus history, best symbolized by the increasingly common use of the concept of the Negro church as a reflection of the desire for racial unity. Institutional divisions among black Protestants were not ignored, but the concept of a racial church shaped the types of questions scholars posed about their source materials, consistently moving discussion away from denominational distinctions among blacks. Interestingly, even those scholars who most adamantly asserted that Protestantism had been a source of oppression for African-Americans, such as E. Franklin Frazier, also employed the notion of the black church as an organic entity with inherent qualities that separated it from other religious forms. In *The Negro Church in America* (1964), an extended essay on and an overview of the history of African-American Christianity, Frazier conceded that the Negro church historically provided racial refuge, facilitated a "structured social life" in which blacks were able to articulate deeply held feelings, and served as a "refuge in a hostile white world." But it did so at a tremendous cultural cost, because its otherworldly outlook prevented blacks from confronting white oppression directly and aided in black accommodation to an inferior social status. Frazier characterized the rise of independent African churches as the institutional manifestations of black exclusion from participation in white denominations.[15]

Frazier's analysis, in conjunction with the larger debate about "Africanisms" of which it was a part, shifted the scholarly dialogue but did not significantly alter some of its fundamental premises. The overriding concern for Frazier was whether the Negro church, a "nation within a nation," had ultimately detrimental or beneficial effects for American blacks and whether any African characteristics survived within it. As important as these questions were, they moved discussion still further away from the issue of whether the black church, as an entity, even existed and whether one could reasonably generalize about it. Conferring upon it sovereign status as a "nation," one could hardly question the loyalties of the individual states of which it was comprised.

The normative shaping of these questions, moreover, privileged certain strands of the historical narrative of black religion. Seeing the evolution of the church as an organic development has led scholars to look for historical precedents in certain kinds of activities and beliefs, such as early accounts of racial consciousness and black separatist ideologies. More recent works, including ground-breaking studies by Gayraud Wilmore and by C. Eric Lincoln and Lawrence Mamiya, have probed important questions about the political involvement of the black church and the influence of the African religious worldview in the historical formation of black Protestantism. Yet Wilmore, Mamiya, and Lincoln have also cast their studies in terms of a debate about the black church and have premised their conclusions on the existence of a broad consensus in the African-American Christian community.[16]

The black church has served as a useful and instructive paradigm for understanding African-American religion. Indeed, it has enabled scholars to ask vital questions about black nationalist movements; about the interaction among race, political protest, and religion; and about differences between Euro-American and African-American worship, theology, and ecclesiology. But recognizing that it is a paradigm with a specific genesis and lifespan should also enable us to move elsewhere, to ask different kinds of questions of historical materials, and to probe different kinds of issues, as well as to note areas of research that have been previously obscured by the biases of our own conceptualizations. One of the areas that has been most neglected is the significance of denominationalism in African-American culture.

Before the Black Church

The twentieth-century emphasis on the black church as a sociological and historiographical construct has thus highlighted racial, cultural, and religious unity among African-Americans. But an overview of some issues in the history of nineteenth-century church life suggests that it has also obscured the full context of black denominationalism. As Will Gravely has noted, two distinct but not mutually exclusive historiographical modes have traditionally characterized the rise of separate black churches in the late eighteenth and early nineteenth centuries. Scholars have tended to emphasize either white racism and the oppression of African-Americans that compelled religious separation or the development of a distinctive black culture and its communal infrastructure that made possible and desirable the formation of independent black churches. In both scenarios the linkages between racial identity and church affiliation are clear and are connected to prevalent assumptions about the organic nature of black church life.

What neither of these explanations takes into account, observes Gravely, is the extent to which early "African" churches were also influenced by and forged in response to the same set of circumstances that shaped the development of Euro-Protestant churches in the post-Revolutionary period, that is, the positive valuations of religious liberty, voluntarism, and denominationalism.[17] Just as the Revolutionary legacy of religious disestablishment brought tumult and revitalization to the biracial and predominantly white churches, so too were black church leaders and laity encouraged to assert themselves spiritually and ecclesiastically by the message of newly legitimated religious dissent.[18] Local black church studies and denominational histories[19] from the nineteenth century reveal an ecclesiastical world filled with division, differentiation, and competition, an environment in which racial identity played a complex and even ambiguous role. These denominational accounts suggest that alongside the history of racial unity and the evolution of the "soul" of the black church, scholars must also begin to analyze and evaluate the historical pluralism within black churches.

A sharply defined denominational consciousness, not unlike that found among Euro-Protestant church leaders in the antebellum era, was an early and persistent feature of the AME Church. Bishop Daniel Alexander Payne, a respected educator and the official AME historian in the nineteenth century, placed the virtues of the Allenites within the context of the wider Protestant spectrum. He viewed his church as one denomination among many, all of which were working toward the same end: "The different denominations may be compared to so many regiments in the 'Grand Army,'" Payne claimed, and "the African Methodist Episcopal Church is one of the regiments of the grand division of the 'Grand Army.'"[20]

Although the AME Church did not fight the Christian battle alone, it could claim a privileged status as the true heir of Wesleyan spirituality. Payne portrayed the AME Church as the direct spiritual descendent of British Methodism, the "saving remnant" that carried Methodism through a time of division and tribulation. "There was," he asserted, "no essential difference between the Methodism that came from the hand of Wesley . . . and that which was chosen by the Founders of the AME Church."[21] Moreover, he noted, the formation of the AME Church also paralleled that of the Wesleyan organization. Payne hailed the Wesleys as apostles who courageously battled the evils of the oppressive and corrupt church establishment, eventually separating to form a faithful and morally elevated religious body. Similarly, when American Methodism veered off course, falling away from its scriptural mission to "love thy neighbor as thyself," the persecuted but spiritually pure African-Americans fled in order to preserve true religion in the AME Church.

Payne thus relied on distinctly American and Protestant precedents for his justification of ecclesiastical separation. Religious liberty, for Payne, meant not simply the ability to establish a racially defined church but the opportunity to extend and express the fundamental biblical principle of spiritual equality before God.[22] In his fairly brief description of the founding of the Bethel church in Philadelphia, Payne vaguely mentioned the "unkind treatment" afforded blacks by their white brethren, but he focused more extensively on the legal and ecclesiastical battles that led up to the organizational separation of the Allenites—battles that had counterparts in many Euro-Protestant churches.[23]

Yet the church spokesman did not ignore the question of race. He deemed Richard Allen a racial as well as a religious leader, "chief of the noble band of heroes . . . a lover of liberty, civil and religious—he . . . felt himself highly honored and sincerely happy in doing and suffering to secure the blessings of ecclesiastical liberty for his despised and insulted race."[24] Payne also emphasized how beneficial the AME Church had been to the race as a whole, inasmuch as it had forced blacks to utilize their own resources, giving each one "an independence of character which he could neither hope for nor attain unto, if he had remained as the ecclesiastical vassal of his white brethren."[25] But salvation was not, ultimately, a matter of color or culture, and the future of Christianity did not rest in the separation of the races: *"The Eternal sets little value upon races, but much upon humanity.... Races perish. Humanity lives on forever."*[26] For Payne, the question of race was only one part of a larger issue of Christian life and leadership.

Bishop Benjamin Tucker Tanner, editor of the denominational *Christian Recorder,* founder of the AME *Church Review,* and author of scores of historical works, also ruminated extensively on the importance of denominational identity. Like Payne, Tanner objected vigorously to the racist "crime" of white Methodists, who had "locked, bolted, and barred" the doors of schools and conferences to the church's African-American members. Nonetheless, he, too, located the AME Church within a spiritually pure religious line that superseded questions of race, a line squarely rooted in the American Protestant tradition of "justifiable" religious separatism:

> Allen and his liberty-loving coadjutors learned these lessons of religious manhood.... They had heard the stories which make up the religious history of the country; of the Mayflower and its heroic band, who braved the perils of the deep, the greater perils of the land, all that they might not be ecclesiastically oppressed. They had heard of Roger Williams and the city which he built for all those who might be distressed on account of conscience.... But the most potent of all, was the lesson taught them by the Methodists themselves. If the rise of Anglo Methodism is to be excused, that of African Methodism is to be plead for; and if the former is to be countenanced, the latter is to be most strenuously defended.[27]

The primary aim of the AME Church, in Tanner's view, was "to help convert the world to Christ—the world, and not simply Africans, real or imagined."[28] In this respect, he agreed with Payne that the denomination was only one among many engaged in a common enterprise, albeit the most "attractive, interesting," and "worthy" of the Methodist alternatives.[29] Despite the inclusion of "African" in the organization's name, Tanner also insisted that the church was "simply a Methodist Episcopal Church, organized largely of 'Americans' by 'Africans' and for 'Africans.' " Attempting to distinguish between doctrinal and racial issues, he declared that the AME Church was not a "race church" but was instead a place where the "doctrine of the Negro's humanity" could be fully realized. In demonstrating the importance of this claim, the journalist pointed out that the church contained Euro-American members, "to say nothing of the host who by reason of mixture cannot be so written."[30]

For both Tanner and Payne, the idea of the AME Church as a unique vehicle for racial uplift existed in some tension with their denials of racial exclusivity. Both believed that religious humanism would ultimately prove of more lasting importance than the temporary claims of race, and both understood the AME Church to be serving the broader needs of humanity. Ironically, Tanner flatly denied that the AME was a "race church," while Payne contended that all American churches were "race churches."[31] Yet both claims tended toward the same idea that race was a contingent factor within a larger context of ecclesiastical and historical considerations. Both churchmen, too, encountered opponents within their traditions, men such as Henry McNeal Turner, who criticized their assimilationist positions. But their defenses of the AME Church suggest that denominationalism and its relationship to racial identity were complicated and even contested issues among African-Americans in the nineteenth century.

The organizational sensibilities of Tanner and Payne may seem self-evident, given their status within the denomination. Alternatively, one might reasonably attribute their views to personal temperament or even to institutional idiosyncrasies of the AME Church as a whole.[32] But other sorts of evidence make it clear that the worldviews of these religious historians were part of a tradition of ecclesiastical consciousness that divided black churches just as it did predominantly white churches. The rise of the notion of voluntarism in antebellum America inevitably led to religious competition, and Protestant African-Americans were not exempt from this schismatic fever. The beliefs of the laity, while not as well publicized as the opinions of leaders such as Tanner and Payne, can be traced through church records; congregations often expressed their commitment to particular denominations by voting with their feet as well as with their voices.

A brief survey of some of these conflicts underscores the complex nature of the relationship between race and denominationalism and suggests many avenues for future research. First, although the historiography of the rise of black churches emphasizes the gradual separation of the races into independent organizations, it is important to recognize that many African-Americans chose to remain within biracial churches, in some cases because of their deep attachments to their denominational affiliations. These members also pushed for racial inclusion and sought means of gaining equal rights within ecclesiastical structures, but they did so within predominantly Euro-Protestant contexts. In the late 1840s, for instance, black members of the Methodist Episcopal Church, North, desiring recognition of their local preachers and a larger voice in church affairs and cognizant that they were quickly losing members to the AME and AMEZ churches, requested a separate conference for black members.[33] The request was denied, but such an appeal demonstrates that African-American denominational identity was hardly an either/or proposition—either complete ecclesiastical separation or complacent submission to white authority. On the contrary, black church members sought various means of reconciling their religious loyalties with their desire for equal rights and full participation within their congregations.

The relationship of whites to the founding of separate African churches also reflects the complex nature of black denominational life. Sought out by African Methodists, early white defenders of separate African churches in cities such as Philadelphia and New York raised money and provided organizational support. In the early years after separation, sympathetic white Baptist clergy in the Northeast preached in African and Abyssinian Baptist churches in the absence of qualified blacks.[34] Moreover, as both Tanner and Payne intimate, African-Americans who joined "black" churches found themselves worshipping in multiracial congregations, albeit ones with many more blacks than whites. "Already we have them from alabaster to ebony. . . . In no sense are we a race Church . . . whose people in color of skin, general contour of face and texture of hair indicate oneness," asserted Tanner, estimating that one-half of 1 percent of the membership of the AME Church in 1891 was "of pure European extraction."[35] His remarks remind us of the extent to which racial divisions—and, by extension, racially delineated denominations—have been defined by social convention and must in themselves be reexamined.

Substantive doctrinal, ecclesiastical, and social differences also split black membership in the early years of denominational formation. Disagreements between Episcopalians and Methodists divided members of the African Church of Philadelphia as they sought organizational independence in the 1790s. Richard Allen, in his autobiography, related that the congregation held an election to determine which denomination to join; he recalled that the "large majority" favored the Church of England, and only he and one other preacher, the Rev. Absalom Jones, desired a Methodist affiliation. When the African Church later requested his offices as minister, he explained his institutional commitments: "I told them I could not accept their offer, as I was a Methodist. . . . I informed them that I could not be anything else but a Methodist, as I was born and awakened under them, and I could go no further with them, for I was a Methodist."[36]

Allen's assertion of institutional loyalty was among the first in a large number of conflicts that separated black churches along denominational lines. Questions of leadership, authority and access to power initially prevented the founders of the AMEZ from uniting within the Allenites in the 1810s; over the century that followed, at least five different merger proposals were presented and voted down or dropped for lack of support. On several occasions the stumbling block proved to be the inability to agree on a new denominational title. In 1885 a joint commission of the two organizations advanced the name First United Methodist Episcopal Church, thus omitting entirely a racial designation.[37] In 1892 another joint commission, after comparing the respective Books of Discipline, agreed that the churches concurred in doctrinal and disciplinary matters. They proposed the name African-Zion Methodist Episcopal Church, but a minority opinion by two AME members objected strenuously to the merger:

Now to impose the term Zion or African Zion Methodist Episcopal Church upon us, is to literally absorb us, and to blot out our individuality as a Connection. We were willing to accept the terms African Methodist Episcopal Zion Church, but to accept African Zion Methodist Episcopal Church would be no union at all. It would be the simple absorption of the African Methodist Episcopal Church, from which every sense and emotion of our nature revolts.[38]

While such disagreements may seem like trivial points, they demonstrate the profound nature of attachments to black denominational identity, allegiances that frequently outweighed racial and cultural points of connection.

Political and social differences also divided black churches during the last century, becoming, in effect, doctrinal issues. George A. Levesque suggests that arguments over the appropriate response of African-American Christians to slavery led to schisms in African Baptist churches in Boston in the 1820s and 1830s, with congregants disagreeing over new abolitionist currents of thought.[39] Another extremely sensitive issue that separated blacks along denominational lines was the formation in 1870 of the Colored Methodist Episcopal Church, an offshoot of the Methodist Episcopal Church, South. Organized during Reconstruction by former southern slaves, the CME was caught up in the intense denominational competition arising from the work of AME and AMEZ missionaries in the southern states. A sizable number of southern blacks resented northern blacks for their imposition of an intellectualized religious tradition and their cultural insensitivity, while northerners deemed the CME Church "the old slavery church" and considered its members illiterate and submissive to white ecclesiastical and social authority.[40] The disagreement over the appropriate African-American relationship to southern white culture continued for decades after the founding of the church.[41]

A final area of research that requires further attention is the relationship between black denominations and the variety of transdenominational structures that have claimed the allegiances of—and caused disagreements among—large numbers of African-Americans. As has been mentioned previously, the abolitionist movement affected the constituencies of black churches; similarly, efforts to colonize Africa found strong support as well as vigorous resistance within congregations. Perhaps the most intriguing example of tension and interaction between black denominations and other sorts of cultural organizations is Marcus Garvey's Universal Negro Improvement Association, an interdenominational movement in the 1920s that mobilized large numbers of African-Americans. As Randall Burkett has suggested, the UNIA effectively utilized religious imagery and symbolism in "nearly every facet of its organizational life," in a way that complemented, rather than competed with, denominational activities. Despite its emphasis on self-identity, nationhood, and the destiny of the race, the movement had a membership that included sizable numbers of Baptist preachers who retained their denominational loyalties. And although some members did push for the creation of a separate religious denomination that would explicitly embrace and reflect the goals of the UNIA, Garvey himself insisted on maintaining its status as a transdenominational movement.[42]

Conclusion

On January 1, 1808, the Rev. Absalom Jones, rector of St. Thomas's African Episcopal Church of Philadelphia, preached a Thanksgiving sermon on the occasion of the abolition of the slave trade. Jones outlined the trials of the African people under slavery, likening them to those endured by the ancient Israelites. He thanked God for delivering the nation from its bondage and asked that "the history of the sufferings of our brethren, and of their deliverance, descend by this means to our children to the remotest generations."[43] As Jones pointed out, there was much that united African-Americans, and the Bible provided a shared narrative that made sense of their collective struggle for equal rights.

This narrative of shared suffering and shared deliverance has long been a central feature of what Will Gravely has termed the "elusive dream of a black communal unity,"[44] a goal that has animated and sustained twentieth-century historical and sociological studies of African-American religion. But even a cursory overview of the significance of denominationalism in the history of black churches suggests that there are counternarratives of division, differentiation, and conflict that must be acknowledged as vital aspects of the African-American past. Long ignored as the unwanted stepchild of an emerging black religious separatism, denominationalism must be appreciated by scholars as a crucial aspect of American religious life for blacks and whites alike.

NOTES

1. This trend is notably in keeping with Russell Richey's characterization of denominations as a "nineteenth-century artifact." The present article suggests, however, that the reasons for the twentieth-century turn away from interest in denominationalism are somewhat different in the African-American religious community than they are among white Protestants. See his foreword to Russell E. Richey, ed., *Denominationalism,* (Nashville, Tenn.: Abingdon, 1977), p. 13. The diminishing ability of black churches to generate internal histories has also been noted by Albert J. Raboteau, David W. Wills, et al., in their extremely useful historiographical essay "Retelling Carter Woodson's Story: Archival Sources for Afro-American Church History," *Journal of American History* 77 (June 1990): 185.

2. Raboteau and Wills, "Retelling," p. 185.

3. Henry Louis Gates, Jr., *The Signifying Monkey: A Theory of African-American Literary Criticism* (New York: Oxford University Press, 1988); Charles

T. Davis and Henry Louis Gates, Jr., eds., *The Slave's Narrative* (New York: Oxford University Press, 1985).

4. Lawrence N. Jones, "The Black Churches: A New Agenda," in *Afro-American Religious History: A Documentary Witness,* ed. Milton C. Sernett (Durham, N.C.: Duke University Press, 1985), p. 491.

5. William B. Gravely, "The Social, Political and Religious Significance of the Formation of the Colored Methodist Episcopal Church (1870)," *Methodist History* 18 (October 1979): 12.

6. As early as 1810, the black Methodist preacher Daniel Coker drew attention to the nascent African church movement, likening its ministers and congregations to the "chosen generation" and the "holy nation," biblical images taken from I Peter 2:9–10. See William B. Gravely, "The Rise of African Churches in America (1786–1822): Re-examining the Contexts," *Journal of Religious Thought* 41 (1984): 58.

7. W. E. B. Du Bois, *The Souls of Black Folk* (1903; reprint ed., New York: Signet Classics, 1969), pp. 213–215, 225.

8. Sernett, *Documentary Witness,* p. 309.

9. Booker T. Washington, *The Story of the Negro,* vol. 1 (New York: Doubleday, Page, 1909), p. 278, quoted in Sernett, *Documentary Witness,* pp. 3–4.

10. Carter G. Woodson, *The History of the Negro Church,* 2nd ed. (Washington, D.C.: The Associated Publishers, 1945); see especially chs. 12–15.

11. Carter G. Woodson, *The Rural Negro* (Washington, D.C.: The Association for the Study of Negro Life and History, 1930), quoted in Sernett, *Documentary Witness,* p. 331.

12. Du Bois characterized the AME as the "greatest Negro organization in the world" (*Souls,* p. 217). It should be emphasized, however, that his relationship to black folk religion was complicated and ambiguous. He simultaneously appreciated its uniqueness and romanticized it, yet remained uncomfortable with its anti-intellectual biases.

13. Mays and Nicholson, *The Negro's Church* (New York: Institute of Social and Religious Research, 1933); Drake and Cayton, *Black Metropolis: A Study of Negro Life in a Northern City* (New York: Harcourt, Brace, 1945).

14. Mays and Nicholson, *Negro's Church,* p. 292, quoted in Sernett, *Documentary Witness,* p. 348.

15. E. Franklin Frazier, *The Negro Church in America* (New York: Schocken Books, 1964).

16. Gayraud S. Wilmore, *Black Religion and Black Radicalism: An Interpretation of the Religious History of Afro-American People,* 2nd ed. (New York: Orbis Books, 1983); C. Eric Lincoln and Lawrence H. Mamiya, *The Black Church in the African American Experience* (Durham, N.C.: Duke University Press, 1990). Lincoln and Mamiya, like other sociologists, provide a large amount of data on specific black churches that elucidates the wide diversity of religious patterns, yet they also refer, in their introduction, to a "black sacred cosmos," an "experiential dimension" of African-American culture that gives rise to a variety of social institutions. This hierarchy of experience over social institutions is crucial to their understanding of the black religious community as an organic whole, just as it was for W. E. B. Du Bois.

17. Gravely, "Rise of African Churches," p. 68. Gravely's article details how the issues of church leadership, governance, and ownership and the ability to administer congregational discipline shaped the formation of "African" churches:

"Those were the power factors being contended for generally in the shaping of the popular denominations, and black members and preachers were in the middle of the conflict."

18. On the many dimensions of religious revitalization in the post-Revolutionary era, see Nathan O. Hatch, *The Democratization of American Christianity* (New Haven: Yale University Press, 1989). Hatch briefly discusses the rise of separate black churches during this period but limits his analysis to the role that religious "democratization" played in the formation of a unified African-American identity and culture. Significantly, he does not mention the debates or divisions that religious competition and division also encouraged.

19. My interest lies not so much in the kinds of factual evidence provided in a denominational account as in the worldview or "metanarrative" described therein. As Russell E. Richey has suggested, a denominational history "perhaps best serves . . . as primary rather than secondary resource. It becomes data for other assessments of the movement" ("Institutional Forms of Religion," in *Encyclopedia of the American Religious Experience: Studies of Traditions and Movements,* ed. Charles H. Lippy and Peter W. Williams, 3 vols. (New York: Charles Scribner's Sons, 1988), 1:33.

20. Ibid., ix. For a more extended discussion of Payne's views about the mission of the AME Church in the context of the universal Christian church, see David W. Wills, "Aspects of Social Thought in the African Methodist Episcopal Church, 1884–1910" (Ph.D. diss., Harvard University, 1975), pp. 34–38.

21. Daniel Alexander Payne, *The Semi-Centenary and the Retrospection of the African Methodist Episcopal Church* (Baltimore, Md., 1866; reprint ed., Freeport, N.Y.: Books for Libraries Press, 1972), p. 22.

22. Ibid., pp. 5–33.

23. Daniel Alexander Payne, *History of the African Methodist Episcopal Church* (Nashville, Tenn.: AME Sunday School Union, 1891), pp. 2–7.

24. Payne, *Semi-Centenary,* p. 33.

25. Payne, *History of the A.M.E.,* p. 12.

26. Daniel Alexander Payne, "Thoughts About the Past, the Present and the Future of the African M.E. Church," *A.M.E. Church Review* 1 (July 1884): 3, quoted in Wills, "Aspects of Social Thought," p. 35.

27. Tanner, *An Apology for African Methodism* (Baltimore: n.p., 1867), pp. 22–23. It should be noted that Tanner was speculating on Allen's motives for separation; thus these passages serve as a record of Tanner's own views on the founding of the AME, rather than a verifiable account of Allen's reasoning.

28. Tanner, "The African Methodist Episcopal Church," *Independent* 43 (March 5, 1891), p. 11.

29. Tanner, *An Outline of Our History and Government for African Methodist Churchmen, Ministerial and Lay, in Catechetical Form* (Philadelphia: Grant, Faires and Rodgers, 1884), p. 10, 13–14. Interestingly, in his extensive catechism Tanner did not require the catechumen to say that the AME Church was the best church but instead that it was "better for me" than other denominations (Baptist, Presbyterian, Episcopal, Catholic).

30. Tanner, "African Methodist Episcopal Church," p. 11.

31. Wills, "Aspects of Social Thought," p. 35.

32. The AME Church, to be sure, has exhibited much more historical and denominational consciousness than many other black denominations, if the numbers of institutional histories are any indication. But the historiographical empha-

sis on the AME Church also reflects many of the biases in the scholarship that this essay seeks to address. Only additional research into the organizational worlds of other denominations will furnish scholars with sufficient data to study black denominations in a comparative fashion.

33. Woodson, *History,* pp. 167–168.

34. Gravely, "Rise of African Churches," pp. 65–66.

35. Tanner, "African Methodist Episcopal Church," p. 10–11.

36. Richard Allen, *The Life Experience and Gospel Labors of the Right Reverend Richard Allen,* with an introduction by George A. Singleton (Nashville, Tenn.: Abingdon, 1960), pp. 29–30.

37. Charles Spencer Smith, *A History of the African Methodist Episcopal Church* (1922; reprint ed., New York: Johnson Reprint Corporation, 1968), pp. 380–381. Consideration of the agreement was indefinitely postponed in 1887 after bishops from the denominations could not agree upon a meeting date.

38. Ibid., p. 386. Interestingly, one of the two authors of the dissenting opinion was Henry McNeal Turner, an ardent supporter of black colonization and an early advocate of black nationalism. Yet Turner also felt deeply about his ties to the AME Church. Smith credits him with singlehandedly defeating the merger proposal.

39. George A. Levesque, "Inherent Reformers-Inherited Orthodoxy: Black Baptists in Boston, 1800–1873," *Journal of Negro History* 60 (1975): 491–525.

40. Clarence E. Walker, *A Rock in a Weary Land: The African Methodist Episcopal Church During the Civil War and Reconstruction* (Baton Rouge: Louisiana State University Press, 1982).

41. On the CME tradition of abstention from politics, see Gravely, "The Social, Political and Religious Significance," p. 23. As late as the 1890s, historians of the denomination acknowledged the fierce opposition encountered from other blacks. Bishop L. H. Holsey remarked in 1891 that the church "has been opposed by strong hands and accomplished leaders among the colored people, from its birthday till the present; tho, happily for us, these oppositions are now subsiding and the young organization is taking on a firm and expanding aspect that is most interesting and extraordinary" ("The Colored Methodist Episcopal Church," *Independent* 43 [5 March 1891]: 11).

42. Randall K. Burkett, "The Religious Ethos of the Universal Negro Improvement Association," in Gayraud Wilmore, ed., *African American Religious Studies: An Interdisciplinary Anthology* (Durham: Duke University Press, 1989), pp. 60–81. For more on the involvement of church leaders in the Garvey movement, see Burkett, *Black Redemption: Churchmen Speak for the Garvey Movement* (Philadelphia: Temple University Press, 1978).

43. Absalom Jones, "A Thanksgiving Sermon, preached January 1, 1808, in St. Thomas's, or the African Episcopal, Church, Philadelphia: On account of the abolition of the African slave trade" (Philadelphia: Fry and Kammerer, Printers, 1808), in *Early Negro Writing 1760–1837,* ed. Dorothy Porter (Boston: Beacon Press, 1971), p. 340–341.

44. Gravely, "Rise of African Churches," p. 65.

Denominations and
Denominationalism:
An American Morphology

RUSSELL E. RICHEY

Of late, both denominational leaders and the academics who study the religious landscape have pondered the poor health of and the future prospects for mainline denominations and denominationalism. The leaders, desperate for antidotes to staunch membership losses and financial reversals, grasp for diagnoses and cures.[1] For their part, scholars wonder whether American denominations and denominationalism are actually breaking up.[2] They see signs thereof in the massive losses suffered by mainstream Protestantism; the alienation of members and congregations from national leadership; resultant diversion of resources away from denominational coffers into local and regional projects; the growing division within denominations between liberals and evangelicals (and the persisting division between white and black); the emergence of quasi-independent caucuses and struggle groups, each bent on pressing its agenda and capturing power; and the muting of mainstream Protestant denominations' public voice and/or its eclipse in American society by evangelical and non-Protestant voices. Denominations, at least in their mainsteam Protestant form, seem to have lost their directions.[3] Such disorientation and cataclysmic change have sufficiently worried the Lilly Endowment that it has invested millions in projects such as the conference from which these papers issue in an effort to understand and to describe mainstream American religion. The resultant enquiries, including particularly the major studies of the Disciples of Christ and of Presbyterianism,[4] help us appreciate the nature and the extent of the change in mainstream Protestantism.

This essay suggests that radical change is not a new experience, either for denominations or for the collectivity that we call denomination-alism. Both the form (denomination) and the family (denomina-tionalism) have changed, evolved over time, metamorphosed.[5] That indi-vidual confessions have changed dramatically over the years the serious student of history should concede. Less obvious, perhaps, is the equally drastic change in the ecology within which denominations functioned, both the larger organizational ecology of American society and the more immediate ecology comprising other denominations and religious institu-tions. The change in the latter has gone unremarked, perhaps because the topic itself is disdained; indeed, of late the term *denominationalism* has been such slur that the serious scholar has been above treating it or has found a less opprobrious rubric under which to attend to the dynamics of American religious institutions. For such analyses, scholars prefer reli-gious freedom, voluntarism, pluralism,[6] and, recently, the independent sector.[7]

Definitions

Such terms, however, do not readily indicate that the American denomina-tional world has possessed, in any given epoch, fairly clear boundaries; that certain groups belonged and others really did not; that denomina-tionalism functioned as the form of the current religious mainstream; that denominations had, again for each period, a recognizable shape such that individual denominations of quite different polities and theologies resem-bled one another; in short, that the denominational definition was period-specific. Within and in relation to this larger denominational universe, the individual denomination defined itself and functioned, as also in their respective realms did both political party and business enterprise. And denominations of a given period resembled one another more than they did their own confessional ancestors or progeny. Hence the constellation of denominations, no less than the individual denomination, has taken different forms, redefined what denomination means, renegotiated bound-aries. For want of a better term we will call that constellation *denomina-tionalism* and will here attempt to sketch its development. Whether such division of Christians is, in ethical or eternal perspective, a good thing will not concern us here. That is quite a legitimate concern but not one that should prevent us also from giving serious attention to the history of Protestant institutions.[8]

Denominationalism presents the denomination as a voluntaristic ecclesial body.[9] It is *voluntary* and therefore presupposes a condition of legal or de facto toleration and religious freedom—an environment within which it is possible, in fact, willingly to join or not join and that provides "space" to exist alongside or outside of any religious establish-ment. The denomination exists in a situation of religious pluralism, typi-cally a pluralism of denominations. It is *ecclesial,* a movement or body understanding itself to be legitimate and self-sufficient, a proper "church" (or religious movement.)[10] It is *a* voluntary church, a body that concedes the authenticity of other churches even as it claims its own.[11] It need not, however, concede that authenticity indiscriminately; it need not, and typically does not, regard all other denominations as orthodox. And it is an ecclesial *body* or *form,* an organized religious movement, with intentions and the capacity for self-perpetuation, with a sense of itself as located within time and with awareness of its relation to the longer Christian tradition.[12] It knows itself as denominated, as named, as recognized and recognizable, as having boundaries, as possessing adherents, as having a history. In these several regards, the denomination differentiates itself from reform impulses that may take similar structural form but construe themselves as belonging within;[13] from the church that does not regard itself as voluntary or as sharing societal space with other legitimate religious bodies; from the sect, which, although also voluntary, does not locate itself easily in time or recognize boundaries or tolerate other bodies or concede their authenticity.

The term *denomination* and, if Winthrop Hudson is correct, the theory antedate the phenomenon itself.[14] The term was used initially in the seventeenth and eighteenth centuries to identify religious postures that could be identified and hence named, such as Arminians. The theory derived from the ecclesiology of the Congregationalists or Independents, a view of the church as institutionalizing itself plurally (and locally) but not in separation or schism, as distinct but not schismatic.

Denominationalism, on the other hand, is a term of more recent vintage, considerably postdating the phenomenon itself. It now functions to describe both denominational theory and the resultant condition or situation of institutionalized division. The accent, particularly in theological and ecumenical hands, tends to fall on the latter part of the definition—"institutionalized division"—and seemingly requires no further comment. While not ignoring division, we will attend here to the condition or situation and its (often implicit) theory. Our argument is that, like democracy or capitalism, denominationalism persists as a complex of theory and practice, of process and form, and has taken very different complexions over its life. Indeed, one feature of denominational complexion has been its relationship with society, commerce, and the state, the "face" that the denominations presented to the culture within which they functioned.

Denominations as we know them may well be breaking up. If so, it need not mean the end to the religious movements now denominated, many of which (for example, Lutherans, Presbyterians, Mennonites, Baptists, Congregationalists) had a predenominational ecclesial existence and have no reason to confuse their essence with its current denominational expression. Denominationalism is a relatively recent phenomenon and may have outlived its usefulness. It may, on the other hand, be simply going through another of its metamorphoses.

The Stages of American Denominationalism

Five American denominational styles or stages can be discerned, each representing something of an ideal type, a predominant trend in the rich texture of American institutionalism, an expressive style of organization.[15] The first, ethnic voluntarism or provincial voluntarism, characterized movements in the religiously pluralistic middle colonies of the eighteenth century, with Presbyterians serving as the best example. The second, purposive missionary association, emerged in the early national period, the form fabricated by Methodists and Baptists and the theory worked out by the Reformed. The third, "churchly" style qualified the second, rather than transforming it fully. It flourished after the Civil War, drew some inspiration from Romantic currents, derived impetus from massive immigration and resulting competition, and took expressive form in both high-church and primitivist movements (Episcopal, Lutheran, Landmark Baptist, Christian).

In the late nineteenth and early twentieth centuries, corporate or managerial organization, the fourth stage, swept virtually the entire Protestant mainstream, producing the structures of denominational organization familiar today. The fifth style, perhaps like the third qualifying rather than displacing its immediate predecessor, emerged in the late 1960s and the early 1970s. Dykstra compares it with its secular counterpart, the regulatory agency. We prefer to see it as combining a number of contemporary cultural forms—the franchise, the regulatory agency, the caucus, the mall, the media.

As the last example should suggest, each style partook of organizational materials of its day. The denomination did not simply derive itself from secular institutions.[16] In several of the periods, religious groups took organizational initiative; Protestants experimented with methods, principles of order, and organizational forms that would find their uses also in political or economic life. This typology, then, does call attention to social origin and social uses of organization. Indeed, it posits that denominationalism served primarily to define the relation of religious movement to the social order. Each type or style functioned with a distinctive vision of American society and of Protestant responsibility therein. Implicitly, the styles delineated rules for, if not a genuine theory of, denominational collaboration or relation. The differences in denominational relations in the several periods are, in part, responsible for the quite contrary judgments that interpreters have rendered about denominationalism—some viewing it as inherently competitive and combative, others noting unitive and cooperative features.

The typology also focuses on the adhesive principle, the commitments, ideals, or purposes that held each religious movement together. This adhesive, too, has differed markedly in different periods. The typology does, however, exaggerate the differences. It isolates the new adhesive principle for each period and, in so doing, obscures the inertia of styles from earlier period(s); as a result, the typology needs to be qualified with the recognition that earlier styles and their adhesive principles continue to live on in later periods; ethnic voluntarism resurfaces to haunt the Presbyterians, and Methodists revert jeremiadically to purposive missionary association. In the present, then, all five types or styles can be detected, in some instances all within a single denomination.

The typology functions, as do typologies generally, to isolate features for purposes of analysis and interpretation. This one serves especially to highlight the dynamic principles internal to the individual denominations, the rules of interdenominational interaction, and the goals they shared vis-à-vis the social order. It is designed for historical uses, to identify for each period the new or predominant denominational style. It does not pretend to embrace the full range of religious institutions, as do sociological typologies. Outside or beyond its purview lie church, sect, and cult structures.[17] Nor is it intended to array churches in terms of their own ecclesial self-understanding.[18] Rather, this typology focusses on "life and work," not "faith and order." It should, however, serve to indicate that both denominations and denominationalism change.

Ethnic Voluntarism and Its Background

Behind the emergence of the first denominational style lie several centuries of European and especially Anglo-Saxon struggles over church order and its uniformity. In the immediate foreground, the Glorious Revolution and the Toleration Act loom especially large as creating actual legal and societal space for loyal but dissenting religious bodies. In England, this space was occupied by the "three old denominations," Presbyterian, Congregational, and Baptist, with Quakers eventually also finding room. By occupying that space, even under what seemed imperfect indulgence, these groups participated in turning the concession of toleration into an ideal, a principle, a theory or theology of the church, a view of ecclesial legitimacy. They borrowed the ideas and metaphors for what would become a denominational theory from various parties, including, as Hudson has suggested, the Independents but surely also the Whigs or liberals and probably also that inchoate population that called itself "catholic" Protestants[19] and certainly also the Quakers. At any rate, tolerated denominations, and they called themselves that, found greater toleration in England than did their counterparts in the colonies. Law, practice, and advocacy would eventually extend the right of toleration to the colonies; Quaker toleration extended over much of the area where denominationalism first succeeded.

In the deeper background belong the Puritan movements, which contributed in a variety of ways to the emerging American denominational pattern. First, the efforts to purify the Church of England generated the several aforementioned movements that would imprint themselves deliberately, fully, successfully on the American landscape. Both Congregationalists and Baptists functioned with ecclesiologies that made every local body, every institutionalization, in principle authentic and self-sufficient, a legitimation that would over time have infectious power. So, first, Puritanism contributed to the actual plurality of groups and generated principles of ecclesial legitimacy under colonial conditions.[20] Second, the Puritan movements functioned, as did other impulses with Reformed origins, with an imperative for godly order and the eschatological urgency to get the form of the church right.[21] In its initial expression, this passion for order was quite intolerant and the very antithesis of the denominational tolerant, branch theory of the church. But the premium put on structure and order would, like so much of Puritanism, have value in transmuted, noneschatological form, in this case as preoccupation with constitution and polity. So, second, Puritanism contributed to American denominationalism the Reformed concern for order, law, and structure. A third, related indebtedness to Puritanism was just this sense of the larger, even eschatological context within which the church undertook its ordering. Polity, important though it was, served larger ends—the renovation of society and world and service for the true church, which remained invisible. Fourth and again related were covenantal views, Puritan public theology and its penchant for careful attention to the relation of civil and ecclesiastical realms, a contribution that would loom larger in the second stage of denominationalism than in the first.

The process by which the ideal of toleration, the several principles of order, and the various notions of ecclesial legitimacy were turned into the fabric of denominationalism (the first stage) was the religious turmoil historians know as the First Great Awakening. This process carried itself through most completely in the Middle Colonies, where Dutch Reformed, Quaker, Scots Presbyterian, Baptists, Anglicans, transplanted New England Congregationalists, and German-speaking peoples of various persuasions (Dunkers, Lutherans, Reformed, Moravians, Schwenckfelders, Mennonites) sought space, identity, and community.[22] Many found their fulfillment in processes that would be known as revivals—spiritual struggles through which strangers became "brothers" and "sisters" (religious family), moral anarchy became discipline, social cacophony became congregation.[23] Its methods of conversion, the testing of one another's religious experience and commitment to a common walk and each other, produced both revival and religious community. And once emergent, the individual communities of Presbyterians or Lutherans sought support from one another and from appropriate European authorities. Out of those relatively spontaneous struggles came modest denominational structures, associations of congregations and of leaders. Typically understanding themselves as under the authority of some home country judicatory, these associations nevertheless found themselves to be quasi-independent and forced by the sheer distance to resolve problems, adjudicate moral and theological disputes, and identify, train, and authenticate leadership.

Such communities delineated themselves sociologically in one way and theologically in quite another. These denominations and the communities that made them up typically drew together persons on some basis of affinity—national origin, language, prior involvement with that religious group, theological posture. Ethnicity defined actual community.[24] However, denominations affirmed their new unity and proclaimed their purposes in eschatological terms, viewing the conversions and revivals that had brought them into being as putting them center stage in God's dramatic work for the redemption of humanity.[25]

In this first stage, denominations talked about themselves in grandiose terms but actually focused inward. Cohesion depended upon consent, the acceptance of the authority exercised, the support of laity. These were voluntary communities that might mete out discipline roughly or establish rigid clerical patterns but that required communal assent even in such coercion.[26] Associations concerned themselves with problem solving— ministerial supply and credentials, hymnals and service books, catechism, discipline, and the like. Mission or evangelization typically honored ethnic boundaries. And most bodies, even including the Presbyterians at this point, operated with little in the way of a public theology or policy. The notable exceptions to this rule were the established bodies, Congregationalists in New England and Anglicans particularly in the South, neither of whom, in areas where they were established, functioned in this denominational fashion.[27] Indeed, insofar as the denominational pattern evidenced itself in New England and the South, it did so in dissenters against these establishments—Separates and Baptists in New England, Presbyterians and Baptists in the South. Denominationalism at this period was an ethnic voluntarism. Since virtually all of the denominations understood themselves to be ultimately under European authority,[28] this denominationalism was provincial and, in a sense, provisional, bound confessionally to Halle, Amsterdam, London, Berlin, or Edinburgh and to those colonial peoples who accepted that confession. Denominations initially adhered as ethnic communities; denominationalism was ethnic voluntarism.

Purposive Missionary Association

The second stage of denominationalism is the one most frequently described and is presented as its norm.[29] It emerged in the national period as the several denominations, recently themselves independent, established new joint purposes in and specifically in relation to the new American society. The new style and theory of denominationalism derived from many hands; indeed, the various religious bodies all played their part. Of special note, however, were the Reformed traditions,[30] particularly the Congregationalists and the Presbyterians, who drew on Scottish moral philosophy, the rubrics of republicanism, and the deeper Reformed tradition, including especially the elements outlined above, to elaborate a public theology and to define collective denominational purposes in terms thereof. Speaking in providential, at times eschatological, language, the Reformed applied covenantal imagery to the nation, tied both civil and religious well-being to a society appropriately ordered, began the invention of societies and structures through which order might be established, and summoned their constituencies to action with notes of concern, alarm, even paranoia.[31]

Such histrionics have, at times, been credited with motivating the Second Great Awakening. A more plausible influence, and one that indeed motivated both revivals and denominationalism, came in the evangelistic efforts of Baptists, Methodists, and Christians (Restorationists).[32] Drawing on diverse strands of Pietism, these popular movements pursued adherents, requiring only, as the Methodists put it, "a desire to flee the wrath to come." This missionary impulse and self-understanding, initially illustrated in the efforts of Shubal Stearns in my area of North Carolina, broke denominations free of the ethnic constraints of voluntarism and offered them, in principle, the entire American society and all its peoples. To be sure, denominations proved, in practice, to be more selective, and they, in fact, employed various class, ethnic, regional, language, and racial screens. Race-specific (African Methodist and Baptist) and language-specific (German and Scandinavian Lutheran particularly) denominations, in fact, emerged very early in this period. But denominations nevertheless saw the nation and eventually the world as their horizon and their domain. The older boundaries of parish, of ethnicity, of confession, they ignored, indeed, violated. The presumption in such attitudes and behavior, the intrusion on one another's turf, the audacity to think one authorized to Christianize the already Christian, offended religious bodies with traditional notions of parish and ministerial authority, particularly offending the established Congregationalists and Anglicans. The popular movements responded by pressing for greater religious freedom, collaborating in that cause with other enemies to establishments. And they persisted in the expansive, aggressive, competitive, entrepreneurial, expressive boosterism that thereafter would be the business of religion and, for that matter, of America. This style accented initiative, risk taking, mobility, openness, experimentation, vernacular idioms, popular expression—traits that Baptists, Methodists, and Christians both espoused and institutionalized.

These denominations functioned, as Nathan Hatch has observed, as a powerful democratizing and creative force.[33] The creativity and the obvious results in such missionary enterprise captivated the more established denominational bodies, notably Presbyterians and Congregationalists, who embraced but redirected this institutionally creative energy. They oriented purposive association towards the building of a Christian America. This coalescence of mission and covenant produced purposive missionary denominationalism. Reformed public theology and missionary pietism unleashed an incredible institution-building effort. Some of that effort channeled itself into the denominations themselves, which adapted the modest associational structures for national ministerial deployment and governance. Much of it went into voluntary societies, which could be erected for whatever the urgent cause, which drew together supporters and workers from various traditions, and which collaborated loosely with one another and with the denominations. Eventually, much of the agenda of the voluntary societies, and some of their structure, would be internalized by the denominations, creating within agencies devoted to missions Sunday schools, tracts, Bible, temperance, colonization—a process not without much trauma and ecclesiastical soul-searching. Purposive missionary association created new institutions and new procedures faster than formal theologies and ecclesiastical polities could adjust. The adjustment crisis would yield the third style of denominationalism.

Churchly Denominationalism

Purposive missionary association did indeed pose crises for movements that, for whatever reason, objected to or were objected to by this increasingly dominant denominational style. R. Laurence Moore calls our attention to the religious outsiders in American history, the self-consciousness with which groups claimed that status, the creativity such self-consciousness elicited, and the ironic way in which outsider status functioned to establish both group and American identity.[34] While the popular movements—Methodists, Baptists, and Christians—initially viewed themselves and were viewed as outsiders, they did participate in expanding and defining what would be the new norm of missionary denominationalism. That new norm turned old insiders, some of the established churches of Europe, into outsiders. It created great difficulty for Episcopalians, Lutherans, and some of the Reformed who valued their churchly, sacramental, and catechetical traditions, and even greater difficulty for what Robert Baird termed "non-evangelical bodies," including Catholics, Jews, Unitarians, and Mormons.[35] Such groups found themselves repelled by missionary denominationalism and at the same time impelled to adopt some of its measures for sheer survival.[36] This accommodation produced unease among leadership conscious of the normative expressions and forms of their faith. Such unease took eloquent expression in the Mercersburg theology; the two major theologians of the German Reformed seminary at Mercersburg, Philip Schaff and John W. Nevin, issued trenchant criticisms of revivalism, the anxious bench, and the whole "methodistical" scheme—in short, purposive denominationalism—and called the Reformed back to the hallmarks of their tradition. Charles Philip Krauth performed similar service for Lutherans and John Henry Hobart and Calvin Colton for Episcopalians. Inspired by Romanticism, an appreciation for the richness of tradition, the nuances of the confession, the value of the catechism, and the importance of one's own ecclesial identity, such criticisms, voiced in the 1840s and 1850s, heralded a new denominational style.[37] Nonliturgical movements reclaimed a more exclusive sense of church by appeal to non-Romantic versions of tradition. Important and illustrative was the Landmark movement led by J. R. Graves. It also discerned its own apostolic succession that distinguished it from all other religious bodies and warranted critical distance from the expansive, open, cooperative missionary association of the early nineteenth century. It opted instead for localism and close communion.

Paralleling this self-conscious confessionalism and producing a revived quasi-confessionalism across American religion were divisive developments within the purposive missionary denominations, specifically, the reemergence of the issue of slavery. Abolition proved the most explosive of a series of "ultraisms" that exposed the fault line in purposive association, namely, that, like another invention of that day, the railroads, denominations and voluntary societies could gather great momentum along their tracks, but a new direction, a new issue, particularly one that exposed profound differences among the travelers (that is, within the membership), could derail and crash the whole train. That, in fact, occurred, beginning with the division of the Presbyterians in 1837, followed by divisions of Baptists and Methodists in the 1840s.[38] Each of these controversies exposed vital unresolved issues in purposive missionary organization—its underlying quasi-Arminian theology; the power conveyed to voluntary, often cooperative organizations, which acted on denominational behalf but not under formal, judicatory authority; the appropriateness of cooperative or interdenominational ventures; the theological accountability of parts of the church to one another; the level or office within which ultimate authority was to be vested; the relation of missions and missionary efforts to regular judicatories; the right of denominational officials and media to suppress controversy and dissent. Whether such ecclesiastical issues or slavery divided the churches, historians debate and will doubtless continue to debate. What needs to be affirmed here is that slavery exposed important ecclesiastical issues and that after the divisions, if not before, each of the sectional churches found it important to construe its purposes in theological and ecclesiastical terms. So Old and New Schools, the Wesleyans, and both northern and southern Baptists and Methodists emerged from their respective division intensely committed to and defining themselves in terms of certain ecclesiological principles. A new quasi-confessionalism, then, derived from the slavery and sectional crises, from the divisions, and intensified itself greatly during and after the Civil War, especially in the border states and in other places of overlap, as the churches fought each other altar to altar, laid blame on one another for the war, waved the bloody flag, and proclaimed themselves the true sons of the founder (Wesley, Calvin).

In the northern churches, this heightened churchly emphasis embraced the covenantal, providential, and millennial Christian American themes, actually accenting them. The northern churches typically made loyalty to the Union almost a creedal test. The southern churches reworked their civil religion into a religion of the lost cause, espoused the spirituality of the church, repudiated northern political activism, and so put denominationalism into a cultural rather than a political or a national context.[39] Eventually, northern denominationalism also gathered stronger cultural accents as, toward the end of the century, a trans-Atlantic Anglo-Saxonism swept over both regions. The denominations increasingly construed the furthering of a Christian culture as their evangelical and shared mission,[40] a purpose readily embraced as well by churches not divided by slavery and less embroiled by sectional factors. Culture, then, served to unite denominations in common cause but also reinforced the churchly emphasis or quasi-confessionalism by inviting attention to roots, to the tradition.

Also reinforcing theological and cultural impulses to heightened inward-facing denominationalism were the trans-Atlantic initiatives in forming denominational fellowships—Lambeth Conference (1867), World Presbyterian Alliance (1877), Methodist Ecumenical Conference (1881), and International Congregational Council (1891). A Baptist World Conference was mooted earlier but not held until 1905.[41] These too encouraged denominations to think about themselves. And so the latter half of the century witnessed an increased denominational consciousness, as each denomination attended to itself. The churches focused on issues of polity, of improved governance, of the structures for mission. They elaborated new youth and men's organizations, worried over the relation of women's missionary structures to those of the denomination, improved Sunday schools and Sunday school literature, packaged model plans for church buildings, erected new buildings at a frenzied pace, put up elaborate congregational educational wings, and refined the grammer of denominational life. Culture in denominations and denominational culture prospered. Such efforts would pave the way for the development of the fourth style of denominationalism, corporate organization, but in this third stage the accent fell on denominational culture, rather than on business culture. So denominations put renewed efforts into making their colleges more explicitly Baptist, Methodist, Presbyterian, Episcopal, Congregational.[42] New systematic theologies appeared, and denominational and seminary journals flourished. The churches endeavored to get their own houses in order presuming, to be sure, that their efforts served the building of a Christian civilization. And the evangelical or mainstream denominations continued to collaborate, participating in the Evangelical Alliance and in various common educational and missional projects. But the emphasis fell on caring for internal matters.

Corporate Organization

In the late nineteenth and the early twentieth centuries, the denominations continued to work on matters of internal structure. Indeed, they intensified those efforts, but did so as a way of gearing up for even more intensified expansion, mission (abroad), reform of American society, and cooperation. Churches shouldered "the white man's burden" and transformed ongoing missions into imperial enterprise, albeit in the name of ideals—the gospel, civilization, democracy, health, decency, free enterprise.[43] Denominationalism became once again instrumental; denominational attention focused outward. The effective building of this Christian civilization required, so realized the leaders (and especially lay leaders, who increasingly played national roles), the application to themselves and to their work of the procedures, techniques, and structures of the then emerging corporate world. "A managerial revolution"[44] in consequence swept the major denominations.

It was undertaken in solution of vexing and important problems, a point now lost on the many critics of denominational bureaucracy. Purposive voluntarism and confessionalism had generated within denominations a complex of essentially voluntary societies, typically run rather independently by an executive secretary. This single person, perhaps with a very small staff, might oversee, as in the case of denominational and women's missions, an army of employees across the world. Counterparts supervised publications, education, Freedman's aid, Sunday schools and Sunday school literature, church extension, home missions, and temperance activities. Each agency secretary pushed his or her own agenda, developed this agency's particular constituency, raised money by separate appeals to congregations, negotiated relations with regional judicatories, and dealt with the formal authority structure of the denomination. Seemingly uncooperative, unchecked, competitive, free enterprise ruled within denominations, as, of course, between and among them. And the embarrassment and chaos at home was magnified in the mission field, where a denomination competed with itself and, of course, with other Christian bodies.

Out of such embarrassment and an appreciation of needed cooperation would emerge the modern ecumenical movement. Some of the same dynamics fed progressivism and the Social Gospel and also professionalization. These larger currents informed the bureaucratization of Protestant denominations, which addressed the duplication, competition, and inefficiency of effort but did so in the interest of ideals—missions, reform, order, unity—and in the recognition that the existing system posed knotty theological, particularly ecclesiological, issues. One of the most vexing ones, appreciated by the Old School Presbyterians earlier in the century, actually at the threshold of the third stage, had to do with the society's or the agency's relation and accountability to formal denominational authority. Enunciated by the cry "The denomination is itself a missionary society" and in protest against Presbyterian investment in interdenominational societies, this concern had eventuated in the establishment of missionary and benevolent societies within denominations, thus achieving a level of accountability.

By the end of the century, the growth and multiplication of these intradenominational structures made the once external problem an internal one.[45] Were the agencies really accountable to the denomination's national assembly, council, convention, or conference? Were these powerful societies through which the denomination did much of its business subject to the denomination's formal authority structure? If so, through what mechanisms? And did such accountability involve coordination between and among the various agencies? And could it also bring into some order the then disparate appeals that agencies made to individual congregations for money, purchase, sponsorship, or whatever?

Denominations answered such questions with the managerial revolution—staffing agencies with professionals; encouraging specialization and relying on expertise; increasing staff; resorting to systematic finance; appointing denominational boards to govern the agencies; elaborating procedures and structures for coordination and collaboration among the agencies and between agencies and local churches; prescribing an organizational grammar so that every level of the church, from congregation to state to regional to national, structured itself with the same bodies, with the same names; consequently centering the denomination nationally through bureaucracy. The efficiency transformation did not happen overnight;[46] it built on developments from earlier periods and continued throughout the twentieth century, indeed, continues today, drawing on current business fads.

Simultaneous with their corporate restructuring, denominations addressed other partially related developments—professionalization of the clergy, allowance for significant lay participation, (partial) desegregation, and admission of women into governing and clergy roles. These developments interplayed in very complex fashion. For instance, the initial phases of bureaucratization and lay empowerment were clearly taken at the expense (among others) of women, who saw their own organizations brought under (male) denominational control, a control now to include lay participation (but not initially of women). Similarly, the centering of denominational business in national boards seems to have permitted the regional judicatory—presbytery, conference, diocese—to assume much of the role of a professional organization for clergy.[47] At a later stage, integration brought significant numbers of blacks and other minorities to board and agency positions but, in so doing, apparently drained much needed leadership from local churches and regional judicatories.

Each of these developments, like bureaucratization, represented an effort on the part of the churches to reform, and each brought the churches into engagement with the larger societal dynamics of differentiation, secularization, and modernization. The embrace of such trends constituted an aspect of the liberal Protestant agenda.[48] This modernization, through self-conscious appropriation of culture, elicited vehement protests, denominational divisions, and the elaboration of a counterdenominational style and culture, one initially normed against modernism and modernization.[49] Beginning in protest against the ideas and the institutions of modernity, fundamentalism and evangelicalism elaborated a vast new array of institutions, some patterned on older Protestant forms, some borrowing the most recent technology.[50] By the end of the twentieth century, this new denominational culture had begun in significant ways to enter the public forum and was doing so just as the older denominationalism was showing clear signs of fatigue.

Postdenominational Confessionalism

The four denominational styles described thus far have been named for their adhesive and dynamic principles. So, appearances to the contrary, has this stage. The name "Postdenominational Confessionalism" is intended to suggest that denominations have lost or are losing long-familiar adhesive and dynamic principles and are groping, often desperately, for tactics that work and unite.

The most profound factor in explaining both present-day so-called mainstream Protestantism and the emergence in the public sphere[51] of the conservative denominations is what Robert Handy terms "the second disestablishment," which he locates between the world wars.[52] That displacement of Protestant denominations from cultural hegemony has, in fact, robbed them of what had been the larger end or purpose that denominationalism served, namely, the building of a Christian society, and made adhesion itself problematic. To put the matter bluntly (and with perhaps some exaggeration), mainstream denominationalism now lacks a credible adhesive and dynamic principle.

Its once-constitutive Christianizing purpose now has been grasped by the evangelical denominations and the transdenominational conservative para-organizations. They contend with or sidestep one of the disestablishing forces—pluralism—by transforming "Christian America" into a set of specific moral campaigns—abortion, school prayer, homosexuality—on which they can make common cause with Roman Catholic, Mormon, and even, at times, Jewish groups. Their denominationalism prospered within a cold war ethos, the shooting cold war that made a conservative moral vision an antidote to communism and the shouting cold war that put conservative rhetoric to use against what they considered the bleeding-heart liberals in church and state. Within that ethos, conservatives and evangelicals erected seminaries, effective publishing enterprises, radio and television ministries, large missionary forces, Christian schools and colleges, megacongregations, and various formal and informal associations—in short, a new denominationalism and a new voluntarism clearly serviceable to a cold war and increasingly appreciated for that service. With the Carter and Reagan presidencies, evangelical denominationalism came into respectability and responsibility. What this new respectability and the end of the cold war will mean for politically conservative denominations we do not yet know.[53]

At any rate, the campaigns of conservative Protestantism are being fought also within the old mainstream and constitute one of several factors that have altered corporate denominationalism.[54] In most denominations, conservative groups lead often vitriolic attacks against the bureaucratic structures and the "liberals" within them. The corporate structure suffers—from erosion of respect, loss of resources, consequent diminished power and smaller staffs, relocation of function to regional judicatories, competition with other national structures, and resurging claims over it by national president, assembly, or conference.[55] The latter prove most newsworthy and certainly take expressive form—for instance, in the Southern Baptist conflict.[56] Less effective and sometimes more symbolic victories occur in decisions to relocate headquarters so as to punish agency staff and to extricate leadership from locations, such as New York, that are perceived to be ideologically liberal.[57]

Such warfare frequently comes from conservative groupings and points to one important reality of contemporary denominationalism, mentioned here initially and documented by Robert Wuthnow, that denominations split badly and fairly cleanly into theologically conservative and liberal camps.[58] An evangelical-liberal cleavage runs both between and through denominations. Liberals tend to have access to denominational power. In reaction, conservative groups have created alternative structures, some of them operating as caucuses in behalf of one or another cause, others functioning as a shadow denominational structure dedicated to publishing more orthodox literature, sending missionaries, training persons of the right complexion for the ministry, holding rallies, and creating "orthodox" quasi-conventions or -conferences.

The temptation is strong, for the academics who interpret such patterns as for the corporate leadership under attack, to locate the problem in contemporary denominational life in the attackers, in this warfare, and in the division of the denomination into liberal and evangelical camps. Might the cleavage and the warfare be more symptom than problem, more effect than cause?

Might the problem, the cause, lie in the collapse of denominational purpose and in the loss of real reason for hanging together? Conservatives after all do not hold the license on the caucus or political action form. Liberal, women's, gay, and ethnic organizations also function like political action groups. The caucuses have, individually and collectively, a divisive effect—the denomination divides itself into caucuses. These movements have also a unitive function—they constitute alternatives to the corporate structure in uniting the denominations nationally, albeit along these particular "struggle" lines. In some instances, they gain agency status, as has the United Methodist Commissions on Religion and Race and on the Status and Role of Women. Or they may function under denominational blessing, as did Presbyterian groups until recently in what that body recognized as Chapter IX organizations. But whether incorporated within, sanctioned, or merely tolerated, caucuses and caucus-like groups press themselves on (other) denominational agencies, demanding, in effect, agency adherence to the caucus norm or cause. Thus they behave like the monitoring or regulatory agency so common now in American political life.

That regulatory behavior also increasingly characterizes all denominational agencies, which find themselves resorting to a variety of new mechanisms to achieve the results that used to come easier—to effect policy, to implement program, to disseminate resolutions. So agencies function at times like regulatory agencies, controlling through expectation or rule. In so behaving, denominations internalize one prevalent mechanism for continuing the rule from the top down. As Dykstra has effectively demonstrated, denominations here borrow from the repertoire of national and state regulatory agencies. Regulation—rule making, monitoring, on-site visiting, indicting, exposing, forcing adherence—reaches for the cooperation, unity, and coordination that used to link congregation to state, to region, to nation in denominational life. Regulatory behavior substitutes for the older dynamic and adhesive principles. Regulation, often adversarial in premise or tone, suggests a collapse of denominational cohesion and purpose.

Regulation, however, is only one of an array of mechanisms to which denominations now resort in quest of once-easier unity and purpose. Denominations seek also to behave like foundations, influencing through grants. This is a friendlier style, giving rather than demanding, but it is no less coercive. And it is prevalent and spontaneous. Boards seek funding from outside or sequester funds and immediately set up their own rules for awarding these funds. By making their own grants, they advertise purpose, communicate with regional judicatories or congregations, and achieve cooperation. Agencies also behave at times like consulting firms, generating within some marketable expertise, then hiring themselves out for a project; at times like franchisers, marketing specific product lines in spirituality or stewardship for congregational or judicatory use; at times like educational systems, credentialing through training.[59] Regulating, granting, consulting, franchising, marketing, training—these tactics do not energize, do not adhere, do not unite the denominations in the way that the grand cause of a Christian America once did. Indeed, these new board and agency mechanisms further fragment denominational life. But absent some lofty purposes, the agencies struggle on.

The same problems and struggles, the same regulatory, grant-making, consulting, franchising, and training mechanisms, the same quest for unity and purpose can be seen on other levels and in other sectors of denominational life. Regional judicatories, for instance, have begun claiming more of the resources and producing more of the program for congregations. In doing so, they create more regionalized patterns of denominational life, effectively competing with their national counterparts and inevitably disrupting the once-uniform denominational style. The top-down, imposed, common denominational grammar begins to erode.

Congregations also increasingly chart their own courses. Less preoccupied with denominational identity and less impressed with denominational delivery systems, congregations, particularly those with sufficient resources to function independently, buy program modules or curricula from various places.[60] They behave like consumers, influenced by and influencing consumerist religious mentality among the people. The ultimate in that style emerges in the megachurches and family life centers, mall-like congregations offering both superstore and boutique religion. Some replicate the entire set of services once rendered by denominations, setting up their own publishing operations, significant television and radio ministries, community service programs, missions, and theological education programs. Such congregations boast of their family atmosphere, their family-like unity. Other congregations evidence the family discord characteristic of other levels of denominational life and "adhere" through the array of regulating, grant-making, franchising, caucusing, consulting, and training functions. In either case, as quasi-family or as a local arena for organizational experimentation, the congregation drifts from denomination and so contributes to the diffuseness of denominational identity.

At the other extreme, and partly in response to denominational consumerism or indifference, can be found an exaggerated denominationalism. Bishops and their counterpart judicatory officials struggle to regain direction, to maintain program momentum, to keep the ship financially afloat. At times, they put high premiums on denominational identity and loyalty, virtually shouting denominationalism. Adherence to denominational practice and structure attests or tests denominational integrity. Polity rather than creed or confession becomes the denominational norm. Exaggerated denominationalism also characterizes institutions dependent upon denominational personnel, resources, or support. Seminaries, for instance, can preach high denominational doctrine.[61] So in areas having to do with ministerial recruitment, training, and credentialing, hyperdenominationalism surfaces, while amid laity and congregations consumerism and indifference prosper.

All of this—the damaged corporate structure, the caucuses, the regional initiatives and variety, the congregational independence, the hyperdenominationalism—shows mainline denominations groping for a new order and for new purposes to replace those once given by a Christian America. In the meanwhile, they focus attention within, as though their purposes were to be discovered there. And the conservative denominations, until recently seemingly impervious to modernity, now begin to show some of the same strains. They face their own disestablishment and a similar struggle as they cope with the end of the cold war. The two styles of denominationalism may well mark a transition to a yet unclear style, or perhaps to another form of the church altogether.[62]

Implications

Denominationalism and denominations have changed. That is the main point. Each of the five stages or styles has had its own complexion—a

dynamic and adhesive principle, distinctive goals vis-à-vis American society, rules of interdenominational interaction, and boundaries that
marked off mainstream denominationalism from sectarian, churchly, or
counterdenominational religious styles. Each stage's dynamic, rendered
in its name, oriented denominations toward society. Of note is the way
in which denominationalism has oscillated between relatively introspective and expansive modes. The first, third, and fifth stages have been
introspective, with denominations preoccupied with internal order; in
the first and third, getting the form of the church right served to build
the kingdom, while in the fifth stage, mainstream Protestantism seemed
to lack for dynamism and lacked also a clear sense of its role in American society.

The second and fourth styles of denominationalism have been expansive, with instrumental conceptions of denominational order and clear
commitments to transforming society and world through effective effort
and organization. These stages also saw the most self-conscious unity and
collaboration between and among the denominations. In the second
stage, denominations collaborated through the evangelical united front,
the network of voluntary societies, as well as through revivals and camp
meetings, in building a Christian America. In the fourth, denominations
found common cause in corporate cooperation through explicitly ecumenical organizations; agencies collaborated to divide missionary turf,
and executives struggled towards unity in both faith and order and life
and work. The first, third, and fifth stages put less of a premium on
cooperation, produced fewer new efforts at unity, and sustained existing
collaboration with lessened enthusiasm.

The matter of boundaries can only be touched upon here. Adequate
treatment would involve discussion of the successively larger boundaries
of each period and the ways in which renegotiation of boundaries created
each stage. In each instance, outsider groups seem to have provided the
creative impulse towards a new dynamic principle, forcing wider the
boundary of denominationalism, negotiating their own way in, and ef-
fecting by their entry a new denominational order. In the first awakening,
Presbyterians, various German groups, Separates, and Baptists forged revivalism into a new principle of ethnic voluntarism, establishing thereby
new space for religion in the colonies and forcefully stating their own
legitimacy. Baptists, Methodists, and Christians played a similar role in the
second awakening, expanding denominationalism with their new expansive principle. Various confessional groups, including perhaps the Old
School Presbyterians, added that principle to denominational legitimacy
in the Civil War period. Around the turn of the twentieth century, corporate reorganization came from outsiders within, reformers and Social
Gospelers, who saw in efficiency and rationalized structure a more effective witness at home and abroad. And the fifth style, perhaps only partially
emergent, clearly owes much to critics within, as well as to the whole
evangelical impulse both within and without. A new denominational or-

der, we suggested, might well radically redraw boundaries so as to embrace both mainstream and conservative denominationalism.

The fifth style may represent another of these periodic stages of withdrawal. Alternatively, as we have indicated denominationalism as we know it may well be breaking up. If so, it need not mean the end to the religious movements now denominated, many of which (for example, Lutherans, Presbyterians, Mennonites, Baptists, Congregationalists) had a predenominational ecclesial existence and have no reason to confuse their essence with its current denominational expression. Denominationalism is a relatively recent phenomenon and may have outlived its usefulness. It may, on the other hand, be simply going through another of its metamorphoses.

NOTES

1. Denominational publishing houses serve up healthy doses of preventive and curative medicine. For instance, Cokesbury, the distributing and sales arm of the United Methodist Publishing House, features Lyle E. Schaller, a guru of church growth, among its "Bestselling Authors," markets similar items in a regular "Effective Church Series" and under the rubric of "Church Leadership," and devotes a section of its catalog to "Evangelism & Church Growth." From the latter, Bishop Richard B. Wilke's volumes *And Are We Yet Alive?* and *Signs and Wonders: The Might Work of God in the Church* can be purchased in either book or video form. Kennon L. Callahan offers *Twelve Keys to An Effective Church,* a *Leader's Guide* to the same, an additional *Twelve Keys: Study Guide,* and *Effective Church Leadership: Building on the Twelve Keys.* In all, the catalog makes available some fifty books, each offering "keys" to the church's survival and recovery.

2. See Wade Clark Roof and William McKinney, *American Mainline Religion* (New Brunswick, N.J.: Rutgers University Press, 1987), and Robert Wuthnow, *The Struggle for America's Soul* (Grand Rapids, Mich.: William B. Eerdmans Publishing Co., 1989) and *The Restructuring of American Religion* (Princeton: Princeton University Press, 1988).

3. The question of how the recent growth and public prominence of evangelical and non-Protestant bodies figure in the denominational saga will be dealt with below.

4. See the multivolume series *The Presbyterian Presence,* ed. Milton J Coalter, John M. Mulder, and Louis B. Weeks (Louisville, Ky.: Westminster/John Knox, 1990–92). The last volume is a synthetic essay by the editors pulling together the findings from the previous seven and entitled *The Reforming Tradition: Presbyterians and Mainstream Protestantism in the Twentieth Century* (Louisville, Ky.: Westminster/John Knox, 1992). See also *A Case Study of Mainstream Protestantism: The Disciples' Relation to American Culture,* ed. D. Newell Williams (Grand Rapids, Mich.: William B. Eerdmans Publishing Co., 1991).

5. This analysis draws on the essay by Craig Dykstra and James Hudnut-Beumler, "The Ecology of Denominational Organization," in *The Organizational Revolution: Presbyterians and American Denominationalism,* ed. Milton J Coalter, John M. Mulder, and Louis B. Weeks (Louisville, Ky.: Westminster/John

Knox, 1992), and also on my own *Denominationalism* (Nashville, Tenn.: Abingdon, 1977) and "Institutional Forms of Religion," in *Encyclopedia of Religion in America,* ed. Charles H. Lippy and Peter W. Williams, 3 vols. (New York: Charles Scribner's Sons, 1988), 1:31–50. The latter treats the literature on denominationalism in some detail, relieves this essay of that burden, and lays the groundwork for this typology in the distinct disciplinary approaches to denominationalism.

6. See William R. Hutchison's chapter, "Denominational Studies in the Reshaping of American Religious History," in this volume.

7. See, on the latter, *Religion, the Independent Sector, and American Culture,* ed. Conrad Cherry and Rowland A. Sherrill (Atlanta: Scholars Press, 1992).

8. This essay does not attempt to cover Roman Catholic and Jewish patterns with any care but does assume, as Gibson Winter and others have shown, that with certain qualifications denominational dynamics do apply. See the essays herein by Marc Lee Raphael, Jay Dolan, and Robert A. Orsi; see also Gibson Winter, *Religious Identity. A Study of Religious Organization* (New York: Macmillan, 1968).

9. This definition draws on classic statements by Winthrop S. Hudson, "Denominationalism as a Basis for Ecumenicity," and Sidney E. Mead, "Denominationalism: The Shape of Protestantism in America," both reprinted in Richey, *Denominationalism.*

10. Or "religious body." Obviously, when Jewish groups assumed denominational form, they did so by claiming their legitimacy and self-sufficiency not as Christian ecclesial but as Jewish bodies.

11. The denomination typically functions with a branch theory of the church, the notion that the church exists and is known in the present as an organism with many branches. That affirmation entails an act of self-recognition, that one is only a branch, and the realization that the church has other legitimate, even vital branches.

12. One of several items of self-consciousness that differentiate the denomination from a sect.

13. Early Puritans (colonial as well as British) who persisted in believing themselves part of the Church of England and British Methodists during Wesley's life thus would not be termed denominations, whereas American Methodists after 1784 would be. As these examples should suggest, one may have some difficulty in determining the point at which a reform or parachurch movement actually achieves independent status as a denomination.

14. Hudson, "Denominationalism as a Basis for Ecumenicity."

15. These were not inevitable stages, either for individual movements in adjusting to American society or for the collectivity of denominations. A given movement, indeed, would typically have within it all the prior stages. And certain denominations might resist the style of a period, although even that resistance often picked up certain aspects of that very style.

Compare the qualifications and the three types isolated by Dykstra and Hudnut-Beumler in "The Ecology of Denominational Organization": confederacy, corporation, and regulatory agency.

16. This point is effectively made by James H. Moorhead in this volume in "Presbyterians and the Mystique of Organizational Efficiency, 1870–1936."

17. It is my own belief, although not one that can be elaborated here, that typologies designed to make sense of the American religious scene do need to put in the center the denominations and denominationalism and to array off-center,

perhaps considerably off-center, the church type as well as sect and cult movements, each of which ordinarily defines itself vis-à-vis the denominational mainstream. Such a graphing differs from the traditional European one that places church in the center and views other religious movements as defined against it. Here denomination, rather than church, is the norm. In the American experience, classic European churches, for example, the Lutheran and the Roman Catholic, have found their way into the religious establishment as they have appropriated denominational form and self-understanding.

18. For that point, see Arthur Carl Piepkorn, *Profiles in Belief: The Religious Bodies of the United States and Canada,* vol. 2, *Protestant Denominations* (1978). (New York: Harper & Row, 1977–79).

19. See my " 'Catholic' Protestantism and American Denominationalism," *Journal of Ecumenical Studies* 16, no. 2 (Spring 1979): 213–231.

20. The Middle Colonies would also "benefit" from the presence and immigration there of religious bodies from Holland, Germany and elsewhere in Europe.

21. See John F. Wilson, *Pulpit in Parliament: Puritanism During the English Civil Wars* (Princeton: Princeton University Press, 1969); William Lamont, *Godly Rule: Politics and Religion, 106–1650* (New York: St. Martin's Press, 1969); David Little, *Religion, Order, and Law* (New York: Harper & Row, 1969); Michael Walzer, *The Revolution of the Saints* (New York: Atheneum, 1969); and the various works of Christopher Hill.

22. As the subsequent citations of Timothy Smith will indicate, I follow him in assessing the relation between the Awakening and ethnicity, an assessment that differs from the more traditional reading that saw the Awakening as substituting a new and shared, indeed, transcolony identity for the linguistic and national divisions of the Middle Colonies. The argument here is that the Awakening did not destroy but transmuted linguistic and national differentia in terms of which people had previously defined themselves. By lodging identity in the new birth of conversion, the Awakening gave a new "evangelical" face to differences—a specifically theologically ethnic face—such that congregations found themselves less reliant on European norms, less subservient to European authority, more conscious of commitments shared with neighbors, but nonetheless bonded along lines of family, language, and national background.

23. For two very different interpretations of this process, both influential in this reading, see Timothy L. Smith, "Congregation, State and Denomination: The Forming of the American Religious Structure," *The William and Mary Quarterly,* 3rd ser., 25 (1968): 155–176, reprinted in Richey, *Denominationalism;* and Jon Butler, *Power, Authority, and the Origins of American Denominational Order: The English Churches in the Delaware Valley, 1680–1730,* American Philosophical Society Transactions, 68, pt. 2 (Philadelphia, 1978), and his more recent *Awash in a Sea of Faith. Christianizing the American People* (Cambridge, Mass.: Harvard University Press, 1990), especially pp. 164–193. Smith views the ordering process as an essentially positive popular initiative taken by groups who found congregation and eventually denomination the viable resource for identity, community, order, authority, and direction. Butler reads that same process as coercive, authoritarian, and elitist.

24. It needs to be recognized that ethnicity was itself a fabrication and this process of denomination forming a key element therein. Denominations gave shape and legitimacy to ethnic community. There were, of course, exceptions to

this pattern of ethnic voluntarism—individuals who affiliated with a group because of proximity, persuasion, marriage, or religious experience—with the major exception religious movements that gradually gave religious attention to, and in some fashion embraced, Africans. Ethnic voluntarism serves nevertheless as a useful rubric for describing the dynamic in denominational formation for this period.

25. For this paradox of ethnic particularity and universality, see Timothy L. Smith, "Religion and Ethnicity in America," *American Historical Review* 83 (December 1978): 1155–1185.

26. A point that Jon Butler seems to have understated.

27. The prior discussion does not imply that revival and conversion confined itself to the ethnic voluntary denominational communities. It did not. Congregationalists and Anglicans did, of course, participate in various ways in the Awakening. However, the Awakening did encourage patterns of divisiveness in those areas.

28. A point of self-understanding distinguishing the denominations from the established Congregationalists in New England.

29. See Sidney E. Mead, *The Lively Experiment* (New York: Harper & Row, 1963); his essay and those by Elwyn A. Smith, Fred J. Hood, and myself in *Denominationalism;* and Winthrop S. Hudson's *Religion in America,* 3rd. ed. (New York: Charles Scribner's Sons, 1981).

30. See especially Fred J. Hood, *Reformed America* (University: University of Alabama Press, 1980), and the considerable literature on voluntarism discussed in my "Institutional Forms of Religion" in *Encyclopedia of Religion in America.*

31. The literature on these developments is immense. A fine collection that engages much of it is Mark A. Noll's *Religion and American Politics. From the Colonial Period to the 1980s* (New York: Oxford University Press, 1990).

32. The contribution of the primitivist, restorationist movements to this denominationalism was vital but ironic. They grasped, articulated, and institutionalized what would become a central theme in denominational self-understanding, namely, that the evangelical mandate was to unite Christians, reform the church, and renovate the world through the restoration of primitive Christianity. To that end, they repudiated, explicitly and forcefully, denominationalism and the denomination. That repudiation, ironically, gave expression to what in other movements and in denominationalism generally would be a contradiction, or at best paradox or tension—belief that the labor was in behalf of an undivided kingdom (of God) but through highly competitive denominational action and structure. Eventually, the Disciples of Christ recognized its denominational character, an ironic development, perhaps, but an irony important to denominationalism generally—unity despite division.

33. Nathan O. Hatch, *The Democratization of American Christianity* (New Haven: Yale University Press, 1989).

34. R. Laurence Moore, *Religious Outsiders and the Making of Americans* (New York: Oxford University Press, 1986).

35. Robert Baird, *Religion in America,* abr. and ed. Henry Warner Bowden (1856; reprint ed., New York: Harper & Row, 1970).

36. See, for instance, Jay Dolan, *Catholic Revivalism* (Notre Dame, Ind.: University of Notre Dame Press, 1978), and *The Immigrant Church* (Baltimore: Johns Hopkins University Press, 1975). Dolan stresses the Catholic and European origin

to patterns that have been frequently ascribed to Protestant influence. One can concede a measure of truth to that point and still observe that Catholics found it appropriate to accent such patterns to succeed in the American environment.

37. The novelty and over-againstness is widely recognized. For instance, see H. Shelton Smith et al., *American Christianity*, 2 vols. (New York: Charles Scribner's Sons, 1960, 1963), vol. 2, specifically the section "Resurgent Churchly Traditions." Sydney E. Ahlstrom in *A Religious History of the American People* (New Haven: Yale University Press, 1972) points to similar dynamics in a large section entitled "Countervailing Religion," pp. 541–632. For a superb case study of this denominationalism, see Robert Bruce Mullin, *Episcopal Vision/American Reality. High Church Theology and Social Thought in Evangelical America* (New Haven: Yale University Press, 1986).

38. Here I follow H. Shelton Smith, *In His Image, But... Racism in Southern Religion, 1780–1910.* (Durham, N.C.: Duke University Press, 1972), in accenting the importance of the slavery issue in divisions that generated incredible ecclesiastical and theological posturing and have been, in consequence, often interpreted in polity terms. The latter, as we will suggest, were and would thenceforth prove very important.

39. Charles Reagan Wilson, *Baptized in Blood: The Religion of the Lost Cause, 1865–1920* (Athens: University of Georgia Press, 1980), and *"God's Project": The Southern Civil Religion, 1920–1980, Religion and the Life of the Nation,* ed. Rowland A. Sherrill (Urbana: University of Illinois Press, 1990), pp. 64–83.

40. On this great inversion, the making of culture rather than kingdom the denominational objective, see Robert T. Handy, *A Christian America,* 2nd ed. (New York: Oxford University Press, 1984).

41. See Henry R. T. Brandreth, "Approaches of the Churches Towards Each Other in the Nineteenth Century," in *A History of the Ecumenical Movement, 1517–1948,* ed. Ruth Rouse and Stephen Charles Neill (Philadelphia: Westminster Press, 1967), pp. 263–306.

42. For a case study of such efforts, see David B. Potts, *Wesleyan University, 1831–1910. Collegiate Enterprise in New England* (New Haven: Yale University Press, 1992).

43. See especially William R. Hutchison, *Errand to the World: American Protestant Thought and Foreign Missions* (Chicago: University of Chicago Press, 1987), and Jane Hunter, *The Gospel of Gentility. American Women Missionaries in Turn-of-the-Century China* (New Haven: Yale University Press, 1984).

44. The term derives from and this discussion is informed by the insights of Alfred D. Chandler, Jr., *The Visible Hand: The Managerial Revolution in American Business* (Cambridge, Mass.: Harvard University Press, Belknap Press, 1977). For a superb discussion of these developments within Presbyterianism, see in this volume James H. Moorhead, "Presbyterians and the Mystique of Organizational Efficiency, 1870–1936." The literature on the managerial revolution and denominationalism is reviewed in my "Institutional Forms of Religion." As this essay shows, the phrase organizational revolution also is applied to these developments and is employed in a fine collection, a case study thereof: Coalter, Mulder, and Weeks, eds., *The Organizational Revolution.*

45. The classic study of these issues is Paul M. Harrison, *Authority and Power in the Free Church Tradition* (Princeton: Princeton University Press, 1959). For extension of this treatment to the Protestant, Catholic, and Jewish

communities, see Gibson Winter, *Religious Identity. A Study of Religious Organization* (New York: Macmillan, 1968).

46. See Rolf Lunden, *Business and Religion in the American 1920s* (New York: Greenwood Press, 1988), for careful scrutiny of a decade of fairly crass celebration of business technique in religion.

47. This point, if accurate, needs study and particularly study that would look at the regional judicatory in relation to some of these larger patterns. How, for instance, have the particularly professional concerns been balanced with governance and program concerns? And how, given significant lay participation in judicatory affairs, have clergy professional matters and more general issues been related?

48. Adjustment to these aspects of modernity was a goal of what would be liberal Protestantism and was initially a positive good. For the larger agenda, see William R. Hutchison, *The Modernist Impulse in American Protestantism* (Cambridge, Mass.: Harvard University Press, 1976).

49. George M. Marsden, *Fundamentalism and American Culture: The Shaping of Twentieth-Century Evangelicalism* (New York: Oxford University Press, 1980).

50. George M. Marsden, *Reforming Fundamentalism: Fuller Seminary and the New Evangelicalism* (Grand Rapids, Mich.: William B. Eerdmans Publishing Co., 1987).

51. On this topic see Richard John Neuhaus, *The Naked Public Square: Religion and Democracy in America* (Grand Rapids, Mich.: William B. Eerdmans Publishing Co., 1984).

52. Robert Handy, *A Christian America,* pp. 159–184. A "third disestablishment" has been proposed by Roof and McKinney, *American Mainline Religion,* pp. 33–39, but the developments they describe might be construed as catch-up adjustments or later phases of Handy's second.

53. Perhaps the result will be some rapprochement with the old mainline, the reinventing of denominationalism, and the redrawing of mainline and denominationalism's boundaries.

54. Again, see Dykstra and Hudnut-Beumler, "The Ecology of Denominational Organization."

55. For a case study portrayal of these factors and indeed this phase of denominationalism, see Coalter, Mulder, and Weeks, *The Reforming Tradition.*

56. Among the discerning treatments are two that have decidedly informed my estimation of denominational patterns within Southern Baptist experience: Bill J. Leonard, *God's Last and Only Hope. The Fragmentation of the Southern Baptist Convention* (Grand Rapids, Mich.: William B. Eerdmans Publishing Co., 1990), and Nancy Tatom Ammerman, *Baptist Battles. Social Change and Religious Conflict in the Southern Baptist Convention* (New Brunswick, N.J.: Rutgers University Press, 1990).

57. Ironically, these attacks on fourth-phase corporate denominationalism are typically justified by an appeal to its central principle, efficiency and cost-effectiveness (The move out of New York to some more central place will "save money and time.")

58. *The Struggle for America's Soul.*

59. Mainstream denominational agencies envy conservative use of the media and would certainly try to behave more like producers or broadcasters if they had the resources.

60. Some of this may well be stimulated by denomination switching, which makes the switchers' experience in other denominational contexts available to the new congregation and, of course, makes the denominational identity of the switcher an issue for the new congregation.

61. At other times and especially when dealing with constituencies from other denominations, the seminaries sound as ecumenical as ever.

62. In this perspective, the recent events within the Southern Baptist Convention may take on a slightly different aspect. Southern Baptists have at once typified, even magnified, these trends *and* also constituted a special and, one hopes, unique pattern. The postdenominational trends are well documented by Ammerman, Leonard, and others; the pattern unique to Baptists is one also prevalent in American society—the leveraged buyout, the hostile takeover. Leonard, *God's Last and Only Hope,* shows the complex traditions and impulses brought into denominational coherence through a shared culture, piety, theology, and program. Ammerman, *Baptist Battles,* demonstrates how that cooperative program gradually edged Southern Baptists out of Southern establishment into mainstream Protestantism and corporate-bureaucratic denominationalism: "Each side was seeking out a viable place in the newly pluralistic world in which they found themselves. To accept the modern rules of religious civility and individual choice was indeed to make a home for oneself in the modern situation, even if other aspects of modernity were questioned. This is the world to which moderates sought to adapt themselves. They were willing to leave their Southern church-like status to become a denomination in the larger American religious mosaic. The dissidents within this denomination, however, were responding differently to change. In a newly pluralistic setting, they were seeking to reestablish homogeneity. They would recreate inside the religious world what was no longer viable in the world outside" (p. 166; see also pp. 213–214, 159).

To an outsider, Leonard's version of denominational identity helps explain why Ammerman's mainstreaming came as such a crisis. At any rate, to this outsider it appears if Baptists arrived just as the party was breaking up but in time to be caught in the ensuing squabble; Southern Baptist corporate leadership came to the mainstream and ecumenical Protestant party just as mainstream Protestantism was discovering that the party was over—that it could not Christianize America and the world, that a denominationalism so premised and so geared for such evangelization was hollow, that its "missional" structures and programs lacked a plausible energizing principle. Other denominations experienced the consequent revolt against "headquarters" as warfare on many fronts. The effective war against corporate culture within the SBC had one front—the conservatives. All the postdenominational trends we have described—the antibureaucratic, anticentrist mood, the consumerism, the caucusing, the PACS, the regulatory behavior, the parachurch structuring, the hyperdenominationalism—when polarized ideologically produced a leveraged buyout. Other denominations may be breaking up. The SBC went private.

The Question of Denominational Histories in the United States: Dead End or Creative Beginning?

CHARLES H. LONG

I do not know exactly why I was asked to comment on the topic of denominational histories in the United States, since this has not been one of my scholarly areas of concern. As a matter of fact, the history of the Christian church in the United States, at least from a conventional point of view, has not occupied a great deal of my time. I suppose, therefore, that I was invited precisely because I might express views regarding the nature of religion in the United States that could enhance or offer alternatives to the present malaise in which research and writing in denominational histories find themselves. Whatever problems I have are probably shared by most of the contributors to this volume. I can best discuss them by asking several sorts of questions about the study of religion in the United States.

Let me begin with this general observation. If you examine the curricula of the major theological or divinity schools in this country, or those of any respectable religious studies department, you would be hard-pressed to find serious attention given to denominational history or histories. At any point there might be references to Baptists, Methodists, Jews, or Roman Catholics, but not in relationship to their historical meanings as denominations or to the cultural impact that a specific religious meaning as denomination had on history at a particular point in time. We need to ask why this is so. Why has the denomination as the form of religious institution in the United States received so little attention in the study of the history of religion in America? I think that there are several reasons for this neglect.

Denominations and the Study of Religion in America

To follow up from my first query, if denominational histories are not being studied in our divinity schools and our departments of religious studies, how are the structures and the meanings of religion in the United States being presented? Until a generation ago, the answer to this question was fairly straightforward: The history of religion in America was understood as the general history of Protestantism. Religion in America, I sense, is still characterized in this way in most of the popular texts in use, with some attention given to Jews, Catholics, and blacks (those who do not fit clearly into mainstream Protestantism).

More recently, religion in America has been contextualized by the problematic of secular or civil religion in America. At least since the 1960s, this has been one of the major topics of scholarly conversation and debate. When the question of religion in America is raised, the issue behind the question is one of locus—where can we locate religion in America, or, to put it in Sidney Mead's terms, what is the religion of the Republic?[1] Asking the meaning of religion in the United States in this manner immediately raises the question of the relationship of religion to the integration and cohesion of any viable community, whether on the local or on the national level. How does a nation that has eschewed the formal and conventional meaning of religion as church in its foundational formulation locate a viable meaning of religion that enables it to represent a primordial and foundational meaning to its national community?

I think that the discussion of civil religion from Mead through Bellah and the continuing conversation about it frame a new and viable context for our problem, rather than resolving the issues at stake. For example, one study that is well-nigh a classic now, H. R. Niebuhr's study of the relationship of sociocultural situations to the rise of American denominations, takes on a new meaning within this context.[2] It is not simply the issue that the people who call themselves Americans in the United States are not the aboriginal inhabitants of the land; more to the point is the fact that they do not conceive of themselves as people who have an aboriginal reflection or experience of the land. Thus, the formation of their notion of being in a place is primarily one of "self-construction" as a primordium of their being. And this self-construction is as varied as the different communities of the various immigrant populations that inhabit the land. For the most part, these groups possess a vague primordiality related to their origins and formation as a people or ethnic group in locations prior to their immigration to America.

If, therefore, you want to look at the history of black religion in the United States, you necessarily have to take account of the sociocultural situation of the black community in the United States as well as the vague primordiality of blacks' sensitivity to their places of origin in Africa. The same might be said of several other communities, such as the various Roman Catholic communities from Ireland, Italy, and Eastern Europe and several Jewish communities. In the case of the Mormons and other groups that emerged from the "burned-over" district of upstate New York—the Noyes group, the Amana—we see in them an attempt to create a purely American primordium as the basis for their meaning of religious communities.

From this perspective, the "civil religion" or the "religion of the republic" tends to serve as a kind of umbrella that allows for the expression of the particular orientations of specific immigrant groups within the American landscape. It is for this reason that the peculiarly American religious organization, the denomination, is expressive of a seemingly endless proliferation of religious orientations that do not fit neatly into the older Troeltschian classification of church-type and sect-type.[3]

Professor Hutchison alludes in his chapter in this volume to a statement by Professor Richey, who suggests that too often denominational histories are written from a purely confessional and self-congratulatory point of view and thus are seldom valuable to persons and groups outside the particular denomination.[4] The issue is not so much whether the writings are scholarly enough but whether they imaginatively grasp the full implications of the formation and the complex origins of their particular formation as an important aspect of the American experience. Denominational history must always deal with two aspects of religion or, more precisely, with two aspects of religious experience—first, the contextuality of the generality of religion in America, some dimension of the religion of the republic or "civil religion," and, second, the more intense and precise meaning of religious experience as it relates to specific historical, social, and cultural situations of individual communities within the broader structure of American culture.

The critique, however, cuts both ways. In my experience in divinity schools and in departments of religion, several of my colleagues received a notion of their vocation from their background in their specific denominations. Once they became scholars of religion, however, the specificity of the denominational background receded in importance as far as their scholarly research into religion was concerned. In other words, the more generalized notion of a Protestant mainstream as the basis for the study and the meaning of religion in America is as unimaginative as the confessional and self-congratulatory denominational histories. The tension and the dialectic between the founding meaning of religion as a national community and religion as the experiential pole of specific communities has been lost, leaving both kinds of religious scholarship in America lacking.

The dilemma of denominational history is shared by the regnant scholarly teaching and research regarding religion in America as the Protestant mainstream. Neither of these approaches has yet come to terms with the specific peculiarity of the meaning of religion in the United States. Although we know that the older Troeltschian classification does not work, our studies still seem to bear the marks of this

European kind of classification. It seems as if we still think of religion in America as simply the transplanting of the European churches to the American soil. It may be that the religious situation in America might enable us to change both our notion of religion and the religious institution itself.[5]

Denomination, Democratization, and Modernity

It is somewhat surd that the name given to the religious institution in the United States—the denomination—is most commonly thought of in terms of a mathematical metaphor. The denominator is the number in a fraction that is below the line and that states the size of the parts. As such, the denominator implies that there is a *common,* and the numerator gives precision to the quantity of the common in a particular case. From this point of view, the notion of the religious body as a denomination simply suggests that aspects of religion are common without having to give any definition as to what this entails. If this question is pushed, one then looks at the numerator that gives a specific name to the fraction of the common that is presupposed in the denominator. It is a way of having a religion without being forced to say what it is.

In this manner the constitutional order of the country avoids having to deal with religion in the positive sense. It is there, to be sure, but it is not the business of the Constitution to define what it is. This allusiveness regarding the meaning of religion in the modern national state begins with the American republic and is directly related to the problem of ultimate authority in the nation-state. It is clear that the American republic intends to deny the meaning of a religiously conceived authority as the *ultimate common authority* for the legitimation of the state. This has come to be one of the hall marks of all democratically conceived constitutions. As such, the notion that lies behind the denomination takes on a new and different meaning in the modern world.

Seen from this point of view, the denomination in some ways begins to resemble those phenomena that have been called "new religions" in Japan. This nomenclature has been used to designate the proliferation of several new religious communities in Japan since the Second World War. If one looks closely at those communities that have been designated as "new religions" in Japan, it is clear that several of them began long before 1945. As Byron Earhart states, "There seems [sic] to be three major criteria for distinguishing new religious movements: 1) chronologically, those movements that appeared from late Tokugawa or early Meiji to the present; 2) in origin those movements that arose as renewal or 'revitalizing' forces; 3) in formation, those movements that led to permanent socio-religious organizations."[6]

The structure of the denominational form is thus directly related to the issue of authority. On the American scene, if we take the New England settlements, denominationalism arose in antagonism to the authority of the ecclesiastical orders in England and then later to the authority of the Puritan settlements themselves in New England. The issue of authority in America was directly related to geographical space, first the space of the Atlantic Ocean and later the almost limitless space of the North American continent. In Japan, the proliferation was dependent not on geographical space but more on the creation of a new sociocultural space. In both cases, however, the religious institutions, whether as denominations or as "new religions," placed the religious experience of the citizens of the state above or at least on an equal level with the authority of the state.

While this structural similarity might hold at this level, there is a fundamental difference between the American denomination and other forms of democratizing and modernizing forms of religion in the modern world. In the case of Japan, for example, in the midst of the proliferation of new religious communities and orientations, the identity of the Japanese people was never at stake. In the case of America, a country that denies the efficacy of an aboriginal orientation in regard to its experience of religious ultimacy, the identity issue remains unresolved, both as denominator and numerator. In one sense, the "civil religion" does not resolve the issue as denominator, nor does the proliferation of religious bodies settle the matter. Rather, the denomination defines the field of contestation not only in regard to the meaning of absolute authority (God) but equally in regard to civil authority and identity. For both Mead and Bellah, the words of Abraham Lincoln are prophetic in regard to the religion of the republic and civil religion, respectively. The irony here is that Mr. Lincoln's words were stated in a period of intense crisis about the very identity of the American people as a culture and nation.

The theological problem in America, at least since the founding of the republic, has become an issue of civil religion rather than one arising at the level of the denomination. The American denominations have by and large acquiesced to the practical meaning of comity, the practise of live and let live, in relationship to the wider doctrinal issues of constitutional government. It would, however, be interesting to see what has been the denominational interest in the theological issues of concern to the public over time and how and why certain denominations expressed these concerns through their practices—in other words, how various denominations have responded to and interpreted not only their own freedom of religion within their several bodies but, equally and simultaneously, how they have understood the meaning of American constitutional freedom.

The Religious Institution as Denomination: A Challenge to the Study of Religion

It is hard to imagine the form of the religious institution as denomination apart from the Puritan incursions into North America. For that matter, as has been stated by Immanuel Wallerstein, it is hard to imagine the modern world without the Protestant worldview.[7] The modern world, from an intellectual and an ideological point of view, is an amalgam of the Enlightenment and the Protestant orientations. These two orientations must be seen in the complexity of their contradictions and tensions as well as in their mutualities. We must also acknowledge that the hold that these orientations have had on the modern world is waning.

Paul Tillich reminded us several decades ago that we were experiencing the "end of the Protestant era." All around us in intellectual circles there is, under the aegis of structuralism or some form of deconstruction, a concerted critique of the intellectual validity of the Enlightenment notions of reason and objectivity. Protestantism and the Enlightenment were expressed as the outward objective, as well as the inner stylizations, of most the cultural forms that came into being in the modern world. With their decline, the representations, structures, and forms of life sustained by them no longer appear to be the only or the dominant way of understanding the world.

The denomination as a classificatory order that emerged only within the structure of modernity might well be the entrée into the problematic of religion in a postcolonial, post-Protestant, and post-Enlightenment world. The category itself as a product of Protestantism was never well suited to dealing with the religious reality of all the peoples who occupied the space of the United States. Nonmainline Protestant groups, Jews, blacks, and Roman Catholics, for example, do not fit easily within this category; the category must suffer from too many qualifications to be adequate to the religious experience and expression of such diverse groups. In like manner, that wide variety of religious phenomena that falls under the name of cults in America demonstrates the inadequacy of this mode of classification. And what is one to make of the religious life of Native Americans?

Denominational history can become an exciting place in which to probe the meaning of religion in the postmodern world. This research, however, must be carried out within a wider context, one that includes the point of view of the dialectic between the civil religion and the religion of the republic and, more than this, the perspectives of other forms of religion and religious communities that have emerged in the modern world (for example, the "new religions" in Japan). The notion and the meaning of the denomination itself should become the basis for theoretical work in the study of religion. We often forget that the great Max Weber, who taught us so much about Protestantism, also wrote and published on religion in India and China. We need to continue along these lines; there need to be more studies that compare the categories of religious forms and groups in this country with the forms of religious groups and communities in other parts of the world. We might be surprised to see certain structural relations between the western church and the Hindu *sampradya,* for example, or between the denomination and the Islamic madabut. In other words, if the denomination remains so unique that it is comparable to nothing else, this uniqueness may force us into silence or, worse into trivial confessional and self-congratulatory texts as the limit of the meaning of this important religious form in the modern world.

The denomination looms as one of the most important experiential poles of the meaning of religion in the modern and postmodern worlds. In the denomination we find the self-conscious expression of communities and their experience, search, and adjudication of the nature and modes of power and authority for the ordering of their personal and social lives. Denominational history may be a rich source of data that can throw new light on the complexity of the ordering power of the sacred within the structures of a diminishing notion of human authority in a world made by humans.

NOTES

1. Mead's views were developed in successive articles, collected in *the Lively Experiement* (New York: Harper & Row, 1963); *The Nation With the Soul of a Church* (New York: Harper & Row, 1975), and *The Old Religion in the Brave New World* (Berkeley: University of California Press, 1977). Robert Bellah's article "Civil Religion in America," in *Daedalus* 96 (1967): 1–21, although suggested by Mead in his earlier works, was the signal for the widespread discussion of "civil religion."

2. H. R. Niebuhr, *The Social Sources of Denominationalism* (New York: Henry Holt and Co., 1929). This work has had several reprintings since its original publication.

3. See Ernst Troeltsch, *The Social Teaching of the Christian Church,* 2 vols., trans. Olive Wyon (Chicago: University of Chicago Press, 1976). See especially vol. 1, pp. 331ff.

4. See William R. Hutchison's chapter, "Denominational Studies in the Reshaping of American Religious History," in this volume.

5. In this regard see Joachim Wach's "Church Denomination, and Sect," in *Types of Religious Experience, Christian and Non-Christian* (Chicago: University of Chicago Press, 1950). In this essay Wach addresses the problematic of the Troeltschian classification in light of the American experience. He goes even further and implies that after the Reformation it is difficult to maintain the Troeltschian classification even in Europe. He goes so far as to say, "We have avoided the term *church* as much as possible in this classification because it implies a theological (normative) decision which at this point we are not ready to suggest" (p. 197).

6. See H. Byron Earhart, *The New Religions of Japan* (Tokyo: Sophia University Press, 1970), p. 6. The structure of this distinction might be applied to history of American religious institutions. Compare, for example, Joachim Wach's discussion in his essay "Church, Sect, and Denomination."

7. See Immanuel Wallerstein, *The Modern World System,* vol. 1, *Capitalist Agriculture and the Origins of the European World Economy in the Sixteenth Century* (New York: Academic Press, 1974).

II
MODELS

The past thirty years have witnessed a flowering of methodological approaches and options among historians. The essays in this section pick up on some of these new possibilities and offer new models or venues for the study of denominations.

Sociology, suggests Nancy Ammerman, can aid in the conceptualizing of denominational history. When denominations (and, more particularly, real congregations of people) are observed, one sees the concept of denomination functioning on three distinct levels: that of the theological or doctrinal, that of the organizational, and that of cultural identity. All these meanings of denomination must be taken into account in any full denominational history. Ammerman also discusses how the apparent present loss of ascriptive meaning of denominations will affect them in the future.

Part of the thrust of the new social history that has flowered since the 1970s has been the study of real local communities in their actions and practices and a critique of the supposed neutral or "objective" status of the examiner. Robert Orsi uses his studies of the devotees of Saint Jude to explore how one should study communities of belief. Orsi argues for a model that transcends the dichotomy between insider studies (or those in which the observer shares the assumptions of the community) and outsider studies (in which the observer claims a neutral or objective stand). Rather, explains Orsi, the student of religious communities should strive to enter existentially into the experience of those studied.

New insights in theology can also contribute to historical understanding. As Henry Bowden has argued, many of the important historical works of the 1930s and 1940s (perhaps most famously H. Richard Niebuhr's *The Kingdom of God in America*) were inspired by the theological vision of Neo-Orthodoxy. Robert Bruce Mullin, in turn, suggests that the movement in postliberal theology associated with George Lindbeck and others, with its emphasis on religious communities as communities of discourse, may likewise provide a new basis for understanding denominational history. He goes on to suggest that this linguistic approach may also help clarify the relationship between a denomination and its wider culture.

Finally, Jan Shipps returns to some of the questions raised in Charles Long's essay, particularly, what is religious about religious history. For Shipps, like Long, many of the assumptions of the old style of denominational history were based on a no-longer-tenable Protestant hegemony. The history that has replaced it, however, has often ignored the role of religious history for the religious communities themselves. Shipps suggests that the insights found in the history of religions methodology can best bridge the gap between the understandings of the scholarly community and the faithful. Furthermore, she argues for the elevation of the tightly knit confessional community as the paradigm for future study of religious communities. The reader will note that she offers a far different interpretation of the value of confessional or insider history than that found in the Bowden essay.

Denominations:
Who and What
are We Studying?

NANCY T. AMMERMAN

This, we are told, is an opportune moment for reassessing how we do
denominational studies. For much of this century, denominational study
fell on hard times because denominations had become something of an
embarrassment to the sort of scholars who inhabited most universities. If
religion was a concern at all, it was certainly in a more universalistic (or,
at the other extreme, more exotic) form than denominations. As H. Richard Niebuhr pointed out, American denominations were more a matter of
region and ethnicity, race and class, than matters of differences in deeply
held beliefs and practices.[1] In an eagerness to heal these human divisions,
scholars paid more attention to ecumenism than to the stories of individual denominations.

Curiously, we are now returning to the particular stories of these
human groups, each of which claims its own ways of being the "people of
God." In part, this probably represents the broad-ranging retreat from
universalism to particularity that is part of what we are coming to call
"postmodernity."[2] We are being reminded that local traditions are worthy
of attention and preservation, even as we attempt to find ways to live
together in our large and complex world. For many, the goal is no longer
a humanity indistinguishable along ethnic, religious, or gender lines but
perhaps a humanity able to honor those distinctions while building a
vision of the common good.

The honoring of distinctions and particularities is taking place alongside a new valuing of the varieties of our ways of knowing.[3] The privileged eye of the impartial observer is being challenged. Description
oriented toward the categories defined by academic guilds is giving way

to description that follows indigenous categories. A new generation of religious studies scholars is beginning to do scholarship in new ways, a development signaled by Robert Orsi's essay in this volume. Rather than paying attention only to that from which we can generalize, we are paying attention to the particular. Rather than reducing all knowledge to cognitive categories, we are attempting to find a place for affective and experiential learning, as well.

While particularity and local knowledge are certainly gaining attention among scholars, not many of those scholars have yet thought of denominations as one of the local traditions to be celebrated. Indeed, renewed attention to lived and experienced religiosity may reveal just how tenuous denominations really are. There is increasing evidence that ordinary Americans are less and less firmly identified with them. People marry across denominational lines, transfer membership when they move, and drop in and out with impunity. The denominations themselves have lost members and money and are wondering just what their futures will be. We will explore all of this in more detail in this essay, but for now it is sufficient to note that a return to the writing of denominational history in these changing times might turn out to be an exercise in writing epitaphs.

The writing of denominational history, then, does not take place in a cultural vacuum. That we have chosen this historical moment to do it at all reflects the very forces of social change that, as I argue here, make it hard for us to define the subject we wish to study. When we are unsure of ourselves, we almost always return to our history. Our attention to denominational history at this point in time is an indication, I suspect, of how pivotal this moment is in the history of denominations. In a variety of ways, the ideas, institutions, and identities that have formed our sense of what a denomination is are in the process of changing. Protestant hegemony has been challenged; the Protestant way of believing, living, and organizing has been de-centered. At a time when we are all wondering who we are and if there *is* a center in our society, we are returning to this old social form to see if there is yet any life in it.

The changing nature of denominational life has become all the more clear to me as I have participated, of late, in creating new ways for Baptists to cooperate in doing their work.[4] The recurring question we "disgruntled Baptists" are asked, especially by reporters, is, "Are you forming a new denomination?" Sometimes the reporters do not take no for an answer. In March 1991, after one of our especially mundane committee meetings, Associated Press put out a story declaring that a group of Baptists had met in Atlanta over the weekend and formed a new denomination—something that was definitely news to all of us! Whether we *are* a new denomination, of course, depends entirely on how one defines the word. Gaining some definitional clarity may, then, have both scholarly and practical benefits. My own reasons for seeking to answer this question are indeed both scholarly and personal/political.

This paper suggests three ways in which scholars have tacitly defined denomination.[5] What all three definitions have in common is their reliance on the American experience of voluntarism and pluralism in religious life. All three definitions assume that denominations are translocal clusters of religious identifications and behaviors (and the people and organizations connected to them) that are chosen and developed by their members and exist alongside other, similarly constructed, more or less-distinct religious clusters. Denominations are clusters of language and meaning, practices and habits, that exist so long as there are people willing to claim that the cluster is somehow distinctive. Denominations are something bigger than local congregations, to which most (but not all) congregations are connected and which identify individuals and congregations as somehow connected to each other.

Just what that "something" is, however, can be quite variously defined, and it is that variation we explore below. For each definition, we look for the ways in which definition and data are mutually implicated, and we examine the effects of building on one definition and base of data rather than another. Then we look at the ways the practical and cultural meanings of each of those definitions are shifting under our feet.

Denominations as Beliefs and Practices

Set out to write about denominations, and one can hardly avoid writing about beliefs and practices. That, after all, is what denominations are supposed to be. The great reformers of the sixteenth, seventeenth, and eighteenth centuries argued over how best to honor God and reach heaven. They argued that what one believed, how one worshipped, the religious devotions of one's life mattered. Certainly there were matters of politics and money involved, as well, but these men wrote theology in such persuasive and voluminous fashion that people began to try to live as good Calvin-ists, Luther-ans, Menno-nites, and, later, Wesley-ans. As Christians began to transform the Church Universal into the Church Denominational, they did so with differences over beliefs and practices at the forefront of their fights. Whatever else may have gone into denominational creation, we have reason to believe that those early denominational pioneers really cared about election and transubstantiation and believer's baptism.

Ask a person today about the differences between, say, a Baptist and a Methodist, and the answer is likely to be something about infant baptism. Ask what a Catholic is, and you may hear about the pope and birth control and the Mass. In some quarters, an inquiry about Episcopalians may get a reply about clerical collars and incense. The person on the street, like the theologian in the seminary, knows that denominations are supposed to be identifiable by their beliefs and practices. Defining denominations by the ideas and rituals that distinguish them from others is the commonsense thing to do.

It is also the practical thing for a historian to do. Most of the denominational "data" that survive to be written about consist of sermons and theological treatises. In formative times of change, when ideas and ways of life are being contested, people (at least for the last several millenia) write about those ideas.[6] There are tracts and court records and books and letters. In later times of stability and routine, people write different things, but they still write. In those times there are handbooks on being a successful pastor and lessons for new members. Many aspects of religious life disappear from our retrospective view, but words usually do not. Those who have carried on the conversations out of which denominations have sprung leave behind records of their talk.

Today, in addition to these long-standing evidences of religious ideas and practices, we also have survey data, theoretically a valuable resource to the future historian. Unfortunately, most national survey data are only marginally useful to the historian who wants to examine denominational beliefs. While most social scientists define religion in terms of beliefs and practices, they rarely define denomination in those terms. Denominations are defined in terms of some measure of membership or identification, while the beliefs and practices usually measured are generic, cross-denominational, "orthodox" Christian ideas—belief in God, life after death, and the like.[7] On the basis of these blunt instruments, we are then told about which denominations are most orthodox—with the same measure of orthodoxy for every group. The differences measured are differences in degree, not kind. Rarely do we find out whether the people within each denomination believe anything distinctive, although such distinctives occasionally appear in unexpected ways. Stark and Glock, for instance, found out something about denominational peculiarities in language when they discovered that Southern Baptists, otherwise more orthodox and active than almost any other group, had shockingly low rates of "taking communion."[8] Baptists, they discovered too late, usually "celebrate the Lord's Supper"; they think only Catholics (and other high-church folk) "take communion."

While national survey data on beliefs may be only marginally useful to future denominational historians, denominational survey data can occasionally prove more substantially helpful. Many denominations either have their own research offices or commission special studies of their constituents. Those who wish to examine the beliefs and practices of a denomination would do well to seek out such data. They are unlikely to provide a history that extends very far back into the past or yields great theological subtlety. But they do provide a modest check on the pronouncements of official theologues about what members of this denomination "really" believe.

A similar reality check is provided by denominational studies that begin at the congregational level, rather than in the library. Stephen Warner has argued that American culture has produced a de facto congregational polity among all American religions. In practice, the expression of denominational life people know most intimately is the lived experience of a congregation. Those congregations, as Jackson Carroll and his coauthors of the *Handbook for Congregational Studies* argue, have their own particular local identity and story, but that story is connected to the larger religious traditions of which they are a part.[9] This interaction between the theological work of the local congregation and the "official" theological work of the scholars and pastors is the stuff of which denominational theological traditions are made. Those who choose to study denominations through the lens of beliefs and practices would do well to seek out empirical windows on congregational life.

We know all too well, of course, that the practical realities of available data always pose problems of interpretation. We have begun to realize how our understanding of history has always been shaped by those who had the power to write and to preserve their version of events. In the case of religious history, those who were literate and had access to printing presses were likely to be those who were already in the idea business—and probably in the religious idea business, at that. Both their vocations and their natural inclinations led them to filter the events they observed through the sieve of the ideas they spent their lives creating. Whether or not denominational life in the seventeenth century was one endless theological debate, the materials that have survived lead us to see it that way.

Today, the official voices of the denominations are still likely to promote a theological definition of denominational studies. Those who occupy the pulpits, teach in the seminaries, and write adult education materials for churches are likely to look toward beliefs and practices as the core of their denominational identity. When you write their history, they will want you to tell about how their distinctive ideas came to be, how they have been changed and challenged over the years, and how they shape the lives of adherents today. Those who choose to write that kind of history will have ample materials. Those of us in the idea business are still quite willing to record and preserve our stock-in-trade. Denominational archives and libraries are full of the stuff from which good historians can discern the intellectual currents that have shaped each particular religious tradition.

Denominations as Organizations

If denominations began in the heat of theological battle, definable in terms of distinctive beliefs and practices, what they have gradually become—especially in this century—is modern organizations definable by their bylaws, budgets, and headquarters buildings. While the student of Presbyterianism would certainly want to know something about John Calvin, that student would also want to know about the programs created and the decisions made on Witherspoon Street in Louisville, Kentucky.

During the nineteenth century, American denominations began to form and to join a wide variety of voluntary associations.[10] Local churches joined forces for more than the occasional ordination, revival, or theological dispute. They began to be bound together by more than their common ties to a bishop. As their world got bigger—through immigration, commerce, and wars—they wanted to do bigger things, everything from running missions in China to distributing Bibles. Some of these early "societies" were aligned with a particular denomination, but others were not. Most were supported by a mixture of churches, individuals, and other religious organizations; they were dependent on the sporadic gifts of their supporters. By the end of the century, American Protestants had discovered just how much they could do, and the pressure was mounting to bring some order out of the organizational chaos that had developed.

Not surprisingly, the order that was created was strongly shaped by the organizational currents at work in the society. American denominations were pulled toward the models of centralization and efficiency that seemed to be working so well for business.[11] Indeed, DiMaggio and Powell have argued that a kind of institutional isomorphism is at work in American society, pushing organizations more and more toward homogeneity of structure, partly because certain forms have been demonstrated to work, partly because those forms are seen as normal and legitimate, partly because interactions with other organizations (especially a regulatory state) produce mirror images among departments that must deal with each other.[12]

Whatever the sources of this development, by the 1920s American denominations of all polities were consolidating their missions, publishing enterprises, and other ventures under one organizational roof.[13] Soon they could draw charts showing the relationship of each part to the whole. Budgets were centralized, and fund-raising was turned over to professionals who advised their constituents that "if the Lord doesn't provide, systematic finance will." Gradually, the people who worked for these organizations were expected to have specific educational credentials, and everyone had a job description.[14] They worked out long-range plans and proposed integrated programs of study. And they began to keep records.

There had been records before, of course, but modern organizations are by their definition creators and keepers of rationally organized documents. In his classic definition of bureaucracy, Max Weber lists paperwork as one of its distinctives.[15] Rather than pass along the lore of the group by oral tradition, modern bureaucrats write it down and put it in a file. (Postmodern communicators type it into a computer and store it on tape.) The point is, however, that the stuff of which the organization is made (in this case members, churches, programs, and causes) is turned into standardized, countable, recordable units.

In the denomination that I know best, the Southern Baptists, the paperwork imperative can be illustrated vividly. Long-standing tradition—

beginning before the 1920s—had called for each church to send messengers to an annual meeting of the local association of churches bearing a letter of greeting. The churches all reported on the triumphs and struggles of their congregations during the year and perhaps even posed a perplexing theological or disciplinary question or two.[16] Once centralized national organizations had been put in place, the patterns of reporting began to change. Today the old tradition remains, but vastly transformed. What the church sends is now called a *Uniform* Church Letter (UCL, to the bureaucrats who handle them), and it resembles IRS Form 1040 more than it does a friendly letter. It is full of technical language, with boxes to be filled in and columns to be added. It assumes that the programs in each church correspond to the plans and materials that have been formulated at headquarters, therefore making their outcomes reportable in uniform fashion. If your church does not do missions education in the prescribed way or divide its choirs into the usual age categories, the person who completes the UCL will struggle like a taxpayer with an odd deduction. It is the perfect example of the standardizing and quantifying Max Weber would have expected. And it is handled in the hierarchical fashion he would have expected, as well. Once the UCL has gone to the association, it is passed along to the state convention and then to the chief keepers of records in Nashville.

All of this centralizing and standardizing has created denominations with much clearer organizational boundaries than had existed before. There are now bylaws and organizational charters setting out lines of authority and ownership. There are also programs and procedures and personnel who give national identity and predictability to the assortment of churches that are part of the denomination. There are budgets and audits and pledges and "apportionments." The denomination now is defined by the administrative structure that takes in the dollars and carries out the mission of the collective churches it represents.[17] Denominational agencies claim the legitimate authority to embody the religious ideas contained in the theological traditions of the group. They are concerned both with external relations (missions and the like) and with the internal life of the body.

In their heyday, denominational agencies were able to formulate policies and programs that permeated the lives of local churches. Even without any coercive power, they could exercise persuasive power based on the religious legitimacy granted to them.[18] Even in polities where there was not a bishop to place every pastor, the official seminary (with courses designed around official denominational programs) trained the pastors and helped them get jobs. Even where there was no official creed, the Bible study materials and the teacher training manuals all came from the same source. Even where there was no official prayer book to shape the liturgy, the ubiquitous denominational hymnal and the standardized liturgical planning resources created enough worship uniformity that visitors always knew where they were. This was certainly the Southern

Baptist experience, a fact that may strike some as ironic, given Baptist
traditions of local autonomy. However, as Mark Chaves points out, it is,
ironically, the very absence of strong regional ecclesiastical hierarchies
that left congregationally based denominations susceptible to such strong
national control.[19] While the strength of the relationship between denomination and congregation has been considerably eroded (as we shall
see in more detail), denominations as agencies still operate as if they have
a primary role in shaping the religious lives of local churches. Denominational agencies claim the legitimate right to be the keepers of religious
identity.

The extent to which modern organizational criteria have shaped our
definition of denomination can be seen, I think, in a common source used
by students of American religion—the *Yearbook of American and Canadian Churches.*[20] When scholars or reporters want to know how many
denominations there are, they go to this invaluable book and count.[21] In
each brief entry are recorded addresses (headquarters), a bit of history
(usually detailing when the group organized but also containing some
theology), some mention of the group's agencies (the interconnected
organizational structure), and statistics on members, budget, and the like
(the standardized units that can be counted). If there were a religious
group without headquarters or agencies or budget or official membership records, we would not likely call it a denomination, and it would not
be included here.

Once these tightly defined organizational structures came into being,
they gained the legitimacy that the modern world grants on the basis of
such rational and legal criteria.[22] They claimed, as well, the right to define
and to maintain the heritage on which they have built. Legitimacy implies
the ability to create and to tell one's history. It is these organizations,
then, that are likely to commission scholars to write denominational
histories, and it is largely these organizations that keep the records from
which future historians will work.

In extreme cases, the organizational definition of denomination has
led to the writing of organizationally defined history. Taking the office-
holders and statistics of the bureaucracy as primary data can result in
very dull stories (witness the 1954 and 1973 officially commissioned
histories of the Southern Baptist Convention, written by Barnes and by
Baker, respectively).[23] Almost the only actors on those pages are programs, agencies, and bureaucrats.[24] Nearly absent are ordinary members
or churches. But also absent are theological developments or any sense of
the mission of the church.

While such plainly institutional histories make a good foil for our
criticism, we cannot ignore the other ways in which defining denomination as a modern organizational structure affects the work of the historian. We take the official organization's word about what membership
means and what the mission of the church is. The churches create and
define the positions occupied by the people we interview. They maintain

the archives from days gone by, and they generate the documents that will become the archives of tomorrow. What we know about comes largely through this definitional filter. Developments that seemed to lead inexorably to the denomination of today are preserved and highlighted; beliefs, practices, and other organizational forms that seem to lead in other directions may be ignored.

Those who write histories of denominations in the late twentieth century, then, almost inevitably begin by assuming that they are writing the story of a particular group that has a logo and an address. We go to them for records, but we also think of them as the "actor" about whom we are writing. We may move on from there to think about the task in other ways, but this twentieth-century organizational reality cannot be escaped.

Denominations as Cultural Identities

Every year since 1972, the National Opinion Research Center's General Social Survey has asked a random sample of the American population about their religious preferences. Interviewers ask first whether the respondent is Protestant, Catholic, Jewish, or something else. If the respondent says Protestant, he or she is asked which specific denomination is preferred.[25] A look at the GSS codebook would prove humbling for denominational bureaucrats and pastors who struggle to inculcate a sense of identity and heritage in their members. This cross-section of the population gives all sorts of very ambiguous responses to questions about their denominational affiliations; Baptists are notorious for not knowing what kind of Baptist they are, and a few souls each year reply that they prefer "First Church." This lack of specificity about identification with a denomination should certainly make us cautious about the meaning of whatever preferences people do express.

The other source of caution is that these preferences are often quite unanchored in any actual participation. People claim that their preference is Presbyterian, but they do not belong to any church, have not attended in quite some time, and probably know little (if anything) about what Presbyterians believe and practice. Even those who do belong and attend often have very limited knowledge. In 1968, for instance, Stark and Glock reported a 1954 Gallup poll showing that 64 percent of American Protestants did not know who delivered the Sermon on the Mount, and 41 percent could not name the first book in the Bible. Being Presbyterian or Methodist or anything else, for these people, clearly does not mean participation in an ongoing theological tradition of any great depth or detail.

Still, Presbyterians identified by so tenuous a connection to the denomination can be shown to be different from Methodists or Baptists or Catholics identified by equally tenuous connections. The national surveys have consistently demonstrated that denomination (even so tenuously defined as a preference) does make a difference. People who say they are one thing are different from people who say they are something else. Kirk Hadaway, in his studies of disaffiliation, terms these "mental members."[26] There is admittedly more difference among denominations if the preference is accompanied by actual organizational membership and attendance, but even the preference alone makes a difference.[27]

What this seems to imply is that there is out there in American culture something defined as Presbyterianism that is not simply a theological tradition or an organizational membership. After a few hundred years of existence, denominational identities have taken on a cultural life of their own. The more established the denomination is, the more pervasive is its cultural identity; the more sectarian and separate the group, the more its cultural identity may be at odds with its actual practices and the less likely it is that someone not actually a participant will claim a preference for that group.

We perhaps recognize the fact of such cultural denominational identities in the jokes we tell. We can tell an "Episcopalian" joke, and people will understand enough to laugh.[28] That we have some preexisting, culturally transmitted sense of a denomination's identity can also be seen in our surprise when our expectations are violated—shaking our heads, for instance, over incense in a Baptist church. We cannot be surprised if we do not have presuppositions. At least part of the story of a denomination, then, exists in the images and the anecdotes of the larger culture.

While we might wish to dismiss these cultural images as uninformed and irrelevant to the actual life of the denomination, I suggest that they may not be. On one side, they are probably not manufactured out of thin air. They arise from widely reported events, the actions of famous persons, the insistent preachments of articulate spokespersons. They are formed by publicly visible buildings and programs and billboards. They come, as well, from everyday observations of ordinary people who claim those identities. They may also be tied—as are the denominations themselves—to an ethnic heritage. Out of all the bits and pieces of knowledge that make their way into our cultural consciousness, we and our fellow citizens have constructed what it means to be Lutheran or Methodist or Catholic.

On the other side of the causal chain, these culturally constructed images are not without their real effects. If people who have never been members or studied the histories of denominations nevertheless have ideas about them, those ideas will shape their actions. People will make decisions, for instance, about whether they are likely to fit in a given congregation on the basis of their image of both the congregation and the denomination to which it belongs. Jon Stone found, for instance, that despite disclaiming any strong denominational loyalty, the Presbyterians he interviewed did admit that denomination had something to do with their choice of a church to attend in the first place.[29] The sorts of people who do and do not assume they fit—on the basis of those images—will shape the constituency that in fact emerges. Even people within a denomination may make their decisions on the basis of subtle notions of what is expected of their denomination—Baptists have simply never done such things, they think. In other words, the images can be self-fulfilling prophecies. They are not unchangeable or utterly determinative, but they are real.

The study of denominations as cultural artifacts is something more likely undertaken by social scientists than by historians. Whenever we use national survey preference data, we are implicitly working with this cultural reality. But it is a reality also found in literature, in the arts, and in other media where ideas about various religious traditions may be communicated. Attention to this cultural level allows us to look at the way various culturally constructed religious identities fit into the larger social system. We can look at how they are related to the educational systems of the culture, where they fit in the economic order, how they relate to political culture, and so on. These amorphous denominational identities may be among the best indices we have of the relationship between denominations and the various other institutional systems of the culture. Each of those systems is operating with implicit ideas about the place of various denominations within American culture.

Tracing the outlines of these cultural artifacts over time offers us a different angle on the denominational story. It is important to remember, however, that while these culturally defined images are surely related to the traditions and organizations that make up the other dimensions of denominational life, they are not the same thing. When we study preferences, we are simply studying something different from the realities defined by organizational membership or beliefs and practices.

What does it mean, then, to write the history of a denomination? Is it primarily a theological task, an effort to understand the origin and the evolution of ideas and practices that have made a group distinct? If so, the primary sources of data will be the writings of preachers and theologians and the recorded musings of reflective laypeople. Is denominational history primarily the story of the origin and the evolution of organizations? If so, the primary sources of data are to be found in the records and statistics collected by those organizations. Or does denominational history also exist at a cultural level, tracing actions and images and links that exist beyond the taught traditions and official organizations?

The answer, of course, is that denominational history has to be all three. Denominations are sets of beliefs and practices; they are organizations; and they are culturally constructed identities. Those who wish to study denominations may approach their subject from any one of these angles. They may enter the field by way of the organizations that claim the label "Baptist" or "Presbyterian"—even if those organizations are only unofficially tied to some centralized denominational structure. They may also enter the field by way of the ideas and practices that claim to constitute the religious reality that follows the contours of some denominational tradition. Or they may cast the net more widely in the culture,

seeking out all the ways in which constellations of denominational identities, images, and practices are kept intact in recognizable ways.

No matter which manner of entry is chosen, denominational researchers need to recognize that all these aspects of denominational life
affect one another. Beliefs and practices sustain and are sustained by
both cultural images and organizational programs. Organizational programs take their legitimacy from theology and depend for their survival
on consonance with the denominational culture. They, in turn, help to
determine which theology is heard and what the culture contains. And
the cultural identities will not survive long without ideological and
institutional supports.

While the historian might protest that dealing with earlier periods
limits the practicality and appropriateness of such broad-ranging definitions of the topic—that seventeenth-century religious practices cannot
be observed in the same way that Robert Orsi might observe supplicants
to Saint Jude—we need to be reminded that official theological records
are not the historian's only source. Historians can examine diaries and
letters, flyers and everyday artifacts. They can also examine mundane
organizational records and the cultural products (literature, art, and the
like) that may embody denominational images from earlier periods. Admittedly, the historian cannot ask probing new questions of some long-
gone religious person. But sensitized to the multiple layers of reality
present in denominational life, historians can seek the kinds of materials
that will help them paint a more multidimensional picture.

The problem we face at this moment, however, is not the lack of
resources but the lack of clarity about what we are studying. All three
aspects of denominational life are undergoing rapid change.

The Shifting Terrain of Denominationalism

In *American Mainline Religion,* Roof and McKinney document the ways
in which the old ascriptive ties, bonds that had helped to hold American
denominations together, have diminished significantly over the last two
generations.[30] In traditional communities, the social fabric contained a
thread of religion that was woven alongside the threads of ethnicity and
family and place.[31] Historically, so the myth of gemeinschaft goes, we
learned at our mother's knee that we were from fine Norwegian stock,
respectable members of the community (with all the norms implied by
that), Iowans, perhaps, and Lutheran. To deny any one of these identities
might be to endanger them all, and powerful social forces operated to
constrain that possibility. In this century, but especially since World War
II, many of those constraining social forces have waned. More than any
other factors, education and geographic mobility have conspired to dis-
place the forces of family and tradition and place that kept us "down on
the farm."[32] As the social terrain has been rearranged, so has the denominational terrain that has been tied to it. My work in *Baptist Battles*

documents the earthquakes that have rearranged Southern Baptist life, but Roof and McKinney make clear that similar tremors have been slowly reshaping the entire American religious landscape.

In the place of commitments to family and place and religion, a new norm of individual choice now seems to reign.[33] We are no longer willing to allow, for instance, the ties of religion, family, or geography to limit our choice of marital partners, as evidenced by the growing rates of marriage across denominational lines. And whether we marry outside our family's faith or inside, we are likely to migrate back and forth across denominational lines throughout the adult lifespan as we make other moves—to new places, new jobs, new marriages.[34] As the range of choice has expanded in other areas, religious affiliations have taken on the same voluntary character. And the inevitable result of all that individual, voluntary movement is a blurring of the denominational lines. Whatever those culturally constructed denominational identities have been in the past, they are surely undergoing change today.

Such individual choices might be construed as leading us in the direction of diminished "social sources" of our denominations. While it is quite likely that individuals no longer make their religious choices on the basis of the same array of ascriptive social factors, that does not mean that social forces are no longer at work. People moving to an urban region are faced with a dizzying array of religious communities from which to choose—including the "Sunday brunch" option. They may look for traditional ethnic or denominational or liturgical practices, but they are just as likely to look for a congregation that "fits" them in other ways. At the same time that individuals are looking for a fit, the congregation is seeking to establish a recognizable identity in this admittedly competitive religious market. The result of both these processes is that most congregations are recognizable in social terms. They seek a certain identity and attract a certain kind of folk. They vary in ways that the social lives of people vary today. Some are more attuned to the verbal and cultural distinctions created by education. Some assume more of the privileges afforded by high income. In some congregations, technospeak is the language, while in others life is paced by time cards and layoffs. Singles find some congregations especially congenial, while in other congregations "intact" families are the norm. A few congregations are even identifiable as places where gays and lesbians can feel at home.[35]

Social identifiers still remain, but they no longer fall neatly along the old denominational lines. Most or all of the variation that exists across congregations is as likely to exist within denominations as between them. Within the field of Baptist or Presbyterian or even Pentecostal churches, there may be rich ones and poor ones, professional ones and blue-collar ones, high-church and low-church, pro-life and pro-choice. Denominational traditions may set some boundaries on the range of variation, but they do not create anything like a sufficient uniformity to override the other identifiers from which people are making their choices. Those social identifiers, Robert Wuthnow has argued, seem increasingly to be clustering around poles labeled "liberal" and "conservative," more than around denominational traditions. People who think of themselves as "liberal" Methodists may be more likely to choose the "liberal" Lutheran church in their new city than to go to the "conservative" Methodist one that is nearby. Whether Wuthnow is right about the shape of the socioreligious clustering that is going on, I think he is clearly right that a restructuring is happening.[36] The old social forces no longer help us draw the lines on the denominational map, and it is not yet clear whether the lines will simply be redrawn in new places or erased altogether or modified in other ways. If there have been in the past culturally defined denominational identities that could be described and analyzed by historians and social scientists, we must surely ask ourselves today whether those cultural artifacts are about to disappear entirely under the pressure of choice and mobility.

If the cultural identities of denominations are under stress, their organizational structures are, as well. In part, the organizational core of denominational life has been weakened by these same forces of mobility and choice. Increasing numbers of members never make it into a new congregation once educational or occupational mobility has dislodged them from an old one. As Roof and McKinney document, the "no-preference" segment is the fastest growing sector in the American religious market.[37] As younger, well-educated, urban cosmopolitan adults choose to drop out, the sheer numerical strength of the mainline denominations has been affected.[38] What has now become apparent at denominational headquarters is that the organizational apparatus once sustained by 10 million members cannot be sustained by 8 million members, especially with today's high cost of institutional maintenance.[39] Programs and staff are being cut, a process that is likely to leave a much leaner structure—perhaps without some of its functions—in the place of the centralized, comprehensive bureaucracies of earlier days.

At the same time that the denominational bureaucracies are being weakened from within, they are also facing unprecedented organizational competition from without. Part of the "restructuring" that Wuthnow documents is the growth of "special-purpose" groups within the religious economy.[40] Taking on all sorts of religious tasks—from publishing to running missions to lobbying—these groups exist outside the official denominational umbrella. As denominations are less able to provide services, special-purpose groups are thriving, ready to fill the gap. The strength of one and the weakness of the other are mutually reinforcing.

Not only are special-purpose groups part of the weakening of traditional denominational structures, they are at the same time part of the erosion of our definition of denomination. Their customers may be predominantly Baptist or Methodist, but nothing prevents them from seeking sales orders from Presbyterians or Lutherans or even Catholics. They may lobby for causes usually thought of as "liberal" but have members from denominations usually thought of as "conservative." Again, the old denominational boundaries are being redrawn, if not erased.

At the local congregational level, a parallel organizational variety may be present. The name on the door may be Disciples of Christ, but the Sunday School material may be Kerygma, the missions budget may include Habitat for Humanity and Bread for the World, and the liturgy may borrow heavily from a newsletter published by a group of feminist Baptists. The congregation remains connected to its denomination in all the ways it officially must, but it looks to the larger religious community for its full identity, the support of its own sense of mission.

Even the official requirements may be renegotiated as ordinations are increasingly recognized across denominational lines. Recent controversies over the ordination of practicing gays and lesbians have provoked renewed attention to ecclesiastical authority in that realm, attention that may create new de facto, if not de jure, norms for the relationship between denominations and their subunits. What may remain as the sole de facto link between local congregation and denomination is money. In the most concrete of terms, if the congregation refuses to give (or, less likely, if the denomination refuses to accept the congregation's gifts), the congregation has left the denominational fold. Short of that, it may deviate and have alternative allegiances on a host of other matters of policy and practice.

It is at least in part these transdenominational elements in the practice of a local congregation that may contribute to the individual patterns of choice we have already noted. When a liberal Methodist moves to a new town, what makes the liberal Lutheran church feel so like home is that some of the liturgical and Christian Education and missions programs come from the same nondenominational sources that were left behind in a former church. Similar links to nondenominational education and mission agencies have held the fundamentalist network together for most of this century.[41] When fundamentalists moved from one town to another, they were able to find another "Bible believing" church, without the aid of denominational labels, mostly by looking for programmatic and liturgical clues. I have argued that this loosely linked, entrepreneurial organizational strategy was part of the fundamentalist refusal to accept the rational/legal, bureaucratic terms dictated by "modernity." Ironically, other groups that long ago accepted modern organizational imperatives are now moving in postmodern fashion toward structures that look rather like what fundamentalists have been using all along.[42]

The nondenominational market is too far-flung (and by definition too decentralized) to ever achieve the kind of local predictability once achieved in centralized, denomination-based programming. But, as Wuthnow warns, there is enough clustering around the liberal and conservative poles to make it unlikely that congregations will mix elements from those two clusters. You would be surprised to hear, for instance, that a church used David C. Cook literature and took its liturgical inspiration from feminists; it is possible, but surprising. I am not so convinced that the clustering is as rigid as Wuthnow fears. There is simply too much ground in the middle and too many hard-to-classify organizations.

I am convinced, however, that the restructuring now under way will see new relationships evolve among denominations, their state and local constituent units, and the special-purpose groups to which each may be tied. We may find in coming years that denominational headquarters have become (if they have not always been) merely one location on a complex organizational map that includes other affiliated associations, formal and informal networks of communication, links to various suppliers of ideas and services, and even the interpersonal environment in which denominational identity is defined and passed along.[43] We may discover again, for instance, just how important families and friendships have been all along in creating and sustaining religious identities. It is probably no accident that "mental members" still seem to seek out churches for significant rites of passage in their lives.[44] Cultural identity, beliefs and practices, and organizational forms are intertwined in complex ways among these occasional participants.

The Southern Baptists may be merely the most visible and dramatic case of the re-creation of the denominational organizational environment.[45] As those of us in the Cooperative Baptist Fellowship (one of the alternative groups being formed by moderates in the SBC) seek to create new ways of cooperating, we will also be creating new ways to answer the question, "Are you a denomination?" I have begun to describe our organizational model as more like a spider web than like a pyramid: composed of complex linkages, functional, fragile, but easy to reconstruct in ever-changing ways.[46] We can be linked on some sides with the Southern Baptist Convention, but also linked with other Baptist bodies and with a variety of institutions not necessarily linked only to us.

The question of denominational identity, then, is a live one at both the cultural and the organizational levels. It is also alive as a theological question. On one hand, seminaries have never stopped teaching aspiring pastors the essential dogmas of their particular tradition. Methodists know about the quadrilateral, and Presbyterians know about Calvin. But on the other hand, a profound distrust of denomination-based theology has prevailed in the academy for most of this century. While Tillich may be the favorite among many Methodists and Barth among many Presbyterians and Baptists, neither of those theologians did his work from within those traditions. As we have pushed toward the goal of a universalized Christian theology, we have consciously left behind the particular denominational traditions that were seen as unnecessary divisions among us.[47]

That leaves the historian of ideas, the person searching for the theological or intellectual thread that runs through a denomination's history, with an unclear task. As theologians themselves have increasingly shed their denominational identity, how does one trace out an ideological picture with any distinct boundaries? When does the story of one denomination's evolving ideas and practices simply merge with some larger whole? If we have depended on theologians and preachers as our primary reporters of a denomination's beliefs and practices, we may have rather unreliable reports for much of this century. On any given Sunday, it might be very difficult to tell the sermons of a Presbyterian from those of a Baptist or a Methodist or a Lutheran. If theologians have written and preachers have preached as if their audience were a church universal, then their accounts give us little insight into the particularistic worlds of congregations and denominations. We may have to look elsewhere for insights into those particular traditions—perhaps to more popular religious literature or to the reports of laity and clergy who do claim their traditions.

Conclusion

It seems such a commonsense task, this writing of denominational histories. But with each year that passes, the boundaries defining what we have known as denominations become less clear as denominations' theological traditions shift and merge into some larger whole, their organizational structures give way to loose networks of denominational and nondenominational agencies, and their cultural identities blur under the pressure of increasing mobility. Whatever working definition guides the historian's task is likely to be stretched by the ways in which meanings have shifted over the centuries of their existence and continue to shift today.

Definition, of course, is never easy. It may be no more difficult today than ever. But the forces of change at work in American religion make it important to test our assumptions. If we assume that "of course" an agency or congregation or idea or person is Presbyterian, on what are we basing that assumption? Are we using organizational criteria, theological criteria, or some other constellation of culturally defined elements? Because we are products of this century, we are likely to operate with organizational criteria as our starting point. But because we are also products of the academy, we may naturally gravitate toward theological assumptions about what constitutes a "real" Nazarene or Episcopalian. The point of this definitional exercise has been simply to sensitize us to our assumptions and to the way those assumptions are historically located and currently under stress.

Identifying definitional assumptions is an important first step in the historian's task. It will, among other things, help to identify appropriate data sources and the actors whose stories will shape our writing. Knowing that denominations exist at all three levels identified here will also help to keep the story balanced. We can never assume that any one level constitutes the whole. We will watch for the ways each aspect of the denomination affects the others. When do changes in theology affect the organizational structure or the way the denomination is identified in the culture? Or when do changes in organizational program affect real changes in practice and identity? If theologians or bureaucrats proclaim a change, does that really mean that practices and perceptions change? While we can make no assumptions about connections between levels, we can also ill afford to ignore those possibilities.

As the meanings of each of these aspects of denominational life shift, it may be a very opportune moment for reassessing just what denominational labels have meant for these last five centuries. Whenever we are entering a new era, we always seek guidance from a fresh reading of our history. A new look at distinct denominational beliefs and practices, particular denominational organizations, and recognizable denominational identities may help us now to see our way forward.

NOTES

Acknowledgment is due the respondents and the participants at the conference at which this paper was originally presented. Special thanks to Clark Gilpin for his careful reading and his provocative questions. Thanks are also due Laurel Kearns, who assisted with library research, and to the rest of the "congregational studies lunch group" (Mary Ann Zimmer, Jim Nieman, Scott Thumma, Nancy Eiesland, Mike McMullen, Richard Lee, and Tom Frank) for their questions and suggestions. They were especially helpful in reminding me to take everyday experience seriously.

1. H. Richard Niebuhr, *The Social Sources of Denominationalism* (New York: World Publishing, 1929).

2. One classic source of this argument is Clifford Geertz's *Local Knowledge: Further Essays in Interpretive Anthhropology* (New York: Basic Books, 1983). Among recent feminist writings, see Patricia Ann Lather's *Getting Smart: Feminist Research and Pedagogy with/in the Postmodern* (New York: Routledge, 1991). The literature emerging on postmodernism is, of course, voluminous.

3. In addition to Lather's book, see, for example, Mary Belinky, B. M. Clinchy, N. R. Goldberger, and J. M. Tarule, *Women's Ways of Knowing* (New York: Basic Books, 1986).

4. After several years of relatively disinterested (in the political sense of that word) research on Southern Baptists, my imagination was caught by the new groups beginning to emerge out of the ruins. I am now fully an insider, committed to their well-being. I serve on the governing bodies of the Cooperative Baptist Fellowship (the group to which I refer here) and of the Alliance of Baptists.

5. One definitional debate *not* included here is the perennial struggle among sociologists to distinguish among church, sect, and denomination (and sometimes cult). Russell E. Richey's "Institutional Forms of Religion," in *Encyclopedia of the American Religious Experience,* ed. Charles H. Lippy and Peter W. Williams, 3 vols. (New York: Charles Scribner's Sons, 1988), 1:31–50, offers a helpful historical overview of the usage of these terms, and Rodney Stark and William Sims Bainbridge offer a theoretical overview in *The Future of Religion* (Berkeley: University of California Press, 1985). In his article on "Religious Organizations" in *The Sacred in a Secular Age,* ed. Phillip E. Hammond (Berkeley:

University of California Press, 1985), pp. 125–138, James Beckford argues that sociology of religion's continued dependence on the Troeltschian formulations has impeded our understanding of the ways in which religious groups organize.

In the "church/sect" tradition, denomination is used to denote religious organizations that do *not* enjoy a monopoly in their culture and accept the pluralism that goes with such a situation (David Martin, "The Denomination," *British Journal of Sociology* 13 (March 1962): 1–14). It is usually noted that such pluralism has as its corollary a high level of individualism and choice. Denominations, then, are relatively accommodated to their culture—at least, to the structural arrangements it imposes on them. See Arthur Farnsley, "The Southern Baptist Convention as an essentially American denomination" (Paper presented to a meeting of the Society for the Scientific Study of Religion, Virginia Beach, Va., 1990).

The biggest problem this definition has had is that its empirical referent has often been unclear. It is primarily a conceptual category (an "ideal type"), and the constellation of factors constituting the definition rarely occur so neatly in the real world. There are, for instance, bureaucratically organized groups that are strongly at odds with their culture and denominations that have enjoyed quasi-monopolies—at least within subcultures. There are also problems in applying the definition thus construed at various levels of analysis. As N. J. Demerath's study *Social Class and American Protestantism* (New York: Rand McNally, 1965) demonstrates, very accommodated denominations might have very sectarian members.

I have found most convincing Benton Johnson's strategy of reducing the original constellation of defining factors into one central variable—tension with the culture—defining as more "church-like" organizations that are more accommodated and as more "sect-like" those that try to maintain distance between themselves and the dominant ways of life around them ("On Church and Sect," *American Sociological Review* 28 (1963): 539–549). Even that usage requires, however, specificity by region and time—that is, tension with whom? See my discussion in *Baptist Battles: Social Change and Religious Conflict in the Southern Baptist Convention* (New Brunswick, N.J.: Rutgers University Press, 1990), pp. 164–166.

None of the sociological debate helps us very much when it comes to defining what we mean empirically when we say "denomination." These are arguments about religious orientations toward culture. They are arguments about the adjective "denominational," more than the noun "denomination."

6. Here I am following the arguments made by Ann Swidler in "Culture in Action: Symbols and Strategies," in *American Sociological Review* 51 (1986): 273–286.

7. See especially Rodney Stark and Charles Y. Glock, *American Piety: The Nature of Religious Commitment* (Berkeley: University of California Press, 1968). Among the myriad recent studies using "orthodoxy" as a measure of religiosity are C. K. Jacobson, Tim B. Heaton, and Rutledge M. Dennis, "Black-White Differences in Religiosity," *Sociological Analysis* 51 (1990): 257–270; and Bruce Hunsberger, "A Short Version of the Christian Orthodoxy Scale," *Journal for the Scientific Study of Religion* 28 (1989): 360–365. An earlier overview of the literature can be found in Wade Clark Roof, "Concepts and Indicators of Religious Commitment," in Robert Wuthnow, ed., *The Religious Dimension* (New York: Academic Press, 1979).

8. Stark and Glock, *American Piety,* pp. 89–91.

9. *Handbook for Congregational Studies,* ed. Jackson W. Carroll, Carl S. Dudley, and William McKinney (Nashville Tenn.: Abingdon, 1986).

10. The role of voluntary societies in foreign missions is evident in William Hutchison, *Errand to the World: American Protestant Thought and Foreign Missions* (Chicago: University of Chicago Press, 1987). Robert Wuthnow, *The Restructuring of American Religion* (Princeton: Princeton University Press, 1988), pp. 101–106, describes this history.

11. Ben Primer, *Protestants and American Business Methods* (Ann Arbor: University of Michigan Press, 1979).

12. Paul J. DiMaggio and Walter W. Powell, "The Iron Cage Revisited: Institutional Isomorphism and Collective Rationality in Organizational Fields," *American Sociological Review* 48 (April 1983): 147–160. On the role of the state, see Robert Wuthnow's *The Struggle for America's Soul* (Grand Rapids, Mich.: William B. Eerdmans Publishing Co., 1989).

13. In addition to Primer's description of this process, see also Gibson Winter's "Religious Organizations" in vol. 1 of *The Emergent American Society,* ed. W. L. Warner (New Haven: Yale University Press, 1967), 408–491. He argues that by the 1950s, Protestant denominations were indistinguishable organizationally, defined primarily as agencies, and that indeed Catholic and Jewish organization was distinguishable but apparently moving in similar directions.

14. Mark Chaves, in "The Intra-Denominational Power Struggle: Declining Religious Control of Protestant Denominational Organization (paper presented to a meeting of the American Sociological Association, Cincinnati, Ohio, 1991), has argued that the shift from a "religious authority" structure to an agency structure actually constitutes a struggle between the two for power—I would say for the power to define what constitutes the denomination. Chaves has shown that over time, denominational chief executives have been increasingly likely to come from within the agency system, rather than from parishes, seminaries, and the rest of the ecclesiastical system. Still, the vast majority have spent substantial portions of their careers in the "religious authority" structure, rather than just in agencies. The victory of the expert seems far from complete.

15. Max Weber, *The Theory of Social and Economic Organization,* trans. A. M. Henderson and Talcott Parsons (1947; reprint ed., New York: Free Press, 1964), p. 332.

16. On the role and functions of associations, see Leon McBeth's *The Baptist Heritage* (Nashville, Tenn.: Broadman, 1989), pp. 243–246; also H. K. Neely, Jr., "Baptist Beginnings in the Middle Colonies," in *The Lord's Free People in a Free Land,* ed. W. R. Estep (Fort Worth, Tex.: Southwestern Baptist Theological Seminary, 1976), pp. 27–38.

17. Chaves, "The Intra-Denominational Power Struggle," argues that the "agency structure" and the "religious authority structure" can be distinguished as two separate organizational dimensions of denominational life. Problems of membership, he claims, are the purview of the religious authority structure, while the agency structure has employees, rather than members. That distinction, it seems to me, misses the extent to which agencies are also concerned with defining membership—not so much for theological reasons as for reasons of record keeping.

18. While Chaves, "The Intra-Denominational Power Struggle," sees the relationship between the agencies and the ecclesiastical authorities as a tug-of-war, I

am more inclined to agree with Paul Harrison's *Authority and Power in the Free Church Tradition* (Princeton: Princeton University Press, 1959) on the way bureaucrats were able (indeed, were required) to appropriate religious legitimation for their work. The two forms of authority are not nearly so neatly divided as Chaves would like to argue.

19. Chaves, "The Intra-Denominational Power Struggle." I think, however, he misses the extent to which the agency and the ecclesiastical structures are intertwined, with the regional religious authorities themselves often highly bureaucratized.

20. Constant H. Jacquet, ed., *Yearbook of American and Canadian Churches, 1989* (Nashville, Tenn.: Abingdon, 1989).

21. The *Yearbook* served as one data source, for instance, for Robert C. Liebman, J. R. Sutton, and Robert Wuthnow, "Exploring the Social Sources of Denominationalism: Schisms in American Protestant Denominations, 1890–1980," *American Sociological Review* 53 (1988): 343–352; also for Robert S. Ellwood and Donald E. Miller's research note, "Questions Regarding the CUNY National Survey of Religious Identification," *Journal for the Scientific Study of Religion* 31 (March 1992): 94–96.

22. See Weber's discussion of rational-legal authority in *The Theory of Social and Economic Organization.* See also Jürgen Habermas, *Legitimation Crisis* (Boston: Beacon, 1973) 97ff.

23. W. W. Barnes, *The Southern Baptist Convention, 1845–1953* (Nashville, Tenn.: Broadman, 1954), and Robert A. Baker, *The Southern Baptist Convention and Its People, 1607–1972* (Nashville, Tenn.: Broadman, 1974).

24. Ellen Rosenberg leveled this criticism at official Southern Baptist historiography, seeing it as a way to avoid the denomination's "real" history. See her *The Southern Baptists: A Subculture in Transition* (Knoxville: University of Tennessee Press, 1989), esp. p. 52.

25. James A. Davis and Tom W. Smith. *General Social Surveys, 1972–87: Cumulative Codebook* (Chicago: National Opinion Research Center, 1987), pp. 130–131, 573–575.

26. Hadaway says, "Increasing numbers of Americans continue to maintain a religious identity but are no longer counted as members by their denomination of choice" ("Denominational Defection: Recent Research on Religious Disaffiliation in America," in *The Mainstream Protestant "Decline": The Presbyterian Pattern,* ed. M. J Coalter, J. M. Mulder, and L. B. Weeks (Louisville, Ky.: Westminster/John Knox, 1990), p. 110.

27. This was especially clear in Wade Clark Roof and William McKinney, *American Mainline Religion* (New Brunswick, N.J.: Rutgers University Press, 1987). Among other recent studies using similar national data sources with "denominational preference" as a significant predictor variable are Clyde Wilcox, "Religion and Politics Among White Evangelicals: The Impact of Religious Variables on Political Attitudes." *Review of Religious Research* 32 (1990): 27–42; Nicholas Babchuk and Hugh Whitt, "R-order and Religious Switching," *Journal for the Scientific Study of Religion* 29 (1990): 246–254; and Robin Perrin, "American Religion in the Post-Aquarian Age: Values and Demographic Factors in Church Growth and Decline," *Journal for the Scientific Study of Religion* 28 (1989): 75–89. The widely reported CUNY "national religious identity" survey is sharply criticized by Ellwood and Miller, "CUNY National Survey," for the apparent ineptness of interviewers and coders who did not know enough about the

American religious landscape to use sensible clarifying probes or to combine categories in a way that conforms to the existing religious bodies the respondents may have been trying to reference. Not surprisingly, the more "established" the denomination, the easier it apparently was for respondent, interviewer, and coder to name the religious identity involved.

28. This assertion has prompted a rash of denomination jokes, many of them answers to the question, "How many X does it take to change a light bulb?" Two of my favorites are about Episcopalians, and the answer in both cases is three— either "one to change the bulb and two to serve sherry" or "one to change the bulb and two to reminisce about how good the old bulb was."

29. Jon Stone, "The new Voluntarism and Presbyterian Affiliation," in *The Mainstream Protestant "Decline"*, pp. 122–149.

30. Roof and McKinney, *American Mainline Religion*, pp. 63–71.

31. Phillip E. Hammond, "Religion and the Persistence of Identity," *Journal for the Scientific Study of Religion* 27 (1988): 1–11, documents the various ways in which religion remains linked to other primary and secondary identities.

32. The effects of education and mobility are discussed both by Roof and McKinney in *American Mainline Religion*, and by Robert Wuthnow in *The Restructuring of American Religion*. Noting these effects seem to imply the classic secularization arguments about the diminishment of religion in the modern situation. It does follow Thomas Luckmann's arguments about the disjuncture between individual belief and institutional religion in the modern period (*The Invisible Religion*, New York: Macmillan, 1967), but I am building more explicitly on Peter Berger's argument in *The Sacred Canopy* (New York: Anchor Books, 1969), esp. chs. 1–2, about the necessary ties between belief and plausibility structure. What is being argued here is not secularization but the transformation of religious institutions as the social base (cultural and interactional) changes.

33. See especially R. Bellah et al., *Habits of the Heart* (Berkeley: University of California Press, 1985).

34. This movement is only partially caught by our usual measure of "switching," that is, whether we still identify with the denomination to which we belonged at age sixteen.

35. Stephen Warner has argued that a de facto congregationalism has become pervasive in American religion (Catholic, Jewish, and other, as well as Protestant). These robust congregations, creating a place for themselves and for their members at the local level, have arisen alongside the decline of denominationalism. See his "The Place of the Congregation in the Contemporary American Religious Configuration," in *The Congregation in American Life*, ed. James Wind and James Lewis (Chicago: University of Chicago Press, forthcoming).

36. Dan Olson and William McKinney have found in a survey of denominational leaders that Wuthnow is right about the clustering of attitudes around two key factors—the Social Gospel and evangelism—and that these factors are correlated with a number of other attitudes. However, at least among these leaders, there is a sizable middle rather than polarization, and there are differences between denominations as well as within them. See their "Restructuring Among Protestant Denominational Leaders: The Great Divide and the Great Middle" (paper presented to a meeting of the American Sociological Association, Cincinnati, Ohio, 1991).

37. Roof and McKinney, *American Mainline Religion*, pp. 99, 236.

38. Over the last two decades, explaining "the decline of the mainline" has

become something of a growth industry among academics and church leaders. Among the works produced are Dean Kelley, *Why Conservative Churches Are Growing* (New York: Harper & Row, 1972); Dean Hoge and David A. Roozen, *Understanding Church Growth and Decline, 1950–1978* (New York: Pilgrim Press, 1979); Robert S. Michaelsen and Wade Clark Roof, *Liberal Protestantism: Realities and Possibilities* (New York: Pilgrim, 1986); and, of course, Coalter, Mulder, and Weeks eds., *The Mainstream Protestant "Decline."*

39. Peter Steinfels, "Churches Are Caught in Economy's Grip," *New York Times,* 20 June 1991, pp. 1, 11.

40. Robert Wuthnow, *The Restructuring of American Religion,* ch. 6.

41. Nancy Ammerman, *Bible Believers: Fundamentalists in the Modern World* (New Brunswick, N.J.: Rutgers University Press, 1987), pp. 114–119.

42. The irony of this is particularly uncomfortable for Southern Baptist moderates who worshipped their centralized "Cooperative Program" for most of this century. As they now establish special-purpose groups, they are visibly eating crow. Meanwhile, fundamentalists who always condemned bureaucracy are having to develop rationales for running one. This latter tension is explored in David Ray Norsworthy, "Rationalization and Reaction Among Southern Baptists," in *Southern Baptists Observed: Multiple Perspectives on a Changing Denomination,* ed. Nancy T. Ammerman (Knoxville: University of Tennessee Press, 1993).

43. This model of the organizational environment follows the ideas developed by Stewart Clegg in *Modern Organizations: Organization Studies in the Postmodern World* (London: Sage, 1990).

44. Hadaway, "Denominational Defection."

45. Marcia Hood-Brown and Robert Liebman have demonstrated that the kind of religious diversity that has always characterized Protestantism results in a variety of organizational innovations that only sometimes become true schisms. Without enough centralization in the SBC to enforce conformity and so long as the CBF does not insist on an exclusive counterorthodoxy, no schism is likely. They see the CBF remaining a special purpose group within the SBC. See their "Paths to Schism: Orthodoxy, Polity, and Dissent in American Protestantism" (Paper presented to a meeting of the American Sociological Association, Cincinnati Ohio, 1991). Given greater exercise of central control (which the new fundamentalist SBC leaders seem inclined toward) and their own concern for orthodoxy, the CBF may yet, however, be forced out (the pattern they term "purge").

46. With my advocacy hat on, I have written about this in "Share My Dreams for Cooperative Fellowship," *Baptists Today* 10 (23 April 1992): 2.

47. Some, indeed are calling for a renewal of theological bases for identity— core beliefs and practices that can shape an enduring denominational community. See Edward Farley's "The Presbyterian Heritage as Modernism: Reaffirming a Forgotten Past in Hard Times," and Benton Johnson's "On Dropping the Subject: Presbyterians and Sabbath Observance in the Twentieth Century," in *The Presbyterian Predicament: Six Perspectives,* ed. M. J Coalter, J. M. Mulder, and L. B. Weeks (Louisville, Ky.: Westminster/John Knox, 1990).

"Have You Ever
Prayed to Saint Jude?":
Reflections on Fieldwork
in Catholic Chicago

ROBERT A. ORSI

I am sitting toward the back of the church of Our Lady of Guadalupe in South Chicago, watching clusters of people arrive for the night's novena service in honor of Saint Jude Thaddeus, patron saint of hopeless cases and lost causes, whose national shrine is housed there. The people coming into the warm glow of the church's electric candles from the darkened, already chilly October streets are wearing windbreakers emblazoned with the names of local unions, fraternal organizations, sports teams, and police and fire auxiliaries over old sweaters. One young woman sports a white quilted sateen bomber jacket with the words "Club Flamingo" arching across her shoulders above the bird itself, silhouetted against a blazing hot-pink tropical sun.

The neighborhood around us is dominated by the abandoned piles of old steel foundries along the lake. In good times, I have been told by older residents, when the mills were working, the skies over South Chicago were darkened already at noon from cinders cleaned out of the tall smokestacks all around the church at regular intervals during the day. But it has been a while since times were good in South Chicago, and the skies are clear now. A big sign outside a dry cleaning establishment half a block from the church promises, "Not just cleaned—disinfected."[1]

The people coming to the shrine are of all ages, although the younger ones—couples sitting close together in the pews, family clusters of many generations—are Hispanic mostly, while the older ones, among whom women significantly outnumber men, are from the old eastern and southern European immigrant enclaves that surrounded Guadalupe in the days of steel but have been shrinking ever since. The church itself was founded in 1928 as a Mexican national parish by a Spanish congregation of priests, the Missionary Sons of the Immaculate Heart of Mary. But Saint Jude's shrine, opened in 1929 as a way of supporting the order's various works, has always drawn more on the Anglo population (as Chicanos in South Chicago refer to everyone else), both locally and across the nation, than on the Mexican community immediately around it.[2]

I think as I watch the pews fill up that all these people have once had (or may be having) an experience so terrible and disorienting that they identified it as hopeless and called on Jude for help, since this is the saint's special province. By this point in my research I know well what sorts of crises these could be: long unemployment, bitter family troubles, abandonment and betrayal by loved ones, difficult challenges with changing technologies at work, problems with drug and alcohol addiction, and life-threatening illness. I am struck by all the stories of pain Saint Jude has already heard (and will be hearing again tonight). The shrine is a place where awful things may be talked about, aloud to friends, family, and clergy, silently to Jude, as part of a larger process of healing. Tonight the place seems charged with all the needs, fears, and hopes brought to it over the years.

Then immediately after this thought come two others, which jar me by the contradiction between them.

First, flushing with pride edged by anger, I think I am here among these working-class people in this postindustrial landscape because I want to hear their stories. I take their voices seriously. This is what research in religion means, I fume, to attend to the experiences and beliefs of people in the midst of their lives, to encounter religion in its place in actual men and women's "lived experience."[3] Where are the theologians from the seminaries on the South Side, I want to know, with all their talk of postmodernism and narrativity? When will the study of religion in the United States take a empirical, and so more realistic and humane, direction?[4]

But then, still warmed by these satisfying feelings, I hear another voice in my head. Do these people really want you here? it asks me. They could care less about your *discovery* of their spirituality, your reclamation project, like the ones periodically proposed and forgotten by the steel industries.[5] Their prayers and their relationship to Saint Jude existed long before you came to study them and will continue after you leave. What need do they have of you, the voice taunts, and what do you contribute to their experience? You are studying them, which means that many of them have sat down and told you stories about their experiences of hopelessness and what they asked Saint Jude for in those times. But what have you given them, or what will you give them, especially after you translate what you understand of their experience into other, academic idioms so that they will not be able to recognize it any more as their experience?

What could have been responsible for this unsettling convergence of pride and doubt? I spent the rest of the service meditating uneasily on my ambivalent place in the congregation that night.

The Space Between Two Challenges

My discomfort was deepened the next morning by an exchange I had with a woman I will call Clara, who first turned to Jude three decades ago when she was nursing her father through his last illness.[6] We had met very early, before Clara went to work, and now the sun was up and we were finishing our talk. The tape recorder was off. Suddenly, Clara turned to me with her coat half on, half off, and asked. "Have *you* ever prayed to Saint Jude?"

No, I told her, I had never prayed to Saint Jude. I explained that, although I had grown up in a devout Italian Catholic household, none of my relatives had had a special devotion to this saint. Since then my own relation to the tradition had become unsettled and tenuous and so I could not really bring myself to pray for the intervention of the saints as I once had.

"Then how do you expect to understand what we're doing when we pray to Saint Jude?" she asked.

This was not an unfamiliar question to me, and I was prepared for it. I told Clara that I hoped to learn something about the meaning of the devotion to Saint Jude by talking to women like her and attending carefully to the specific ways they described the saint's place in their lives. I would ask them to tell me about their feelings toward Saint Jude and examine the various ways they engaged him in their everyday experience. I was also reading all the historical material I could find about the devotion, such as the letters published in the shrine's periodical, *The Voice of Saint Jude.* But Clara interrupted me.

"You have to promise," she said, "that someday you'll ask Saint Jude for something you really want, at a time when you really need him." She insisted that I do this "not just because I asked you to or because you think it'll help your research" but in order to experience the saint the way his devout do: "Then maybe you'll understand what we're doing." I might even get helped, she added.

I made a noncommittal response, agreeing at least to think about her suggestion, and this is how the conversation ended. But Clara's challenge stayed with me. I have always assumed that because I belong[ed] more or less to the same culture as the people I study, I had special access to their worldview and could count on an intuitive grasp of the point of their practices. I knew these people in a deep and intimate way, I assured myself, so my work was not comparable to that of the ethnographer who goes far from home to study a culture that is alien to him or her, at least initially. But Clara forced me to recognize the error of this belief. However I had grown up, my childhood was long ago, and since then I had been trained in disciplines that generally sought to conceptualize religious experiences in categories other than those of practitioners. I was asking outsider questions now, mostly. Furthermore, my own complex autobiographical relationship with the community I was working on was as much barrier as meeting ground. I was less inside the tradition than I had thought, or, more precisely, I seemed both thoroughly inside and outside it at the same time, which now, after Clara's question, seemed a uniquely difficult place to be.

Could I really take Clara's suggestion? Even though I was brought up with the saints all around me and still obviously found them (and people's relationships with them) fascinating, they were no longer part of my own intellectual or spiritual life. What would it even mean for me to "pray to Saint Jude"?

Other women would later broaden Clara's challenge by inquiring into my motivations. Why are you interested in us? they wanted to know. Why do you want to understand practices and beliefs you do not share? I might have protested that I once did share these practices and beliefs, again more or less, or that my grandmothers did and my mother still does (which is more interesting and relevant in terms of my motivation), or that I do in fact still consider myself a Catholic, albeit in my own way. I also could have told them that I believed their questions reflected the devaluation of women's experience in this culture (and many others), the belief that women's lives were not as important as men's. But I had to acknowledge the justice of the implication of their inquiries. There has been a break between myself and the world I study, and the rupture has occurred on an intimate level, involving central intellectual, emotional, spiritual, and existential issues. I was no longer confident that I could ever find my way to anything like Ricoeur's second naiveté, the revived sense of the *mysterium tremendum* on the other side of suspicion. I would have to be content with the more prosaic satisfactions that came from disciplined and precise analysis, which is what last century's practitioners of the field had prided themselves on anyway. But I was humbled by these reflections and my confidence in my intuitions undermined. Now it seemed to me that of all the traditions I might study, I was least equipped, emotionally, existentially, and intellectually, to study my own.

Back in the university, meanwhile, a colleague of mine offered another sort of challenge, this one coming from within what she understood to be the canons of the discipline of religious studies. "They're wrong, of course," she said after hearing me describe women's prayers to Jude and their beliefs about his response. "It seems to me that your interpretation of the material has to begin with the recognition, at least to yourself, that imaginary beings do not change men's work schedules or military orders or help women find places to live. This isn't the way the world works." The women who believed that Jude acted in their lives in these ways, my colleague continued, drawing out the implication of her perspective, are deluded, and the more fervent their faith, the deeper their delusion.

Clara's question had to do with hermeneutics, and in this she was a closet Schleiermachian, claiming that shared experience necessarily precedes understanding; my colleague's remarks also had to do with hermeneutics, and she was aligning herself with the modernist traditions of suspicion that still dominate the field. It may have been possible to engage either one of them separately, but it was very difficult to remain in meaningful conversation with both simultaneously. As a student of my own tradition's recent history and contemporary practice, I was something betwixt and between, an inorganic intellectual, not in enough to contribute to the ongoing life of the tradition, share its consolations, or experience the power of its account of the world, but not out enough to assent to my colleague's charge. I suspect this is the predicament of many denominational researchers.[7]

My assignment here is to comment on the interplay between denominational studies and the experiences of religious practitioners, specifically on the question of how the interests of the academy and those of the religious community can be balanced, or how studies can be organized to coordinate the interests of the sociologist or the historian with those of the members of the religious community. I want to approach this question by examining the terrain between Clara's challenge to pray to Saint Jude and my colleague's interpretation of the necessary suspicions of the discipline.

The Anomalies of Home: Studying One's Own Denomination

My conflicting feelings on the night of the novena were not unique or unusual; instead, they reflect the peculiar position of religious studies as a discipline, caught somewhere between belief and analysis, sometimes in different people but often enough in the same ones. Clara's challenge and my colleague's counterchallenge mark out the dominant poles between which the discipline exists, and for this reason the question about the relationship between denominational studies and the lives of practitioners is one expression of the larger issue of the nature of religious studies and its engagement with the people and worlds it takes as its subjects.

I have experienced two levels of difficulty as a scholar of my own tradition, one historical and historiographical, the other existential and psychological. These inherent but historically specific dilemmas make up the first level of the interplay between the researcher, with his or her methods and questions, and the perspectives and needs of members of the religious community under study.

Historical Contexts

In the heady days of liturgical experimentation and church renewal following the Second Vatican Council, the eminent church historian Thomas A. McAvoy warned that American Catholics were in danger of losing their history. "The mood of so many Catholic writers of the past two years has been a kind of fear to look back," McAvoy wrote in *Ave Maria,* "as if opening the windows of the Church to let in fresh air means closing the door on the past."[8] McAvoy's caution was not heeded, however, and now indeed a great divide seems to separate contemporary American Catholics from what has gone before them.

The convergence of several factors in the mid-1960s, including but not limited to the Council, begins to account for this alienation. The social landscape of American Catholicism had changed dramatically since the end of the "new" immigration in 1924. The generations born and raised in this country had moved away from the old ethnic enclaves their parents had built as a way of defending themselves against the brutalities of industrial capitalism. Intermarriage among ethnic groups (and even with non-Catholics) had increased steadily in the middle years of the twentieth century, fundamentally altering the meanings of ethnicity and communal and personal identity in the younger generation. American Catholic women first and then their brothers, husbands, and sons had begun to leave the blue-collar world for places in the emergent postindustrial economy. Although the 1950s witnessed a resurgence of anti-Catholic sentiment around the nation, distinguished this time by its origin in educated and upper-middle-class Protestant quarters, American Catholics by these years had already moved into the national mainstream.[9]

This became clear in 1960, not so much by the fact of Kennedy's election as by the clear evidence of the kind of Catholic he was. Kennedy wore his faith more lightly (very lightly indeed in certain areas of human experience) and more gracefully than some members of the American hierarchy, hardened veterans of the long struggle both with American anti-Catholicism and Roman anti-Americanism, really liked, and he was confident in a way they could never have been that there was no problem being both American and Catholic. This is what made him a hero to the new generations of American Catholics. When the president broke ranks with the hierarchy on a number of issues dear to them, including the matter of American diplomatic representation at the Vatican, he signaled the end of an era. What mattered now in the American century was what was happening here, not what was happening in Rome. The Holy See itself seemed to acknowledge this in its various, strenuous efforts to lobby the American government on important international economic and political issues after the Second World War.[10]

The ties to the old world of European Catholicism, both among the children of immigrants and among the younger members of religious

orders with European foundations, had been severed long before the first
vernacular Mass was celebrated. It was this generation of American Catholics, inspired by the liturgical reform movement, confident of its place in
national life, and encouraged by two sympathetic popes (John XXIII and,
at least up to the debacle of *Humanae Vitae,* Paul VI, who seemed to like
Americans and their ways), that set about to change American Catholicism in light of conciliar decrees. For our purposes, it is necessary to note
that they went about this work with a vengeance.

The everyday texture of American Catholic life was attacked with a
ferocity not easily accounted for, given the widespread popularity of the
maligned practices just a few short years before; popular religion, that rich
world of saints, perambulating virgins, perpetual novenas, block rosaries,
and pagan babies, came in for particularly savage scrutiny. What is most
surprising about the years of change in American Catholicism is how little
affection, respect, or understanding there was (or has been) for the world
the reformers were so eager to bring to an end, how little curiosity since
about its sources, motivations, or creativity. American Catholics then and
now have been distinctly humorless in their engagement with the exuber-
ance and occasional extravagances of devotionalism.

A mocking article published in the devotional periodical *Ave Maria*
(itself once a bastion of popular piety) in 1965 reveals the general tone of
the period. "We must do away with superstition and quaint old-world
folklore emanating from the ghetto," Ethel Marbach, a laywoman active in
church affairs proclaimed:

> Down with nine hour storm novenas, nine First Fridays so you can die
> happy, sewing sequins on the Infant of Prague's nightie, and dressing little
> Mary Hermoine in blue for the first year of her life. Thank goodness we've
> outgrown all that nonsense, and now, with the help of authentic sources,
> we can really get down to the roots of liturgical living.[11]

It is all here: the contempt for popular religion (and, in particular,
women's religious practice, since all of Marbach's examples of contempt-
ible pieties were the work of women); a complete lack of interests in
those practices or the circumstances in which they evolved; the denigra-
tion of the immigrants' world and its ways; and the peculiar but characteristic historiography of American Catholics, which applies the metaphor of
stages of personal psychological growth to history in order to designate
what came before as juvenilia and what is now as mature adulthood, a
kind of Gestalt whiggery.

In another article at the same time in the same periodical, a young
mother superior taunts her aging, widowed father by telling him that she
is taking his beloved statue of the Sacred Heart "to the dump." When the
old man asks why, his daughter snaps, "It would break your heart to know,
but for too long you have nursed your piety on this sickening, saccharine
symbol of impiety." She comes back the next day for the family's statue of
the Infant of Prague, that most scorned of all preconciliar icons, which

had been dressed in a little gown sewn by her mother. Later she tells the old man that now "it too lies smashed among the egg crates of the city dumping ground." When her father turns for comfort and consolation to the pastor of his parish, all the priest can do is warn him not to be "an old fogey" and "to keep up with the rest of us."[12]

Contemporary Catholics assumed a variety of poses toward the old popular culture. Some treated the plethora of devotional practices (most of which had been generated in the United States in the 1920s and 1930s, an extraordinarily fertile period in the history of Catholic popular piety) as if they were exotic imports from European Catholicism, utterly strange to the American ethos.[13] Others attempted to recast devotionalism in new idioms. At a conference he convened at Notre Dame in 1966 to determine what could be salvaged in the new spiritual environment of his once enormously popular Family Rosary Crusade, Father Patrick Peyton was told by a panel of distinguished theologians to break from "magical mathematics and mechanical indulgences" (in the words of Bernard Haring). They advised him to incorporate a concern for social justice in his promotions of the rosary by studying and addressing the material conditions of the people in areas designated for crusades and to allow greater time for Scripture study and interior prayer.[14] In the emergent postconciliar culture, the saints and the Virgin Mary were to be reimagined in the languages of friendship, morality, or mythology, deemphasizing what the reformers considered an inappropriate and extravagant emphasis on the emotional and the miraculous.[15]

Above all, however, the reformers insisted that popular devotions, if they were to remain a feature of the postconciliar American Catholic church at all, be surrounded by *words:* one way of understanding the transitions of the early 1960s, which continue to shape the intellectual climate of contemporary studies of American Catholicism, is as a shift from an ethos of charisma and sacred intimacy toward a culture bounded by, and even obsessed with, words. This is clear in Marbach's reference to the "appropriate sources"; the new spirit was one of justification by text. Words were not absent from preconciliar popular culture, of course, with all its prayer cards, novena booklets, and pious ejaculations. The difference is that the words of the old devotionalism were efficacious not simply in themselves but in relation to specific cultic practices and disciplines, such as vows, perpetual novenas, and devotion to particular saints. The new words belonged to a professionalized class of ritual specialists, whose development reflects the higher educational levels attained by middle-class American Catholics in these years. The new words derived their legitimacy from a strict and precise connection to church authority and not from their association with a beloved saint.

Devotions were necessarily now to be accompanied by some sort of discursive practice—explanatory sermons, clerical reflections on the meanings of particular expressions of piety, readings of Scripture or some other devotional text, as if by hedging these practices about with the written and spoken word their improvisatory and disruptive potential could be controlled, or at least diminished.[16] It is not an accident that the patron saints of these years are Thomas Merton, who managed to write scores of books after dedicating himself to a vow of silence, and Dorothy Day, a journalist.

The development of the hegemony of the word over the deed among American Catholics parallels a similar trajectory in the history of the academic study of religion in the United States.[17] One of the great archeological mysteries of the discipline is what became of the field's initial orientation toward psychological examinations of what William James called "the feelings, acts, and experiences of individual men in their solitude in relation to whatever they consider the divine," such as those of Starbuck, Leuba, Kardiner, and others, and toward ethnographic studies, principally of Native American religions.[18] To study religion in the United States today is to study texts. The briefest review of papers given at meetings of the American Academy of Religion over the last two decades shows how few studies are empirically based. The written and the spoken word, rather than engaged behavior studied in its place, are what occupies practitioners, and this resolutely textual orientation, among American Catholics and scholars of religion both, is one of the obstacles to the study of contemporary Catholicism.[19]

The community's own scorn for its past, the shame and embarrassment associated with it and the accompanying anger and denial in the broader setting of the orientation toward words in the study of religion, constitute the historiographical difficulty besetting contemporary students of American Catholicism. It is virtually impossible to work in the denomination without becoming embroiled in controversy. People expect the researcher to condemn or defend, and I have found myself alternately denounced as a liberal and castigated as a conservative. Since the immigrants and the working classes that made up most of American Catholicism for most of its history left so few written records, there seems to be little to study there, anyway.

Existential Considerations

Just as there was obviously a generational impulse to the reformers' contempt for the old ways, so my own fascination with those ways has a child's spirit about it. I feel that I know the people at the shrine so well because not only do they do the same things my mother and father do, they look like them too, and I admit, when I reflect on the question scholars of religion are most often (and most appropriately) asked by students and friends— "What got you interested in this in the first place?"—that when I am working in the field or in archives I often feel like a child again, peering into the strange and mysterious world of adults and trying to figure out what is going on in there. This is the existential ground of studies of one's own denomination, and perhaps more generally of our curiosity about religion, and there is both promise and dread here.

That question about the origins of my interest in religion has always provoked annoyance and uneasiness in me. It is like asking me why I fell in love; I used to counter those students bold enough to ask it. But this peevish displeasure was hiding something else, as I might have suspected. In a commentary on the relationship between anthropologists and their informants, Vincent Crapanzano writes of the prominence in such engagements of a "guilt-inspiring voyeuristic intention that can be rationalized away no more in the anthropological endeavor (by science) than in the psychoanalytic endeavor (by cure)."[20] What is this intention in religious studies, and specifically in the study of one's own denomination? By what do we rationalize our voyeurism, and to what end?

When I try to remember my childhood curiosity about my mother's and my father's religious worlds (and it is already significant that this is where I naturally wanted to begin this account of the roots of my professional life), it seems to me that I was fascinated first of all by the depth of their emotion; clearly something very important was going on here. I was also frightened by it. My parents and my grandparents withdrew from me in the intensity of their prayers in a way they never did otherwise, except maybe in grief. They seemed so completely absorbed and at the same time so vulnerable (a projection, perhaps, of my own unease) and powerless. They had entered a world apart from me, one presided over, furthermore, by someone much greater than they. Who or what was so much bigger and more powerful that they bowed to it, pleaded and argued with it, sometimes were bitterly angry toward it, and at other times made joyous by it?

My family's engagement with this power was not limited to extreme moments, however, although they prayed more intensely at such times. The Madonna and the saints were household companions, as familiar and unpredictable as my aunts and uncles. The grown-ups around me were forever bringing their pleas, hopes, and furies directly to these apparently ubiquitous holy figures. The first memory I have of a religious practice that intrigued me (and still does, actually) was hearing about a cousin who rushed home from the hospital where his wife had just died in childbirth to smash all their religious statues and images. What was going on in these fierce engagements between the grown-ups I could see and those I couldn't?

From a psychoanalytic perspective, peering into the adult world is hardly an innocent enterprise. The adult domain is fascinating and dangerous. Grown-ups do things to each other there that are fraught with implications for children's lives, as children themselves know well, so a child's curiosity is always, to some greater or lesser extent, defensive, depending on specific family situations. Sneaking peeks into the territory of adults, children are trying to figure out what the adults are up to and what this will mean for them; the stakes are high. They are gathering information not on the way the world *is* but on the way the world is for this group of adults (which is the only world particular children really know). And the key religious question is: What do these invisible beings contribute to the local configuration of reality?

Prayer in this way becomes the analog to the primal scene:[21] to come upon an adult in prayer is mesmerizing, compelling, frightening. It is to be aware that something of extraordinary power and complexity is happening, that the world is being constructed and engaged in a compelling and authoritative way. It is also to experience oneself as excluded, awakening the desire to enter this world for oneself, to explore it, perhaps also to master it and make it safe.

This is how I understand the anxiety I feel in the field, the inevitable discomfort that grips me just before I sit down with someone (most recently, women) to talk with them about their religious understandings, practices, and experiences. This is not bad faith; I am not guiltily anticipating debunking them, and the analogy here is not of going behind the curtain, like Toto in Oz, to uncloak the impostor (although this is right for the modernist impulse in the discipline). Rather, the parallel experience is of a child glancing over his own folded hands at his mother at prayer beside him or picking out her voice speaking in tongues above the din of an excited church or watching her cry on a riverbank above a muddy baptism. Of the many feelings that characterize and shape fieldwork, mine have always included a sense of intrusion, of interrupting and prying, which seems to be built into the enterprise. "No matter how far 'participation' may push the anthropologist in the direction of Not-Otherness," Paul Rabinow has written in his autobiographical examination of his fieldwork in Morocco, "the context is still ultimately dictated by 'observation' and 'externality.'"[22] And we feel uneasy about this spectating because we realize, however dimly, that we are looking for something that frightens as much as it intrigues and excites us.

Furthermore, the powerful feelings I had of recognizing the people I was working among—recognizing not only what they were saying but the look on their faces as well, their postures and their gestures, hearing familiar echoes in their voices and their laughter—evoked in me always a range of emotions that included contradictory impulses to protect them and to accuse them, as well as the need to be taken in and accepted by them.

The consequences of all this for our work is that unless we recognize first the elemental fascination and power of religious goings-on, and then all the things we want to do with them—share them, control them, mute their power over us and our memories—our writing will become an unconscious exercise in boundary making. This is the emotional ground of the impulse toward functionalism in the field: to tame what is wild and threatening and dangerous *specifically to us, because of the details of our particular childhoods,* about different forms of religious experience and practice. This is what makes so much religious study dull and beside the point. It is also the reason why scholars of religion spend so much

time in making sterile taxonomies, gridding what we study into safe—
and discrete—categories.

These various complex anxieties, needs, and discomforts constitute
the existential difficulties of field work in one's own religious tradition.

Conclusion

Recent critics of ethnography have sharpened our awareness of the
narrative and epistemological strategies of the genre and, more broadly,
of the work of studying and representing other peoples. They point out
that ethnographies are generally plotted in three acts. First there is the
scene of arrival in a distant place, often in the middle of the night.
Highlighting the exoticism of the locale, this shadowy beginning represents the anthropologist's initial confusions and disorientation as it impli-
cates the reader in them. Then, after a disorienting and dangerous initia-
tory crisis, comes acceptance by the local people. The balance between
inside and outside has tilted toward the former. Finally, there is the
achievement of a special kind of understanding (which the reader, having never arrived in the middle of the night nor been accepted by the
natives, cannot claim).[23] In this way, through the skillful manipulation of
the dialectic of otherness-not otherness, the anthropologist establishes
his or her voice and interpretation.

Harsher critics of the genre go on to say that this is also how
ethnographers occlude the people they have lived among as they establish the authority of their texts and foreclose alternative readings. This
may be, but the drama of anthropological understanding in three acts as
outlined seems a useful model of how to approach people whose ways
and values are alien to us. The field-worker sees (and should respect) the
differences between him- or herself and the other; but gradually, as the
exchanges across the difference multiply in common experience and
conversation, otherness can become a heuristic tool that opens understanding of the ways and the mores of both cultures, the anthropologist's
and the local people's.

The dilemma of fieldwork in one's own religious culture, however, is
that difference is never clear and sharp enough, for the historical and
existential reasons I have just described. The people we are talking to are
simultaneously and disconcertingly both other and not, and we cannot
respect and use the distance between us because we cannot establish it
securely. Difference is constantly being undermined by memory, desire;
rejection, and anger, and we are in danger of being swamped by the
undertow of the unconscious. The first two acts in this drama of research
and interpretation are a muddle of unacknowledged transferences. In act
3, either the natives (confused themselves by our ambivalence and ambiguity) reject us, with resentment and misunderstanding on both sides, or
we come to identify with them so closely that we lose the distance

necessary for understanding and yield to expectations of defense and celebration.

These then were the two concurrent, subterranean, and not completely discrete levels of meaning and experience, historical and psychological, that shaped both my work in the field and my sources' attitudes toward me. Now I want to show how they played themselves out in my actual experience in Chicago.

A Diary in the Strict Sense of the Term

The following are some selections from my fieldwork journal, followed by brief commentary.

October 30, 1987. The older woman (maybe seventy years old) sitting in front of me at the 2:00 service—the one who elbowed her husband in the ribs when the priest made the joke about retired men driving their wives crazy—handed her well-worn novena booklet to her husband to put into his pocket after the novena. People come with these booklets in their purses and pockets.

October 30, 1987. One woman, V., refers to me as "Father" Orsi, even after I've told her I'm not a priest.

October 30, 1987. After the 5:30 service, a *very* obese woman, who looked to be more than seventy years old, came over to me to tell me about a miracle Saint Jude had accomplished for her. (She smelled very bad, was wearing old, grey, stained slacks and a greasy brown quilted ski jacket.) Her sister and brother had stopped talking to each other, "wouldn't even eat at the same table," and this, she insisted several times, was "real suffering," "real trouble." She prayed to Saint Jude for them, and they started talking again, and—this is how she ended her story—"they sat down together again at the same table." She was very emotional while she was talking to me; her eyes were filled with tears, and several times she had to stop, overcome.

October 31, 1987. At the 5:30 service this evening, a woman going down the side aisle toward Jude on her knees. Father D. is careful in his sermons to make sure that people understand that Jude points the way toward Jesus and that the important thing is not to make of this a private cult. D. also spends a great deal of time in his sermons on Central America and points out that this is Jesus crucified again. He says that the church, taking its stand with the "emarginated," is itself being crucified in Central and South America by the "power structure."

November 1, 1987. I overheard the following conversation at the shrine: one woman says to another, "Have you filled out the questionnaire?" [some very general questions I distribute as a way of inviting people to think about their attachment to Jude and then either talk to me in person or on the telephone or write to me]. "Who has the time to do that?" her friend replies. "Oh, come on," says the first, "you can sit on the toilet and do one question at a time."

December 29, 1987. I am reluctant to discover that Catholics under 30 have a devotion to Saint Jude, perhaps because this would obliterate the neat periodization of Before/After the Council.

January 7, 1988. S.A. called tonight to cancel her [I crossed this out and over it wrote "our"] appointment tomorrow. "If it's not inconvenient, Professor, I'd like to know if I can cancel my appointment." What could I say? I was apprehensive about the power relationship implicit in her question. Could she cancel? What would she have done if I'd said, "No, S., tomorrow we must meet"? I had a feeling throughout our conversation that her husband was on the other side of the phone table. She said that her husband was home on vacation and they were wallpapering the house, "and tomorrow night I go running with the kids, and they have basketball and everything." We agreed to meet in June, when I'll be back.

January 8, 1988, 12:40 PM. From outside, the sounds of the school children on their lunch break. A neighborhood street person circles the church, perhaps making the stations of the cross, more likely just wandering around; I'd seen him reading the paper in Sonny's this morning when I went in for breakfast.

January 8, 1988. Long and deep reflection on certain essential religious and existential questions can lead Jude's devout into heterodoxy. C.G. used to believe in reincarnation; less so now, she says. But this emerges out of their serious engagement with Catholic questions, and not necessarily through an encounter with other currents in American religion.

The first thing that even this brief selection of entries illustrates is how minor a part of the total religious experience words are. If American Catholic spirituality, liturgical practice, and religious aesthetics (all those banners proclaiming "pax" and "agape" in the spaces where the saints once stood, as Paul Hendrickson has written[24]) have come to be ordered around words and the safety they provide against the embarrassing spontaneity of practice, my time at the shrine pointed me away from words, and especially from official words (from creeds to liturgical rubrics). Fieldwork forces an acknowledgement of and engagement with something messier than the controlled marshaling of letters on a page, something less predictable, and demands a different kind of attentiveness. The world of the text is really not the world.

While the priest was speaking about the political concerns that do indeed occupy many American Catholics, a woman was crawling toward him down the aisle of the church. Which represents the contemporary life of the denomination—either one, both, or the contradiction between them? What matters—the sermon or the range of interactions and exchanges taking place among the congregation in the interval of the sermon's time? My attention was inevitably drawn away from the official words and postures occurring on the main altar and toward the secret, subtle, but persistent interpersonal connections—nudges, glances, thighs pressed against one another, hands held or withheld—going on all around me during the service. I noticed that women kept their prayer-books in their purses, tucked in among their other private things. What relationship did this indicate between the shrine, with all its powers to heal and comfort, and the intimate spaces of a woman's life? What kind of place is a pocketbook, and how is it connected to the other places—desk drawers at work, kitchen counters, bedside tables and bureaus—where Jude also resides? I became interested in the movement of prayerbooks from hand to hand during the service. What was a woman doing when she asked the man accompanying her to hold her prayerbook? What kind of bond was she establishing, confirming, or enforcing? What places did the invisible persons occupy *between* the visible ones? These are the questions of an inquisitive child, and from the perspective of the pew they seem like the right ones.

The sounds of the children that filtered into the shrine illustrate the porousness of such spaces. Among the sounds that matter here are not only those coming from the organ, choir, and priest up front but those that penetrate from the outside, too, posing both challenges of endurance and possibilities of interpretation for believers.[25] So too did the appearance in the sacred space of the confused street person and the drunken (a detail I omitted in my notes for some reason) and troubled woman. Any honest description of very many religious spaces in contemporary America would have to include some reference to the inevitable presence in them of strange, disturbed, possibly psychotic people, loudly sharing their distress with the worshippers. Yet these people are almost always excluded from our presentation of such sites.[26] I have been saddened by these old people when I have come across them and uncertain about what to do with them in my analysis; the worshippers, however, long familiar with them, must learn to deal with such eruptions. What else do we routinely edit out and what do our elisions disclose about our anxieties and the limits we want to impose on our material? How are these figures to be included in our understanding of denominational space?

My own lingering allegiance to the preeminence of the word is clear in my reluctance to see clearly what was around me: These can't be young people I am seeing, because we all know (the books tell us) that devotionalism has declined among young Catholics, and so I must be imagining them.

Finally, the notes also illustrate the density of the interpersonal world in which the denominational researcher takes his or her place. Because Jude is the patron saint of hopeless cases and lost causes, when women spoke to me about him they necessarily had to talk about some very bleak moments in their lives, and the ones who sought me out to tell me their stories (often over many hours) brought their needs and hopes to me as I brought mine to them: to be recognized, praised, respected, heeded. At times, listening to tales of illicit romance or of the consequences of bad choices, I knew I was being called on at least to bear witness to their lives but perhaps also to offer some sort of absolution. Certainly, confession was a close analogue to the kind of conversations we were having. While women talked about mastectomies, abandonment, domestic violence, adultery, and loneliness, I could feel myself being transposed, without any encouragement on my part, into other men in their lives, not only the protagonists of their stories but also doctors, priests, and counselors.

Furthermore, working beside all field researchers are dreaded doubles, figures like Malinowski's missionaries, who are close enough in education, class, and style to make them particularly vexing figures, since we need to distinguish ourselves from them in order to get work done.[27] Their numbers in my own experience have included journalists (who often spread mistrust and suspicion), church officials, parish workers, overly zealous parishioners, and clergy. Our being confused with these other categories of persons can complicate our conversations with people, and I have always felt that these proximities demanded a certain delicate diplomacy from me. As my conversation with the very nervous S.A. indicates, however, this was not always successful. The researcher is perceived through multiple frames and becomes the object of displaced resentments and expectations. All his or her conversations with practitioners about important things take place in this charged setting.

Clearly, a lot more goes on at a shrine (or a Pentecostal meeting, or a Baptist summertime revival, or a neo-pagan festival) than its sponsors, promoters, and spokespeople intend or hope, and a lot more takes place in denominational research than a simple exchange of information. What happens at the ritual center represents only the tiniest part of the total interaction of the event, and the explicit topics pursued by researcher and subject are just one dimension of their encounter. A season in the field shatters the givenness of the various borders we seem committed to maintaining and serves to de-center denominational research first and then to re-center it in the broader domain of human experience, just as it calls into question the way we structure our research (with questionnaires and research instruments of various sorts). There is always an earthier, material ground for what happens in a sacred space, as my notes indicate. The laughter in the old woman's eyes as she teased her husband with her sharp elbow during the novena reflected the complexities of aging, the strains of retirement, and the pleasures of a long life together. That the gesture took place in a shrine, amid many other gestures, official and not, opens this space up to the rest of experience. As Robin Horton insisted, religion cannot be understood apart from its place in the everyday lives, preoccupations, and commonsense orientations of men and women.[28]

What Is One Studying When One Studies Denominationalism?

Although historians say that the dilemmas of ethnography are not their concern since the past is not a place we can visit (all such metaphors aside, and despite the efforts of Le Roy Ladurie and his students), I think the preceding examination of what I saw at the shrine has some relevance for how we understand the appropriate domain of denominational studies.

Such studies, of course, are necessarily concerned with the origins, achievements, struggles, institutional organization, dilemmas, and controversies of particular communities. But the gesture of the old woman at the shrine, the ravings and wanderings of the street people there, the discrepancy between Father D.'s sermon and the behavior of the woman in the aisle, suggest that on another level, and often working against what we have generally preferred to study, there are other aspects of denominational life and experience that must be included in our purview and attended to. Fieldwork certainly suggests such an expansion.

On this other level, denominational study is the examination of particular patterns of response to shared human situations and dilemmas. The patterns have evolved over time, and they carry deep within them— often out of the conscious reach of the people whose lives they shape— the marks of this development, the impress of old conflicts, circumstances, and strategies. They are an example of what Ernst Bloch called the "simultaneity of the unsimultaneous." They have been crafted and recrafted by many hands, in many different places, and in contradictory circumstances. They constitute the way that living people experience and construe events in their social world (war, economic distress, the organization and experience of work, for example) and perennial human problems (always encountered within specific historical constructs, although never completely and safely so).

This is what characterizes a denomination historically and existentially: the forms within which everyday realities are construed and engaged, the idioms in which the imagination is exercised and (most important) constrained, and the channels through which desire and hope are made to flow. Such idioms are rich in theological and spiritual resonance. They represent the way a community's history is physically internalized—embodied—by its members and made vivid as styles of thinking, living, feeling.

Thomas Simmons's account of growing up in a Christian Science household offers an eloquent and moving instance of what I mean here. Simmons describes how his parents' God was pressed into his flesh and bones in times of sickness, an ironic incarnation given his church's understanding of matter: "When I had earaches, for example, or when the metal swing tore into my forehead, I would repeat the Scientific Statement of Being or other passages I'd memorized from Mary Baker Eddy's *Science and Health with Key to the Scriptures* until I was dizzy with pain and exhaustion." As a result, "God became ... the presence that would not heal."[29] Denominational idioms shaped the boy's experience of illness, of his body, of the meaning and limits of hope and endurance; in turn, these idioms were marked by the pain of earaches and the boy's rage at his mother's cruelty.

What I am saying here appears to resemble what some contemporary historians of mentalities have concluded about the forms of a people's mental activity, except that I want to leave much more room than they do for creativity in the manipulation of inherited forms in response to changing circumstances. The forms do not simply remain constant over the long duration; instead, as they are wielded, as they must be, in people's efforts to deal with the vicissitudes of their experience, they are always subtly altered, just as the people and their worlds are. People are free to the extent that they may make something of what has been made of them, according to Sartre, and for religious men and women in this country, one of the ways they have exercised this freedom is by improvising with the inherited idioms of their tradition that constrains them as they enable them to live and change at the same time.[30]

Denominationalism (defined now as a cluster of idioms for patterning lived experience) serves to provide men and women with existential vocabularies with which they may construe fundamental matters, such as the meaning and the borders of the self, the relations of self to others, the sources of joy, the borders of acceptable reality, the nature of human destiny, and the meaning of the various stages of their lives. It is through these various denominational idioms that the necessary material realities of existence—pain, death, hunger, sexuality—are experienced, transformed, rendered meaningful, and endured. These idioms are neither sufficient nor discrete. They interact with other competing, alternative, or complementary, configurations of experience that are available outside the denomination. Growing up in a denomination at a particular moment in its history—and it is the work of researchers to delineate these moments with precision—is to be provided with what Clifford Geertz calls a "sentimental education," a training in ways of feeling and patterns of thought.[31]

The patterns, gestures, and styles of thinking and feeling that are characteristic of denominations are not completely congruent with the overall institutional structure and the official ethos of those denominations, nor are they internally consistent or completely appropriate to contemporary situations. Ways of feeling and thinking are, to some extent, under certain circumstances (and just which circumstances is another historical problem), detachable from the official or organizational life of a community. A recent example of this potential for the disassociation of idiom from institution was the Rev. Troy Perry's use of Pentecostal modes of spiritual authority and religious experience to ground a completely new, non-Pentecostal, denomination, the Metropolitan Community Churches, that otherwise diverges from Pentecostal cultural and aesthetic styles, especially its ethical teaching in the matter of sexuality.[32]

This way of understanding denominationalism opens it up to another set of questions. How do patterns of religious feeling and experience intersect with others originating elsewhere in culture—with the sentimental education offered by the movies, for example, or by popular music, or with the expectations and disciplines of different kinds of work places, the blandishments of advertising, the styles that signify class membership, or the politics of gender? What is the relationship between various religious construals of anger in this country and the opportunity afforded by different religious settings for the expression of such powerful emotions with the fate of these feelings elsewhere in the culture, at home, for example, or at work?[33] Denominational idioms compete with all these others, sometimes working against them, at other times conforming to them.

Denominations, then, function as one of the primary mediators between historical circumstance and individual experience and response.[34] Denominationalism, in the way I have described it here, has provided Americans in the turbulent and distressing circumstances of life in an industrial, capitalist society—with its high geographic mobility, periodic economic fluctuations and consequent unemployment, and fierce competition among groups for work—with a repertoire of feelings and orientations with which to make sense of and to live in their world. Michael Jackson writes that "our concept of culture must . . . be made to include those moments in social life when the customary, given, habitual, and normal is disrupted, flouted, suspended, and negated, when crises transform the world from an apparently fixed and finished set of rules into a repertoire of possibilities, when a person stands out against the world and, to borrow Marx's vivid image, forces the frozen circumstances to dance by singing to them their own melody."[35] In American history and experience, many of the dance tunes have been limned by denominational culture.

Toward a Conversational Model of Religious Ethnography

My argument has proceeded so far from an examination of the specific difficulties, historical and existential, of doing research in one's own tradition, to the reorienting lessons of fieldwork, and, finally, to the revision of the meaning of "denominationalism" suggested by them. Now I want to return to the issue of interplay, by way of conclusion.

It has become virtually axiomatic in the last several decades that understanding human culture requires a different kind of inquiry than that which characterizes the natural sciences. The psychologist Stanley Leavy's comment about psychological insight seems broadly applicable to the human sciences: "Meaning, and the interpretive process through which meaning is disclosed, exists in dialogue." Understanding in this context emerges out of a conversation, through the process of interaction; it was not there at the beginning waiting to be discovered. As Leavy says, "When we interpret personal meaning, we must ask one another, for this kind of meaning exists between us."[36] The nature of what is learned through this kind of research will be different, too. "A person differs from any other 'object' in that it is a person alone whom I address as 'you,'" to quote Leavy a last time. "As soon as I recognize that, I can see that my explanations with regard to persons must be fundamentally different from any other explanation."[37]

The interplay between believers and researchers is not a stage at either end of a project for setting the agenda of the inquiry (what might be called programmatic interplay) or exchanging information (this is what we have discovered about the history of your community—informational interplay). Both of these possibilities, important as they are, ignore the complexity of what is actually learned in the field and, more important, how it is learned. Nor would it be the modernist version proposed by my colleague (tell me what you believe, and I will analyze it according to my categories). All of these perspectives keep practitioners safely in the camp of the other, constituting them as a "they" that can be studied, written about, and taught, without challenging their status of otherness and without being actually engaged with them. They also ignore the psychological undercurrents and biographical circumstances that render this academic imposition of "otherness" ludicrous.

Interplay is, instead, the ground of the whole undertaking.

The same is true more generally for studies of religion. In the last few years, Clifford Geertz's writings on the study of culture have dominated historical and cultural studies in religion. Disciplinary practitioners for various reasons have found his methodological paradigms compelling. It may seem that I am calling here for something like Geertz's thick description, but in fact I am proposing a break with this orientation at last. Influenced by Ricoeur's hermeneutics, Geertz's approach to religion is relentlessly textualizing. He is a master hermeneute, who explicitly transforms the world into text, upon which he then performs virtuosic acts of "reading" (Geertz's own word for his cultural work). Religion, in this perspective, functions as a highly privileged form of cultural theater in which the ethos of a people's world, "the tone, character and quality of their life, its moral and aesthetic style and mood," and their understanding of the way the world is are brought together with great authority—and publicly, making it available for outside observers. It is this devotion to the text—not the many years he has spent in various field settings—that have made Geertz's work so intriguing to our text-besotted discipline.

All Geertz's metaphors to describe his interpretive activities reveal this inclination towards spectating, but perhaps the most revealing is his famous definition of ethnography as "trying to read (in the sense of 'construct a reading of') a manuscript—foreign, faded, full of ellipses, incoherences, suspicious emendations, and tendentious commentaries, but written not in conventionalized graphs of sound but in transient examples of human behavior."[38] I am proposing instead that in the study of contemporary denominational cultures we step around the informant and talk with him or her face-to-face as Geertz himself has always done.

But how exactly would this conversation proceed? What will we be talking about, and on what grounds will we meet? Does this mean that Clara was right after all and that I do need to pray to Saint Jude?

Clara's Challenge Again

About two and a half years after my initial conversation with Clara at Saint Jude's shrine, I found myself in circumstances that I felt were hopeless in the way that I think Jude's devout mean this term. One terrible evening as I was agonizing over my situation, I recalled Clara's challenge.

"What would it be like," I asked myself, "to pray to Saint Jude now?"

I have a big statue of the saint in my study, and it would have been easy to look in his eyes, as the devout do, and plead with him, but I just could not do it. I had to respect my own intellectual and spiritual culture as much as I did Clara's. So I shifted the ground of the experiment, and, instead of actually praying to Saint Jude, I tried to find some analogue to this act in my own emotional and behavioral repertoire on the basis of what I already knew of the nature of women's prayers.

Women who call on Saint Jude in these circumstances tell him what they want. They make their desires explicit, naming what they see as the best possible outcome of their hopeless dilemma. Strictly speaking, their prayers are petitions. So I did this, although I did not direct my petitionary "prayer" to Saint Jude (I might have called a friend but could not). In this way I learned my first real lesson about the devotion: It is tremendously difficult to put one's desires and hopes into words, even to oneself, when realistically one knows, as the devout claim they do, that there is no earthly chance these will be realized. It is easier for the purposes of endurance and survival to hunker down and accept the situation without the unsettling distraction of hope.

But I did it (to the extent that I understood what I really wanted, or that what I allowed myself consciously to want was really in fact what I wanted—levels of complexity that are shared by Jude's devout). This taught me the second lesson: It is a tremendous relief to admit to oneself clearly and as honestly as one can just what one would like to have happen. Once I had spoken aloud in the empty room what I wanted, I found I had opened up the closed space of my despair a tiny crack. It was as though this other possibility now had a more substantial presence, just for having been spoken and acknowledged. I could reimagine the world and my situation in ways I couldn't just moments before. At the very least, it made it clear to me what I had been denying or repressing.

Now I was at the edge of hope (another lesson: This process of hoping has many stages). Would I take the next step, as Jude's devout do, and actually surrender myself, not simply to the hope that I would get this one thing that I acknowledged wanting but, again as they do, to whatever would happen, which they express by adding to their prayers the proviso that they were prepared to accept Jude's decision for them, whatever it was? Could I go through this difficult movement from despair to admission to resignation and hope?

By using my own experience as a way of probing Clara's suggestion, I was slowly working my way not into the devotion itself (this is impossible) but into the experience of vulnerability, risk, and acceptance that serves as the ground of the devotion. "Experience in this sense," Jackson writes, "becomes a mode of experimentation, of testing and exploring the ways in which our experiences conjoin or connect us with others, rather than the ways they set us apart."[39] I had had to involve my life in the process of reflection; I could not withhold myself.

It was a night of rich (and, to my relief, distracting) discoveries. I learned in particular the courage of Jude's devout by observing in my-self the enormous strength of will it took simultaneously to risk hoping while conceding that I had come to the end of my own powers in the situation. (This is in sharp contrast with the usual perspective on peti-tionary prayer, which sees it as weak and self-interested.[40]) Most of all, as the possibility of hoping and the recognition of accepting both grew stronger, I felt a subtle shift in my experience of the world, a slight realignment, a change in atmospherics, and this helped me understand the feeling that women describe after praying to Jude.

I had set out to study one denomination's characteristic forms of construing and responding to psychological and physical suffering. In the process, under the prodding of the people I was working with, I was forced to admit our estrangement from each other; we inhabited different cultural and intellectual universes. But coming around in a circle again, what I learned as I tried to take Clara's challenge seriously is that we were alike nonetheless in our vulnerability, need, and risk. This was, to para-phrase Ricoeur, a second solidarity, the recognition after the necessary discipline of distanciation of a common project. I had gone from other-ness to a new conjuncture of otherness/not otherness, different from the one I started with, an appreciation of shared experience on a level other than that of specific religious practice or belief.

To reach this, however, I had to respect the integrity of my own convictions, and I was clear on the difference between Clara's experience and understanding and my own. Distance remained important, not only for the quality of my work and the reach of my understanding, but as the ground of this experience of a second not-otherness. I could not pretend to pray to Jude, and I was not identifying with Clara or participating in her religious practice. Instead, I respected the disciplinary and personal necessity of what Gananath Obeyesekere calls a "disengaged identity" or "distanciation" as necessary to the kind of study I am describing here as "the capacity to imaginatively and empathetically project oneself into an alien life world."[41]

"Participation," Obeyesekere goes on to say, "is participation in dialogue, not identification with the other culture."[42] Clara and I together had identified the ground of our dialogue. "One does not have to believe in *santería* in order to understand it," a scholar of the tradition has recently proposed, "but one must be willing to believe in something."[43] I understand the intention here, but I want to modify the dictum slightly: To understand one does not have to believe, only to acknowledge a common human project, within the framework of different histories and idioms. Then fieldwork becomes a matter, not of taking notes, but of comparing them.

Interplay: Comparing Notes

That I ever thought I could engage other people's responses to pain and suffering without putting my own on the line is now a great embarrassment to me, but I believed that this is what was required by the discipline. I held on to this mistaken sense of disciplinary propriety even though I already knew that Clara was not as different from me as my colleague suggested. She and I had discovered that we were both nervous about raising daughters in the conditions of modern American culture, uneasy about our parents' deepening dependence on us, and afraid of driving on dark country roads, preferring instead the comfort of city streetlights. But I felt I had to occlude myself in order properly to analyze her experience. Now I know that the best moments of our conversations were precisely these recognitions of shared fears and hopes and our acknowledgement of the different idioms we relied on to experience and to endure them.

Furthermore, it is not clear that what I was doing on that bad night—testing, exploring, pushing at the edges of my experience with whatever came to hand (including Clara's challenge itself, which in fact offered me another medium for engaging my situation)—is any different from what Jude's devout themselves have always done when they called on him in similar situations. They have also been improvising with the materials at hand, not always certain what the outcome of their experiment would be. The devout usually say that they tried turning to Jude when all else failed, to see now if this would work instead. So the kind of research I am proposing here—a tentative, interpersonal examination of particular denominational beliefs and practices that constitutes the ground of the conversation as it explores it—resembles the nature of many kinds of praying and religious acting, too; in the cases both of prayer and of research, the telos is not simply there at the start of the process but begins to be clarified only through the process.[44]

"Research is a relationship between men," Sartre wrote, "and the relationship itself must be interpreted as a moment of this history."[45] Things happen in the course of this sort of conversation. Emotions are

generated, fantasies provoked; there are projections and counterprojec-
tions as the two people create and recreate each other in desired or
feared images, and this complex process too must be monitored and
studied.

The space between the challenges, then, is rich terrain. Its examination may require that we try some methodological experiments, such as
those suggested by James Clifford in his critique of ethnographic practices.[46] We may want to include the voices of our sources somehow in
our texts, for example, allowing them to challenge and to question our
interpretations of them, to dissent from our analysis, to propose their
own alternative narratives, to question our idioms in relation to theirs,
and in general to break into the authority of our reading and to reveal its
tentative character. We might want to examine openly and critically the
emotional and intellectual sources of our own implications in the practices and the beliefs we study.[47] We could foreground the process of
mutual constitution that characterizes the initial encounters between us
and our sources, critically examining the fantasized versions of each
other that parade across the space between us, and we can be clear about
the changing nature of this engagement over time.

This is not an argument for "subjective" research. I have stressed
the necessary disciplines of fieldwork, the need for scrupulous and careful attention to the practices encountered, the resolute otherness and
autonomy of our sources, as well as the importance both of respecting
one's own culture and of being attentive to the conscious and unconscious sources of the motivations for our work and the direction of our
inquiries. It is not sufficient to append an autobiographical prologue or
epilogue to the old studies. We need to rethink the nature of cultural
research itself. Furthermore, the point of all these experiments and all
this critical attention to the unfolding of relations in the field is to
clarify and to understand denominationally inflected ways of living and
thinking.

Of all the dichotomies we use to structure our work in religion, says
Jonathan Smith—popular/official; heresy/orthodoxy; good/bad—the most
fundamental is us/them.[48] At the very least, the discipline would benefit
from a season of experimenting with ways of rethinking this great modernist boundary that has been so long and so carefully enforced. Fieldwork in
the denominations provides an interesting opportunity to conduct this
sort of experiment. In this way, the interplay of denominational research
would make a contribution to contemporary practice in the field. The
outcome of this experiment would not necessarily be the dismantling of
the border, but even rendering it problematic would be something. Our
work then could become as porous as the shrine itself, a site of many voices
talking on top of each other and against each other, a place of unexpected
intrusions and uncertain borders, built in the middle of and from the same
stuff as what Sartre calls the "equivocal givens of experience."

NOTES

I want to thank Ronald Numbers and Colleen McDannell for their sharp and helpful critiques of an earlier version of this paper.

This essay is affectionately dedicated to Michael Jackson and Francine Lorimer and to their son Joshua.

1. Critics of ethnography would have some questions about the specific tropes employed in this opening description. Why am I in the back of the church? What does this suggest about my sense of my place in the community, and how does it position the reader in relation to what follows? What is the point of the opposition between cold/warm; dark/light; outside/inside? Does the appearance of the young woman in the bomber jacket disclose an erotic current or a voyeuristic impulse? Why have I emphasized the "abandoned" quality of the neighborhood and the "diminishing" of the old ethnic worlds? To secure its sense of otherness in the reader's mind? To anchor my authority as a person who has bravely gone into a marginal urban neighborhood? For critical essays in this spirit, see James Clifford and George E. Marcus, *Writing Culture: The Poetics and Politics of Ethnography* (Berkeley: University of California Press, 1986).

2. This spatial anamoly is the subject of my article "The Center Out There, In Here, and Everywhere Else: The Nature of Pilgrimage to the Chicago Shrine of Saint Jude," *Journal of Social History* 25, no. 2 (Winter 1991): 213–232.

3. I am borrowing the phrase "lived experience" from Jean-Paul Sartre, *Search for a Method* (New York: Vintage Books, 1968) and from Michael Jackson, *Paths Towards A Clearing: Radical Empiricism and Ethnographic Inquiry* (Bloomington: Indiana University Press, 1989).

4. By "empirical" here I do not mean "realistic" or "objective," and this is not a call for a return to the old positivist orientation of the social sciences (as will be clear later in the essay). Instead, I mean an encounter with human beings in the everyday circumstances of their lives, of which religious practices constitute one part (and not always a discrete one, as we might hope or believe). The specific interpersonal nature of this encounter, the relationship between the researcher and the people he or she is studying, is one of the concerns of this essay and will be discussed below.

5. The anthropologist Jack Kugelmass, who has reflected systematically in his various writings on the implications of working in one's own tradition, describes the fantasy that possessed him of being the "repository" of the vanishing world of the elderly South Bronx Jews he was studying. See *The Miracle of Intervale Avenue: The Story of a Jewish Congregation in the South Bronx* (New York: Schocken Books, 1986), p. 202. The synagogue continued on its fragile way long after Jack's work was finished there. James Clifford calls this fieldwork fantasy of the "disappearing object" "salvage ethnography." See Clifford, "On Ethnographic Allegory," in Clifford and Marcus, *Writing Culture*, p. 112–113.

6. I have used the same fictitious names for my sources in all the writing I have done on the devotion to Saint Jude, so more information about Clara's experience of the saint and her understanding of the devotion can be found elsewhere.

7. "Inorganic intellectuals" refers to Gramsci's typology of the various patterns of connection that might characterize different social classes and the men and women who articulate, define, and explore their values, purposes, and histories. An "organic" intellectual is rooted in the praxis of his or her working-class

people; "traditional" intellectuals are the familiar educated elite, which practices its arts apart from the customs and concerns of the working classes. See *Selections from the Prison Notebooks* (New York: International Publishers, 1971), pp. 5–23, 326–343.

8. Thomas A. McAvoy, C.S.C., "The Ave Maria After 100 Years," *Ave Maria* 101, no. 18 (1 May 1965): 6–9, 21.

9. An excellent discussion of this revival of American anti-Catholicism can be found in Lawrence H. Fuchs, *John F. Kennedy and American Catholicism* (New York: Meredith Press, 1967), pp. 71–150.

10. I have benefited here again from Fuchs, *John F. Kennedy and American Catholicism,* and from Gerald P. Fogarty, *The Vatican and the American Hierarchy* (Stuttgart: Anton Hiersemann, 1982). For an interesting discussion of the changing patterns of Cardinal Spellman's relations with Vatican officials in these years, see John Cooney, *The American Pope: The Life and Times of Francis Cardinal Spellman* (New York: Times Books, 1984).

11. Ethel Marbach, "Liturgical Customs from Many Lands for the Family Through the Year We Have Tried at Our House," *Ave Maria* 102, no. 4 (24 July 1965): 14–15.

12. Robert F. Griffin, "De Senectute," *Ave Maria* 96, no. 16 (20 October 1962): 20–22, 28.

13. See, for example, Frank Calkins, O.S.M., "Our Lady of Childbirth," *Ave Maria* 96, no. 14 (6 October 1962): 23–25.

14. Gary MacEoin, "Has the Rosary Survived the Council?" *Ave Maria* 104, no. 2 (9 July 1966): 12–14, 28.

15. See, for example, C. J. McNaspy, "The Fracas About Saints," *America* 120 (24 May 1969): 608; "The Case of Therese Neumann," *Ave Maria* 96, no. 14 (6 October 1962); Joachim DePrada, C.M.F., "The Meaning of Saint Jude," *Voice of Saint Jude* (October 1954): 8.

16. This theme of the word runs through the literature of the period. See, for example, Valentine A. McInnes, O.P., "The Liturgy of the Word and the Rosary," *Homiletic and Pastoral Review* 65 (May 1965): 648–654, and A. Longley, "Make Christian Burial Christian," *Ave Maria* 99, no. 25 (20 June 1964): 289–297.

17. One of the clearest and most succinct reviews of this history is Murray G. Murphey, "On the Scientific Study of Religion in the United States, 1870–1980," In *Religion and Twentieth-Century American Intellectual Life,* ed. Michael J. Lacey (Cambridge: Cambridge University Press, 1989), pp. 136–171; see also Eric J. Sharpe, *Comparative Religion: A History* (LaSalle, Ill.: Open Court, 1986).

18. James's phrase is from *The Varieties of Religious Experience* (New York: New American Library, 1958), p. 42.

19. American Judaism has fared better, beginning with Barbara Meyerhoff's important *Number Our Days: A Triumph of Continuity and Culture Among Jewish Old People in an Urban Ghetto* (New York: Simon and Schuster, 1978) and since then by her students and others, but this has been mainly the work of anthropologists and folklorists, not of scholars of religion. See Jack Kugelmass, ed., *Between Two Worlds: Ethnographic Essays on American Judaism* (Ithaca, N.Y.: Cornell University Press, 1988).

20. Vincent Crapanzano, *Tuhami: Portrait of A Moroccan* (Chicago: University of Chicago Press, 1980), p. 144.

21. When Freud used this term, he was describing occasions on which he believed children actually witnessed some form of sexual exchange between

their parents. I am using it more broadly to refer to encounters of many different forms between child and parent that the child understands to be of particular importance and gravity. Because such glimpses are had in the exciting world of the family romance, they may be charged with libidinal energies and shaped by all the varied mechanisms of the unconscious.

22. Paul Rabinow, *Reflections on Fieldwork in Morocco* (Berkeley: University of California Press, 1977), p. 79.

23. See Mary Louise Pratt, "Fieldwork in Common Places," in Clifford and Marcus, *Writing Culture,* pp. 27–50.

24. Paul Hendrickson, *Seminary: A Search* (New York: Summit Books, 1983), pp. 36–37.

25. James Baldwin's description of his father's storefront church in *Go Tell It On the Mountain,* for another example of this, includes the noise of the fallen world coming in through the big, covered, plate-glass windows of the saved and offering them a further reminder of their difference and specialness. Malcolm X took the squeals of pigs about to be slaughtered coming from the packing house next door to the Detroit temple as signs of the uncleanliness and the depravity of the non-Muslim world outside and his need to be ever vigilant about it.

26. A wonderful exception to this is Kugelmass's treatment of marginal members of the synagogue in *The Miracle of Intervale Avenue,* see especially pp. 55–81, 109–117.

27. Bronislaw Malinowski, *A Diary in the Strict Sense of the Term* (New York: Harcourt, Brace, and World, 1967), p. 41.

28. Robin Horton, "African Traditional Thought and Western Science," in *Rationality,* ed. Bryan R. Wilson (Oxford: Basil Blackwell, 1970), pp. 131–171.

29. Thomas Simmons, *The Unseen Shore: Memories of a Christian Science Childhood* (Boston: Beacon Press, 1991), p. 55.

30. Sartre, *Search for a Method,* p. 91. Sartre, in an interview in the *New York Review of Books* (26 March 1970), identified this as his understanding of freedom.

31. Clifford Geertz, "Deep Play: Notes on the Balinese Cockfight," in *The Interpretation of Cultures,* ed. Clifford Geertz (New York: Basic Books, 1973), p. 449. The transmission of religious idioms to children offers an illuminating perspective on the ways a sentimental education is acquired and functions; see David Heller, *The Children's God* (Chicago: University of Chicago Press, 1986).

32. Rev. Troy D. Perry, with Thomas L. Spicewood, *Don't Be Afraid: The Story of Troy Perry and the Metropolitan Community Churches* (New York: St. Martin's Press, 1990).

33. For a provocative study of the changing place of anger in American culture, see Carol Zisowitz Stearns and Peter N. Stears, *Anger: The Struggle for Emotional Control in America's History* (Chicago: University of Chicago Press, 1986).

34. I am working here from Sartre's definition of "mediations" as those that "allow the individual concrete—the particular life, the real and dated conflict, the person—to emerge from the background of the *general* contradictions of productive forces and the relations of production" (*Search for a Method,* p. 57).

35. Jackson, *Paths Toward a Clearing,* p. 20.

36. Stanley A. Leavy, *The Psychoanalytic Dialogue* (New Haven: Yale University Press, 1980), p. 30. Paul Rabinow, writing in *Reflections* about anthropological research, notes that understanding is "mutually constructed" by ethnographer and informant in a process that transforms both (p. 38).

37. Leavy, *Psychoanalytic Dialogue,* pp. 29–30.

38. Clifford Geertz, "Thick Description: Toward an Interpretive Theory of Culture," in *The Interpretation of Cultures,* p. 10. Elsewhere in this volume Geertz notes that the "culture of a people is an ensemble of texts, themselves ensembles, which the anthropologist strains to read over the shoulders of those to whom they properly belong" ("Deep Play: Notes on the Balinese Cockfight," p. 452).

39. Jackson, *Paths Towards a Clearing,* p. 4. For Jackson, this exercise reveals the "the grounds of a common humanity," "the continuity of experience across cultures and through time."

40. For a powerful account of the use of one's own experience in the process of understanding another person's (in this case in a culture different from the ethnographer's), see Renato Rosaldo, "Grief and a Headhunter's Rage: On the Cultural Force of the Emotions," in *Text, Play and Story: The Construction and Reconstruction of Self and Society,* ed. E. M. Bruner (Proceedings of the American Ethnological Society, Washington D.C., 1984), pp. 178–195.

41. Gananath Obeyesekere, *The Work of Culture: Symbolic Transformation in Psychoanalysis and Anthropology* (Chicago: University of Chicago Press, 1990), p. 230.

42. Obeyesekere, *The Work of Culture,* p. 226.

43. Joseph M. Murphy, *Santeria: An African Religion in America* (Boston: Beacon Press, 1988), p. 129.

44. This point itself became clearer to me in a long discussion of this paper with a graduate student, Sarah Pike, and I am grateful for her help.

45. Sartre, *Search for a Method,* p. 72.

46. James Clifford, *The Predicament of Culture: Twentieth-Century Ethnography, Literature, and Art* (Cambridge, Mass.: Harvard University Press, 1988), pp. 51–52.

47. Karen McCarthy Brown's *Mama Lola: A Vodou Priestess in Brooklyn* (Berkeley: University of California Press, 1991) is an important effort at this kind of experimentation.

48. Jonathan Z. Smith, "Fences and Neighbors: Some Contours of Early Judaism," in *Imagining Religion: From Babylon to Jonestown* (Chicago: University of Chicago Press, 1982), p. 6.

Denominations as Bilingual Communities

ROBERT BRUCE MULLIN

In the year 1863, in the midst of one the bloodiest years of the American Civil War, an ecclesiastical squall erupted within the Episcopal Church concerning, of all things, who should be reckoned the true founder of the Episcopal Church. For John Henry Hopkins, Jr., writing in the *Church Journal,* the true patriarch of the church was Samuel Seabury, the first bishop of Connecticut. The editors of the Philadelphia-based *Episcopal Recorder* were equally adamant in claiming the title for William White, the first bishop of Pennsylvania.[1] Incidents such as this pepper the histories of America's religious denominational communities but usually fail to find a place either in traditional denominational historical accounts or in general American histories such as those of the Civil War. What, if any, relationship such an incident might have to the broader culture and how one might illumine the other remain unexplored.

I

Let us, however, begin at the beginning. This essay attempts to formulate a new model for understanding the role of a denomination in its society, but it recognizes that denominationalism has always been something of an enigma for the historian interested in neat categories. Although the term is constantly used, the student of denominations admits they are neither fish nor fowl—they are like neither an historic church nor a sect—but are in some ways a tertium quid. What interpretive paradigm can be invoked to make sense of this phenomenon?

It must be further acknowledged from the outset that the term denominationalism also has a certain looseness of meaning. The term originally arose to characterize a distinctly Protestant ecclesiastical compromise, and as late as 1960 it was often used in this restrictive sense. Since that time it has taken on a more general connotation and has been used to categorize most American religious communities.[2] As its perimeters have been expanded, its definition has become less precise. Nonetheless, although there is no universal consensus as to a precise definition, most persons would agree that a denomination almost always is a nonexclusive community—in practice, if not in theory. The church historian Winthrop Hudson has argued, "The basic contention of the denominational theory of the church is that the true church is not to be identified with a particular ecclesiastical institution."[3] The theme of nonexclusivity as the defining mark of the denomination has also been emphasized by the British sociologist David A. Martin, who has written, "[T]he denomination merely claims that while there are doubtless many keys to many mansions it is at least in possession of one of them, and that anyone who thinks he has the sole means to open the heavenly door is clearly mistaken."[4]

Denominations (and especially members of denominations) find it easier to cooperate and to find common ground with members of other religious communities than do members of more exclusive communities, and this has led some to emphasize the implicit ecumenical aspect of denominationalism. It is readily acknowledged that there are often exclusive claims embedded in the theology of individual denominations, but on the practical or functional level cooperation and nonexclusivity seem to win out.[5] Furthermore, denominations are usually seen as occupying a position different from that held by sects or churches vis-à-vis their culture. Denominations neither include the culture they inhabit nor separate from it but exist in ambiguous relationship with it, sometimes affirming it but at other times striking out on their own. All in all, compromise and ambiguity, rather than boldness and precision, have been the adjectives employed to describe denominationalism.

Recognition of this ambiguity has made the study of denominations more problematic in recent years. If the historical health and success of denominational families in American life had earlier led some scholars to an overestimation of their importance, the crisis of identity more recently experienced by the older denominations has in turn cast a shadow upon the past. Were denominations ever meaningful in shaping or guiding the lives of their members, or were they merely meeting places for persons of very different worldviews and agendas? Were they not always distinctions without a difference, more analogous to bus stations (where people with individual itineraries met) than to families? Indeed, the thrust of some of the most fruitful of recent scholarship has argued that the important religious categories are either broader than that of denominationalism (such as evangelicalism or gender) or more restricted (such as regional or ethnic subcategories).[6] The study of denominations (so this argument continues) may be of antiquarian value, but it sheds little light on either the real religious life of individuals or on the wider historical narrative.

I believe that these conclusions are mistaken. It is true that denominations have a different relationship with both the society and other religious communities than either do churches or sects, but this makes them more important, not less.

II

It has become something of a commonplace in recent years to speak of religious communities as communities of discourse or, more generally, as language communities. Inspired originally by anthropologists such as Clifford Geertz, this understanding has been central to the modern renaissance of postliberal theology, particularly through the labors of the theologian George Lindbeck. A central assumption of these theologians has been the power of language to shape human perception and understanding. Lindbeck, for example, appeals to the now famous example of a tribe that, not possessing a verbal category to differentiate between green and blue, seemed unable to discriminate between these two colors. According to Lindbeck, religious systems function in a similar way:

> A religion can be viewed as a kind of cultural and/or linguistic framework or medium that shapes the entirety of life and thought. It functions something like a Kantian *a priori* although in this case the *a priori* is a set of required skills that could be different. It is not primarily an array of beliefs about the true and the good (though it may involve these), or a symbolism of expressive attitudes, feelings, or sentiments (though these will be generated). Rather, it is similar to an idiom that makes possible the description of realities, the formulation of beliefs, and the experiencing of inner attitudes, feelings, and sentiments. Like a culture or language, it is a communal phenomenon that shapes the subjectivities of individuals rather than being primarily a manifestation of those subjectivities. It comprises a vocabulary of discursive and nondiscursive symbols together with a distinctive logic or grammar in terms of which this vocabulary can be meaningfully deployed. Lastly, just as a language . . . is correlated with a form of life, and just as a culture has both cognitive and behavioral dimensions, so it is also in the case of a religious tradition. Its doctrines, cosmic stories, or myths, and ethical directives are integrally related to the rituals it practices, the sentiments or experiences it evokes, the actions it recommends, and the institutional form it develops. All this is involved in comparing a religion to a cultural-linguistic system.[7]

The British philosopher Janet Martin Soskice has also emphasized this parallel between religion and cultural-linguistic communities with her call for a social theory of doctrine that ties religious statements to particular communities.[8]

A religious tradition, from this perspective, is a social way to talk about and to respond to the divine. A corollary notion for these theologians is that of narrative or story. All communities possess a story, that is, a common memory or history. The story serves a variety of functions. It not only provides a sense of coherence and self-definition but serves as the central framework for the language of the community. The more one internalizes the story, the more the rules of discourse become apparent. The biblical story of the passion, for example, becomes formative of the way in which we may make theological assertions about Jesus. Furthermore, the story in turn provides a lens through which the community can interpret the larger world. The tradition serves as a "vast loosely-structured non-fictional novel."[9] As these writers continue, meaning is shaped by the narrative and the text and then flows from the story to the world as interpreted through the story, which they contrast with the alternative tendency of liberal theologies to bring to the text meaning systems that have their roots outside the text. Finally, according to this view, an essential practical function of the community is to initiate its members into the story, through socialization and/or catechesis.

Although the postliberal theory has been largely used by theologians, it nonetheless provides many helpful hints to historians of denominations (though to be sure, many persons other than the current postliberal theologians have employed the metaphor of a religious community as a community of discourse).[10] It has long been recognized that whatever the role of theology within denominational communities might be, it is not often definitional. But it is from the postliberal theologians that one gains an awareness of what might be the function of theology—namely, to provide the grammar for discourse.[11] Hence, on first glance the postliberal theory appears particularly useful in making both historical and sociological sense of religious communities such as the denominations and in highlighting the nature of their particularism. A central function of a denomination (like any religious community) is the inculcating of a common language and story. It is undoubtedly true that a community like the Episcopal Church can be understood far more as a linguistic and cultural system than as a theologically defined community. Its liturgy provides a classic form of sacred vocabulary that reverberates in the public utterances of numerous historical figures. When one reads the notes and letters of the early Elizabeth Ann Seton (who, although better known as a Catholic saint, was earlier a devout Episcopal laywoman), for example, one finds the language of the Anglican liturgy shaping her religious experience; of her newly baptized daughter she wrote, "Oh that we may receive the fulness of his grace and remain in the number of his faithful children—that being stedfast [*sic*] in faith, joyful thro hope and rooted in charity she may so pass the waves of this troublesome world that finally she may enter the land of everlasting life." Here Seton is paraphrasing a prayer for baptism, but throughout the early pages of her journal one hears the echoes of liturgical language, and these words she admitted "sooth and encourage ... and insensibly diffuse a holy composure."[12] Indeed, evidence of Episcopal liturgical language reverberates even in the public proclamations of Franklin Delano Roosevelt.[13]

Although a liturgical denomination is the most obvious example of an inculcator of language, other communities also are linked by a common language or vocabulary rooted in any number of areas (hymnody, spirituality, catechesis). Many of the essays contained in this volume have accurately noted the role of denominations as preservers of a distinctive story that provides meaning to its members.

Yet, when pressed, the analogy bogs down. Let us remember that one of the central characteristics of those denominations we are here examining is their nonexclusive nature. This factor, coupled with the recognition that denominations often appeal to persons who are to a large degree assimilated within the general society and culture, suggests a paradoxical positioning of the denomination with regard to the larger society. Part of a denomination's self-understanding is grounded in a unique ecclesiastical tradition that links it to an older past, whether churchly or sectarian. At the same time these denominations have recognized that they also shared membership in a wider culture that marched, if not to a different drummer, at least to a different cadence. If the narrow ecclesiastical tradition serves as a community of discourse linking the American denomination both to its pre-American roots and to its non-American compatriots, the culture of the society likewise offers a second community of discourse that allows fellowship across denominational boundaries. An obvious example of this latter point is the power of national festivals such as Thanksgiving, which derives not only from the civil religion but from the fact that such holidays reflect a spirit of functional ecumenism within the denominational worldview. This ecumenism stands in contrast to other strands that emphasize denominational particularity.

To isolate this tension between particularity and ecumenism, one has only to reflect on how different hymns and sacred songs affect individuals and communities. The hymn "A Mighty Fortress Is Our God" has a powerful meaning for American Lutherans. As the most famous hymn associated with their founder, it evokes a sense of the specialness of the Lutheran story and the connectedness of American Lutherans with other Lutherans throughout the world. Other communities have their own special hymns.

In contrast, some hymns inspire not a particularism but a sense of commonality. The great appeal of many of the well-known Christmas carols (probably most especially "Silent Night") is grounded in a common religious sensibility that transcends particularity. The power of these common hymns should not be underestimated; indeed, many observers have commented upon them.[14] A close reading of American history shows that these hymns have often popped up when Americans desired to emphasize their unity. In the American South through the Second World War, for example, the song "Onward Christian Soldiers" was often sung at at high school graduation ceremonies, and in 1952, when the delegates pledged to Senator Robert A. Taft entered the Republican presidential nominating convention, they expressed their solidarity and their unity of purpose by singing the same hymn. In both cases, the appeal was not only the bouncing melody (although this of course should not be underestimated) but also the song's imagery of a unity of belief and purpose. One of the hymn's great images is contained in its line "we are not divided; all one body we," which has often been used to express the solidarity of the wider transdenominational community. A denomination hence straddles two cultures, one made up of a particular tradition and the other comprising the wider social tradition. The cultural-linguistic world of a denomination, whatever its inner logic, generally does not make exclusive claims. During most periods of history one did not have to convert to a denomination's language in any absolute sense that involved the eschewing of all other traditions in order to be a member of the community. Rather, one merely shared in it with the community and accepted the community's tradition as an alternative reality that could inform but need not necessarily dictate an understanding of the larger world. Likewise, as a community itself the denomination did not feel constrained to act in accordance only with its ecclesiastical past, at times it could chart its course of action by accepting the guidance of the general culture.

Let us take again an example from the Episcopal Church. Perhaps because of that denomination's long-standing place in the society, it is easy to overlook the dissonance between the world as symbolized in nineteenth-century Episcopal worship and that of the national culture. The world of worship used a different language and a different concept of time. The anachronistic language of Elizabethan England continued to be the norm, and the church year was pointedly out of step with all other ways of rendering time. Its use of vestments and ornaments also suggested a concept of aestheticism and a hierarchy of values very different from that found in other parts of nineteenth-century American culture, with its concern for republican simplicity. Similarly, one easily forgets how the bodily actions called for in Episcopal worship—bowing, kneeling, breast beating—clashed with almost every other aspect of an egalitarian and democratic society. All were bodily actions having few if any parallels within the broader society. In its language, ceremony, and architectural setting, Episcopal worship evoked the ideas of hierarchy and subordination, reverence for tradition, and a distancing from the concerns of the secular world. It offered to the worshipper a very different reality from that found outside the house of worship. Nor was this accidental. As one writer commented, "It is conformable to a law of our nature that the excitement and expression of feeling of devotion should be aided by those exterior embellishments that delight the eye and gratify the taste, and thus—for there is an intimate association between all our powers—enlighten the understanding and elevate the heart."[15] The experience of this reality offered in turn a vantage point from which to view anew the society as a whole. Later writers were adamant on this point.

[P]ublic worship is the voicing and ... making operative of public religion,
and this is in a sense a "new creature," an entity that ... is something
more than the sum of personal religion of the several individuals. ...
There may be something implicit in the spiritual atmosphere that incar-
nates itself in one or more persons, and that thereafter the power that
becomes operative for good or ill is the energy contributed by the coalesc-
ing in a dynamic unity of so many individual souls, to whom, in one unit,
is vouchsafed a certain outpouring of the Holy Spirit ... that exalts it to
new altitudes of attainment and accords it a greater force. ... Personal and
corporate action towards political, economic, industrial, social reform is
good, but "these actions that a man might play" and they can be but
palliative and temporary unless there is behind them the spiritual regeneration that will change the tempor of the people as a whole, and by its
very nature, public worship ... is, as it has always been, one of the most
fruitful agencies of operation.[16]

As a sometime student of the history of the Episcopal Church, I could
multiply such examples and have, in arguing for the importance of a
distinctive Episcopal vision in American culture that provided a lens for
seeing the world in the way described by the postliberal theologians. Nor
is this true only in the realm of worship; others have shown how this
distinctive vision shaped much of the Episcopal Church's understanding
of its place in the social order.[17] Its worldview or language was remarkably consistent and well worked out. Yet I am always conscious of my
selectivity with the historical record and realize that, if I were so inclined,
I could supply an equal amount of Episcopal rhetoric (some indeed from
the same people) that would be virtually indistinguishable from the language of other religious (or even nonreligious) contemporaries. Other
historians have looked at the same period and seen a decline in ecclesiastical distinctiveness.[18]

I suspect that this paradox can be found in other communities. There
is no single unified voice in denominational discourse. At times it is
rooted in a distinctive and exclusive denominational consciousness; at
other times it is based upon the grammar of the larger culture. This
paradox most likely grows out of the nonexclusive nature of denominational self-identification. Part of the denominational compromise has
been that its alternative perspective is not dictated to members of the
community but rather exists for the taking.

Let us return, then, to our metaphor and refine it slightly. The
denominational communities we have set out to examine are in one
sense cultural-linguistic communities, but what is significant is that their
participants are "bilingual"—members of the community are fluent in
both the language of their particular community *and* that of the wider
society, either religiously or sociopolitically conceived. The average
well-catechized denomination member has at his or her own disposal
two independent structures of discourse, each with its own distinctive
symbols and stories and each with its own grammar and rules of dis-

course. Once one acknowledges the bilingual nature of the denominational community, one can plumb the metaphor. There has been, for example, an inordinate amount of scholarly research on the phenomenon of bilingual communities.[19] For linguists, the central question is why a person or group with two languages at its disposal chooses to use one or the other. These scholars note that one standard bilingual pattern is what is called "diglossia," in which members of a community organize language use into divided spheres, with a separate language appropriate for the distinctive spheres. Charles V, of France is probably the most famous example of an elaborated diglossia. "To God I speak Spanish," he is supposed to have said, "to women Italian, to men French, and to my horse—German."[20] A more common example of diglossia is a person bilingual in German and English who speaks German at home and English in the business world. These two worlds, the German and the English, however, remain largely separate.

Once one chooses to picture denominations as bilingual communities, it becomes apparent that for large parts of their experience the relationship between the language of the inner theological/linguistic tradition and that of the broader culture (whether socially or even religiously conceived) broadly resembles that of diglossia. The fact that an Episcopal businessperson worships in a gothic revival building using an archaic language does not often affect the worshiper's understanding of his or her secular calling. The two worlds exist simultaneously and in a nonconflicting way. Yet linguists refer to a second phenomenon common to bilingualism known as "code switching," or switching from one language to another, sometimes within the same thought. It is "a communicative resource that builds on the participants' perception of two contrasting languages. . . . [It] is meaningful in much the same way that lexical choice is meaningful: it is a verbal strategy, used in the same way that a skillful writer might switch styles in a short story."[21]

Reasons for code switching are many, but two stand out. The first has to do with the limitations of one language in expressing an accurate or precise meaning, or the perceived inability to express something essential. Since English has no appropriate simple term with which to compliment the graciousness of a host as he or she sets down a plate of food before a guest, a bilingual guest may inadvertently say *"Bitte,"* even though the rest of the conversation is in English. A second reason for code switching is for the sake of emphasis and to establish an intimate relationship with members of the audience who share the common language. This idea of code switching seems to me to be important in pinpointing the central dynamic of a denomination in American society. As we have suggested, the two languages of a mainline denomination— the special or esoteric language of its particular tradition and the common or exoteric language of the wider society—allow its members to position themselves either as insiders or as outsiders, depending upon the situation. Whereas these two languages often function in an independent and complementary way, there are periods in a community's history that are parallel to code switching, that is, when either the special language of the community affects and shapes the relationship of persons to the larger society or the language of the larger society forces its vocabulary upon the language of the denomination.

III

Let me use as an example an aspect of the history of the Episcopal Church in America. As I have argued elsewhere, one of the side effects of the American Revolution and of the extended debate over the place of the church in the new American society was the emergence of a distinctive Episcopal high-church ethos that emphasized the dissimilarity between the spirit of the church and that of the larger society.[22] Whereas there had always been (at least implicitly) a disjunction between Episcopal liturgy, theology, and worship and the broad cultural patterns of antebellum society, these high-church writers consciously chose not only to emphasize the dissimilarity but to use the language and the concepts of the ecclesia to offer criticism of the democratic cultural trends that Nathan Hatch has sketched so well in his *Democratization of American Christianity*.[23] Their community was viewed as an ark of refuge, a place psychologically outside the democratic social swirl where cultural trends might be evaluated and critiqued. Thus, in the works of writers such as John Henry Hobart, John Henry Hopkins, and Calvin Colton one can observe this psychological separation of self from the dominant trends of public discourse and an appeal to the vision of the true church as a corrective to the spirit of the age. The titles of the works themselves—*An Apology for Apostolic Order, Protestant Jesuitism,* and *The Primitive Church*—reflect this sense of distancing from the more popular trends of the society, usually castigated as "the spirit of the age." They seem to glory in the exceptionalism of the Episcopal Church and its angularity toward the general cultural ethos.

For a person like Hobart, the position of the Episcopal Church was analogous to that of the early church in the pre-Constantinian era—a small but distinct community in an alien environment. A central assumption was that the church was a community automous from the general culture, subject to its own values and presuppositions. In defending his views Hobart proclaimed, "I shall . . . have the consolation of having faithfully borne my testimony to the principles of the Apostolic and primitive Church, to principles which 'the noble army of martyrs' confessed in their writings, in their lives, in the agonies of those cruel deaths, to principles which in every age have ranked among their advocates . . . intrepid champions of divine truth."[24] It is hard to overestimate the rhetorical and psychological importance of this identification with the early church. Even the most cursory readings of either the works mentioned above or of the private papers of their authors convinces one that they were far more caught up in the world of John Chrysostom than that of John Quincy Adams. Indeed, in order to maintain the desired psychological distance between the church and the world, clerical leaders often did not vote in political elections, and even the propriety of praying for deceased political leaders was hotly debated.

Finally, as I have also tried to show, this vision of the Episcopal Church as a denominational community out of step with its contemporaries grew in persuasiveness, first during the 1830s as other Protestant churches began to divide over questions of revivalism and social reform and even more so during the decades of the 1840s and 1850s as the nation itself seemed to be moving towards disunion. The crisis in the general culture made the alternative reality of the Episcopal community more attractive and persuasive, and by the 1850s what had begun as a peculiarity of the high-church party had become a standard part of Episcopal self-description.

Let us return to the historical incident with which I began this essay—the debate in the midst of the Civil War as to who was the true founder of the Episcopal Church. The Civil War was a time of great crisis for this theological community. As James Moorhead and others have shown, northern evangelical Christians became caught up in a millennial understanding of the war and saw its ramifications in religious categories such as "the coming of the Lord," to use Julia Ward Howe's famous phrase (or at least the coming of his kingdom).[25] The excitement gave a religious significance to the war effort and served to unite northern Protestants in a great crusade that had strong ecumenical implications. Those Episcopalians, however, who maintained the traditional high-church language and worldview were separated from such trends. Their language offered no vocabulary or structure conducive to expressing these themes of millennial expectation and ecumenical cooperation. Their situation was somewhat analogous to that tribal community that, lacking a verbal category to distinguish green and blue, was unable to discriminate between these colors. An examination of Episcopal public pronouncements at the outbreak of the war reveals a coolness in rhetoric that stands in marked contrast to the exalted millennial language of others. A study of private Episcopal responses to the war shows, in contrast, that from the very beginning many individual Episcopalians were drawn to the attractiveness of the millennial discourse with its nationalistic and ecumenical assumptions and felt constrained by the limitations imposed upon them by the traditional esoteric high-church Episcopal categories. The journal of the prominent Episcopal layman George Templeton Strong gives evidence of the growing attraction to the current millennialism; in the diary one finds by the early war years clear examples of code switching, or the employment of religious language and rhetoric that had its roots not in the narrow ecclesiastical tradition but in the larger societal tradition. Such language is almost completely absent in his earlier entries but emerges with force in the early 1860s. An example is his reflections on the hanging of the American flag on the tower of Trinity Church in New York. Earlier in his diary he had spoken confidently in the language of the independence of the church from the spirit of the age. But with the firing upon Fort Sumter, his language changed dramatically. The placing of a national symbol on the church was

> an unprecedented demonstration, but these are unprecedented times. . . . [T]he ideas of Church and State, Religion and Politics, have been practically separated so long that people are specially delighted with any manifestation of the Church's sympathy with the State and recognition of our national life on any fitting occasion. The flag was the symbol of the truth that the Church is no esoteric organization, no private soul saving society.[26]

Strong used the word *esoteric* here in a way different from the way it has been employed in this essay, yet we can sense the irony. Earlier the esoteric nature of his church had been part of its strength and identity; here it is seen as part of its weakness.

The debate, then, over the iconic role of Samuel Seabury or William White was symbolic of this debate over code switching, or, more precisely, over the appropriate code or language with which best to make sense of the crisis of the 1860s. Seabury represented (to his defenders) a rigid high-church tradition. During the American Revolution he had been willing to endure condemnation by the patriotic forces in order to be true to his ecclesiastical tradition. He symbolized the integrity and the uncompromising spirit of the ecclesiastical tradition and, by implication, the sufficiency of the intraecclesiastical language. White, in turn, represented the spirit of openness to the political and psychological world of the new republic. He was willing to accept the language from outside of the church and the necessity of balancing internal and external discourse. White accepted appointment as chaplain to the Continental Congress and was always willing to seek a common ground that might help anchor the Episcopal Church in the broader community. It is perhaps significant that iconographically Seabury and White were pictured by their supporters in fundamentally different ways. The favorite portrait of Seabury showed him with the visage of an Old Testament prophet, windswept against a stormy background, yet standing against the storm. White, in contrast, was often pictured in a style reminiscent of the later portraits of George Washington, as a patriarchal figure, reflecting the wisdom of years. The differing styles of portraiture suggested two decidedly different visions of the role of the Episcopal Church.

One might see the tension between the religious visions of Seabury and of White as a central organizing tension in the story of the Episcopal Church in America, but I want to return again to my thesis. If my analysis is correct, the tension between Seabury and White is the Episcopal reflection of a tension that lies deep within many denominations and is part of their bilingualism.

The idea of a nonexclusive alternative worldview plays a crucial part in the story of the mainline religious denominations in still another way, by providing their members with a dual citizenship. As Laurence Moore has argued, a central issue in American history has been the tension between insiders and outsiders.[27] Moore has used the insider/outsider distinction to explore the dynamic of outsider groups in American life and has suggested that communities such as the Mormons gain strength by juxtaposing their perceived outsider status with their participation in insider values. The reverse phenomenon also is the case. Few religious communities would more classically fit Moore's category of insider than the traditional denominations. Yet we have seen that their story involves both periods of active identification with the larger society and times of withdrawal and critique. Like other communities, at certain times they desire to be insiders; at other times, outsiders. Their bilingualism allows them to achieve this fluidity. When they use their fluency in the language of the general culture, they can speak as insiders, but when they choose their own special language, they take the role of outsiders. Historians of ethnicity have long noted the tension within ethnic communities between assimilation and pluralism, between a desire to identify with a larger culture and desire to maintain a particular identity, and the dialectical operation of these desires over time, with sometimes one predominating and sometimes the other.[28] To a lesser degree, denominational identity operates in a similar way. In times of crisis it serves as an alternative reality and the escape hatch of the insiders.

The tension between the inner life of the denominational community and its participation in the broader culture is the great unexplored facet of denominationalism. Here we should note that historical psychology and theology come together. As students of history we recognize that groups within a society always express some ambivalence about the society. At times they identify with and actively participate in it; at other times they feel estranged and psychologically withdraw from aspects of it.[29] Similarly, Christian theologians have recognized that the biblical injunctions to be "strangers and pilgrims" or to fear God and honor the king (I Peter 2:11, 17) and to be in the world but not of it have led to a variety of Christian attitudes about participation in the larger world. Both these understandings fit into my model of bilingualism. Hence the ambiguity: These churches' members find themselves occupying two worlds of discourse with varying degrees of comfort. This paradox, however, does not make denominationalism less important as a historical phenomenon, but more. Indeed, it raises a bevy of questions: Why is it that these two language systems can coexist for long periods without conflict? What happens when conflict does come? Are there any patterns in this religious code switching like those that seem to exist in linguistic code switching? Such questions may help breathe new life into the study of denominationalism.

NOTES

I would like to thank Grant Wacker and Russ Richey for their critical readings of earlier drafts of this essay and my colleague Mary Kathleen Cunningham for help in clarifying some of the theological ideas underlying the essay.

1. The debate, which took place in a number of other journals as well, is summarized in "The First Bishop of Connecticut and the *Episcopal Recorder,*" *The American Quarterly Church Review* 15 (1863): 30–76.

2. See, for example, Andrew Greeley, *The Denominational Society: A Sociological Approach to Religion in America* (Glenview, Ill.: Scott, Foresman and Co., 1972). For Greeley, a denomination was "any religious organization which emerges in a society which has no established church (official or unofficial) but permits and encourages the practice of religion by the various organized religious communities" (p. 79). Russell Richey has outlined a number of these divisions in his essay "Institutional Forms of Religion," in *Encyclopedia of the American Religious Experience: Studies of Traditions and Movements,* ed. Charles H. Lippy and Peter W. Williams, 3 vols. (New York: Charles Scribner's Sons, 1988), 1:31–50.

3. Winthrop Hudson, "Denominationalism as a Basis for Ecumenicity: A Seventeenth Century Conception," *Church History* 24 (1955): 32. This essay is also in Russell E. Richey, ed., *Denominationalism* (Nashville, Tenn.: Abingdon, 1977).

4. "The Denomination," *The British Journal of Sociology* 13 (1962): 5.

5. Even communities that formally maintain certain exclusive claims often deemphasize them in practice. For an interesting account of this phenomenon, see John Murray Cuddihy, *No Offense: Civil Religion and Protestant Taste* (New York: Seabury Press, 1978).

6. The literature on all of these topics is immense, and any list must be somewhat arbitrary. Of the many works on the question of religion and gender, Nancy Cott, *The Bonds of Womanhood: "Woman's Sphere" 1780–1835* (New Haven: Yale University Press, 1977), and Carol Smith-Rosenberg, *Disorderly Conduct: Visions of Gender in Victorian America* (New York: Knopf, 1985), are particularly persuasive. George Marsden and other evangelical historians have argued that evangelicalism functioned as a unifying force in many periods of American history and was of more importance than denominational particularity. See "The Evangelical Denomination," in *Evangelicalism and Modern America,* ed. George Marsden (Grand Rapids, Mich.: William B. Eerdmans Publishing Co., 1984). Historians of southern religion have often argued for the preeminence of regional identity in understanding American religion. See, in particular, the essays included in *Religion in the South,* ed. Charles Reagan Wilson (Jackson: University of Mississippi Press, 1985), and the many works by Samuel S. Hill, including his article "Religion" in *Encyclopedia of Southern Culture,* ed. Charles Reagan Wilson and William Ferris (Chapel Hill: University of North Carolina Press, 1989). Finally, on the question of ethnicity as the key to understanding American religious movements, see the bibliography provided by Richey in "Institutional Forms of Religion."

7. George A. Lindbeck, *The Nature of Doctrine: Religion and Theology in a Postliberal Age* (Philadelphia: Westminster Press, 1984), pp. 33, 37. Lindbeck, however, admits that this example (on the empirical level) has been challenged by a number of anthropologists. See p. 43, n. 14.

8. Janet Martin Soskice, *Metaphor and Religious Language* (Oxford: Clarendon Press, 1985), p. 151.

9. Lindbeck, *The Nature of Doctrine,* p. 121. Lindbeck is here quoting a

passage from the theologian David Kelsey's description of Karl Barth's view of scripture.

10. See, for example, James Gustafson's treatment of the church as community of language, interpretation, and memory in his *Treasure in Earthen Vessels: The Church as a Human Community* (New York: Harper and Brothers, 1961).

11. For an early (and classic) critique of the role of theology in defining denominations, see H. Richard Niebuhr's famous study, *The Social Sources of Denominationalism* (New York: Henry Holt and Co., 1929), p. vii.

12. See Ellin Kelly and Annabelle Melville, eds., *Elizabeth Seton: Selected Writings* (New York: Paulist Press, 1987), pp. 83–88.

13. See the Thanksgiving Day proclamation for 1932 in *The Public Papers and Addresses of Franklin D. Roosevelt,* 13 vols. (New York: Random House, 1938–50), 1:595.

14. Sydney Ahlstrom records a humorous example of the appeal of these hymns taken from the Broadway musical *Say Darling* (1958), in which hardened New York theatrical producers join in on the singing of the revival hymn "Let the Lower Lights Be Burning." See *A Religious History of the American People* (New Haven: Yale University Press, 1972), p. 846n.

15. John Henry Hobart, *The Worship of the Church on Earth, A Resemblance of that of the Church in Heaven . . .* (Philadelphia, 1823), p. 14.

16. Ralph Adams Cram, *Convictions and Controversies* (Boston: Marshall Jones, [1935]), pp. 226–227.

17. For a recent example, see David Hein, "The High Church Origins of the American Boarding School," *Journal of Ecclesiastical History* 42 (1991): 577–595.

18. See, for example, William H. Swatos, *Into Denominationalism: The Anglican Metamorphasis* ([Storrs, Conn.]: Society for the Scientific Study of Religion, 1979).

19. The literature on this subject is immense, but I have found of particular use Suzanne Romaine, *Bilingualism* (Oxford: Basil Blackwell, 1989); Francois Grosjean, *Life With Two Languages: An Introduction to Bilingualism* (Cambridge, Mass: Harvard University Press, 1982); and Wallace E. Lambert, *Language, Psychology, and Culture* (Stanford: Stanford University Press, 1972).

20. "Je parle espagnol à Dieu, italien aux femmes, français aux hommes et allemand à mon cheval." *Oxford Dictionary of Quotations,* 2nd ed. (New York: Oxford University Press, 1953), p. 136.

21. Grosjean, *Life With Two Languages,* p. 152. Grosjean has a full discussion of diglossia and code switching in ch. 3, and my discussion of these subjects (as well as the example of the use of the word *bitte*) is taken from him.

22. Robert Bruce Mullin, *Episcopal Vision/American Reality: High Church Theology and Social Thought in Evangelical America* (New Haven: Yale University Press, 1986).

23. Nathan Hatch, *Democratization of American Christianity* (New Haven: Yale University Press, 1989).

24. John Henry Hobart, *An Apology for Apostolic Order and its Advocates,* 2nd ed. (New York: Stanford & Swords, 1844), p. 16.

25. James H. Moorhead, *American Apocalypse: Yankee Protestants and the Civil War, 1860–1869* (New Haven: Yale University Press, 1976). See, too, Ernest Lee Tuveson, *Redeemer Nation: The Idea of America's Millennial Role* (Chicago: University of Chicago Press, 1968).

26. *The Diary of George Templeton Strong,* ed. Allan Nevins and Milton Halsey Thomas, 4 vols. (New York: Macmillan, 1952), 3:124–126.

27. R. Laurence Moore, *Religious Outsiders and the Making of America* (New York: Oxford University Press, 1986). See, too, his earlier essay "Insiders and Outsiders in American Historical Narrative and American History," *American Historical Review* 87 (1982): 390–412.

28. See, for example, Harold J Abrahamson, "Assimilation and Pluralism" in *The Harvard Encyclopedia of American Ethnic Groups* (Cambridge, Mass.: Harvard University Press, 1980).

29. For one case study of this phenomenon, see T. Jackson Lear, *No Place of Grace: Antimodernism and the Transformation of American Culture, 1880–1920* (New York: Pantheon Books, 1981).

Remembering, Recovering, and Inventing What Being the People of God Means: Reflections on Method in the Scholarly Writing of Denominational History

JAN SHIPPS

The fire fed by the bodies of Bishops Latimer and Ridley in 1555 still burns, but scholarly studies of the Reformation seem almost to have reduced the story of how the blood of Anglican martyrs became the seed of English Protestantism to that lovely quotation from Foxe's account in which Latimer told Master Ridley to "be of good cheer." For, said he, "we shall this day light such a candle, by God's grace, in England, as I trust shall never be put out."[1] This is not to say that modern critical histories of the English Reformation entirely ignore religious matters or even that they completely neglect the story of the persecutions endured by the Protestants during Queen Mary's reign. What happened where, when, and to whom is typically described, sometimes very well indeed. But modern scholars tend to look beyond religion for explanation, predicating the establishment of the Anglican Church on the crisis in the aristocracy, the politicization of the culture, the rise of the middle class, and other social factors.[2] Similarly, the flame that warmed John Wesley's heart flickers only faintly in the accounts of scholars who see the modernization of England in Methodism and use the Wesleyan movement to explain the "making of the English working class."[3]

Many critically acclaimed scholarly studies focus on these and other religious events, dealing with them directly and thoroughly. Yet because the authors of so many of these histories explain what happened to the faith of people, as well as the organization of the ecclesia, primarily in

terms of politics, economics, social class, or—since it is English history—
the amorous desires of kings, it is hard to find among them many particularly fine models for the scholarly writing of England's religious history.
Many historians also describe religion in America as a means to some end,
a way to make Americans, for example, or a means of masking the seeking
of power and social status.[4] Such studies explain a great deal about American society and culture, but they do not recount and explicate what
happened in a manner that makes their histories meaningful for the members of faith communities.

This historiographical circumstance points to the fact that two audiences exist for histories of religion. One is made up of the members of
communities of believers—in common parlance, the church. The other
is what those in religious communities call the world—which, in matters
historiographical, is represented by academia. No matter which audience
they intend to address, those who write the history of the religious
dimension of human experience, especially as it is manifested in corporate forms, must deal with essentially the same historical sources, the
same data sets. Yet the concerns of the historians who write for communities of believers and of those who write academic treatises diverge. These
two groups of historians pose different questions and consequently produce distinctively different accounts of what happened.

In the United States before World War II it was not really obvious just
how different these two forms of history are, at least insofar as the history
of American religion is concerned. Before that watershed conflagration,
this nation's multicultural character was hidden beneath a widely shared
impression of North America as a white, Anglo-Saxon, Protestant culture,
and the bases for such a perception were not hard to find. Despite consti-
tutionally mandated church-state separation, school prayer was virtually
a universal ritual, religious rhetoric was a staple of political discourse, and
all sorts of civic occasions opened with invocations that asked the blessings of Almighty God and closed with benedictions that ended by calling
on "the name of Jesus Christ."

Since these symbols and rituals represented the religion of white,
Anglo-Saxon Protestants, they and other symbols and rituals present at
key points in the public arena supported the conception of a WASP-ish
"Christian America." Furthermore, whether they were Protestant, non-
Protestant, non-Christian, or even unchurched, most citizens of the
United States saw the nation's Constitution as a civic covenant and consequently understood themselves as somehow exceptional, a covenanted
people. And this understanding was supported by the narratives that
informed Americans of their past, especially the text used in the public
schools that emphasized Puritans and pioneers and scripted the settlement of the country as a journey to a land of promise.[5]

Back then, the current lines of demarcation between audiences in
faith communities and those in the larger culture were not so sharply
drawn. As a result, the histories that interested one type of audience very

often appealed to the other, which is not surprising since institutions and leaders were emphasized in both. Whether describing the building of America for a scholarly or for a popular audience, the authors of histories of the nation concentrated on key figures—founders and pacesetters—and on the structures of government, business, and society. Whether penned by ministers or by members of college or seminary faculties, histories of American religion focused on clergy and institution, bricks and mortar.[6]

In such a situation, religious history was almost as acceptable as a scholarly pursuit as the political, economic, or what then passed for social history that provided the foundation for scholarly accounts of the nation's past. Although surveys of national history rarely recounted the story state by state, proceeding chronologically and thematically instead, whereas American religious history was generally organized within a denominational framework, each had a major theme. Civic history rang the changes on the growth of freedom (including religious freedom) and democracy. Religious history privileged Protestantism and pictured non-Protestant faith communities as more or less marginal. Like U.S. history texts, religious history was also written in a triumphal vein, and, because both kinds of historical accounts were dominated by the actions of white Anglo-Saxon men, it was quite as chauvinistic as the political and economic history of the day.

In spite of the fact that the importance of women to the religious life of the nation was seriously underestimated, they were at least integrated into the main text. By sheer dint of numbers, Roman Catholics also generally became a part of the narrative, even though an earmark of American religious history was its clear qualitative differentiation between Catholic and Protestant Christianity. But Protestant or not, the faith communities that historians of American religion regarded as sects and cults were relegated to the margin that brief capsule accounts signify. By cultural definition, Jewish and African-American communions likewise inhabited the margins.

In the decades following World War II, the consensus assumptions underlying civic history started to unravel, as did the unquestioning acceptance of mainstream Protestant hegemony, and historians and their readers alike began to be dissatisfied with a historiographical situation that posited substantive agreement about the way things were and are. In the area of religious history, the civil rights and the women's movements of the 1960s and '70s started to make denominational histories that were focused almost exclusively on white men seem outdated. And the reality of religious pluralism made accounts that privileged Protestantism appear hopelessly old-fashioned, particularly to intellectuals aware of the magnitude of the changes going on in American culture.

In addition, perceptions about the pertinence of standard denominational history were revised as many people switched their denominations as well as their residences when they moved from place to place. Left

with what might be described as religious orientations rather than enduring affiliations with particular faith communities, many readers became
less interested in the details describing a specific denomination's unfolding doctrine, institutional development, reform movements, and schisms.

Moreover, it was not just the audience for religious history that
changed. Many of the historians who had engaged in the writing of
religious or (as it was then called) church history—and many more of
their students—also became dissatisfied with its conventional forms.
This is evidenced by the shift that took place after mid-century away
from the study of ecclesiastical and institutional matters and toward a
focus on the experience of the people in the pews generally and especially of the women and the minorities who theretofore had been left
out. Although Sydney Ahlstrom's classic *Religious History of the American People* (1972) was, finally, more distinctive in the way it was organized than in the approach to the topic revealed through the text, the
shift in focus pushed religious history toward social history, a disciplinary subfield that, as a result of the increasing ease of electronic data
manipulation, was itself in the throes of methodological transformation.
Consequently, a number of church historians, chiefly those holding faculty positions in public institutions and private colleges and universities without close denominational affiliations, became enamored of technology and statistics.

It would be an overstatement to say that church historians suddenly
discovered power, money, and social class where before they had placed
the people in the communities of faith they studied in lay and clerical
categories and along continuums that ranged from pious to apathetic,
active to inactive, and generous to parsimonious. Yet it is certainly true
that when some of them started to take advantage of the data preserved in
census reports and church statistics, they began to write a very different
kind of history. And if there were not really large numbers of church
historians who themselves started to draw detailed information about
occupation, economic status, location and size of residence, and birth-
places of citizens and their parents (that is, ethnic data) from the manuscript census and then to link census and church records for sequential
decades both to determine demographic and social mobility and to define the ethnic character of local congregations and denominational bodies, the profession was influenced, perhaps inordinately, by those who
did. Histories that failed to address questions of social class, ethnicity, and
the place of women in the organization took on a musty, antique tone.

At about the same time, the altered cultural situation also led scholars
who wrote synthetic treatments of American religion to become more
inclusive, incorporating and frequently giving equal time to the stories of
many of the communities of faith that once had appeared to be marginal.
This mandated a more empirical approach that sometimes led scholars—
sociologists more often than historians—to organize the nation's multi-

plicity of religious groups according to criteria that made more sense in the academy than they did in chapels, churches, synagogues, or mosques.

The expanding fissure in the audience for studies of religion in America may be detected by examining the reaction to the altered approaches to the history of faith communities both in academia and in the communities themselves. In the Church of Jesus Christ of Latter-day Saints—the case I know best—the "new history" become a matter of concern to church authorities at the very highest level.[7] If this is at all indicative of a general trend, the change in the way professional historians were beginning to write religious/denominational history proved much less satisfactory to the faith communities whose histories were being written than to the scholarly community as that community is reflected in the book review sections of historical journals, as well as in the annual, semiannual, and regional meeting programs of the American Society of Church History and the North American Religion Section of the American Academy of Religion.

The principal ground for the dissatisfaction of both the leaders and the rank-and-file members of religious communities was (and is) not so much that the works themselves are filled with mistakes as that scholarly works somehow seem to tell their stories from the wrong angle, addressing questions of greater importance to the culture than to the faith community. In academia, the new history describing the interpenetration of religion and culture and measuring the impact of culture on religion were (and are) highly praised.[8] Traditional narrative histories of faith communities, on the other hand, have often been criticized as old-fashioned and their lack of intellectual rigor derided.

Few academicians seemed to appreciate how religious history serves faith communities as a sort of holy grail, failing to see that it is the vessel that contains the stories of beginnings and of God's dealing with humanity in past times that spark faith and pass belief from one person to another and from one generation to the next. But religious history does this only if it is the sort of account in which the hand of God is not removed from the action, a narrative that preserves the religious story and provides in it a recognizable a place for believers in both past and present times. For faith communities, the new social history and those revisionist histories that explain religion almost entirely in human terms simply do not fill the bill, whereas they are precisely the kinds of studies that receive scholarly acclaim.

Despite the dramatic changes in the culture and in the scholarly approach to the study of history sketched above, denominational histories written by members of the academy have not disappeared from the scene. Seminary faculty members and members of the history faculties of various institutions of higher learning continue to compose such accounts, often of their own denominations' histories. But as the process that transformed story telling into an academic discipline—a process that had been under way for decades—steadily accelerated after World War II, what once had been a steady stream was reduced to a trickle. And neither historians nor religious authorities seem to have fully anticipated what turning the chronicler's vocation into a profession would mean for the writing of histories of faith communities.

The emerging prominence of social history generated a substantial literature on method in the late 1960s and the 1970s, much of it having to do with the application of statistical techniques and sociological analysis to historical data.[9] For the most part, these methodological discussions recommended that religion be treated as one among a variety of variables to be investigated as a part of multivariate analysis. The goal was a demonstration of the direct connection between religious leadership and economic power, for example, or between gender and piety, or between any number of other pairs of variables. But the sanguine expectation that religion—and practically everything else—could be explained if enough data that could be digitized could be collected and analyzed did not go unchallenged. The late 1970s and the 1980s saw the emergence of neopragmatism in philosophical theology, a movement that generated a substantial body of discussion about how historical reality emerges from historical interpretation. William Dean, one of the leading thinkers in this area, describes this an "an unexpected development in recent American intellectual history" and points out that, among other things, neopragmatism calls into question the "cliometric historicism that seeks verification of historical claims through the strict use of quantitative methods."[10]

Notwithstanding this postmodernist critique (to which historians of religion would do well to pay close attention), the work of Paul Kleppner, Robert Swierenga, Richard Jensen, and a host of others demonstrates that explorations that treat religion as a function of economic status, for instance, or ethnicity, or social class can be perfectly legitimate and sometimes extremely useful academic enterprises.[11] As long as they treat religion as an epiphenomenon and deal membership in faith communities as just one of several key variables to be analyzed in order to explain what happened in the past, however, historians can write about the belief and the behavior arising from faith commitments without addressing the fundamental question of how to write about religion without reducing it to something that occurs with and seems to result from something else.

While the discussion of how to handle the study of religion as it functions in and is influenced by culture has proceeded apace, the bifurcation of the audience for works on religion has thus far failed to prompt much explicit methodological inquiry regarding writing about the faiths around which communities of believers coalesce and the history of the experiences of believers in such communities. There is an increasing awareness, however, that historians cannot treat religion as a dependent variable if they wish to study communities of faith and preserve religion as an irreducible element in the histories they write. That awareness led to the consultation that gave rise to this book.

What follows here are some observations, reflections, and recommendations about the writing of the histories of communities of faith from one who been directing her energies to that enterprise for decades. These include: (1) some general observations about an approach that holds out the possibility of building a bridge between religion as a part of social and cultural history (what many academics describe as the "scholarly" approach to religious history) and the scholarly enterprise of writing the history of faith communities; (2) some suggestions about how the work of historians of tightly bonded faith communities might be of help to those who write about communities of faith—particularly mainstream Protestant denominations—whose boundaries are so highly permeable in both directions that it is sometimes difficult to make distinctions between faith communities and the surrounding culture; and (3) some observations about the advantages and the disadvantages of writing religious history from outside and from inside particular faith communities.

In order to diminish the distance between history written for the church and that written for the world, historians of communities of belief, which for the sake of convenience will hereinafter be called denominational historians, should pay close attention to religion itself. One way a historian can do this is by naming and defining religion's constituent elements and pointing to their embodiment in the denomination under consideration. Referring with specificity to myth (which, in addition to Scripture, includes the stories of those who first believed), institutional structure (formal and informal), doctrine, ritual, and the social, ethical, and experiential dimensions of the religion being studied provides a set of categories, a shared language of analysis that makes intellectual rigor easier to demonstrate to the scholarly world. When they explore the interactions of these elements and dimensions, historians can more readily illustrate how religion generates belief and behavior that are amenable to analyses in which belief is treated as the independent variable, with behavioral variables dependent on belief—and vice versa. If it is used skillfully, this approach does not make the denomination's story inaccessible to the members of faith community.

Of perhaps even greater importance from the standpoint of re-imagining the scholarly writing of denominational history, this set of categories allows denominational historians to explore the interaction between Scripture, history, and faith. This examination inevitably leads to a recognition that early histories written by or about the founders of religious communities are not ordinary histories. This approach is helpful to denominational historians as they go about their work, and it also allows them to explain convincingly that, as the world understands history, such accounts are, in fact, not histories at all. In the eyes of the members of the faith communities in question, they take on the characteristics of Scripture (which is true by definition), rather than being seen as merely accounts and interpretations of what happened, accounts that are always open to continuing revision on the basis of new evidence. Since they tell of a time of direct divine-human interaction, within the bounds of faith communities, such accounts are sacred history and must be so recognized.

In addition to exploring sacred history, denominational historians are in a good position to treat the issue of canonization in connection with the religious history of the faith communities they study. While the canonizing of historical accounts occurs in the political, as well as the religious, arena—as recent developments in the histories of the former Soviet Union have made clear—the canonizing process is rarely well documented and consequently is often ignored. But canonization is sometimes so overt and so easily traced in religious communions that denominational historians can make significant contributions to historical knowledge by examining canonization in the historiography of the faith communions they study.

As is the case with so much else in denominational history, both the recognition of the historical accounts that have gained the status of sacred history and the explication of the process of canonization are easier to accomplish when fixed and stable boundaries surround a community of faith.[12] This is, however, only one of the exceptional advantages that come with studying communities of faith that are so tightly bonded that they function as ethnic groups.[13] Even when these communities are what sociologist Bryan Wilson calls "world-indifferent," rather than "world-denying," they maintain sharp and well-defined boundaries between themselves and others, insiders and outsiders, "them and us."[14] Consequently, participants in sectarian and cultic groups as well as members of non-Protestant and non-Christian communities are provided with positive as well as negative identities; from the standpoint of their relationship with the divine they know who they are (chosen, saved), as well as who they are not (gentile, damned).[15] Furthermore, because all communities of faith have a mechanism for conscious appropriation of membership (for example, confirmation and adult baptism and affirmation of faith), the state of being a part of the community is, at least theoretically, voluntary. There is, however, a great deal that is involuntary about being a member of such communities, and this involuntary side of things is likewise a part of the identity of community members.

This two-sided aspect of personal identity is illuminated, as is so much else, by the work of Robert Wuthnow. In a recent discussion of religion and personal identity, he separates the latter into what he calls *ascribed* and *achieved* dimensions, with the former referring to given attributes (such as gender and ethnicity) and the latter to statuses or features that are embraced or earned (church member, college graduate).[16] Applying Wuthnow's insight as an analytical device reveals more than one might expect about the population of tightly bonded communities of faith.

If members are "birthright" members or members of very long standing, they are not only connected to the group through the continuing affirmation of its religious claims that regular and wholehearted participation in public and private worship signifies; they are also connected to it ethnically and culturally, thus unifying the ascribed and the achieved dimensions of their personal identities within the framework of the faith community. Even if, at some point in their lives, members reject the theological and doctrinal underpinnings of the community's institutional structure and make a conscious decision to disclose their unbelief, they do not so easily shed the ethnic and cultural dimensions of their identity. As a result, much of its meaning-making and value-imparting structure stays with them.

By way of illustration, I recall the remark of a Latter-day Saint who had been "born in the covenant" but had lost his faith. Refusing an offer of coffee—as all Mormons must if they comply with the Mormon prophet's "Word of Wisdom" that forbids the consumption of coffee, tea, and alcohol—he said ruefully, "There's just no 'checkoutability' in this system." In LDS circles he was one of those who had moved over into the "Jack-Mormon" category, but what had happened to him is not unique to Mormonism. Many (perhaps all) faith communities have such categories—for instance, cultural Jews and ethnic Catholics. The people in these categories have given up active participation in the strictly religious facets of the corporate life of the community, but they retain their understanding of themselves as community members and often continue normal interaction with others in the community.[17]

This is not to say that people do not leave Mormonism, Roman Catholicism, the more sectarian forms of Protestantism, or any of the many other communities of faith that maintain high boundaries between themselves and others. Many do. But they seem to have more difficulty simply drifting into inactivity than do the many Protestants in the American mainstream who move away from birthright denominational domiciles. Some do not drift away, of course; they are converted to the acceptance of alternative theological and ecclesiastical systems, but their difficulty in fully "checking out," escaping the ethnic and cultural dimension of the personal identities that were ascribed and internalized as they grew up, is captured in the names of the groups some of them join: "Jews for Jesus," for instance, or "Saints Alive in Christ." Recognizing the dual character of personal identity also helps in making sense of how it is that some denominations seem readily to make converts, yet have real difficulty in turning them into members who stay the course.

From the perspective of denominational history, it is interesting to note the incredible interest in the history of their community shown by many of the people who have forsworn the theological tenets that are the reason for the community's existence and rejected the authority of the institution around which it is organized. In some instances, study of the community's history appears to be a surrogate for lost faith. In other instances, however, it becomes an effort to find hard evidence that can serve as justification for abandoning the community's creedal base. If the latter, and if the interest in history becomes a preoccupation that leads to writing about the community, very often the outcome is history that is tendentious in the extreme—history the community dismisses as "apostate." Although such slanted accounts do not provide good models for the scholarly writing of denominational history, they are useful to scholars as evidence of what can happen when the religious basis of personal identity is shattered.

Scholars who have learned to appreciate the utility of membership profiles from social history can take advantage of personal identity's double strand by drawing from within the community's belief and behavior patterns measures of the intensity of members' identification with the community along both dimensions. For the religious dimension, some possible measures are level of attendance and participation in worship, offices filled, and contributions of time and money; for the ethnocultural dimension, some possibilities are level of interaction with other members in community activities that are not specifically religious (parent-teacher organizations, service clubs) and commitment to the preservation of the community's cultural heritage. Although gathering such data would be very difficult and time-consuming, it would be feasible to use such measures to construct membership profiles of the community at different points across time.[18] These profiles would very probably differ from socioeconomic profiles of the same community at the same points in time, but perhaps not. Correlating the place of individuals in religiocultural profiles with their place in socioeconomic profiles of faith communities would surely be extremely revealing. Perhaps correlations of this sort could even provide enough convincing empirical evidence about the connection between money, power, and religion to test theories about their interconnections. But even without the socioeconomic comparison and even without rigorously constructed statistical profiles constructed from measures on the ascribed and the achieved dimensions of personal identity, an analysis that takes account of the double strand of members' identities may come closer than strict socioeconomic analysis to describing the faith community as experienced at different points in time.[19]

In this same vein, historians may make efforts to describe the community as experienced by directing attention to that part of personal identity that stipulates the nature of divine-human relationships. Although such knowledge is ultimately purely perceptual, the student of communities in which the notion of being the chosen people or the perception of presiding over the sole avenue to salvation is present has the benefit of being able to determine whether tensions in the community are a part of intragroup dynamics or whether the sources of anxiety and stress come from the outside. Moreover, explorations of the mechanisms of boundary maintenance and the impact of perceptions of chosenness on individual and group behavior are also fruitful as lines of inquiry that can open to view the specifically religious dimensions of the life of communities of faith.

Yet another advantage in studying communities that have both well-defined boundaries and authoritarian systems (historic Roman Catholicism, Mormonism, the Unification Church) is that historians have no trouble recognizing who it is that speaks for God within the community. With such a fundamental "fact" established, delineating human responses to what are understood as divine mandates is a much simpler task than is the case when both mandate and response must be teased out of the sources—diaries, letters, personal essays, sermons, testimonies—that open individual perceptions to history. In this and in many other ways, definite boundaries lend a clarity and a power to a faith community's story that is often missing when boundaries are indefinite and porous, allowing members to move in and out as the winds of faith blow hot and cold.[20] Historians of denominations without clear and unmistakable boundaries cannot manufacture them to make consideration of a particular denomination's history more accessible to analysis. But if tightly bonded communities are treated as something like ideal types, comparison on points of structure, the various elements of personal identity, intragroup dynamics, and other factors might shed light on the workings of communities whose boundaries are so porous that they are almost nonexistent.

Despite all the advantages of doing the history of tightly bonded communities of faith that traditionally have been at the margins of American religion, questions about the scholarly writing of their histories are probably more pervasive and pressing in these communities than they are in mainstream American Protestantism.[21] The reasons are not hard to find. The stories of the genesis of indigenous religions like Mormonism, Christian Science, and the Unification Church make these communities particularly vulnerable to apostate accounts and exposé, but they are not alone. Almost any faith community founded or led by a charismatic leader is likewise vulnerable to historical accounts that, at the very least, are unflattering. The history of such communities reveals that most of their leaders have understood that unanswered negative versions of their history pose a danger, not so much to their image in the world as to the health of the communities themselves. Accordingly, community leaders have a record of countering negative renditions of their history by issuing histories that are subsequently recognized by the community as its official (that is, canonized) history, reissuing previously canonized histories in a more accessible format—often in larger print with pictures added—or commissioning and/or otherwise putting their stamp of approval on new renderings of the conventional canon.[22] Confronted with the cool medium of scholarly history, however, many leaders and most rank-and-file members have not been entirely sure how they ought to respond.[23]

If the scholarly writing of denominational history seems a cool medium to the community of faith, however, it often seems just the opposite to historians in the academy. This may simply be the nature of things, but if the scholarly writing of denominational history is separated from the traditional kind, the situation can be clarified and an answer can be advanced to the question of whether scholarly writing of denominational history is an oxymoron. In addition, consideration of the several kinds of accounts of the history of communities of faith points to connections, not only between religion and personal identity, but also between religion and ethnicity.

When the Islamic specialist Bernard Lewis delivered the Gottesman Lectures at Yeshiva University in 1974, lectures that were subsequently published as *History—Remembered, Recovered, Invented,* he was more concerned about the connections between history and contemporary events than about the association of religion, history, identity, and ethnicity. But because he dealt with the history that religious people write and how such history serves to locate modern believers inside their respective traditions, Lewis's division of history into remembered and recovered varieties, as well as his reflections on how history is invented, can be used to make distinctions not only between the types of religious history written for the church and the world, that is, traditional (or confessional) history and scholarly (or critical) history, but also between subdivisions within the genre of confessional history.

With regard to this last, since the Protestant Reformation and the division of Protestantism into denominations, its history (at least in English) has nearly always been written by Protestants. The same cannot be said for faith communities outside the Protestant mainstream. Roman Catholic history was written both by Catholics and rabidly anti-Catholic Protestants, and the outcome was not just history seen from two angles but two very different histories. Two different histories of the Shakers, the Mormons, the followers of John Humphrey Noyes, the Christian Scientists, and of many other communities of faith outside the Protestant mainstream also exist. As different as the two basic renderings of each community's history are, however, both must be classified as confessional, for each version reflects and is determined by the different authors' particular understandings of reality, truth, and the historical process.

In the admirable discussion of denominational history he includes in his description of the "Institutional Forms of Religion" in the *Encyclopedia of the American Religious Experience,* Russell E. Richey avers that, whatever the situation for the scholarly writing of denominational history, the confessional genre is alive and flourishing inside nearly all faith communities. Written by insiders for insiders, these accounts are, finally, not efforts to recover history so much as they are a form of corporate remembering whose purpose is preserving particular understandings of the past. Whether the subject is the recent period of a particular faith community's experience, the beginnings of a religious movement (the story of its founders and those who followed first), the church fathers, or Jesus and the apostles, the goal of remembered history is effective communication, history written so that it will be meaningful to new generations of readers.[24]

That most examples of this type of remembered history are Whiggish in interpretation and supportive of the status quo is to be expected. But it is not always so. Even when they write from the inside, denominational historians also manage to find, in the existing storage bin of available incidents to recount and stories to tell, precedent for reform, change, and a turn to new directions. For all that, however, if the truly significant difference in confessional and scholarly history is to be isolated and named, it is crucially important to recognize that, whether or not they are trained as professional practitioners of Clio's discipline, historians who do confessional history must work within a genre whose resources are limited to a particular body of data.

Although it often appears to historians in the academy that historians who write confessional history are forever "pulling their punches," a close analysis of any large bibliography of confessional history reveals that this is not what always happens in such writing. While there are people who write denominational history by doing little more than recycling existing accounts, there are also many denominational historians who employ the canons of the profession in gathering evidence, determining whether each source from which data are to be drawn is authentic and, if so, whether it is trustworthy and deciding where each piece of evidence fits in the overall context of the community's history. Within the confessional form of the genre, however, the historian's main purpose is not the discovery of new information about the past, that is, recovering history, but strengthening the chain of corporate memory by writing an account that stretches from the very day in which the history is being written back through time to the point of beginnings and returns by moving forward through the ages to the present.

While the program of the writer of confessional history is thus essentially circular, it is not merely "painting by the numbers." In accomplishing their task, confessional historians are, in fact, at liberty to shape the story as they like as long as they do not mix new colors. What this less than subtle analogy intends to suggest is that the authors of confessional history cannot reach outside what amounts to a canonized body of evidence that is composed of the testimony believers have left behind in their writings and in the stories of their lives, as well as in the records kept by the members of the faith community. When these historians extend their search into other portions of the historical record, they are constrained to include only that which serves to support and to confirm the memories of believers.

Circumscription of the available body of evidence has an inevitable impact on the history that can be written, for it removes the chronicling of events from the ongoingness of experience, producing a narrative that—for all its detail, its precise location in particular times and places—stands outside history. Confessional accounts are, finally, ahistorical because all explanation is internal to the community. Latter-day Joshuas fight battles in which they are outnumbered a hundredfold, but the walls come tumbling down nonetheless and there is one and only one acceptable explanation—as an actor in the drama, God determined the outcome. Evidence drawn from outside the community might be available to establish the existing weakness of the walls and the likelihood that they should have crumbled in any case, but historians who write confessional history do not have access to that body of evidence.[25] No matter how sophisticated the handling of the evidence drawn from the recorded memories of believers, and it is often very sophisticated indeed, the result is a history shot through with accounts of divine-human interaction that do not lend themselves to disinterested historical analysis.[26]

As explanation and support for a community's most-favored-people status, confessional history does more than strengthen and fortify the faith of individuals. It also serves as a bridge between individual religious experience and corporate perceptions of the faith community as a distinct and esteemed people with whom the divine is directly concerned. The reality of a shared history in which divinity and humanity have participated jointly provides a basis for kinship that may begin as fictive and symbolic but that across the generations becomes the real kinship that underlies ethnicity.

As vital to the life of the community as is confessional history written from the inside, however, such accounts rarely go unchallenged for long. Whether written before or after a faith community's story assumes its elemental configuration, history written by nonbelievers very often becomes a mirror image of the community's faith story. Instead of depending primarily or exclusively on evidence drawn from the memory of believers, the historians who write this sort of history base their accounts on the memories of those who were present at the creation but failed to participate, those who never believed, or—and more important—those who believed for a while before becoming disillusioned and leaving the movement, carrying with them in their memory banks a plentiful supply of insider information. Fashioned into narrative, the histories based on this class of evidence picture the faith community's leaders and members alike in all too human terms—the former filled with cupidity, sexual desire, and a yearning for power, while the latter seek protection, psychic security, and an opiate that will alleviate the pain of the human condition. In all events, any manifestation of the divine is noticeably absent from the narrative.

While the historians who compose such accounts may likewise be skilled gatherers of information who carefully evaluate the authenticity of the evidence they use and assess its trustworthiness, they, too, are constrained by the limited corpus of available evidence. They also draw on a fixed body of data: the memories of those who did not believe, plus the generally ample evidence drawn from any religious community's historical record that can be used to bolster the picture of human folly. As in all history, the result is an account that reflects the historian's mind-set and perceptions of reality and the historical process. The difference is that, to those who are not directly involved, confessional history written by believers is filled with leaders and people who are just too good to be convincing, whereas confessional accounts written by historians preoccupied with their unbelief are filled with leaders who are so bad that they are unconvincing and followers who seem more like caricatures than living souls.

Although scholars may write confessional history of either variety, confessional history is not the sort of scholarly history that is the hallmark of the best historical writing, either in or out of the academy. This is to say that, as good as some confessional history is, because it practitioners allow themselves to be bound by informal but nevertheless very real limits on the data from which evidence may be drawn, the accounts they write cannot be classified as critical history.[27] This matter of not muzzling the ox as the grain is being treaded out is, it seems to me, the crucial distinction between traditional and scholarly history. Those who do scholarly history must be able to proceed through the evidence untrammeled by blinders that place whole categories of data off limits.

When beginning history students are introduced to the concept of perspective, some of them immediately jump to the conclusion that history is all interpretation. Without appreciating what they are doing, these initiates move toward the position of some postmodern philosophers of history who, in response to deconstruction and the limits of historicism, have concluded that, at bedrock, history (even critical history) is ultimately nothing more than an interpretation of reality fabricated from interpretation "all the way down." While I recognize that the emphasis I here place on the crucial importance of full and unlimited access to the historical record to doing critical history could be read as an effort to reclaim the integrity of the idea of a past as it actually was, I do not mean to go so far as to suggest that full recovery of that past was—or ever will be—possible. What I intend, rather, is to defer the issue of interpretation until the matter of putting together the building blocks from which histories are constructed can be addressed.

While fiction may theoretically issue ex nihilo from an author's pen, history never does; the story of the past is fashioned from existing elements into which historians must breathe life and "vent in" meaning. If any history—whether of nations or of denominations—is to represent something more than an individual historian's idea of what happened, as scholarly history must, then gathering sufficient data to answer questions about who, what, where, and how must antedate the creation of that literary invention called narrative history. Historians who are willing to follow the evidence wherever it leads in the search for answers to those fundamental questions can and do write scholarly history. When they take a particular faith community as the subject of their historical inquiry, whether what they write can be classified as scholarly history primarily depends on the locus of their inquiry.

If the story of the faith community is treated as a case study and analyzed as a way to further exploration of larger questions such as modernization, the politicization of the culture, or the nature and management of power, then the result is quite obviously scholarly history. Yet such studies are not examples of the scholarly writing of denominational history. When historians turn their attention to the communities themselves, however, when they describe them in a manner that fully credits their character as communities and when they make a conscientious effort to represent what happened in a way that the participants themselves would recognize, then they are engaging in the scholarly writing of denominational history.

But how are historians to meet the requirements that turn scholarly history into denominational history without returning to the genre of confessional history? These observations will be brought to a close with some final reflections on method that speak to this question.[28] Again, the key concept is identity, this time not the identity of the objects of inquiry but the identity of the historian making the inquiry.

Scholars (especially those in the academy) who wish to engage in the writing of a scholarly history of their own denominations cannot go back inside, using their status as believers unduly to privilege their own denominations. They must always keep in mind their status as historians and proceed in accordance with their historical training, refusing to neglect the canons of history. In gathering evidence, as far as possible they must consider all the available data, assessing the reliability (or lack thereof) of evidence and authenticating any that is questionable. In doing so, they must apply the rules of evidence evenhandedly, and—although a denomination's fundamental religious claims are generally ahistorical—they must determine where and how evidence just coming to light fits into the larger contemporaneous body of historical data. Nevertheless, this does not mean that those who are worthy of being called professional historians must write a secular history of faith communities or a necessarily unsympathetic one.

As important as using the rules of evidence to determine what occurred is listening to what the data really appear to be saying. Here believers have an advantage, for they speak the language and can recognize nuances that are easily missed by scholars unfamiliar with a denominational idiom. Insiders are also familiar with the faith community's formal institutional system as well as with the informal manner in which it operates at both the administrative and the congregational levels. Moreover, in assessing meaning and significance and determining how evidence is connected to later events, historians can look to religious studies, anthropology, and sociology of religion for interpretive models that describe how religion works and how it fits into culture. Such a program for the scholarly writing of denominational history requires insiders to become "outside-insiders" who know their denominations intimately but are willing to develop the ability to see them from the disinterested perspective of the outside.

At the same time, it is equally possible but, in different ways, just as (or even more) demanding for outsiders to engage in the scholarly writing of denominational history. If insiders have to become "outside-insiders," then outsiders must become "inside-outsiders." Before they can apply the rules of evidence, which may be easier for them than for insiders, they must learn enough about the denomination to collect data efficiently. Since the bulk of the historical sources are often held by the denomination, this very often involves gaining the trust of denominational officials. In order to determine the meaning of the evidence they gather, outsiders have to learn both the theological and the popular religious language of the denominations they study. They also have to guard against analyses that make too much of petty intradenominational squabbles on the one hand and that fail fully to credit the importance of believers' commitments to theological positions and worship practices on the other.

Finally and, it seems to me, of the greatest importance when writing about denominations from either inside or outside, historians whose goal is writing scholarly history need somehow to bracket and to suspend judgment about a faith community's truth claims. Unless this approach to basic beliefs is taken, insiders will almost inevitably write tendentious accounts that amount to a defense of the denomination and outsiders will write tendentious accounts that call the denomination's legitimacy into question. A willing suspension of belief (or disbelief) makes it less likely that what a historian writes will be confused with efforts at faith promotion or exposé. But if the basic elements and dimensions of religion are kept to the fore, the suspension of belief (or the lack of it) will not prevent the composition of sensitive accounts of the denomination's past. Such a strategy can provide both inside-outsiders and outside-insiders with a place to stand, one where they can be interested and fair at one and the same time. More than anything else, this may be the key to the scholarly writing of denominational history, for if the disinterestedness that is at the heart of fine history starts to disappear, then what started out as an effort at composing a scholarly account of a faith community's experience will revert to a variant form of confessional history.

In the particular case, the historian will have failed to write a scholarly history. But as the foregoing suggests, this in no way means that the scholarly writing of denominational history is a contradiction in terms.

NOTES

1. John Foxe, *Acts and Monuments,* vol. 7 (New York: AMS Press, 1965), p. 550. This passage is found in many books of quotations, including several editions of Bartlett's *Familiar Quotations* and all three editions of the Oxford *Dictionary of Quotations.*

2. An early example of works in this genre is Conyers Read, *Social and Political Forces in the English Reformation* (Houston, Tex.: Elsevier Press, 1953). See also Steven Gunn, *Recent Perspectives on the Henrician Reformation* (Leicester, England: UCCF Associates, [1985]).

3. Among such works, the best known and most influential is E. P. Thompson, *The Making of the English Working Class* (New York: Vintage books, 1963). A second, expanded edition was published in 1968.

4. R. Laurence Moore, *Religious Outsiders and the Making of Americans* (New York: Oxford University Press, 1986); Paul E. Johnson, *A Shopkeeper's Millennium: Society and Revivals in Rochester, New York, 1815–1837* (New York: Hill and Wang, 1978). In an important paper presented to a joint session of the American Society of Church History and the American Historical Association in December 1990, Stephen Marini directed the attention of the profession to the way in which religion historians are increasingly interpreting religion as an epiphenomenon.

5. Timothy L. Smith reminds us that journeys to lands of promise are "theologizing experiences." See "Religion and Ethnicity in America," *American Historical Review* 83 (1978): 1155–1185.

6. Denominations were species of the genus Protestantism, and their individual histories were species of the genus American church history. Consequently, individual denominational histories written during the first half of the twentieth century reflected the same attitudes and narrative patterns as did sweeping surveys of the nation's religious history.

7. This concern was first expressed in negative reactions to James B. Allen and Glen M. Leonard, *The Story of the Latter-day Saints* (Salt Lake City, Utah: Deseret Book Co., 1976). See my *Mormonism: The Story of a New Religious Tradition* (Urbana: University of Illinois Press, 1985), pp. 106–107. See also Boyd K. Packer, "The Mantle is Far, Far Greater than the Intellect," *B.Y.U. Studies:* 21 (Summer 1981): 259–278. In this diatribe warning against professional history, Packer, a member of the Council of the Twelve Apostles, spoke for the church. Further evidence of the concern of the LDS General Authorities about the writing of history was supplied when Linda K. Newell and Valeen T. Avery, the authors of *Mormon Enigma,* a critical biography of the Mormon prophet's first wife, were forbidden to speak about their work to Mormon women's groups and in any other official church meetings.

8. A prime example in the first category is Ernest Lee Tuveson, *Redeemer Nation: The Idea of America's Millennial Role* (Chicago: University of Chicago Press, 1968). As for the impact of culture on religion, no major work surpasses Nathan Hatch, *The Democratization of American Christianity* (New Haven: Yale University Press, 1989).

9. Many monographs on method in social history have been published since the late 1960s and early 1970s. Early examples are Charles Dollar and Richard Jensen, *Historian's Guide to Statistics: Quantitative Analysis and Historical Research* (New York: Holt, Rinehart, and Winston, 1971), and Robert P.

Swierenga, ed., *Quantification in American History: Theory and Research* (New York: Atheneum, 1970). *Historical Methods Newsletter* (now *Historical Methods*) began publication in 1967. The *Journal of Social History,* which places major emphasis on method, began publication that same year.

10. William Dean, *History Making History* (Albany: State University of New York Press, 1988), contains a broad-ranging and intelligible discussion of this intellectual movement. The quotations are from the preface.

11. Paul Kleppner, *The Cross of Culture: A Sociological Analysis of Midwestern Politics, 1850–1900* (New York: Free Press, 1970); Richard J. Jensen, *The Winning of the Midwest: Social and Political Conflict, 1888–1896* (Chicago: University of Chicago Press, 1971); Robert P. Swierenga and Philip R. VanderMeer, eds., *Belief and Behavior: Essays in the New Religious History* (New Brunswick, N.J.: Rutgers University Press, 1991).

12. To some extent this is explained by the distinctiveness of the stories of the genesis of such communities, stories that are not widely shared and thus are not subject to multiple interpretation.

13. Whether denominations are ethnic groups or whether religious communities simply function as ethnic groups is one of the basic questions that animate ongoing discussion among scholars on the relationship between religion and ethnicity. See the section on ethnic studies in Russell E. Richey, "Institutional Forms of Religion" in *Encyclopedia of the American Religious Experience: Studies of Traditions and Movements,* ed. Charles H. Lippy and Peter W. Williams, 3 vols. (New York: Charles Scribner's Sons, 1988), 1:44–47. Although I believe that this is a fruitful arena of scholarly inquiry, I do not mean to claim anything more here than that tightly bonded religious communities function in much the same way that ethnic groups function.

14. Bryan Wilson, *Religion in Sociological Perspective* (New York: Oxford University Press, 1982), pp. 111–113.

15. Although I have made an effort to generalize from my work with historians studying other faith communities as well as my own experience as a historian of Mormonism, most of my examples are drawn from the Mormon case, not only because it is the one I know best, but because the Mormon examples are so clear and unambiguous.

16. "Religion, Identity, and Ethnicity: A Forum," *Religion & American Culture: A Journal of Interpretation* 2 (January 1992): 2–8.

17. Prominent examples of this pattern in Mormon circles are the feminist activist Sonia Johnson and the philosopher Sterling M. McMurrin, former U.S. Commissioner of Education. See Johnson, *From Housewife to Heretic: One Woman's Spiritual Awakening and Her Excommunication from the Mormon Church* (New York: Wildfire Books, 1989), and the interview with Sterling M. McMurrin published in *Seventh-East Press,* 17 January 1983.

18. Jan Shipps, "Beyond the Stereotypes: Mormon and Non-Mormon Communities in Twentieth-Century Mormondom," in *New Views of Mormon History: A Collection of Essays in Honor of Leonard J. Arrington,* ed. Davis Bitton and Maureen Ursenbach Beecher (Salt Lake City: University of Utah Press, 1987), pp. 342–362, is an effort at classification not unlike the one suggested here, but it is extremely rudimentary and does not make use of the conception of identity as a combination of ascribed and achieved dimensions.

19. Jan Shipps, "Making Saints in the Early Days and the Latter Days" (Paper presented to the annual meeting of the Society for the Scientific Study of Reli-

gion, Salt Lake City, Utah, October 1989), in *Contemporary Mormonism: Social Science Perspectives,* ed. Marie Cornwall (Urbana: University of Illinois Press, forthcoming).

20. Examples of studies that support the claim that distinct boundaries make for historical clarity include Jay P. Dolan, *The American Catholic Experience: A History from Colonial Times to the Present* (Garden City, N.Y.: Doubleday, 1985); Robert A. Orsi, *The Madonna of 115th Street: Faith and Community in Italian Harlem, 1880–1950* (New Haven: Yale University Press, 1985); Ann Taves, *The Household of Faith: Roman Catholic Devotions in Mid-Nineteenth-Century America* (Notre Dame, Ind.: University of Notre Dame Press, 1986); Jack Wertheim, ed., *The American Synagogue: A Sanctuary Transformed* (Cambridge: Cambridge University Press, 1987); Leonard J. Arrington and Davis Bitton, *The Mormon Experience: A History of the Latter-Day Saints* (New York: Knopf, 1979); and Klaus J. Hansen, *Mormonism and the American Experience* (Chicago: University of Chicago Press, 1981).

21. In recent years probably no issue has generated more attention, both in articles published and in letters to the editor, in *Dialogue* and *Sunstone,* the major journals of opinion in the LDS intellectual community. Within conservative evangelicalism, fundamentalism, and pentecostalism, the matter of the scholarly writing of denominational history has also generated a whole corpus of scholarly books and articles, as well as a professional organization of conservative historians that devotes its sole attention to faith and history. See the ample bibliography of secondary works in Grant Wacker, *Augustus H. Strong and the Dilemma of Historical Consciousness* (Macon, Ga.: Mercer University Press, 1985).

22. The canonized *History of Joseph Smith, the Prophet,* a portion of which is included in the Pearl of Great Price, one of the three new books of scripture of the Church of Jesus Christ of Latter-day Saints, originated, as the first verse says, as a response to the "many reports which have been put in circulation by evil-disposed and designing persons in relation to the rise and progress of the Church of Jesus Christ of Latter-day Saints, all of which have been designed by the authors thereof to militate against its character as a Church and its progress in the world." Another example of official reaction to negative history is found in the biographical studies and the several official histories of the Church of Christ, Scientist, written by Robert Peel. These are works clearly designed to answer unflattering pictures of Mary Baker Eddy and the beginnings of Christian Science such as the one found in Edwin Franden Dakin, *Mrs. Eddy* (New York: Grosset & Dunlap, 1929), and in several subsequent accounts that have been perceived by the church as nothing more than scurrilous attacks.

23. The response of Oral Roberts and his followers to David Edwin Harrell, Jr., *Oral Roberts: An American Life* (Bloomington, Ind.: Indiana University Press, 1985), quite a sympathetic biography of the faith healer, is a case in point.

24. In addition to new generations based on age groupings, confessional history must also communicate effectively to generations of new believers—new converts to the faith.

25. A pertinent example of this pattern can be drawn from an incident in the recent history of Mormon historiography. The "miracle of the seagulls" is a well-known part of the LDS story that recounts the appearance of gulls to ingest the horde of crickets that threatened the grain fields whose harvest was crucial to the Saints' survival during their first year in the Great Basin. Memorialized in a stone monument that presides over Salt Lake City, as well as in countless numbers of

"faith-promoting" narratives, it has assumed such a sacred character that a historian in the employ of the LDS Church was censured for looking outside the circle of acceptable sources and reporting that at the time there were many keepers of conscientious chronicles in the area who failed even to mention the seagulls, much less to note that a miracle had occurred.

26. Note that throughout I have conscientiously avoided using both the word and the concept of *objectivity,* a more extreme version of disinterestedness. While this is an issue of great importance, a discussion of objectivity and the extent to which it is possible to attain it is less important to the matters I am concerned with than the effort to find a reasonably disinterested perspective from which to write denominational history.

27. A first-rate example of fine confessional history is Richard L. Bushman, *Joseph Smith and the Beginnings of Mormonism* (Urbana: University of Illinois Press, 1984).

28. These reflections are drawn directly from my own experience as a birthright Methodist who has continued to maintain that denominational connection while devoting almost the whole of the more than three decades of my life as a professional historian to a study of the Latter-day Saints.

III
CASE STUDIES

A reimagined approach to denominationalism benefits both members of the communities themselves and the larger scholarly audience. These essays describe both how these new approaches would look and some of their advantages.

No concern has so revolutionized the historical discipline, particularly religious history, over the past twenty years as has the rediscovery of the role of gender. Gender historians have eagerly turned to the stories of religious communities to explore key aspects of women's lives. As Jean Miller Schmidt notes, however, these insights have not been fully integrated into the discipline of denominational studies. Her essay discusses how gender awareness can inform our understanding of denominations and how, conversely, an awareness of denominationalism can refine our understanding of religion and gender.

Returning to Charles Long's question of whether denominationalism has a clear meaning outside the Protestant Christian world, Marc Lee Rafael examines the traditional divisions or denominations of Judaism. As he observes, the function of a denomination in defining the relationship within a broad religious family such as Judaism is often more complicated than its role in defining the boundary between the member of the denomination and the conscious outsider. Rafael offers a typology with which to understand the placing of denominations within Judaism.

Will Gravely continues themes found in Maffly-Kipp's essay and offers a careful detailed study of African Methodism. He explores how denominational consciousness emerged and functioned in the rise of these communities.

A major contribution that a revitalized study of denominationalism can make is in exploring the intersection between denominational life and larger cultural trends in order to refine our understanding of both. A case in point is the history of the Progressive era. Cultural historians have long noted the fascination this generation had with the question of efficiency and scientific management, and denominational historians have recently noted (as Richey observed in his essay) how crucially important this period was in the development of the modern denomination. James H. Moorhead examines the interrelationship between these two trends and suggests that each illuminates the other.

Bradley J. Longfield suggests that a refined understanding of the nature of denominationalism can help one better understand the role of religion in the founding of colleges during the antebellum period and in turn contribute to our understanding of the history of education.

Finally, Christa Klein in her case study of Lutheranism discusses the problems and possibilities of denominational studies for religious communities themselves. Lutherans, she argues, have not heretofore emphasized the telling of their own story, but a renewed denominational consciousness would both contribute to a better understanding of the role of Lutheranism in American society and offer a distinctive theological conception of denominational studies for other scholars.

Denominational History
When Gender Is the Focus:
Women in American Methodism

JEAN MILLER SCHMIDT

How does one think about denominational history when gender is taken seriously? Since the early 1980s, scholars have begun to recover and to interpret the histories of women in a number of Protestant denominations.[1] My own work has focused on women in American Methodism, including the history of women in the predecessor bodies of the United Methodist Church and the broader American Methodist family of denominations.[2] This essay attempts to use the scholarship on women in American Methodism as a case study to illustrate the fruitfulness of gender-conscious denominational history.

Recent research on women and religion has raised important methodological and interpretive issues. What sources might be used to learn more about the religious lives of ordinary laypeople, including women? How did gender role expectations as well as women's own life circumstances shape their religious experience? How did women utilize the theology and the practices of their particular religious traditions to help them make sense of their daily existence? What can be discerned about the actual presence and role of women in various religious communities as compared to the conception of women's appropriate place as prescribed in the literature? How is the historian to evaluate the relationship between evangelical religion and self-empowerment for women? What can be learned about the appeal of particular religious traditions by observing the response of women? This essay seeks to address these and related issues.

"Grace Sufficient": Women's Religious Lives in
Early America

Nathan Hatch's work *The Democratization of American Christianity* (1989) argued that to understand democratization, a central theme in American Christianity, we must look to the years of the early republic (1780–1830), particularly at the astonishing growth of popular religious movements such as the Methodists and the Baptists during these years. "The rise of evangelical Christianity in the early republic is, in some measure," wrote Hatch, "a story of the success of common people in shaping a culture after their own priorities." Hatch cited the peculiar relationship between clergy and laity, the acceptance of the spiritual experience of ordinary people, and the passion for equality in these popular movements as articulating a profoundly democratic spirit.[3]

There is a curious omission in this important and suggestive work of Hatch's—the women who constituted two-thirds of the membership of these popular religious movements are largely missing from his account. In this essay I want to contribute to our understanding of the religious lives of ordinary people in the early republic by reporting on my examination of the diaries, letters, and spiritual autobiographies ("pious memoirs") of Methodist women. Such exploration can tell us much about the appeal of Methodism for ordinary people and give us a clearer view of the intimate sociability of the early Methodist world that contributed to the democratization to which Hatch's study pointed.

I am arguing that (1) the "grace sufficient" theme of my title (from 2 Corinthians 12:9, "My grace is sufficient for you, for my power is made perfect in weakness") was central to the spirituality of these Methodist women and representative of the Methodist ideology of these early years; (2) that it was useful to women not only in terms of a spirituality of holiness but also as a way to make sense of the experiences of their lives with regard to affliction and vocation; and (3) that an examination of these pious memoirs suggests how evangelical conversion both affirmed women's role in a patriarchal society and subverted some of the assumptions of that society.

Women's pious memoirs,[4] consisting of a short biography by the editor and extracts from the spiritual journals and letters of the subject, were usually compiled and published posthumously by relatives of the deceased or by clergy. Although (male) ministers had a large hand in shaping and interpreting women's published memoirs, female models were crucial for women as they wrote their spiritual accounts. The memoirs of both English and American women were part of what Jo Gillespie called "a functional pious memoir canon . . . all reprinted and circulated among evangelical readers in America."[5]

The pious memoirs of Methodist women give strong evidence of a folk theology in which the notion of "grace sufficient" was central. An early example is certainly the Englishwoman Hester Ann Rogers (1756–

1794), the wife of one of John Wesley's early Methodist preachers, whose spiritual autobiography and letters were widely read by Methodist women in early-nineteenth-century America. Once when she was critically ill, a visiting cousin asked her, "Are you willing to live forty years, if the Lord please?" She later recalled, "A thousand fears suggested, that if I lived, I might lose what I now enjoyed of the love of God; and perhaps be one day a dishonour to his cause. But I said, Lord, thy grace is ever sufficient; thou art as able to keep me a thousand years as one day!"[6] When she struggled with spiritual temptations, Rogers reflected, "Those precious words, 'My grace is sufficient for thee,' shall stand firm as the pillars of heaven: and when the enemy shall tell me— In such and such a trial thou wilt be entangled and overcome, I tell him, 'My Lord hath promised strength equal to my day,' and all his darts are instantly repelled."[7]

These women lived in the constant presence of death, whether the ever-present possibility of their own death in childbirth or the loss of a child or a spouse. With regard to what she called her "bodily distress," Mrs. Mary W. Mason (1791–1868), organizer in 1819 of the first Methodist female missionary society, wrote in her diary: "I found his grace, as heretofore, more than sufficient. I think the Lord does not bestow premature or unnecessary grace. All we can expect is grace equal to our day."[8] Rejoicing at the safe birth of her child, she recorded, "Glory to his holy name for grace sufficient for our day." Those who were with the Southern Methodist missionary Laura Askew Haygood (1845–1900) at her deathbed in China mentioned the motto hanging on a wall near her bed, "As thy days, so shall thy strength be [Deut. 33:25]."[9]

This folk theology seems to have been a crucially important defining element in early-nineteenth-century American Methodism. In describing "the Methodist ideology," historian Donald Mathews claimed that a major difference between early Methodists and other evangelical Protestants was that the new birth event in Methodism was "no guarantee of final perseverance. The Methodist could not say 'I have been saved!' and leave the sacred event at that. The Methodist had to say: 'I have been saved, I am saved, I may be saved, I shall one day be saved.' "[10] In 1824 Elizabeth Lyon Roe, a pioneer in Illinois Methodism, wrote in her journal, "I asked the Lord to take me to that better world, that I might sin no more, but I was reminded that I was a probationer, and that there were many duties and trials before me, but I felt assured that His grace would be sufficient for the day."[11]

Early Methodist women and men experienced the release and the joy of forgiveness and a new relationship to God, but Wesleyan theology and practice urged them not to stop there. By actively cooperating with God's grace, they were to press on toward sanctification and holy living. My own research suggests that trust in the sufficiency of divine grace was central to the spiritual lives and experience of ordinary Methodist women and that it was closely related to the early Methodist quest for

Christian perfection. When Hester Ann Rogers longed to die in order to be free from the power of sin, she was led to trust not in her own heroic strivings but in "grace sufficient." When she finally realized her desire to be perfected in love, she wanted to help others to understand what that meant. She explained in a letter to her cousin: "You ask how I obtained this great salvation? I answer, Just as I obtained the pardon of my sin—*by simple faith.* . . . I knew the faithfulness of my God, and ventured on the promise . . . 'My grace is sufficient for thee.' "[12]

One sees the same phenomenon in the diary of Catherine Livingston Garrettson (1752–1849), a member of the prominent Livingston family of New York state, who was converted the day before her thirty-fifth birthday and later married the Methodist preacher Freeborn Garrett-son.[13] This early Methodist woman longed for sanctification and submitted her daily life to rigorous scrutiny in order that no unknown sin might hinder her relationship with God. In editing Garrettson's journal, Diane Lobody explained: "Methodists were keenly aware that, however much grace was given to believers, they might very well backslide. Grace was not irresistible, and it took enormous effort for the believer to respond to grace affirmatively and energetically. The idea terrified Garrettson: 'a disagreeable reflection on the falling off, of those who had once been favored children of the most high; sent me mourning to my room. Shocked at the fear that it might one day, be my melancoly case, I beged, and prayed of the Blessed Jesus, to make his grace sufficient for me.' "[14] The fear so often expressed in Methodist women's diaries is a fear, not of being damned, but of disappointing God or being separated from God.

Historians of women and American religion have tended to focus on women's religious activity rather than on women's religious lives. Studies of early American theology and spirituality have usually depended on the journals and sermons of Methodist preachers. Careful exploration of this folk theology of "grace sufficient" as expressed in the pious memoirs of Methodist women may tell us much about the religious appeal of Methodism for ordinary people.

A crucial aspect of this appeal that extends well beyond the bounds of this essay is the "radical spiritual egalitarianism" of early Methodism. As one Methodist historian expressed it, " 'Brother' and 'sister' shattered the lines drawn by the world—lines of race, class, family, and language—by drawing a new line between Methodism and the world."[15] Although there were significant ambiguities in this egalitarianism, the countercultural thrust of early Methodism tended to oppose the worldy hierarchies of race, gender, and class. The African Methodist witness to the spiritual power of the early Wesleyan message and the considerable black presence in early Methodist class meetings, love feasts, exhortation, and preaching is important evidence of this.[16]

Donald Mathews has consistently interpreted the appeal of early Methodism to women and African-Americans in terms of the "sense of release from prior restraints" and "entry into a new kind of life" that conversion created; Jo Gillespie has argued that by attributing to Providence (I would say "grace" for Methodist women) a mandate for spiritual self-development, evangelical females in the early nineteenth century began to think new thoughts and to examine new possibilities for their lives.[17] If that meant they overflowed their "woman's place," they seemed not to notice. They told themselves they were simply learning to live their Christian commitment to the full as any individual was called to do.

A study by Virginia Lieson Brereton of women's conversion narratives corroborates this interpretation.[18] Brereton suggests that conversion narratives both affirmed women's role in a patriarchal society and subverted some of the assumptions of that society. For many women religious, submission to God resulted in the loss of inhibiting self-consciousness and a new sense of inner authority. Women were obligated to tell their stories. Claiming obedience to a higher authority, these evangelical women often moved beyond the bounds prescribed for them in the nineteenth century. Through the experience of conversion, it was not unusual for them to find not only God but also a worthy role in this world.[19]

As the spheres of home and world increasingly diverged in the early nineteenth century and as women came to be regarded as primarily responsible for the religious and moral formation of children, "women were surrounded by women"[20] in their everyday religious lives. Carroll Smith-Rosenberg has powerfully described the "female world" of networks of relatives and friends that accompanied virtually every important event in women's lives.[21] Women's informal spiritual networks were nurtured through channels such as camp meetings and sustained through letter writing, visits, and women's organizations at the local level. The spiritual journals and letters of early Methodist women are among our best resources for understanding these female spiritual networks. Hannah Syng Bunting's Philadelphia diaries, for example, are full of accounts of love feasts, class and band meetings, female prayer meetings, camp meetings, and sacramental occasions. Her letters to female cousins, friends, and Sabbath scholars are almost entirely devoted to religious reflection and exhortation, with occasional reports of camp meetings and other edifying spiritual experiences.[22]

Domestic Religion and Popular Evangelicalism

Whereas older denominational studies tended to focus on ecclesiastical structures and issues involving the more public face of the church, more recent scholarship has rediscovered the centrality of domestic religion in the early growth of Methodism and the crucial role women played in this. Membership lists of the early British Methodist societies demonstrate that the ratio of women to men in early Methodism throughout most of the eighteenth century was typically two to one. Women were "conspicuous as pioneers" in the establishment and expansion of early Methodist societies, were encouraged to be sick visitors, and were appointed leaders of the classes and bands (small groups for spiritual oversight and accountability) by John Wesley himself.[23]

Regional studies of early American Methodism by William H. Williams (the Delmarva peninsula), Doris Andrews (Middle Atlantic port societies of New York, Philadelphia, and Baltimore), and, for a somewhat later period, A. Gregory Schneider (the Ohio Valley, 1790s–1840s) are remarkably consistent in depicting the preponderance of women in the membership of the early Methodist societies, the importance of women's roles in the establishment and expansion of Methodism, and the appeal of Methodism for women.[24] Much of early American Methodism was home-based religion. Preaching services were held in homes because there was nowhere else to hold them. Class meetings likewise took place there, and women as well as men served as class leaders. As keepers of the household, women often initiated and promoted meetings. They also exercised considerable influence over the young itinerant preachers who were dependent on them for room and board.

Through public prayer, testimony, and exhorting, women in early Methodism gradually but regularly engaged in "communicating the gospel in all but preaching."[25] All these leadership roles were primarily charismatic in nature, that is, based on spiritual authority and empowerment and "grounded in the evangelical urge to save souls." Praying in public was most accessible for women because it took place initially in the home or in female prayer meetings. Some women became "highly gifted in the art of prayer."[26] Methodists love feasts (informal occasions for Christian fellowship) gave both women and men opportunity to testify publicly about God's work in their lives. Exhorting most frequently followed the preaching of an itinerant and involved urging sinners to repent and be saved. The Methodist network itself provided the training for all this. For example, women naturally moved from praying at home to praying in women's prayer meetings to being asked to pray in larger public gatherings of Methodists. They were led step by step to assume more conspicuous evangelical roles.

"Mother in Israel" was a beloved title given to women among the early Methodist people as an indication of community regard for their spiritual leadership. Mothers in Israel were (like Deborah in Judges 5:6–7) spiritual mothers to their people, revered for their role in the conversion of souls and remembered with gratitude for their hospitality and assistance. Catherine Livingston Garrettson in New York state and Mary White in Maryland were two such women in early American Methodism. After marrying Freeborn Garrettson, Catherine functioned as a spiritual director in a network of evangelical women and was deeply involved in the spiritual and temporal affairs of her community.[27] Together with her husband, she established a home in Rhinebeck, on the Hudson, that became famous for its hospitality to Methodist itinerant preachers and to others seeking rest. When she died at the age of ninety-six, she was widely revered as an example of holy living and dying and praised as "in no trite, ordinary sense 'a mother in Israel.' "[28]

Mary White was one of the "female friends"[29] of Francis Asbury who offered the unmarried bishop the hospitality of their homes as he traveled his circuits. She also encouraged and welcomed the itinerant preachers of the young Methodist movement. The wife of Judge Thomas White, with whom Asbury sought refuge during the American Revolution, Mary White had been important in bringing her prominent husband into the Methodist fold. A frequent worship leader as well as a class leader, she might have "gone further and preached" (said an early Methodist historian) "if Asbury had encouraged her."[30] Benjamin Abbott, about to leave the White home in 1782 for Barratt's Chapel, later recalled: "Mrs. White came to me as I sat on my horse, and took hold of my hand, exhorting me for some time. I felt very happy under her wholesome admonitions." Thomas Ware, another of the preachers, referred to her as a "mother in Israel in very deed."[31]

Early Methodist women were particularly effective in person-to-person evangelism. According to testimonies of the influence of maternal piety, female Methodists played a crucial role in family devotions and in nurturing pious sensibilities in children. Women often acted independently of their husbands in deciding to become Methodists. Perhaps women were attracted to Methodism because it met their needs for intimate sociability as well as for independence and self-esteem. Methodist class meetings, love feasts, and family circles were places to enjoy "the precious seasons of social religion" that fostered an experience of Methodist people as the "family of God" in opposition to the world.[32] In all of these settings, in ways I have suggested, women played a key role.

One of the most remarkable autobiographies of Methodist women, in terms of what it tells us about early Methodism on the frontier and about the religious lives of ordinary Methodist people, is *Recollections of Frontier Life* by Mrs. Elizabeth A. [Lyon] Roe.[33] Elizabeth Roe did not marry a Methodist preacher. She and her husband were active laypeople who moved from Kentucky to Illinois in 1827. Wherever they lived, their cabin became the Methodist meetinghouse until a larger structure could be built. They usually organized the first class meeting in their neighborhood (often John Roe became class leader) and got the circuit preacher to make an appointment to preach there. Elizabeth Roe was always involved in the female prayer meeting. Her account demonstrates the important role she and her family, and other early Methodists like them, played in starting and supporting new churches on the frontier.

Women in Public Ministry—A Long History

Gender awareness makes one more sensitive, not only to the importance of domestic religion, but also to parts of the public history of the denomination that have largely been overlooked. The late-twentieth-century debates over women in public ministry have inspired a rediscovery of a much longer discussion on this subject that was far more complicated than heretofore believed. A case in point can again be seen in Methodism.

In the years 1761 to 1791, women's leadership in the Wesleyan Methodist revival in England was gradually expanded to include female preaching. Sarah Crosby received Wesley's informal authorization to exhort large numbers of people in 1761. In response to Mary Bosanquet Fletcher's defense of women's preaching, Wesley in 1771 defined the "extraordinary call" that allowed room for women preachers. Between 1781 and his death a decade later, John Wesley underwent a change in attitude toward female preachers that led to the official recognition of a number of women in the Methodist system; Sarah Mallett is perhaps the best known. Paul Chilcote identified forty-two women preachers among the Methodists prior to 1803.[34] After Wesley's death, a new generation of women preachers had to contend with the struggle between charismatic and authoritarian views of the ministry in an increasingly institutionalized church. In 1803 the Methodist Conference ruled that any woman convinced that she had "an extraordinary call from God to speak in public" was advised to address "her *own sex,* and *those only.*"[35] After 1803 increasing numbers of aspiring women preachers found it necessary to join groups like the Primitive Methodists or the Bible Christians.[36]

Doris Andrews's research on women as class leaders in the Methodist port societies of New York, Philadelphia, and Baltimore shows that, although women were appointed class leaders in the early years (from about 1770), by 1800 there were no longer women class leaders in those societies. She concluded that women fared better in the smaller societies and that the more institutional Methodism became (after its formal organization as a separate American denomination in 1784), the less access women had to public roles or to official capacities in the church.[37]

Nevertheless, there were women in the Methodist denominations in this country who experienced a call to preach and became (unordained) traveling preachers as early as the 1810s and 1820s. Two of the earliest examples were Jarena Lee, a free black woman born in New Jersey and probably the first female preacher of the African Methodist Episcopal Church, and Fanny Butterfield Newell, the wife of a circuit-riding Methodist Episcopal preacher in the New England Conference. From the published spiritual memoirs of these two women, we know how they experienced and responded to their call.

Jarena Lee's *Religious Experience and Journal,* published in 1836 and 1849, is one of the earliest examples of the genre of nineteenth-century autobiographical writings of African-American women.[38] Published not by ministers but by the women themselves, these writings focused on the authentication of a black female self in a world that denied that self full humanity through the combined forces of racism and sexism.[39] Lee's journal gives a vivid picture of the challenges she faced as an African-American woman preacher. In 1819, eight years after Lee first felt

a call to preach and was told by Richard Allen that "the rules of Methodism did not call for women preachers," Bishop Allen recognized her call
and gave her permission to preach. In the meantime she had become a
pastor's wife, a mother, and then a widow. Almost immediately she began
an itinerant preaching career, first in the Philadelphia area; later she
traveled from upper New York state to Maryland and as far west as Ohio.
In one year in the 1820s, she claimed to have traveled more than two
thousand miles and preached more than 175 sermons. She apparently
spoke to large congregations, both black and white. Like the prophets of
old, she relied fundamentally on the God who says, "I will send by [sic]
whom I will."[40] In 1851 the African Methodist Episcopal General Conference defeated by a large majority a resolution to give women licenses to
preach; however, neither petitions for licensing and ordaining women
nor women's preaching activities subsided after that vote.[41]

Fanny Butterfield's call first came in 1809, when a messenger appeared to her in a dream and told her to take on the mantle of the
Methodist preacher Henry Martin (who had died the previous year and
under whose preaching she had experienced conversion). The following
year she married Ebenezer F. Newell and traveled with him around his
circuits in Vermont and Maine. Her call to preach was reaffirmed by a
powerful religious experience in 1811, when she nearly died in childbirth. Even when her husband volunteered in 1818 to go to Saint Croix,
at the eastern edge of Maine near the New Brunswick border, she accompanied him on the long, difficult trip by sailing vessel to frontier outposts
that had been settled only eight years earlier. She died of consumption
(tuberculosis) in 1824, at age thirty.[42]

In many ways, Fanny Newell must have served as an example to
early (white) American Methodist women who felt a call to preach. The
first edition of her memoirs was printed within months of her death; by
1848, the memoirs were in their fourth edition. The unnamed minister
of the New England Conference who wrote the introduction clearly
understood Newell's call in terms of her willingness to assume the
responsibilities of a Methodist itinerant preacher's wife, even stressing
that her public labors in the church had not caused her to neglect her
domestic obligations. Her husband, Ebenezer, on the other hand, had
recognized his wife's own call. On proposing marriage to her, he wrote
in his journal, "I viewed it my duty to bring her gift into the more
public service of the church."[43]

Although their life circumstances were very different, Jarena Lee and
Fanny Newell experienced their call in strikingly similar ways. In dreams
each woman saw herself preaching to large crowds; yet each felt her call
as a terrible cross for a poor female to bear.[44] Neither woman had spiritual peace except in striving to do what she believed God required of her.
As they expressed it, when they shrank from taking up the cross, they
were pierced through with many sorrows. These women and others like
them experienced themselves as empowered and authorized by God to

preach when the church still refused to grant them official acceptance. They had to overcome what they called a "man-fearing spirit."

At least one woman, Hannah Pearce Reeves, preached among the smaller and more democratic Methodist Protestants from the 1830s. She had been an itinerant preacher in England among the Bible Christians (a Wesleyan sect); on hearing her preach, the Wesleyan Methodist lay preacher William Reeves asked to be introduced to her. In 1831 she joined him in Ohio and, from the day of their marriage until her death in 1868, they "labored together in the gospel ministry" of the newly organized Methodist Protestant Church.[45]

In the 1840s several women applied to the United Brethren for permission to preach. The 1845 General Conference ruled that the Gospel did not authorize the introduction of females into the preaching ministry.[46] In spite of that action, Charity Opheral applied to the White River Conference (Indiana) in 1847 for a license to preach and was given "a note of commendation." Although the United Brethren General Conference of 1857 passed a resolution prohibiting women from being licensed to preach, women of that church continued to be given letters of recommendation to preach. Lydia Sexton was granted a preacher's license by the Illinois Quarterly Conference in 1851, and continued to have it renewed it annually, even after 1857.

In the Methodist Episcopal Church, the holiness evangelist Phoebe Palmer in *The Promise of the Father* (1859) defended women's right to preach on the basis of the gift of the Spirit to the church at Pentecost ("your sons and your daughters shall prophesy"). In 1869 Maggie Van Cott was granted one of the first preacher's licenses to be given to a woman in the Methodist Episcopal Church. During the 1870s numbers of women asked for and received local preacher's licenses in that branch of Methodism.[47]

In 1880 two women, Anna Howard Shaw and Anna Oliver, applied to the Methodist Episcopal Church for ordination. Both women had obtained local preacher's licenses in the 1870s, had graduated from Boston University School of Theology, and had been approved by their conference examining committees as candidates for ordination. When they were presented for ordination at the appropriate session of the New England Annual Conference, the presiding bishop refused to ordain them. They appealed to the General Conference, the major legislative body of the Methodist Episcopal Church, which met in Cincinnati on May 1, 1880. Under the direction of two powerful committees, the Judiciary Committee and the Committee on the Itinerancy, the 1880 General Conference decided against the ordination of women. In addition, it declared that all local preacher's licenses issued to women from 1869 on were to be rescinded. The Methodist Episcopal Church would not grant women local preacher's licenses again until 1920.

When historians of Methodism first explored the beginnings of the struggle to ordain women, they focused on events in the 1850s and

1860s.[48] It was likewise assumed that the women who appealed to the General Conference of the MEC in 1880 for ordination were an exceptional few. However, a letter addressed to that General Conference by a Mrs. Mary L. Griffith of Mauch Chunk (now Jim Thorpe), Pennsylvania, referred to women "rising up all over the land who feel moved by the Holy Ghost to preach" and are "flocking into our theological schools as fast as the doors are opened." Her question to the (male) members of the General Conference was, "if God calls, how can the Church refuse to call?"[49] There is every indication that increasing numbers of women were seeking licensing and ordination and that women experienced the action of the Methodist Episcopal General Conference in 1880 as a severe blow.

Anna Oliver was never ordained. She died an early death, some thought of a broken heart. Anna Howard Shaw was ordained by the Methodist Protestants at Tarrytown, New York, in October 1880. In 1885, after seven years' ministry on Cape Cod, Shaw resigned as pastor to devote herself full-time to the struggles for temperance and woman suffrage. Although the Methodist Protestant Church General Conference voted in 1884 that Shaw's ordination had been unauthorized by the law of the church, the New York Annual Conference continued to recognize her ordination as valid. In 1889 the Kansas Conference of the MPC ordained Eugenia St. John, the wife of a Methodist Episcopal minister. The MPC had obviously begun to be known as a Methodist denomination in which women could be ordained. That same year, the United Brethren (one off two smaller German pietistic groups that became the Evangelical United Brethren Church in 1946 and would unite with the Methodists in 1968 to form the United Methodist Church) ordained their first woman minister, Ella Niswonger.

In 1889 Frances E. Willard, president of the Woman's Christian Temperance Union, published *Woman in the Pulpit,* a strong defense of women's rights in the church. Willard's book appeared the year after she and four other women had been refused seating as official, elected lay delegates to the 1888 General Conference. The exasperated Willard now suggested that if men continued to refuse to share power with the women, perhaps women should "take this matter into their own hands" and form a new church in which they could receive full clergy and laity rights.[50] The October 2, 1890, issue of the *Christian Advocate* reported the formation on November 6, 1889 of a "New Century Club" in the Methodist Episcopal Church to be an advocate for women's rights in the church. Professor Luther T. Townsend, a Boston University faculty member, urged that "these noble women should knock only once more at the doors of the Methodist General Conference, and if their signals and entreaties are again uncivilly disregarded, they should never knock again."[51] He warned that the church would be surprised at the number of Methodist clergy who would be glad to assist the women in an irregular ordination.

Even limited clergy rights would not come in the Methodist Episcopal Church until 1924. In that year the church decided to grant women "partial status," which meant that they could be ordained for a particular location in response to the emergency missional needs of the church; they were not members of the covenant body of clergy of annual conference and were not eligible for a regular conference appointment. At the Uniting Conference in 1939, which resulted in The Methodist Church, full conference membership for women was defeated by a narrow margin. Full clergy rights for women in The Methodist Church finally became a reality in 1956.

Women's historians have described the erosion after 1880 of the rigid Victorian gender ideology of separate male and female spheres, as the "New Woman" gradually but steadily moved into leadership in the public realm through higher education, separate women's organizations (such as the Woman's Christian Temperance Union), new roles in the church, and, finally, woman's suffrage. Betty A. DeBerg's book, *Ungodly Women: Gender and the First Wave of American Fundamentalism,* argued persuasively that the rise and fall of Victorian gender ideology constituted a major cultural crisis in the lives of the late Victorian middle class and that an analysis of popular fundamentalist rhetoric reveals how central gender issues were to this movement.[52]

Here is an excellent example of how our understanding of denominational development is benefited by the growth of gender analysis. During the 1880s, the national WCTU president Frances Willard, a Methodist woman, began to redefine the ideal of womanhood, leading Victorian "ladies" out of their homes to support the causes of temperance and woman suffrage for the sake of "home protection." The Rev. James M. Buckley, on the other hand, a powerful shaper of opinion in the Methodist Episcopal Church for nearly forty years and an archopponent of new roles for women in the church, argued that what the Methodist General Conference needed was not female delegates but more laymen. As the Methodist Episcopal Church denied women clergy and laity rights in the 1880s, it sanctioned women's work in the Sunday schools and as missionaries and deaconesses. (The Woman's Home Missionary Society of the Methodist Episcopal Church was formally recognized by the 1884 General Conference; four years later the General Conference authorized the office of deaconess as a ministry for women.) While women were denied access to roles of authority as clergy and laity within the church, opportunities increased in areas where need and gender stereotypes converged.[53]

Women's Missionary Organizations: Strategies and Benefits

The past fifteen years have witnessed a flowering of interest in the role of missions for American Protestants. Here, too, an awareness of gender has allowed historians to rediscover a crucial activity of women.[54] The Woman's Foreign Missionary Society (WFMS) of the Methodist Episcopal Church was founded in Boston in 1869. It was the first of eight women's home and foreign missionary societies to be organized between 1869 and 1890 in the Methodist, Evangelical, and United Brethren family of churches. Although the women who led these societies were conscious of strategies and aware of the benefits to themselves of being organized for mission, the significance of their work has only recently been noted by denominational historians. Example from the WFMS of the Methodist Episcopal Church, as the earliest of these societies, may suffice to illustrate my point. However, similar studies of women's mission work in the other branches of the denominational family have begun to attend to these issues. Sara J. Myers has demonstrated, for example, that mission work enabled Methodist women in the South to begin the movement out of their homes and into the public arena while at the same time preserving their identity as "true women."[55]

When the Woman's Foreign Missionary Society of the Methodist Episcopal Church was founded, the membership fee was fixed at "two cents a week and a prayer," on the premise that no woman should be excluded from membership because of inability to pay. A journal was founded to provide "constant enlightenment in regard to the world's claim upon our money and energy." The journal's original title, *The Heathen Woman's Friend,* was changed in 1896 to *The Woman's Missionary Friend.*[56] Its counterpart for Southern Methodist women, *Woman's Missionary Advocate,* was published from 1880 until 1910.

From the first, the women had to battle their parent mission boards for the right to raise and disburse their own funds. In 1870 the Woman's Foreign Missionary Society of the Methodist Episcopal Church first adopted a "spirited motion" saying that its public meeting should be "a *woman's* meeting, addressed by *women* only."[57] Before the end of the Society's first year, its officers had perfected a plan for dividing the church into districts, with a Branch of the Society in each district. The executive committee functioned during the annual meeting, and the auxiliary societies reported directly to the Branches. Because of this structure, the corresponding secretaries had enormous influence; they were the real contact between the central group and the workers on the local level.

In newly organized areas like the Western Branch, the president and the corresponding secretary functioned like traveling missionaries as they organized local auxiliaries. The following description of Mary Clarke Nind's work as corresponding secretary of the new Minneapolis Branch was part of a funeral tribute to her upon her death in 1905: "Her courage never faltered, as by faith she laid the foundations of this great organization in Minnesota, the Dakotas, Montana, Idaho, Washington and Oregon, traveling over the unbroken prairie and through the wilderness in wagon or cart or sleigh, in summer and winter, by day and by night, by freight train or day coach (never in a Pullman—the Lord's money was too precious for such luxuries), compassing as many as ten thousand miles in a single year, and counting it all joy to be engaged in her blessed work."[58]

To the women of the WFMS, she was "Mother Nind," or even "Our Little Bishop." It is not surprising that she was one of the five women elected as lay delegates to the 1888 General Conference of the Methodist Episcopal Church. (These women were, of course, not seated; female lay delegates were first admitted to the General Conference in 1904.)

Methodist camp meetings afforded excellent opportunities to reach Methodist women on behalf of the new missionary societies. Anniversary meetings held at the camp meetings each year attracted large crowds. The women's missionary magazines were from the beginning an effective means of advancing the cause, as newly organized auxiliaries were reported in their pages. It is also clear that family connections—mothers, daughters, sisters, aunts, cousins—were important in the leadership of these early societies. The daughter of one of these early officers later reflected on the impact this had on her: "What a large part of my real education it has been to know the beginnings of the Woman's Foreign Missionary Society. Mother in her gentle, brave way doing what she had never done before and doing it calmly, sure it was right."[59]

By 1879 "Uniform Readings" for mission study were published monthly in the *Heathen Woman's Friend.* The system of mite boxes, which became almost a symbol of the missionary societies' ability to enlist the widespread support of women, was introduced by the New York Branch of the WFMS in 1870 and was soon adopted by the other branches. The early pioneers of the Society saw the organizational apparatus as enabling spiritual purposes: "the complex machinery, wheel within wheel, depends for its running upon the current of His mighty power. . . . The treasury has ever been close beside the altar."[60] In the process of all this organizing, Methodist women gained invaluable administrative experience and established networks for support and action with women around the country. Jennie Fowler Willing once remarked, "[O]ur paper ought to be called the 'Christian Woman's Friend,'—such blessed opportunity has it helped us find as co-workers with God; such growth and comfort and sweet fellowship as we have had in His work!"[61]

Any new history of American Methodism that makes the present denomination more understandable will have to pay attention to Methodism's move to respectability in the late nineteenth century.[62] Once again, it will be important to see how the various women's organizations in the Methodism of this period compare with the professionalism and bureaucratization so evident in other aspects of the church's life. A key element in these organizations from the beginning was the strategic linkage between the local and the national level through several intermediate levels. To read the histories of these organizations written by the women themselves is to sense the excitement, the spiritual and social networks, the increasing self-confidence, training, and empowerment, and the movement into more public roles that these organizations represented for the women who were active in them. In Methodist as in other denominational studies, attention to this late Victorian period may offer rich rewards.

By using the Methodist example, I have attempted to demonstrate in this essay that attention to gender shows:

1. the importance of women's religious diaries, letters, and pious memoirs for recovering the religious lives of ordinary women;
2. the role of doctrine, particularly notions of sanctification, in shaping the lives of lay people, especially women;
3. the ways women used the theology and practices of their religious traditions to help them make sense of their daily existence;
4. the religious appeal of Methodism, particularly its radical spiritual egalitarianism, for ordinary people;
5. the impact of life in grace in leading women to transgress the social boundaries defining women's place;
6. the importance of domestic religion, especially in early Methodism, and the large role women played in it;
7. the high percentage of women in the movement, the leadership roles they played, the titles they were given, and the significance of their modeling of the Christian life;
8. the importance of the distinction between charismatic and authoritarian views of the ministry; that access to ministerial roles was more open in the revivalism of the early movement, then actually contracted and only emerged again gradually in an increasingly institutionalized church;
9. the degree to which women were aware of precedent and biblical precept as sanctions for expanded leadership;
10. the relation between resistance to new roles for women in the church and the crisis in the middle class caused by erosion of the Victorian gender ideology of separate male and female spheres; and
11. the strategies and impact of women's missionary organizations and their relation to larger denominational and social patterns of professionalization and bureaucratization.

In terms of agenda for the future, major comparative and synthetic tasks remain. For denominational historians, the issue is how these studies can be integrated into a new synthetic history. Historians of gender will need to be attentive to the area of family studies, particularly with regard to religion, and to press the larger gender questions of the interactive nature of women and men in the church. It will also be important for historians of gender to ask how more nuanced and sophisticated denominational studies can enrich and refine our understanding of gender in American history.

Taking gender seriously in writing denominational history invites and demands new interpretive paradigms, a larger and more encompassing vision, and fresh ways of understanding and evaluating what we knew was there but have never really seen before.

NOTES

1. See, for example, Lois A. Boyd and R. Douglas Brackenridge, *Presbyterian Women in America: Two Centuries of a Quest for Status* (Westport, Conn.: Greenwood Press, 1983); Margaret Hope Bacon, *Mothers of Feminism: The Story of Quaker Women in America* (San Francisco: Harper & Row, 1986); Mary Sudman Donovan, *A Different Call: Women's Ministries in the Episcopal Church, 1850–1920* (Wilton, Conn.: Morehouse-Barlow, 1986); and L. DeAne Lagerquist, *From Our Mother's Arms: A History of Women in the American Lutheran Church* (Minneapolis: Augsburg Publishing, 1987).

2. Jean Miller Schmidt, *Grace Sufficient: A History of Women in American Methodism* (Nashville, Tenn.: Abingdon, forthcoming). See also my earlier articles "Reexamining the Public/Private Split: Reforming the Continent and Spreading Scriptural Holiness," in *Rethinking Methodist History*, ed. Russell E. Richey and Kenneth E. Rowe (Nashville, Tenn.: Kingswood Books, 1985), pp. 75–88, and "The Present State of United Methodist Historical Study," *Methodist History* 28 (January 1990): 104–116.

3. Nathan O. Hatch, *The Democratization of American Christianity* (New Haven: Yale University Press, 1989), p. 9.

4. See Joanna Bowen Gillespie. " 'The Clear Leadings of Providence': Pious Memoirs and the Problems of Self-Realization for Women in the Early Nineteenth Century," *Journal of the Early Republic* 5 (Summer 1985): 197–221.

5. Ibid., p. 197; see also the appendix, pp. 220–221.

6. Hester Ann Rogers, *An Account of the Experience of Hester Ann Rogers; and her Funeral Sermon, by Rev. Dr. Coke. To which are added her Spiritual Letters.* Rev. and ed. (New York: Carlton & Phillips, 1856), p. 38. This work was one of the Methodist best-sellers. See, for example, the accounts of books sold in the papers of Methodist itinerant preacher Benjamin Lakin in William Warren Sweet, *Religion on the American Frontier, 1783–1840,* vol. 4, *The Methodists* (Chicago: University of Chicago Press, 1946), pp. 700–706.

7. Rogers, *Account,* p. 190.

8. Elizabeth Mason North, *Consecrated Talents: or, The Life of Mrs. Mary W. Mason* (1870; reprint ed., New York: Garland, 1987), pp. 93–94.

9. Oswald Eugene and Anna Muse Brown, *Life and Letters of Laura Askew Haygood* (1904; reprint, ed., New York: Garland, 1987), pp. iv, 196.

10. Donald G. Mathews, "Evangelical America—The Methodist Ideology," in Russell E. Richey and Kenneth E. Rowe, eds., *Rethinking Methodist History* (Nashville, Tenn.: Kingswood Books, 1985), pp. 91–99. (Quote is on p. 93.)

11. Mrs. Elizabeth A. [Lyon] Roe, *Recollections of Frontier Life* (1885; reprint ed., Salem, N.H.: Arno Press, 1980), p. 614.

12. Rogers, *Account,* pp. 206–207.

13. Diane Lobody, "Lost in the Ocean of Love: The Mystical Writings of Catherine Livingston Garrettson" (Ph.D. diss., Drew University, 1990).

14. Ibid., p. 89.

15. Russell E. Richey, *Early American Methodism* (Bloomington: Indiana University Press, 1991), p. 6. Richey also explores the ambiguities; see pp. xii, 55–57, and ff. In a richly suggestive way, Richey describes the tension between the several Methodist languages, especially the vernacular language of religious experience that Methodists shared with other evangelicals, and their own Wesleyan

language, that distinguishing tongue that spoke of Methodist classes and quarterly meetings, local and itinerant preachers, love feasts, and Christian perfection.

16. See also the work of Diane Lobody on early Methodist women and of Will B. Gravely on African Methodists for further exploration of this issue.

17. Donald G. Mathews, *Religion in the Old South* (Chicago: University of Chicago Press, 1977), pp. 104–105. See esp. "Evangelical America—The Methodist Ideology," in which Mathews describes the subversive possibilities of Methodist "liberty," the power of self-determination conveyed by the liminal event of new birth (pp. 94–97). See also Gillespie, "Clear Leadings," p. 210.

18. Virginia Lieson Brereton, *From Sin to Salvation: Stories of Women's Conversions, 1800 to the Present* (Bloomington: Indiana University Press, 1991). See esp. pp. 28–40.

19. In her analysis of the rhetoric used by evangelical women to characterize their new relationship to God and Christ as a result of their conversion, Brereton found that the women often spoke of the "sufficiency" of grace (ibid., p. 21). This suggests to me that the centrality of the grace sufficient theme was typical and characteristic of the spirituality of Methodist women, while not unique to them, except perhaps in connection with their quest for Christian perfection.

20. Ibid., p. 37.

21. See Carroll Smith-Rosenberg, "The Female World of Love and Ritual: Relations Between Women in Nineteenth-Century America," in *Disorderly Conduct: Visions of Gender in Victorian America,* ed. Carroll Smith-Rosenberg (New York: Knopf, 1985), pp. 53–76.

22. *Memoir, Diary, and Letters of Miss Hannah Syng Bunting, of Philadelphia, Who Departed This Life May 25, 1832, in the Thirty-First Year of Her Age,* comp. Rev. T[imothy] Merritt. 2 vols. (New York: T. Mason and G. Lane, For the Sunday School Union of the Methodist Episcopal Church, 1837). See also *Walking with Jesus: as illustrated in the Life, Correspondence and Death of Mrs. Sarah Eamess,* ed. Rev. S. H. Platt (New Haven: Publ. by her Husband, Harris Eames, 1876).

23. Paul Wesley Chilcote, *John Wesley and the Women Preachers of Early Methodism* (Metuchen, N.J.: Scarecrow Press, 1991), pp. 45–91.

24. William H. Williams, *The Garden of American Methodism: The Delmarva Peninsula, 1769–1820* (Wilmington, Del.: Scholarly Resources, 1984); Doris E. Andrews, "Popular Religion and the Revolution in the Middle Atlantic Ports: The Rise of the Methodists, 1770–1800" (Ph.D. diss., University of Pennsylvania, 1986); and A. Gregory Schneider, *The Way of the Cross Leads Home* (Bloomington: Indiana University Press, 1993). Andrews's work also provides important documentation of the biracial character of these early Methodist societies [Baltimore, 1800, women 63%: c. 2/3 white, 1/3 black; NYC, 1791, women 66%: 77% white, 23% black].

25. Chilcote, *Women Preachers,* p. 92.

26. Ibid., pp. 92, 94.

27. Diane Lobody, "Lost in the Ocean of Love: The Spiritual Writings of Catherine Livingston Garrettson," in *Rethinking Methodist History,* ed. Russell E. Richey and Kenneth E. Rowe (Nashville, Tenn.: Kingswood Books, 1985), pp. 175–184. See also Lobody, "Lost in the Ocean of Love."

28. Stephen Olin, "Life Inexplicable Except as a Probation: A Discourse

Delivered in the Methodist Episcopal Church, Rhinebeck, N.Y., July 15, 1849, at the Funeral of Mrs. Catharine Garrettson" (New York: Lane & Scott, 1851), p. 40.

29. Abel Stevens, *The Women of Methodism* (New York: Carlton & Porter, 1866), p. 226.

30. Ibid.

31. Ibid.

32. Williams, *Garden,* pp. 107–111; Schneider, *Way of the Cross,* pp. 293, 297. See also A. Gregory Schneider, "Social Religion, the Christian Home, and Republican Spirituality in Antebellum Methodism," *Journal of the Early Republic* 10 (Summer 1990): 163–190.

33. Mrs. Elizabeth A. [Lyon] Roe, *Recollections of Frontier Life* (1885; reprint ed., Salem, N.H.: Arno Press, 1980).

34. Chilcote, *Women Preachers.* See Appendix A, pp. 253–287.

35. Ibid., p. 236.

36. See E. Dorothy Graham, "Chosen By God: The Female Itinerants of Early Primitive Methodism" (Ph.D. diss., University of Birmingham, 1986). Graham's careful study has identified nearly one hundred women itinerants among the early Primitive Methodists; she gives a kind of group biography of twenty of them whose diaries and autobiographies are available. These traveling women preachers were given regular appointments in distinction to women exhorters and local preachers whose roles were more spontaneous and informal.

37. Andrews, "Popular Religion," pp. 196–200.

38. The shorter version was published in *Sisters of the Spirit: Three Black Women's Autobiographies of the Nineteenth Century,* ed. William L. Andrews (Bloomington: Indiana University Press, 1986). The longer and later version appears in *Spiritual Narratives,* one of the volumes of the Schomburg Library of Nineteenth Century Black Women Writers. It was published in 1988 by Oxford University Press, with an introduction by Sue E. Houchins.

39. Nellie Y. McKay, "Nineteenth-Century Black Women's Spiritual Autobiographies: Religious Faith and Self-Empowerment," in *Interpreting Women's Lives* (Bloomington: Indiana University Press, 1989), pp. 139–154.

40. Jarena Lee, *Religious Experience and Journal,* p. 42 (in *Spiritual Narratives*). "But said the Lord, 'I will send by whom I will'—praise the Lord who willeth not the death of sinners—'as I live, saith the Lord, I have no pleasure in the death of the wicked, but that they turn and live.' " The last part of the passage quoted by Lee is from Ezekiel 18:32 and 33:11. The pattern is that of the prophetic vocation reports: I am unworthy, but there was nothing I could do; God says, "I am going to send whom I will."

41. See Jualynne Dodson, "Nineteenth-Century A.M.E. Preaching Women," in Hilah F. Thomas and Rosemary Skinner Keller, eds., *Women in New Worlds* (Nashville, Tenn.: Abingdon, 1981), pp. 276–289.

42. *Diary of Fanny Newell: with a sketch of Her Life, and an Introduction by a Member of the New England Conference of the Methodist Episcopal Church,* 4th ed. (Boston: Charles H. Pierce, 1848).

43. *Life and Observations of Rev. E[benezer] F. Newell* (Worcester, Mass., 1847), p. 138.

44. Diane Lobody's study of Garrettson also explores her desire to exercise ministerial leadership, revealed in her dreams. Lobody quotes Elizabeth Janeway: "[W]omen explore possibilities in their dreams that they cannot allow themselves to do in the working world." See Lobody, "Lost in the Ocean of Love," p. 124.

45. George Brown, *The Lady Preacher: or the Life and Labours of Mrs. Hannah Reeves*... (1870; reprint ed., New York: Garland, 1987).

46. Donald K. Gorrell, ed., *"Woman's Rightful Place"* (Dayton, Ohio: United Theological Seminary, 1980), p. 28.

47. In her introduction to *The Defense of Women's Rights to Ordination in the Methodist Episcopal Church* (New York: Garland, 1987), Carolyn DeSwarte Gifford claimed that over seventy women received preacher's licenses in the Methodist Episcopal Church in the 1870s.

48. See, for example, Elaine Magalis, *Conduct Becoming to a Woman: Bolted Doors and Burgeoning Missions* (Cincinnati: Women's Division, Board of Global Ministries, United Methodist Church, 1973), pp. 108–125, and Frederick A. Norwood, *The Story of American Methodism* (Nashville, Tenn.: Abingdon, 1974), pp. 350–353.

49. *Daily Christian Advocate,* 25 May 1880.

50. Gifford, *Defense of Women's Rights,* n.p.

51. *Christian Advocate,* 2 October 1890, p.

52. (Minneapolis: Fortress Press, 1990), pp. 13–41.

53. Ann Taves, "Mothers and Children and the Legacy of Mid-nineteenth-Century American Christianity," *Journal of Religion* 67 (April 1987): 203–219; quote is on p. 216.

54. Among the important recent studies of women and missions, see Patricia R. Hill, *The World Their Household: the American Woman's Foreign Mission Movement and Cultural Transformation* (Ann Arbor: University of Michigan Press, 1984), and Jane Hunter, *The Gospel of Gentility: American Women Missionaries in Turn-of-the-Century China* (New Haven: Yale University Press, 1984).

55. Sara Joyce Myers, "Southern Methodist Women Leaders and Church Missions, 1878–1910" (Ph.D. diss., Emory University, 1990); see also Ethel W. Born, *By My Spirit: The Story of Methodist Protestant Women in Mission 1879–1939* (New York: Women's Division, Board of Global Ministries, United Methodist Church, 1990); Donald K. Gorrell, "'A New Impulse': Progress in Lay Leadership and Service by Women of the United Brethren in Christ and the Evangelical Association, 1870–1910," in *Women in New Worlds,* ed. Hilah F. Thomas and Rosemary Skinner Keller (Nashville, Tenn.: Abingdon, 1981), pp. 233–245.

56. Louise McCoy North, *Story of the New York Branch* (New York Branch, 1926), p. 39; Miss Frances J. Baker, *The Story of the Women's Foreign Missionary Society of the Methodist Episcopal Church, 1869–1895* (Cincinnati: Curts & Jennings, 1898), pp. 22–24.

57. North, *New York Branch,* pp. 67–71.

58. *Mary Clarke Nind and Her Work,* by her Children (Chicago, 1906), p. 193.

59. North, *New York Branch,* pp. 104–105.

60. Ibid., pp. 191, 193.

61. Ibid., p. 194; Joanne E. Carlson Brown, "Jennie Fowler Willing (1834–1916): Methodist Churchwoman and Reformer" (Ph.D. diss., Boston University, 1983), pp. 80–82.

62. See, for example, William McGuire King, "The Role of Auxiliary Ministries in Late Nineteenth-Century Methodism," in Richey and Rowe, eds., *Rethinking Methodist History,* pp. 167–172; also King's "Denominational Modernization and Religious Identity: The Case of the Methodist Episcopal Church," in *Methodist History* 20 (January 1982): 75–89.

Reform, Conservative, and Orthodox Judaism in America: Is There an Alternative to Denominationalism?

MARC LEE RAPHAEL

In 1981 a publisher invited me to write a history of American Judaism to serve as one volume in a series on religions in America. The senior editor told me to organize it around the major denominations, and I must admit that I never gave this organizing structure much critical thought. True, I wrestled with how to define Orthodoxy: as a self-conscious response to the challenges modernity offers to tradition or as an attempt to reconstruct East European Jewish communities? And, depending on the answer to this, I wondered in what order I should present the branches of American Judaism: Was Orthodoxy always here, together with the earliest Jews, or (as I would argue) did a self-conscious American Orthodoxy emerge only after the rise of Reform and Conservative Judaism? Was Conservative Judaism an American denomination, or did it intentionally imitate the European model in which its origins lay—who was (and was not) a Conservative Jew in the nineteenth century? But the fundamental division into Reform, Conservative, Orthodox, and Reconstructionist Judaism, whatever the actual order, I took for granted.[1]

In this paradigm, of course, I did what scholars before me had done. The late Marshall Sklare, a sociologist, had written an entire book on Conservative Judaism; David Philipson, a congregational rabbi, had written a scholarly history of Reform Judaism; Nathan Glazer, when he wrote about the religious life of American Jews in American Judaism, organized his thinking along denominational lines.[2]

There were a few biographies of Reform, Conservative, and Orthodox rabbis, but none that even hinted at a cross-denominational or supradenominational approach, for American rabbis studied at denominational seminaries, obtained positions through denominational auspices, and served denominational congregations.[3] The only history of the American rabbinate approached its subject in the same manner: one essay on the Reform rabbinate, one on the Conservative, and one on the Orthodox.[4] The same was true for studies of synagogues, seminaries, and rabbinical organizations. Every study I consulted put its subject under one of the denominations.[5]

I organized my study of American Judaism around three major themes: denominations, rabbis, and congregants. Even the available studies and surveys of congregants' beliefs organized their material by denominations. I had few, if any, models, therefore, for a different approach, had I wished to offer a challenge to the publisher's request. But I never considered doing so, even in my mind.

The current assignment led me, for the first time, to rethink all of this. I decided to visit synagogues in two cities, Boston and San Francisco, to talk to rabbis in these communities, to read the institutional publications, and to observe the Jews who attended these synagogues and listened to these rabbis. What made this different from my previous study were two factors: the methodology and the denominational issue.

In my earlier study, I had relied overwhelmingly on printed and archival sources and rarely on observation. This time around, I decided to use my skills as a participant observer, supplemented when necessary with institutional records and local newspapers. I attended numerous worship services of each denomination in both cities; I listened carefully to and formally interviewed rabbis and informally interviewed (usually at the refreshment table) Jews who attended these worship services. In addition, as I continually reflected upon the data I was collecting, I asked myself how I was learning to rethink my traditional denominational approach.

I wish to share two areas—denominations and rabbis—in which I found myself approaching the study of Judaism in America somewhat differently from before and, after exploring these two topics, to make a modest methodological suggestion.

Denominations

In preparing this essay, I gained a much deeper appreciation of the variety of "Judaisms" housed under each denominational label. Although the meaning of the word *tradition* (or *traditional*) needs considerable discussion when applied to Judaism in America,[6] I was struck by the return to tradition in all denominations and the strong reaction to this return (let me call it "modern") in each group. The labels Reform, Conservative, and Orthodox are simply not very useful, except to inform one that a particular synagogue belongs to the umbrella organization of Reform, Conservative, or Orthodox congregations although multiple memberships in national organizations are not uncommon, and some synagogues

perceived as members of one denomination actually belong to the synagogue organization of a different branch).

I want to illustrate the denominational variety by discussing Orthodox Judaism in the San Francisco Bay Area. As recently as the first two
decades after World War II, the San Francisco Bay Area was considered a
backwater of American Judaism. Widely viewed as the most acculturated
and even assimilated Jewry in America, its most prominent Jews were far
more likely to own hotels, baseball teams, and Levi's than to be linked to
Jewish institutions or organizations, secular or religious. Even in the mid-
1980s San Francisco's Jewish community remained perhaps the least
religiously affiliated in the United States. The overwhelming majority (75
to 85 percent) of Jews in most communities, when questioned by poll-
sters about their religious preference, identify with one of the four
branches of American Judaism; in the Bay Area the largest percentage of
Jews in any city thus far surveyed (35 percent) reported their preference
as "just Jewish," "not Jewish," or "other."[7]

By the 1970s a Jewish renaissance was visible, and by the 1980s the
seven counties in the San Francisco Bay Area contained 250,000 Jews
and had emerged as one of the most vital Jewish communities in America. Its institutions included The Magnes Museum (a repository of western Judaica); an annual Jewish film festival; the Pacific Jewish Theater;
the Lehrhaus (a huge adult Jewish education program); the Midrasha
East Bay Jewish Community High School and the East Bay Ritual Burial
Society; several Jewish all-day schools and Jewish newspapers; a Chabad
(Hasidic) House located in a downtown San Francisco neighborhood
containing the city's most fashionable stores, boutiques, and galleries; a
Yiddish Folk Theater; the Jewish Arts Community of the Bay (JACOB); a
Chinese kosher restaurant (situated above a Taoist temple); a 550-
member gay-lesbian congregation; and even two New Age or Jewish
Revival congregations.

Most of the Jews with whom I discussed the Judaization of the Bay
Area pointed to the dramatic growth of a newly affluent, very self-
confident, small (less than 5 percent of the area's population), but vibrant
Orthodox community. Few would have predicted that Orthodoxy would
accompany American Jews into the single-family, split-level houses of
Marin County or the Peninsula or be a critical element in the lives of
those Jews who were building a life in the city. A vital Orthodox Jewish
life was thought to have been impossible in the Bay Area in the 1950s and
even in 1965, when I last studied this community, but by the 1980s its
presence was felt in every corner of the Bay area, including the suburbs.
So much so that what its adherents call "Torah-true Judaism" may be the
most vibrant and the fastest-growing segment of the Bay Area Judiac
community, confirming what Edward S. Shapiro noted in 1985: "The
future of Orthodoxy ... is being determined in suburbia."[8] I visited eight
Orthodox congregations (five in San Francisco, two in the East Bay, and
one on the Peninsula) between 1988 and 1990: almost all had rabbis,

although most of the congregations were quite small by the standards of the Reform and Conservative congregations in the same area.

Every observer of American Judaism knows that Orthodoxy is moving to the right religiously. This move involves a more rigorous interpretation of Jewish law, as well as a lack of tolerance for those Jews who do not live their lives according to Jewish law. The president of Modern Orthodoxy's flagship institution, Yeshiva University, consistently speaks of the Modern Orthodox as "centrists" in an (unsuccessful) attempt to try to maintain links with what other Modern Orthodox dismiss as the "ultraright." Bay Area Orthodox Jews and their institutions reflect this division among the Orthodox: both modern or centrist Jews and those Jews who have moved further to the right together make up the Orthodox Jewish community.

There is a clear division in the Bay Area between the right-wing Orthodox who, to a great extent, reject the contemporary world and the Modern Orthodox who embrace it, between those who assert an absolute dichotomy between Judaism and the secular world and those who attempt to affirm an observant life and a commitment to American society by adapting the Torah to the events and mood of their time. Non-Orthodox Jews call them both Orthodox, not so much because of their ideology of the divine origin and immutability of the Torah, but because of the institutions and organizations to which they belong and, to a lesser degree, because they observe the Sabbath and *kashrut.* The Reform and Conservative Jews of the area seem unaware of the considerable distinctions between these two broad divisions within Bay Area Orthodoxy.

There are, of course, areas of agreement within the variegated Orthodox community. To begin, even the Bay Area Modern Orthodox leaders with whom I spoke, whose sermons I read, or whom I heard speak reject the notion that dialogue with Conservative and Reform Jews will bridge the enormous ideological gap between the Torah community and what the Orthodox call the non-Torah community and lead to the discovery of a common agenda. They correctly note that Reform Jews reject the authority of Jewish law, while Conservative Jews acknowledge its significance but not its binding nature; thus, neither branch accepts the Orthodox allegiance to *halacha.* The Orthodox feel confident that there is but one Judaism, Torah Judaism, as interpreted by Orthodox Jews, and that thus, by definition, Judaism has no branches and no denominations. Since, in fact, Judaism does have several branches or denominations, "unity" dialogues between even Modern Orthodox Jews and non-Orthodox Jews are as rare as Chinese Jews in San Francisco. To the Orthodox, Conservative and Reform Judaism are not legitimate expressions of Judaism.

I must note in passing that the non-Orthodox Jews that I met, while vigorously defending the legitimacy of their ideologies and movements, have little interest in dialogue with Orthodox Jews, even those who call themselves modern. They too see their differences as unbridgeable, and the Orthodox community's preference for phrases such as "the Torah viewpoint," "divine revelation," and "Torah truths" keeps the non-Orthodox at a distance. In fact, however, and in spite of the private rhetoric, during the late 1980s Bay area Orthodox (only Modern Orthodox will talk to non-Orthodox about anything) and non-Orthodox debated frequently in public over issues such as the authority of the Orthodox in Israel, the desirability of amending the Law of Return in Israel, the acceptance in 1983 by the Reform movement of patrilineal descent in determining Jewishness, and the Jewish position on abortion. The speakers that I heard were far more interested in delineating differences than in seeking common ground.

Furthermore, I had no sense that Bay Area Reform and Conservative Jews, whether institutional leaders or laypersons, felt that their Orthodox neighbors were any more "authentic" than they. With one or two exceptions, I found no non-Orthodox rabbis, philanthropic leaders, or other Jewish leaders who felt the Orthodox were the voice of authenticity or that they were "better" Jews or that they provided role models. Bay Area Jews of all branches, as well as those who claimed to be "just Jewish," felt their expressions of Judaism or Jewishness to be as legitimate as those of Orthodox Jews who observed dietary laws and the Sabbath.

This is, I think, a very important observation, since one of the great strengths of Orthodoxy is supposed to be the belief of the non-Orthodox that the Orthodox represent "real" Judaism. The willingness of the non-Orthodox to bend over backwards defending the Orthodox is supposedly a result of non-Orthodox Jews' guilt over their less observant lifestyle. I too heard this in the past, most frequently in the 1970s and 1980s at the allocation sessions of the philanthropic organizations of American Jewry, when non-Orthodox Jews would provide generous funding for Orthodox causes and institutions because of, as they would put it, their belief that "the Orthodox are the real Jews." My San Francisco experience indicates that this rationale has virtually disappeared.

Dominating nearly every discussion I had with Chabad or Hasidic rabbis, synagogue rabbis (the two are not necessarily mutually exclusive), and Jews who attend religious and cultural events at Orthodox institutions and who identify themselves as Orthodox was the differences between the Modern Orthodox and the right-wing Orthodox in the Bay Area, or what one congregational rabbi in the East Bay called (carefully choosing political terminology) the "liberals" (his adherents) and the "reactionaries."

First, there is a strong difference in the attitude toward general culture, as well as toward secular (and even general) Jewish culture. The Modern Orthodox enthusiastically participate in the pleasures of San Francisco secular culture, taking courses and attending lectures on the Bible, modern Hebrew literature, the Jewish short story, and Jewish history (all subjects disdained by those whose intellectual world is limited to rabbinic sacred texts), and generally embrace modernity and the comforts of a middle- or upper-middle-class lifestyle, while still adhering to Orthodox norms.

The right-wing Orthodox have little interest in either general Bay Area culture (the San Francisco Opera, for example, or ballet) or even secular Jewish culture (such as the Jewish Film Festival, or the Pacific Jewish Theater). They limit their cultural activities to those sponsored by the institutions to which they belong, which are almost exclusively Jewish cultural events. Typical activities include attending a lecture by a rabbi from Jerusalem, participating in a Hebrew or Yiddish singing group, or attending a party celebrating a Jewish festival. The right-wing Orthodox reject, as vigorously as they can, not only secular culture (especially, and dramatically, the university, where many of the Modern Orthodox hold positions), but secular Jewish culture. I did note one exception: Hasidic rabbis sometimes took off their distinctive garments and wore trendy (albeit black) Italian suits, or even slacks, shirts, and sweaters. One Chabad rabbi in Palo Alto even admitted a fondness for Rockport shoes— the dressy black kind, of course.

Second, the Modern Orthodox, lay and rabbinic, see themselves as affiliated not just with a synagogue in Oakland, Berkeley, Palo Alto, or San Francisco, but with the Jewish community as a whole. They disagree with Reform and Conservative Jews ideologically but join non-Orthodox Jews at religious and secular events (Soviet Jewry rallies, Israel Independence Day celebrations, Jewish films) under the sponsorship of the larger Jewish community. In contrast, the more conservative Orthodox argue that participation with non-Orthodox is the equivalent of legitimatizing non-Orthodox forms of Judaism, and they reject such joint activity, whether sponsored by synagogues, centers, or the Jewish Community Federation. An occasional event (the anniversary of a great rabbinic authority's birth or death, the annual banquet of one institution) might bring all the Orthodox, left and right, together, but this is exceedingly rare.

Most concretely, the ultraright do not serve on boards of directors of community institutions, although they are heavily dependent on the organized Jewish community for help. The Jewish Community Federation's annual campaign funded the building and has funded the maintenance of the only *mikveh* (ritual bath) in San Francisco, but the Orthodox community, modern or sectarian, is not visible in the various combined institutions of the federation. There was only one Orthodox Jew among the fifty leaders serving on the Jewish Community Federation board in 1990, and the other institutions had only a few Modern Orthodox on their boards. But the Modern Orthodox, unlike the right-wing Orthodox, vigorously campaign for the JCF. Sixty percent of the members of the largest Orthodox congregation in the area, Adath Israel, gave to the 1990 campaign, a figure that compares well with non-Orthodox congregations in the area.[9]

Third, the ultra-Orthodox, or sectarian, Jews are not Zionists and, unlike the Modern Orthodox, they do not build their programs around

Israel. The annual graduation of the Hebrew Academy of San Francisco might feature an Israeli general, and the Modern Orthodox day schools that I visited put Israel at the center of the curriculum and featured Israeli singers at fund-raisers. The right-wing Orthodox, however, subordinated Israel. They complain that Israel is a secular country, that its founders were and its leaders are irreligious, and that, as a rule, it ignores Torah. These ultra-Orthodox institutions have built their programs exclusively around Jewish law and Torah, rather than around Israel-centered activity.

Fourth, their attitudes toward *halacha* (Jewish law) are clearly different. The Modern Orthodox have divided the *halachot* they observe into those they observe in greater or lesser degree and those they ignore. They usually began our discussions of Jewish law by affirming that *halacha* is absolutely binding (the sectarians agree); they continued by explaining that Jewish law must be interpreted (again, the sectarians agree) and that there are two categories of *halacha:* relations between God and man and relations between man and man.

The Modern Orthodox believe that in relations between God and man—matters of divinely ordained ritual, custom, and ceremony—a lenient interpretation is both possible and necessary (their disagreements with the sectarians begin here). If a box of cookies has a "K" or "U" (symbols of *kashrut*), the cookies may be eaten, since food is either kosher or it isn't. The sectarians, on the other hand, have a category of superscrupulous (*glatt*) kosher for meat, and there are serious disagreements over the acceptability of various kosher symbols, especially the "OU"; the modernists I met could not see why "plain" *kashrut* wasn't sufficient to fulfill God's command.

In the area of human relationships, the modernists articulate an ethic at least as demanding as that of the rabbis I met who had come out of a sectarian yeshiva world or defined themselves as Hasidim. In Israel, the central moral issue over which liberal and sectarian Orthodox diverge is the Arabs and the occupied territories; in the Bay Area it is clearly the attitude toward non-Orthodox Jews. The sectarians emphatically deny the legitimacy of the Judaism of the non-Orthodox; the modernists, although certain their own form of Judaism is far more authentic than non-Orthodox forms of Judaism, repeatedly use phrases such as "We are One" to convey their sense of peoplehood and participation with Reform, Conservative, and "just Jewish" Jews. Modern Orthodox Jews do not hesitate to attend mixed-seating bar or bat mitzvah ceremonies at Reform or Conservative synagogues; sectarian Orthodox refuse to participate in worship services that were not celebrated according to *halacha.* Modern Orthodox rabbis in the Bay Area do not hesitate to associate organizationally with Reform and Conservative rabbis; the sectarian rabbis refuse. In general, the "We are One" language of the modernists emphasizes what they have in common with other Jews; the "Torah-true" language of the sectarians emphasizes their uncompromising style.

One area of commonality between Bay Area Modern and sectarian

Orthodox is their enthusiastic embracing of Jews, largely assimilated, who have "returned" not just to Judaism but to traditional forms of Judaism. Although these "returnees" are by no means a homogeneous group, all the Orthodox I met referred to these Jews as *ba'alei teshuva,* or penitents.

There is no monopoly in the Bay Area as to which segment of Orthodoxy these "lapsed" Jews return to. Some "return" to Modern Orthodox synagogues, for these are much closer than are sectarian synagogues to the world from which they came. Others, seeking what they sense to be for them a more authentic traditionalism, attach themselves to Jews and to institutions that have withdrawn as much as possible from modern life.

Most of those active in encouraging assimilated Jews in the Bay Area to accept more rigorous Jewish lifestyle claim that it is largely the personality of the "recruiter" that determines which branch of Orthodoxy returnees choose. If discussions with these penitents are to be trusted, this is no exaggeration. Rarely did returnees cite a personal crisis, a rejection of secularism, or any other major psychological or emotional event as the cause of their return to Judaism. Instead, it was the charismatic personality of an Orthodox rabbi or lay leader, or perhaps the collective appeal of a group of Orthodox Jews, that enticed them to experiment with Orthodoxy, and then it was the larger Orthodox community that embraced them.

The Orthodox community seems especially eager to discover and to integrate *ba'alei teshuva.* Confronted with numerous examples among their own children and peers of people who have abandoned traditions and observance, they enthusiastically welcome those who are searching for a more structured and disciplined religious tradition than they had previously known, who fervently agree to take upon themselves the binding authority of the Torah and its commandments. The "veteran Orthodox" may consistently have exaggerated the number of *ba'alei teshuva,* claiming hundreds where there were dozens, but these penitent, or returnees represent an important stamp of approval for all Bay Area Orthodox. "See," one rabbi told a stranger, "how intelligent, worldly, accomplished men and women, searching for their roots, return to Torah."

My observation of the phenomenon in the Bay Area tends to qualify this triumphalism. A generation or two ago, one proclaimed goal of the Orthodox (the term *Modern* was seldom used because the sectarians were hardly identifiable) in America was to capture the American Jewish intellectuals. To accomplish this, Orthodox rabbis needed to meet them as intellectual equals; hence the emphasis on advanced secular studies as well as Judaic studies, the attempt to master the very culture that intellectuals found so seductive.

In contrast to other communities in which I have studied contemporary Judaism, I rarely found an intellectual among the numerous *ba'alei teshuva* active in Bay Area Orthodox institutions. Far more often, the returnees were unhappy housewives with modest secular educations, working-class Jews with unskilled jobs, or lonely Jewish men and women unable to gain social acceptance among either Jews or non-Jews. They rarely seemed "intelligent, worldly, [or] accomplished."

I now see much more clearly the existence of two camps within the orbit of authentic Orthodoxy,[10] and this seems relevant to an understanding of Orthodox Judaism in the Bay Area and elsewhere. Similar differences, for example, separate moderns from sectarians in New York. Two broad groups within the community feel strongly that they have the Ortho-doxy ("correct doctrine"), and both seem to be increasing, albeit slowly, in size and vitality. For some San Francisco Jews, the discovery of an Orthodox community seems as strange as the identifying of a new planet within the solar system. Nonetheless, it seems likely that a vital, yet highly variegated, Orthodoxy is well-established in the Bay Area.

Rabbis

I want to illustrate an alternative approach to studying the congregational rabbinate according to denomination by presenting a group portrait of non-Orthodox Boston rabbis.

Boston and its near western and northern suburbs contain more than twenty-five Conservative and Reform synagogues, which employ more than thirty-five rabbis. I closely observed eleven of these rabbis in four Conservative and four Reform synagogues. The institutions ranged in size from two hundred-member-unit congregations to those having more than one thousand member units; some were housed in temporary facilities and had annual expenditures of less than $1 million, whereas others imposed annual dues of more than $1,000 and ran multimillion-dollar fund-raising campaigns. They struck me as quite representative of the approximately eight hundred Conservative and eight hundred Reform congregations in the United States.

As a whole, the Reform congregations I observed are among the most traditional synagogues in the national organization of the Reform movement, the Union of American Hebrew Congregations, whereas the Conservative congregations appear quite similar to those I have observed in numerous other cities. Most of the Reform congregations observe the second day of Rosh Hashanah and have Sukkot, Simchat Torah, and Shavout services on the actual day of the celebration rather than on the closest Sabbath. Some have early morning Sabbath prayer groups and Torah study in addition to later Sabbath morning services and even hold *tashlich* (an atonement ritual held near a stream on the first day of the Jewish New Year) ceremonies late in the afternoon on Rosh Hashanah and *aufruf* (calling up the groom, on the Sabbath before the wedding, to the Torah) ceremonies at Sabbath morning services—rituals that are very rare in Reform congregations outside of Boston. Ten of the eleven rabbis were male (about the national average); all but one were more than forty years of age; and most of them had been serving their well-established congregations for some years. My profile of their rabbinates is a group one, and therefore it either omits or obscures marginal and idiosyncratic rabbinical styles. Nevertheless, the Boston rabbinate that I observed is so homogeneous that I became convinced I could best present a portrait of the Boston non-Orthodox rabbinate by delineating its commonalities rather than by highlighting its points of distinctiveness.

Unlike the neighboring Catholic clergy of the same age who were trained during Vatican II and in an era of liberal social currents but who now find themselves expected to preach John Paul II's conservative moral and theological agenda, none of the rabbis I studied seemed particularly confused, outmoded, or overwhelmed by the movement toward tradition in both Conservative and Reform Judaism during the 1980s. Those reared in classical Reform congregations, in which rituals and ceremonies were studiously avoided, indicated no dissatisfaction with "extra" prayer services, *tashlich,* or head covering. The Conservative rabbis (unlike so many of their colleagues, apparently) expressed no doubts or disappointments with their movement.[11] And neither Reform nor Conservative rabbis complained about salaries or fringe benefits, (such as pensions or health insurance).

Nor did they complain about their rather formal liturgical formats, although most of them participated in the omnipresent reforms of the 1960s. These reforms broke down the barriers between rabbi and congregation by moving the rabbi off the pulpit to the level of the congregation, providing alternatives to fixed liturgies, maximizing congregational singing, and minimizing preachy sermons that discouraged congregational discussion. As a group, these were rabbis who were comfortable with their physical elevation, read to (or with) their congregants, told (rather than discussed with) them about history, Torah, and Jewish values, and easily assumed the public role of actor and stage director; they were spiritual leaders who had learned to lead prayers by rote. Nor was their own spiritual questioning—and we will look at this shortly—for public display. None of these rabbis would lay out his or her own fears and spiritual questions for the congregation in sermons or introductions to liturgical selections, their questioning and doubting of the fundamentals of Jewish tradition remained a very private affair.

These congregations must be thought of not simply as religious institutions where Sabbath and holiday services occur but as synagogue-centers where groups run by everything from the Boy Scouts to Overeaters Anonymous and interfaith discussion groups were housed. Although the non-Jewish programs did not require the rabbis' time, this was not the case with regard to the numerous Jewish and Judaica programs housed in the synagogues. A common function of these Conservative and Reform rabbis, notwithstanding the presence of synagogue executive directors, is the task of administration—running the institution.

This does not necessarily mean that the rabbis have studied the financial records of their synagogues (most have not) or that they know how to change the filters in the heating apparatus (they do not). They do claim responsibility for the total functioning of the institution, even if they don't know how to fix one or more of its parts. Surprisingly, these rabbis don't complain much about this role, and it certainly does not seem to be the source of confusion or depression. Although their rabbinic training, whether at the Jewish Theological Seminary or The Hebrew Union College-Jewish Institute of Religion, included no discussion of institutional management, these rabbis seem to be quite comfortable with their administrative or managerial roles.

One of the men, who had served his congregation during three decades (the 1950s, 1960s, and 1970s), invited me to read the minutes of the Board of Trustees from 1965 to 1970 in order to obtain a sense of the managerial role he had played in the congregation. Between 1965 and 1969 he struggled with the congregation's concern over the "changing neighborhood" surrounding the synagogue (a neighboring congregation in a "changing" neighborhood had lost 128 families and 50 percent of its school children, one board member reported). He worried about how to fund the $300,000 annual budget (the 1,200 or so members were billed for $224,000), how the congregation should respond to the civil rights problems of the nation, how to "manage" (the board's term) the congregation without a full-time assistant rabbi, how properly to "mourn" Sir Winston Churchill, and whether to forsake once and for all the synagogue's bomb shelter and turn it into a mimeograph room. He sweated over contract negotiations, finally signing a $30,000-a-year (up to age sixty-five) deal that included biannual salary reviews by the Board of Trustees. The rabbi reluctantly gave in to pressure from the board and from the Combined Jewish Philanthropies of Boston to require all members of the congregation to be contributors "to the best of their ability" and enthusiastically addressed an Advanced Gifts Dinner (prior to the annual High Holy Day Appeal) that raised nearly $20,000 of its $30,000 goal.

The Ritual Committee and the rabbi took three years to work out a compromise over authority; the agreement gave the laymen the final say in all synagogue matters except for those things that are specifically given to the rabbinate (priesthood) in biblical law. The Ritual Committee further debated whether to continue using non-Jewish singers in their choir (the rabbi finally convinced the committee members to use only Jews, but the Board of Trustees, by a vote of 11–2, defeated the proposal) and joined the rabbi in proposing that, despite the by-laws, women be eligible for election to the board. The rabbi was a central actor in all of these matters, no less than in officiating at bar and bat mitzvah ceremonies or at any pulpit activity.

Unlike some of their clergy colleagues in Boston's Catholic and (occasionally) Protestant churches, these rabbis do not have spiritual advisers with whom they meet, even irregularly, to discuss their spiritual well-being. Some of them participate in an unusually stimulating rabbinic study group, but for most the demands upon their time limit their opportunities for reflection and meditation considerably.[12] If a common complaint is voiced by these rabbis, it is the lack of time available for spiritual rejuvenation and the lack of people within their religious movements to whom to turn with theological doubts and questions. One rabbi confessed to wondering, during readings of the liturgy from the pulpit, whether God "understands" prayers in both English and Hebrew (not to mention the other languages in which Jews pray). Another was bothered by the inability to find the time for personal prayer and wondered whether it was really the lack of time or doubts about the efficacy of prayer that kept his pace so hurried that time for prayer was absent.

These doubts remained private, for the rabbis felt that confessing them would be viewed by their congregants as a sign of weakness. They believed (and I could cite considerable impressionistic evidence to support them) that what their congregants want from their rabbis, above all, is not great preaching or teaching or sterling representation to non-Jews but spiritual commitment. They want a truly spiritual person, a rabbi who can pray to God as easily as she or he can talk about God, whose spiritual dimension is as deep and sincere as the educational or psychological or organizational tasks the rabbi brings to his or her rabbinate. Hence, raising questions rather than giving answers about the very basis of the faith process is widely viewed as a sign of weakness, rather than a means for spiritual growth within the worship service or within any other area save the safety of an adult-education course.

Not unrelated to the rabbi's inability to share their struggles with their faith is the lack of such struggle, publicly at least, among their congregants. Just as these rabbis point out that their seminary education, whether at the Jewish Theological Seminary or The Hebrew Union College–Jewish Institute of Religion, was filled with Hebrew Bible, rabbinics, history, commentaries, philosophy, and student pulpits, leaving no time for discussions of faith, so their congregants lead lives in which theological issues occupy none of their public hours or even family conversations. They don't, one rabbi told me, even know what questions to ask. Their congregants want leaders with deep spirituality, and they don't suggest to their leaders any hint of their own doubts, so there is little motivation for the rabbis to initiate such discussions, to take off the robe of surety and put on the dress of doubt. Unable to talk to either congregants or colleagues about these matters, rabbis find their questions and doubts a private but pervasive malaise.

Perhaps this is related to the second most common complaint of these rabbis—that they hardly know their congregants. This is, of course, less true for the rabbi with 210 families in the congregation for those with eight or nine hundred families, but it is noticeable everywhere in the Boston area. (The other side of the shekel—that synagogue members do not get to know the rabbi—is suggested by the rabbis, but I did not get to know the members beyond having brief conversations with some after worship services.) One rabbi actually thought this lack of closeness was good, suggesting that the lack of actual personal knowledge on both sides frees rabbi and congregant to use psychological means to turn the other into whatever one wants him or her to be. This rabbi rather enjoyed the sense of appearing larger than life to the congregation.

For the others, the lack of closeness was a source of concern. Unlike a rectory or parsonage, the availability of which serves as a kind of spiritual firehouse and where occupants respond to various needs of parishioners, the home of the rabbi is not as readily available to congregants, and few bring their personal problems to the rabbi. He or she celebrates life-cycle events with them, but most rabbis remain in doubt about how many congregants they really know and about the quality of that knowing. In a setting where rabbis do not regularly share with their congregants their own spiritual doubts and difficulties, the sense of distance from their congregants is heightened.

The word *rabbi* means teacher and Torah is teaching, and as we turn from the rabbis' malaise to their satisfactions, it is unquestionable that they find their greatest fulfillment in their role as teacher. This is not surprising, for surely what is most distinctive about Boston is its educational vitality. The number (or at least the proportion, however defined) of the Jewish young in colleges and universities in Boston is exceptional, as Harvard, Brandeis, Tufts, Clark, Boston University, MIT, Wellesley, and other schools attract thousands of Jewish students from all over the country. The presence of so many intellectual "stars" on the faculties or in the area may well have given the community its special cast. Surely this has its impact on the local synagogues, which host one of the most extensive assortment of serious educational programs I have observed in American Jewish life.

These rabbis then, beyond all else, see themselves as teachers. Readily acknowledging that the local competition—university-trained academics specializing in Jewish studies—is more deeply grounded in at least one area of Judaica than they, the rabbis rightly stress a crucial distinction. The professors are committed to a dispassionate explanation of the Jewish experience, whereas the rabbis are filled with passion; the academics present Judaism as one among equals, a tradition as legitimate as other traditions taught in the academy, whereas the rabbis present Judaism—its beliefs, customs, history, ideas, and values—as the most meaningful religious system for their congregants. These rabbis, with strong secular and Judaica educations, are advocates of the Judaism they teach, and in this advocacy they find abundant satisfaction.

Like the group of Conservative rabbis surveyed by Abraham J. Karp in the 1970s,[13] these Boston rabbis listed teaching as their highest priority, and they did it extremely well. They brought considerable knowledge to their classes and used it in various ways to help their students (teens through adults) to ask questions, understand the answers, and grow as Jews. I saw little evidence to confirm Gilbert S. Rosenthal's observation that the rabbinate is attracting "second- and third-rate candidates" because the best men and women choose business, medicine, law, and the academy. Perhaps he meant that the women and men entering rabbinical school in the 1980s are second-rate and the middle-aged women and men I observed were those he had in mind when he boasted about the "giants in the rabbinate" in the past?[14] I doubt it. Charles S. Liebman, too, has suggested that "the quality of the conservative and Reform rabbinate has declined."[15] I despair over how to measure quality, especially when rabbinical school committees cannot agree on the criteria to use in selecting a rabbi. Nevertheless, to the extent we can agree on some measures to define good teaching and good teachers (and there is hardly more agreement here), these are excellent teachers seriously committed to teaching.

In the early days of organized Jewish life in America, there were no ordained rabbis in the country. Poorly trained men—sextons, *hazzanim* (cantors), reverends, teachers—served the modest needs of the none-too-demanding congregations. The first ordained rabbi arrived in 1840; until the 1870s, when The Hebrew Union College was founded, and the 1880s, when the Jewish Theological Seminary was established, those American congregations that had rabbinical leadership secured European-trained men, largely from Germany. It was these men who expanded the rabbinic role into more or less the form we know today. With the growth of the two American seminaries, a professionalized rabbinate began to emerge. In addition, American-born and -trained rabbis not only served congregations; quite a few of these Conservative and Reform rabbis established national reputations in the first five or six decades of the twentieth century.

Karp claimed that the "1950s and 1960s were the 'glory days' of the American rabbinate," when rabbis were given "respect and exerted influence."[16] I suspect that the 1920s, 1930s, and 1940s were no less "glory days," as prominent rabbis, with large congregations, considerable control over trustees and administrators, significant local and national reputations, and extensive influence as speakers and writers, dominated the Reform and Conservative rabbinates. The rabbi was, until quite recently, usually the most educated among his congregants (in terms of both Jewish education and secular, general learning), and in the larger congregations, where an assistant did most of the daily nuts-and-bolts work of the congregation, the senior rabbi was free to address not only the Jewish but the national and international events swirling in the news. With his congregation growing and his congregants satisfied, he began to be respected not only for the intellectual acumen and spiritual conviction he brought to his rabbinate but for the synagogue he "managed" and for the sheer size of this congregation.[17]

Boston's rabbis are clearly much less concerned with increasing size of their congregations, dominating their congregants, or gaining a reputation outside the congregation. No Conservative or Reform congregational rabbi in America is any longer a household word, even in his or her own movement; these men and women face enough of a struggle in becoming household names in the homes of their own congregants. There are so many others to whom congregants can now turn for help with their emotional needs; the spiritual needs of the congregants seem modest, and only a small number pray sufficiently regularly for the rabbi to know them as worshippers. This has left the classroom as the primary center of meeting, in the real sense of the word, for most of these rabbis and their congregants.

A Modest Proposal

Nonlinearity has become a commonplace among mathematicians and scientists, and it seems to me that it offers us an alternative to the linear model we have long utilized for explaining Judaism in America: Reform on the left, Orthodoxy on the right, and Conservative Judaism resting somewhere along the middle of a line drawn horizontally across a page. But the massive amount of data available to the student of American Judaism, both as a participant observer and as a researcher, yields a portrait that is not quite so linear. Orthodoxy has at least two major divisions—let us call them "resisters" and "accommodators"—and this is no less true for Reform and Conservative Judaism. All of this adds up to a complex picture that, to some, might seem like chaos and thus, as one scientist has argued, "defies direct analytic treatment."[18]

The obvious manner in which scholars have made sense of this mass of data is to accept the institutional divisions in the American Jewish community and to speak of denominations. Perhaps, however, it is more useful to begin to speak about a number of Judaisms within the three large branches of American Judaism. It is more helpful, then, to imagine some geometrical forms, rather than a straight line, in trying to characterize and classify the behavior of Jews in America—something akin to breaking down the compartmentalization of knowledge that is the culture-bound legacy of a form of linearization derived from the aesthetic of simplicity or imagining alternatives to the prevalent political science "realist" concept of discrete frontiers separating the realms of autonomous nation-states.

Scientists have usually sought to reduce matters to their simplest terms, to group such simplified phenomena under a single law, to rid themselves of all ambiguities, and to attain precision. I think students of American Judaism have been doing something similar; fearful of wallowing in ambiguity and ambivalence, they have constantly tried to reduce the variables and to find a slot for rabbis, synagogues, and congregants. This assignment has suggested to me that I might fruitfully increase the number of variables and search for that which interconnects. Instead of regarding complexity and ambiguity as weaknesses, I sense that to classify and compartmentalize is limiting. My vision, after preparing this paper, is much better able to encompass both similarity and difference.

NOTES

1. Marc Lee Raphael, *Profiles in American Judaism: The Reform, Conserva-tive, Orthodox, and Reconstructionist Traditions in Historical Perspective* (San Francisco: Harper & Row, 1984).

2. Marshall Sklare, *Conservative Judaism: An American Religious Move-ment,* 2nd ed. rev. (Glencoe, Ill.: Free Press, 1972); David Philipson, *The Reform Movement in Judaism,* 2nd ed. rev. (New York: Macmillan, 1931); Nathan Glazer, *American Judaism,* 2nd ed. rev. (Chicago: University of Chicago, 1972). See also "Revisiting a Classic," *American Jewish History* 77, 2 (December 1987), devoted entirely to Glazer's book. (See also Michael A. Meyer, *Response to Modernity: A History of the Reform Movement in Judaism* (New York: Oxford University Press, 1988). We badly need a scholarly history of Orthodox Judaism in America.

3. Melvin Urofsky, *A Voice that Spoke for Justice: The Life and Times of Stephen S. Wise* (Albany: State University of New York Press, 1982); Aaron Rothkoff, *Bernard Revel: Builder of American Orthodoxy* (Philadelphia: Jewish Publication Society, 1972); Simon Noveck, *Milton Steinberg: Portrait of a Rabbi* (New York: Ktav, 1978); Aaron Rakeffet-Rothkoff, *The Silver Era in American Jewish Orthodoxy: Rabbi Eliezer Silver and His Generation* (New York: Yeshiva University Press, 1981).

4. Jacob Rader Marcus and Abraham J. Peck, *The American Rabbinate: A Century of Continuity and Change, 1883–1983* (Hoboken, N.J.: Ktav, 1985).

5. Alexandra S. Korros and Jonathan D. Sarna, *American Synagogue His-tory: A Bibliography and State of the Field Survey* (New York: Marcus Wiener, 1988); Samuel E. Karff, ed., *HUC-JIR at One Hundred Years* (Cincinnati: HUC Press, 1976); Gilbert Klaperman, *The Story of Yeshiva University* (New York: Macmillan, 1969); Louis Berstein, *Challenge and Mission: The Emergence of the English Speaking Orthodox Rabbinate* (New York: Shengold, 1982). See also Nina Beth Cardin and David Wolf Silverman, eds., *The Seminary at 100: Reflec-tions on the Jewish Theological Seminary and the Conservative Movement* (New York: Jewish Theological Seminary, 1987), and Jeffrey S. Gurock, *the Men and Women of Yeshiva: Higher Education, Orthodoxy, and American Judaism* (New York: Columbia University Press, 1988).

6. I discuss tradition and modernity in "Tradition in Modern Dress: Jews and Judaism in a World of Change," forthcoming in *Jewish History* 7, no. 1 (Spring 1993): 107–16.

7. Gary A. Tobin and Sharon Sassler, *Bay Area Jewish Community Study, Special Report: Jewish Identity and Community Involvement* (Waltham, Mass.: Brandeis University, 1988), pp. 20–45.

8. Edward S. Shapiro, "Orthodoxy in Pleasantdale," *Judaism* 34, no. 2 (Spring 1985): 163–170.

9. Personal communication, Brian Lurie, executive vice president, Jewish Community Federation, 9 May 1991.

10. Charles S. Liebman delineated the division of Orthodox into modern and sectarian, as well as uncommitted and committed, in his essay, "Orthodoxy in American Jewish Life," in *American Jewish Year Book* 66 (1965): 21–92. See also Samuel C. Heilman and Steven M. Cohen, *Cosmopolitans and Parochials: Mod-ern Orthodox Jews in America* (Chicago: University of Chicago Press, 1989).

11. Compare Bernard Martin, "Conservative Judaism and Reconstruction-

ism," in B. Martin, ed., *Movements and Issues in American Judaism* (Westport, Conn.: Greenwood Press, 1978), p. 134.

12. A recent study of Reform, Conservative, and Reconstructionist rabbis found that "study" ranked considerably higher than "meditation" when the surveyor asked which aspects of a religious life the rabbis find most meaningful and important. Elaine Shizgal Cohen, "Rabbi Roles and Occupational Goals: Men and Women in the Contemporary American Rabbinate," *Conservative Judaism* 42, no. 1 (Fall 1989): 27.

13. Abraham J. Karp, "The Conservative Rabbi," in Marcus and Peck, *The American Rabbinate,* pp. 98–172.

14. Rabbinical Assembly of America, *Proceedings of the 1987 Convention* (New York: RAA, 1987), p. 111.

15. Charles S. Liebman, "A Grim Outlook," in *The Quality of American Jewish Lives—Two Views,* ed. Steven M. Cohen and Charles S. Liebman (New York: American Jewish Committee, 1987), p. 33.

16. Karp, "The Conservative Rabbi," p. 150.

17. Harold Saperstein noted in the 1970s that "our congregations [*sic*] are often as well or better informed than the rabbi on the problems of society and the cultural content of our civilization." See "The Changing Role of the Rabbi: A Reform Perspective," in Gilbert S. Rosenthal, ed., *The American Rabbi* (New York: Ktav, 1977), p. 162.

18. David Campbell, "Nonlinear Science: From Paradigms to Practicalities," *Los Alamos Science* 15 (1987): 233.

African Methodisms and
the Rise of Black
Denominationalism

WILL B. GRAVELY

At least since 1921, when Carter G. Woodson published his classic survey, *History of the Negro Church,* it has been commonplace to refer to religious separatism in the free black communities of the post-Revolutionary generation as "the independent church movement."[1] A quarter century earlier, Bishop James W. Hood of the African Methodist Episcopal, Zion Church used a similar idiom to describe the origins of northern black congregations. Discounting denominational differences among antebellum black Protestants, Hood argued that a common racial bond made for "a general, grand, united and simultaneous Negro movement." Regretting the scarcity of early sources and the absence of comprehensive histories, the bishop declared, "there was more in it than what appears on the surface," for "it was a general exodus of colored members out of white churches."[2]

Contemporary historians have reinforced the implications of Woodson's and Hood's writings by treating the earliest institutionalization of black religion in the United States, as distinct from the "invisible institution" of slave religion, in terms of incipient black nationalism.[3] Their interpretive perspective emphasizes the natural evolution of separate churches within the expanding African-American community life of northern urban community centers in the late eighteenth century. The social forces that account for their emergence lie in the demography of black communities, the effects of migration and of economic change on their composition, and the presence of intrareligious competition and social dissent within them. Preeminently, black religious independence arose from communal initiative and from a corporate ethnic consciousness that expressed "nationalist aspirations" at a pretheoretical but practical institutional level.[4] Simply put, black churches, as the first public institutions controlled by black people, provided the original context for what E. Franklin Frazier called "a nation within a nation"—the institutional equivalent to W. E. B. Du Bois's insight about the dialectic of double-consciousness in black American experience and identity.[5]

Much of the protonational orientation of the earliest black churches, to return to Bishop Hood's analogy, existed beneath the surface. Obviously, separate black churches served the needs of the black communities in which they resided. Insofar as these communities formed a separate culture, an implied "black nationality" was present from the beginning. The fact that by the 1830s there was a black press, an annual convention system, and numerous voluntary associations alongside the churches gives such an argument strong force. And there were interlocking relationships between free African-American benevolent societies in Boston, Providence, Newport, New York, and Philadelphia as far back as the 1780s, with a coordinated effort to sponsor emigration to Africa.[6] Within the independent church movement, however, local developments with differing connections to biracial denominational structures were primary for a generation. Not until the appearance of separate black denominations with itinerating ministers was there a coordinated effort to create networks linking black communities. Denominationalism, however, brought not only connections to other congregations. It also meant schism and competition within black communities.

The nearest equivalent of a corporate linkage between the first separated congregations appears in Daniel Coker's pamphlet against slavery published in 1810. In his appendix, the black Methodist preacher and schoolmaster used the early images of "chosen generation," "royal priesthood," "holy nation," and "peculiar people" to demonstrate "what God [was] doing for Ethiopia's sons in the United States of America." His evidence was the African church movement, contained in a complication of four lists in which he named thirteen ordained black clergy (excluding himself), an additional eleven licensed Methodist local preachers, eight "descendants of the African race, who [had] given proofs of their talents" in public, and fifteen separated congregations. The churches represented four denominational traditions, all biracial at the time of Coker's writing, and ten cities, including the ill-fated African Methodist congregation in Charleston, South Carolina, to which Denmark Vesey would belong. But Coker saw them all as "African churches," whose common characteristic lay in their nearly simultaneous emergence in less than two decades.[7]

Over the twelve years following the appearance of Coker's booklet, a new institutional structure, black denominationalism, evolved within the African church movement. In that development, Coker was instrumental, becoming a separatist leader among black Methodists in Baltimore and merging his followers with dissidents in the region around Philadelphia to form in 1816 the second of the three African Methodist denominations. (Three years earlier, in 1813, black Methodists in Wilmington, Delaware, had made the first denominational break with the Methodist Episcopal

Church to create the African Union Church.) Then, in 1822 a third African Methodist denomination arose in New York City, culminating more than two decades of separate congregational existence of the Zion church.

This essay, as a retelling of a familiar history, has been motivated by three concerns. First, the renaissance of black history over the past three decades has surfaced new or forgotten sources that flesh out the basic story and make possible comparative analysis across denominational and community boundaries. Methodist developments in Philadelphia, Baltimore, Wilmington, and New York can be seen in the larger context of the independent church movement.[8]

Second, this study concentrates on the shift within the independent church movement from congregational autonomy within patterns of interdependence with biracial denominational judicatories to denominational autonomy. Since the three African Methodist denominations pioneered in this process, my question has been how and why they took religious separatism to its fullest conclusion. By studying this question, I will assess the implications of black denominationalism within American church history generally.[9]

Finally, there are several pragmatic issues that were contested by white and black Methodists during the shift to congregational autonomy and to African-American denominationalism. I draw particular attention to five factors indigenous to the organizational life of Christian churches: access to ordination, representation in denominational governance, consultation about pastoral appointments and services, ownership and use of church property, and participation in congregational discipline. These same factors were present in Baptist, Presbyterian, and Protestant Episcopal settings where, as in Methodist churches, the maintenance of white control and the refusal to share white power with black members triggered the rise of independent congregations. Black churchfolk refused to contain or segregate the sacred power they experienced in Christian faith from these more mundane forms of power. They wanted to elect and to be elected to office, to ordain and be ordained, to discipline as well as to be disciplined, to preach, exhort, pray, and administer sacraments—in sum, to have their gifts and graces acknowledged by the whole community. Where that acknowledgement was withheld, black Christians resisted and protested, organized and created new institutional alternatives for themselves.

I

Our only design is to secure to ourselves our rights and privileges, to regulate our affairs, temporal and spiritual, the same as if we were white people.[10]

Richard Allen and the trustees of Bethel Church to the Philadelphia
Conference of the Methodist Episcopal Church, April 8, 1807

When Bishop Francis Asbury preached the dedicatory sermon on June 29, 1794, the first African Methodist church building, named Bethel, was available for black Methodists in Philadelphia.[11] The event ended eight years of struggle for Richard Allen, a former slave and a local preacher in the Methodist society who formed a class of forty-two black members in 1786 and who first proposed that a separate "place of worship" be erected "for the colored people." His suggestion met with opposition both from the Methodist elder that year, Caleb Boyer, and from "the most respectable people of color in this city."[12] In November 1787 Allen convened black members of "the Methodist Society of Philadelphia" to consider "the evils under which they laboured, arising from the unkind treatment of their white brethren." The meeting apparently followed an incident, told without date in Allen's autobiography, at Saint George's Church in which white trustees pulled black worshippers from their knees during prayer.[13]

Between 1788 and 1791 Allen endured the threats of Richard Whatcoat and Lemuel Green, elders in Philadelphia, who tried, he recalled later, to "prevent us from going on" with an "African church" project.[14] During the same period he was censured and finally excluded from the Free African Society, which organization he helped found in April 1787. As they banished Allen in June 1789, his colleagues charged him with "attempting to sow division among us" and with "rashly calling or convening the members together." He had, according to his own account, continued to support the ideas of an African church, even though the Free African association took upon itself in 1791 the major responsibility for constructing a building and working out "a plan of church government." When that plan turned out to be Protestant Episcopal in polity (a result of the influence of Dr. Benjamin Rush), Allen cooperated with the project but refused an invitation to be the church's first pastor. Intent on remaining Methodist despite the difficulties he had experienced in the denomination, Allen, with a committee of ten others, turned to the community for subscriptions to his Bethel Church. The campaign began in the spring of 1794, just as Saint Thomas's African Episcopal Church, was being completed. St. Thomas's construction was halted for three months during the yellow fever epidemic, resuming in December 1793. It opened for worship July 17, 1794. By summer a blacksmith shop frame had been remodeled into a suitable building for Bethel.[15]

If the dedication of the first Bethel building in June 1794 closed one struggle for Richard Allen, his model for the congregation and its relationship with the Methodist Episcopal denomination ensured that further difficulties awaited him. Allen was officially unordained but was licensed as a local preacher with responsibilities under white elders assigned to Saint George's Church. His initiative had solved the first problem confronting black Methodists who retained fresh memories of "many inconveniences" that resulted "from white people and people of color mixing together in public assemblys [*sic*]." Issuing a "public statement" in November 1794, Allen and the Bethel trustees justified their need for "a convenient house to assemble in separate from our white brethren."

The Bethel proclamation contained ten articles and regulations that confirmed the intent to abide by "the Methodist Episcopal Church for our Church government and discipline with her creeds and articles for our faith." Since the black congregation held the deed for the church property, however, a disclaimer was necessary to protect the "right and proprietory of our house" from denominational ownership. Moreover, the document asserted the goal of the Bethel founders to push for ordination of black "persons endowed with gifts and graces to speak for God." It also declared the "right" of the majority of voting members (males in close communion) of the congregation "to call any brother that appears to us adequate to the task to preach or exhort as a local preacher, without the interference of the Conference, or any other person or persons whatsoever." Beyond that, the statement defined provisions for elections, limited membership to "descendants of the African race" (while retaining "mutual fellowship" with "white brethren" as visitors "in Bands, classes and Love Feasts"), empowered trustees with "temporal concerns," and retained "matters of a spiritual nature concerning discipline" as "now in use in the Church."[16]

The "public statement" was an assertion of black religious independence, not a negotiated agreement with the Methodist Episcopal denomination. The posture of Allen and the Bethel trustees, who insisted on remaining Methodist while holding property for blacks to use and refusing to worship at Saint George's Church, must have been enigmatic to many whites. Allen was publicly committed to the denomination, had its bishop behind him, and opened the building to sympathetic white ministers in the Methodist conference. Yet he did not turn over the property to the denominational officials, and his congregation claimed an autonomy disallowable under Methodist traditions and practice. It was not surprising, therefore, that in 1795 "our warfare and troubles," Allen would later remember, "now began afresh." That year John McClaskey, whom Allen had faced down in 1792 over fund-raising for the first African church, returned to the Saint George's appointment as elder. Determined to respond vigorously to Bethel's autonomy, McClaskey found that it was necessary to turn to Ezekiel Cooper, on leave from the itinerant ministry and trustworthy to blacks because of his strong antislavery position, and ask him to negotiate a compromise.[17]

That compromise included a charter of incorporation, dated September 12, 1796, and entitled "Articles of Association of the African Methodist Episcopal Church." The articles required loyalty to the denomination but placed the Bethel property under a board of black trustees "for the religious use of the ministers and preachers of the Methodist Episcopal Church" and "likewise for our African brethren." They retained the stipulation from the "public statement" that members would always be "coloured persons." A similar provision protected defendants in cases of congregational discipline, allowing appeal beyond the white elder to a jury from the Bethel church. At the same time, the black congregation conceded the right of the white elder to license and to assign local preachers and to officiate sacramentally. It added, however, the qualification "for the time being" after its recognition of the elder's authority over "spiritual concerns." Reiterating the forceful assertion of 1794, the leaders of Bethel anticipated a time when white supervision would end, when "coloured brethren shall graduate into holy orders," as the articles expressed it. Such expectations were established on reasonable grounds of comparison with another denomination; Absalom Jones, a former Methodist and a leader in the Free African Society, had already been consecrated deacon in the Protestant Episcopal ministry.[18]

Three years after the incorporation, the articles were made public, and Bishop Asbury ordained Allen the first black deacon in the Methodist Episcopal Church. A few months later, the General Conference of 1800 approved Asbury's innovation and provided for other such ordinations, but there were still difficulties to be faced. The legislation was left out of the *Discipline,* thus making the office of black local deacon an anomaly in the Methodist system.[19] As it stood, Allen was not a member of the annual conference of traveling ministers but remained under the supervision of the elder for Philadelphia. The unprecedented local nature of the office prevented him from celebrating the Lord's Supper or from officiating at baptisms and weddings outside the appointment or when the elder was available.[20]

The curb on Allen's ministerial authority did not hamper the growth of the Bethel congregation. Moreover, Allen's varied business activities kept him active beyond his pastoral duties. Black membership at Bethel and Zoar, another black mission established in 1794, grew spectacularly, from 211 in 1799 to 738 in 1805.[21] In 1801 Allen published a hymnal for use in the church.[22] He maintained good relations with several of the white Methodist clergy who came to the city and who often stayed with him and Sarah Allen when the visitors officiated at Bethel.[23]

The accommodation of 1796, however, worked only when the white elder in Philadelphia conceded a large measure of autonomy to Allen and the black trustees—an autonomy assumed in the public statement of 1794 and effectively guarded in the Articles of Agreement. When the Virginian James Smith came to Saint George's in 1805, old controversies flared up over congregational discipline and the limits and powers of the white elder. After Smith threatened to lay claim to the Bethel property in behalf of the denomination, Allen was forced to admit how vulnerable the Bethel trustees were, depending on how the Articles were construed. By a two-thirds vote of the members, the congregation amended its charter to become a civil corporation. Consulting a lawyer, he found a way to secure Bethel's interest. The state supreme court approved the document—"The African Supplement"—on March 16, 1807.[24]

The new legal measure addressed the perennial irritants—questions about the ownership and the use of property, the powers of the trustees, and the absence of ordained black elders to function in the congregational life of the Bethel church. In place of "the consent of the elder," its first article substituted a two-thirds ratification by the adult male membership of "one year's standing" as the requirement for approving all property transactions by the trustees. Three other major changes aimed at reducing the power of the elder completed the revisions. Under the amended charter, the trustees could appoint "any other person, duly qualified" according to the Methodist *Discipline* to "preach and exhort" if the elder did not officiate, as was his right, "once every Sunday, and once during the course of the week." The alteration made the elder's right into the trustees' demand and moved the power of selection fully into their hands. Amendments also empowered the local preachers at Bethel to hold quarterly meetings, love feasts, and trials of "disorderly members" when the elder neglected or refused to do so. Disciplinary cases where former members of Bethel who had been expelled had "been received as members of the Methodist Episcopal Church elsewhere" made another change imperative. Having vested the trustees with the right to open buildings to meetings, the Supplement backed them in maintaining excommunication by barring any who had been dismissed from Bethel Church.[25]

The Supplement extended the autonomous authority of the Bethel congregation and challenged, again, the usual requirements of Methodist structure. This action would not have been necessary, of course, had Allen or other black deacons been advanced to elder's orders or become members of the annual conference. As it was, the Philadelphia Conference accepted Allen's notification, signed as pastor, that the Supplement had been legally obtained. Denying independence or separation as a goal, the statement, nonetheless, reasserted black autonomy. "Our only design," it read, "is to secure to ourselves our rights and privileges, to regulate our affairs, temporal and spiritual, the same as if we were white people." On behalf of the conference, Bishop Asbury accepted the memorial, expressing confidence "that our African brethren" remained "Methodists according to our Discipline." The carefully worded response did not approve the Supplement but received it insofar as it was "not contrary to the allowed usages, customs, and privileges of the Methodist Episcopal Church."[26] The two contradictory positions were fated to come face-to-face before some third party. Meanwhile, Allen had weathered another challenge to African Methodism, while remaining, however tenuously, within the denomination structure.

The Supplement did not end Bethel's problems, but it did ensure the congregation's ultimate protection and pave the way to denominational separation. Its passage went relatively unnoticed for four years, but in 1811 the Methodist Conference went on the offensive. First, the trustees at Saint George's Church claimed that the Supplement was void because they had not approved it. The contention accompanied a move to reconnect Bethel to the appointment at Saint George's. Second, the elder, Stephen G. Roszel, sought unsuccessfully to have the Bethel membership repeal the Supplement by the same means that had been used to obtain it in the first place. Neither tactic succeeded. In 1812 Bethel was made a stationed church and placed, with two other congregations, under Thomas G. Sergeant. When that plan was discontinued the next year, the old question, rooted in the refusal of the Methodists to sanction black elders, reemerged. The Bethel congregation appealed to Bishop Asbury for assistance, but he refused to intervene.[27]

A controversy smoldered during the next two years over the fee structure for sacramental services, part of an effort to curb Bethel's financial independence. When Bethel came under Saint George's church, its elder and the black trustees disagreed over money. From the elder's point of view, the black congregation ought to contribute funds to support the larger connectional ministry of which it was part. The issue was not the fees charged for services performed, except in cases of conducting marriages.[28] From the point of view of Allen and the Bethel trustees, the one remaining limit on their autonomy was their lack of access to elder's orders and to the sacramental authority it conferred. Until those privileges could be had, Bethel would pay for the necessary services. The Bethel trustees' resistive position was calculated to force their denomination to open up all levels of clerical orders; the alternative would be continued irritation from black members.[29]

By this time blacks numbered more than thirteen hundred, or about two fifths of the Methodist membership in Philadelphia. By far one of the largest congregations in the denomination, Bethel had achieved a level of success that was viewed ambivalently by white officials. Moreover, significant changes had accompanied the denomination's rapid growth. After 1800, it consistently backed away from its original antislavery standards for church membership and ordination. Had Allen been ordained elder, he would have met with slave-owning ministerial colleagues in conferences in the border states and in the South. Accommodation to proslavery sentiment was so necessary that Bishop Asbury and the General Conferences of 1804 and 1808 approved expurgated versions of the *Discipline* with the chapter opposing slavery omitted. Following the abortive effort to petition state legislature in behalf of emancipation in 1800, the denomination withdrew from taking any official position on the social and political question of human bondage.[30] While these developments occurred without Allen's participation or direct comment, he could hardly have failed to notice them.

As a further complication, there may have been a breach between Allen and Bishop Asbury. Although he had sponsored the black diaconate and had earlier been a staunch opponent of slavery, Asbury had finally compromised about emancipation. His journal in 1809 reflects the denomination's concessions, fatefully conceding that saving the souls of the Africans was more important than freeing their bodies. There is no direct evidence of an overt break with Allen, only Lorenzo Dow's retrospective suggestion, but Asbury made no mention of the black leader or the Bethel church in his journal or letters during the last five years of his life. And, after ordaining eight additional black local deacons for New York and for Philadelphia between 1806 and 1809, Asbury ceased to perform the procedure.[31]

Two events in the summer of 1814 set in motion the actions that led in the next year and a half to a final break between Allen's Bethel congregation and Asbury's denomination. On July 7 John Emory, the pastor of the Academy church in Philadelphia and a future bishop, issued a public letter disowning the Bethel membership as Methodist because the black trustees were exercising the spiritual discipline as outlined in the African Supplement. Later the same month, a legal challenge to their authority forced a showdown. In 1812 Robert Green was excommunicated by a disciplinary committee of ten officials at the Bethel church for breach of rules. As a trustee himself, Green complained to the white elder and then took the case to the state supreme court. His suit was argued on July 30, 1814. The following January, the judges overturned the church's action on procedural defects in the "manner this Committee was selected or appointed" for the disciplinary trial of Green.[32]

A few weeks later, just before the Philadelphia Conference met in the spring, Robert R. Roberts, pastor at Saint George's Church, tested whether the court's action had discredited Allen's leadership or the power of the trustees. He announced his intention to preach at Bethel, as was his right by the original Articles of Agreement. The trustees, not to be outdone, stood on the authority of the Supplement, which gave them the prerogative to choose preachers. When Roberts arrived, he found Jacob Tapsico in the pulpit. Rebuffed, Roberts left the building, but further strife was predictable.[33] In a new effort to thwart Bethel's autonomy, the annual conference tried again to include the black church in the regular appointments. The new elder at Saint George's, an Irishman named Robert Burch, would add Bethel to his pastorate for 1815.[34]

Green's lawsuit raised another challenge to the Supplement, this time over the issue of local control of property. Green's victory forced a sheriff's sale of the land and the building on June 12, 1815; Allen, as highest bidder, retained possession.[35] But the tug-of-war was still not over. In December Burch, following the example of Roberts, sought to preach at Bethel, using Green, the disaffected trustee, as his host. On this occasion the congregation blocked the aisles at the New Year's Eve service, preventing Burch from going to the front of the church. That collective symbolic gesture brought the developments of nearly thirty years full circle. In the early years of incipient black independence, white trustees and black members had clashed in Saint George's church. Now the shoe was on the other foot as the Bethel trustees and the congregation physically prevented the Saint George's minister from officiating in their building.[36]

Burch immediately petitioned the state supreme court for access to the pulpit, but the judges refused to grant his claim. Instead, the Bethel church, standing on the legality of the African Supplement, gained its independent status. Four months after the announcement of the court's decision, it joined representations from Baltimore, Salem (New Jersey), and Attleborough (Pennsylvania) to form the African Methodist Episcopal denomination. After waiting seventeen years, Allen was ordained elder and named, after Daniel Coker became ineligible, the bishop of the new organization. He served in that capacity until his death in 1831.[37]

II

Gone with Coker
> Designation used in the membership records of the black Methodist
> societies of Baltimore to indicate those who had withdrawn to form Bethel
> Church and join the African Methodist Episcopal denomination

The beginning of an independent African Methodist church in Baltimore is difficult to substantiate with primary evidence, given the limited information on the stages that led to a final break for more than two hundred members, exhorters, and local preachers in the black classes in 1815. Secondary sources, in the form of autobiographical recollections and undocumented histories, refer to the roots of a separatist movement in 1787, the second year in which the annual minutes of the Methodist Episcopal Church recorded membership by race. The tradition recounts objections by blacks to seating arrangements in the gallery of the Light Street church, objections that led to separate classes and prayer meetings in houses and businesses such as Caleb Hyland's boot-blacking cellar.[38] The degree of racial separation over the next decade, beyond the division of black members into their own classes (a development that was apparent as early as 1786) is impossible to establish. Black Methodist membership in the city did grow from 111 in that year to 269 in 1788. The numbers seven years later were not substantially higher, with 282 members in the societies of the city and in a separate circuit.[39]

In 1795 there was sufficient interest in forming "a distinct African, yet Methodist Church" that negotiations began with white officials such as Bishop Asbury. No documents similar to the Articles of Association used in Philadelphia and in revised form in New York survive, but Asbury made clear that the same assertive posture that had characterized the Bethel movement under Allen was evident in Baltimore. In October 1795 the proposals that had come to him asked that "in temporals" the African Methodists be "under their own direction." Taken by surprise at the full implications of the plan, Asbury regarded the blacks as asking "greater privileges than the white stewards and trustees had a right to claim."[40] Twenty months later, he was still "trying to organize the African church," but by that time the project to obtain a building had already advanced.[41]

It is not clear whether Asbury's reference in 1797 was to a building that the African Academy first leased for black education by the American

Convention for Promoting the Abolition of Slavery or to a short-lived effort to establish a second African church in rented quarters on Fish Street.[42] The Academy building, which became by deed in 1802 the Sharp Street church, was the single African meetinghouse listed in Baltimore's city directory that year and on a map in 1804.[43]

During the decade 1801–1811, black trustees held and sold land and obtained title to the Academy building in behalf of the African Methodist Episcopal classes in Baltimore. A Bethel congregation, which traced its origins to the abortive Fish Street organization in 1797, may have continued to meet separately from other black Methodists in the Academy, since Daniel Coker's pamphlet of 1810 refers to two African Methodist churches in the city. If that was the case, however, there was still a common identity between all the black Methodist classes of Baltimore until 1815. By 1812 a separate Asbury African church was an additional meeting place for these classes, but it was not until there was a formal break, led by Coker, that the buildings can be said to have spawned identifiable congregations. The Sharp Street and the Asbury congregations after 1815 remained loyal to the Methodist Episcopal Church, thus inheriting the property rights of the original African church of Baltimore even though they did not incorporate until 1832. The separatists, on the other hand, were forced to find new quarters; Coker first rented a former Presbyterian building and then purchased the Fish Street property originally used in 1797.[44]

It is not clear when the white Methodists in Baltimore licensed the first black local preachers and exhorters, but in 1810 Coker, whom Asbury had ordained a local deacon in 1808, listed seven men in those roles. That pattern of leadership, to which black class leaders should be added, remained normative until the secession of 1815. Black classes met in locations around the city, worshipped in two African churches, and depended on white elders for sacramental functions and final disciplinary authority. There was a modicum of black independence in the system, for black trustees owned and controlled property, Coker was a local deacon, black local preachers gave congregational leadership, and black exhorters and class leaders functioned in customary fashion. The city's black population responded to the religious energies of the African Methodists, for the congregation grew from 637 in 1808 to 973 in 1813.[45] By March 1814 the totals were indeed impressive: forty-one classes with 1,552 members, eight black local preachers, and ten black exhorters.[46]

Seeds of dissension were also present, however, as a negotiated agreement between the white elder and the "African Church in Baltimore" in 1814 recognized. The document, designed "to preserve the peace and union" of the black classes with the denomination, spelled out the pastoral expectations of the white elder. The black membership unquestionably felt slighted; it had to request that special attention to given to the visitation of the sick, the baptism of the children, a regular pastoral conference with the classes at least quarterly, and the performance of funeral services, with sermons "if the deceased have been an aged upright official member, who died tryumphant [*sic*] in the Lord." In exchange, the African society agreed "to bear their part of the expense of the preacher."[47]

The agreement of 1814, as viewed by newer members and by the younger leaders, did not meet the real needs for black independence.[48] With Coker at the center, a group of dissidents met weekly to prepare for full separation, according to David Smith, who was part of the circle. By this time, developments in Philadelphia were well known to the Baltimore organizers, and Coker was coordinating his plans with Richard Allen. The "club," as Smith termed the group, agreed to make the break late in 1815, a few weeks prior to the final round of controversy in Philadelphia. More than two hundred members of the black classes kept to the agreement, leaving Methodist Episcopal authorities to strike their names from the rolls with the comment "gone with Coker."[49] Over the next four years, the new Bethel congregation worked out problems of incorporation and obtained its own property. In 1818, when the first session of the Baltimore annual conference of the new African Methodist Episcopal denomination convened, the number at the Bethel church had jumped to 1,096, and nine former local preachers and exhorters were ordained by Bishop Allen.[50]

The connection between Allen and Coker, between the Philadelphia and the Baltimore movements for independence, was forcefully dramatized on January 23, 1816, when the Maryland African Methodists celebrated the Pennsylvania court decision that freed Bethel Church. Preaching to a jubilant audience, Coker claimed that the court had vindicated religious liberty in the United States. The biblical archetype for the victory was the Jewish story of freedom from captivity, when the Jews "were held against their will." Black Methodists had been relegated to a ecclesiastical caste as the Jews had been kept in Babylonian captivity. "Those Jews . . . had not equal privileges with the Babylonians," Coker asserted, "although they were governed by the same laws, and suffered the same penalities." The legal decision cleared the way for African Methodists to embrace "the opportunity that is now offered us of being free," as Coker put it in biblical idiom, "to sit down under our own vine to worship, and none shall make us afraid."[51]

If freedom was the major motif of Coker's sermon, his title insisted that the black seceders had *"withdrawn from under the charge of Methodist Bishops and Conference, (BUT ARE STILL METHODISTS)."* The convention of April 1816 and the subsequent *Discipline* of the new denomination that appeared in 1817 proved as much. Virtually all features of Methodist Episcopal doctrine and polity were carried over to the new church, which added, appropriately, a strong condemnation of slavery to its standards. With ordination in the hands of the independent denomination and with black churchpeople representing their own congregations, the last obstacles to equal power and full autonomy had been overcome.[52]

III

Then that body of us who built the meeting house, could not see our way clear to give up all say.[53]
Peter Spencer and William Anderson describing the African independent
church movement in Wilmington

An observer at the organizing convention of the Bethel Methodist connection, Peter Spencer of Wilmington had, with William Anderson, anticipated by three years the result of the movements for independence and denominational separation in Philadelphia and Baltimore. Failing to join with Allen, the African Union church remained the smallest of the three black Methodist denominations, with a regional base in Delaware and Pennsylvania. Its route to independence, abbreviated to less than a decade, moved through two stages—congregational, then denominational autonomy.

There were black members of the Asbury Methodist Episcopal Church in Wilmington from its founding in 1789, when nineteen of the original sixty-two persons in the church were classed as "colored." Between 1800 and 1802, their number climbed, dramatically increasing two and a half times to reach 117, or eight less than the white total for the latter year. Even though black classes met separately, white officials began to complain of overcrowding and of damages to the main floor of the building, and in June 1805 they acted to force all black classes to meet in the gallery. The resolution instructed black class leaders to "govern themselves accordingly."[54]

As early as January 1805, black members had shown some interest in building an "African Church."[55] An appeal for assistance to the general public became the more necessary when, in late June, Spencer and Anderson rebelled against the command of the trustees and led forty-one other secessionists from the Asbury church. They met in private homes until the African Chapel, or Ezion Methodist Episcopal Church, named for the port of Ezion-geber, where King Solomon kept a fleet of ships (I Kings 9:26), was dedicated.[56]

From the beginning, difficulties paralleling the conflicts that had arisen in Philadelphia and in Baltimore threatened the harmony of the black congregation. It had no local ordained deacons and was, therefore, even more dependent on the white Methodist elder for pastoral attention. The founders of Ezion believed they could "refuse any that were not thought proper to preach," but they ran into stiff opposition in 1812 from the white elder, James Bateman. When the charter members of Ezion resisted him that winter, Bateman summarily "turned out all the Trustees and class-leaders." The two sides ended in court, but Spencer's protesters lost the case. A minority of black members, siding with the white elder, retained the church property for the denomination. The remainder followed Spencer in a second schism within eight years in Wilmington Methodism.[57]

The separatists moved rapidly. Forming a board of seven trustees (four of whom were listed as "labourers" and two as blacksmiths in the city directory), they purchased a lot in July 1813 and opened their building by fall. Incorporating under the Delaware law of 1787, which authorized religious bodies, the African Union Church drew up Articles of Association, dated September 18, 1813, for itself. Forty charter members, six of whom were women, signed the document.[58]

By the end of the first year, the Wilmington church had linked up with a congregation in Pennsylvania and another in New York to develop denominational connections. In 1815 new churches began in Christiana and New Castle, Delaware. Following the death of "Father" Spencer in 1843, the church suffered fragmentation, but it survived to lay claim to the first black denominational break with the Methodist Episcopal Church.[59]

The African Union movement represented the sharpest fracture with the biracial denomination from which it withdrew. In contrast with both our African Methodist communions, the Unionists simplified their polity. They elected five laymen as ruling elders in each congregation, which had the power to license local preachers and to ordain ministers. Rejecting both the presiding eldership and the episcopacy, the African Union church retained ordination of deacons, who could preach and baptize but not celebrate the Lord's Supper or administer church discipline, and of elder ministers who had full authority in these matters.[60]

The struggle for independence in Wilmington was essentially a lay movement, since neither Spencer nor Anderson was an ordained clergyman. It emphasized local automony more than connectionalism. By providing a skeletal structure as a small denomination, however, the African Union church made it possible for other congregations to organize, to own their own property, and to participate in every level of church government in a congregational or "associated" polity. Ensuring black control of local churches, the Unionists gained what had been prohibited them in the Methodist Episcopal Church.[61]

IV

So long as we remain in that situation our Preachers would never be able to enjoy these privileges which the Discipline of the white Church holds out to all its Members that are called to preach, in consequence of the limited access our brethren had to those privileges, and particularly in consequence of the difference of color.[62]

> Statement of the source of the separation of Zion Methodism by Abraham Thompson, James Varick, and William Miller in their "Founders Address" of 1820

A third black Methodist denomination began in an independent congregation that was originally part of the John Street church of New York City. Six black classes under white leaders existed as early as 1793, when there were 143 members.[63] In August 1796 some of that number conferred with Bishop Asbury to request permission to meet separately with their own class leaders. In October that group rented a house on Cross Street, where they gathered during the next four years for prayer meetings and for preaching services. Three of their number, James Varick, Abraham Thompson, and June Scott, were licensed by the John Street quarterly conference, which still maintained formal authority over the black society in behalf of the denomination.[64]

In 1799 the Zion Society, as it was called, selected trustees and announced a "subscription" before the public to erect "an African church in the city." By July of the next year the cornerstone was laid at a site at the intersection of Leonard and Church streets. In September the structure was dedicated. During the next six months the trustees obtained a charter for the church and worked out, as instructed by the General Conference of 1800 (to which they had appealed) "Articles of Agreement" with the denomination. Appropriately, John McClaskey, pastor of the John Street church and fresh from participating in the same process in Philadelphia, acted as formal agent for the New York Conference.[65]

There were two significant differences between what had been negotiated in Philadelphia and what transpired with the trustees of Zion Church, led by Peter Williams, Sr. The document signed in 1801 in New York formed a board of black trustees but limited their function to maintaining property for the denomination. In contrast to their Philadelphia counterparts, these trustees had no authority in matters of church discipline. That restriction kept the Zion Society more dependent on the denomination than the Bethel church was. Second, the agreement in New York defined the process by which local preachers could be granted ordination as local black deacons. Such authorization promised a new level of inclusion but simultaneously restricted ordination to the ambiguous legislation of 1800. Any further advancement by blacks to elder's orders would require new general conference legislation, a procedure limited to the quadrennial sessions of that white ministerial body in which no blacks were members.[66]

Over the next two decades, the Zion Church avoided some of the bitter controversy with denominational officials that had erupted in Philadelphia, but it faced internal dissension over matters left unsettled by the Articles of Agreement. First, blacks had to wait five years before the first three of their local preachers were ordained local deacons by Asbury. In 1808 William Miller and Daniel Coker joined Varick, Thompson, and Scott, who had been made deacons in 1806, in that rank. Without a plan for rotating black preachers who did not belong to the conference's itinerant ministry, there was inevitable competition among the five ordained deacons who served one congregation. By 1810 Coker had moved to Baltimore. In 1812 Thompson and Scott joined the African Free Methodist Society, led by a former Quaker, John Edwards, but it soon disbanded. Thompson kept his standing in the Zion Church by returning apologetically, but Scott left for good. Two years later, in February 1814, Miller, with Thomas Sipkins (a former trustee of Zion), founded a new black Methodist church named African Asbury. By the process of elimination, Varick became the central leader of the Zion Church, with Thompson as his assistant.[67]

Beginning in 1808, the Zion Church had become a community center for free blacks in New York City. It hosted five of the next six annual New Year's Day celebrations of the end of the African slave trade (which became illegal in 1808). The occasion was marked by parades featuring the city's black benevolent associations and by religious services with choral music and orations. The black preachers connected to Zion congregation figured prominently in the festivities. For 1810 William Miller was the orator, for example, while James Varick was the evening preacher for the first commemoration in 1808. George White, a local preacher, prayed in the ceremonies of 1810. So did Miller and Varick in 1811 the next year, when Abraham Thompson was the orator.[68]

Proclaiming their public convictions about the evil of slavery and celebrating their own freedom, these Zion churchmen provoked taunts and vandalism from white mobs. Their response to their white opponents was not passive acceptance. Rather, they complained formally to the Common Council of New York on at least four occasions between 1807 and 1817, charging that the watchmen of the city were neglecting their duties and asserting their rights to have church property protected and to enjoy religious assembly without interruption.[69]

The perennial goals of the Zionite movement, as they had been for the Bethel congregation in Philadelphia, were access to the regular ministry and conference membership for black preachers. For the entire period of its autonomous existence, from 1796 through 1822, Zion Church had as senior pastors white elders who rotated preaching and pastoral assignments throughout the city. Local black deacons (from 1806) and licensed preachers served under white direction. By the time the congregation began construction of a new building to meet the demands of increased membership in 1818, that practice had become a liability, especially after Richard Allen's denomination came to town to form new churches for its connection.[70]

Over the next four years, Zion's leaders petitioned and negotiated, waited and planned, all the while hoping to find a way to remain within or attached to the Methodist Episcopal church. That possibility required what the General Conference since 1800 and the episcopal leaders of the denomination persistently refused to do—ordain blacks as elders into conference membership or create an "African conference" as part of the connection.

After deciding not to join the Bethel movement, the Zion congregation began to move on its own in the summer of 1820. With the backing of the white elder, Williams Stillwell, who was leaving the Methodist Episcopal ministry over differences of polity, the members printed a *Disci-*

pline for themselves. In November Varick and Thompson served their first communion on their own.[71] Meanwhile, they kept pressing for a way to obtain full ordination. Twenty-one months later, after being refused by three Methodist bishops, two annual conferences, and the Protestant Episcopal bishop of New York, the two deacons, with Leven Smith, were consecrated elder by three sympathetic white elders from the parent denomination.[72] A month afterward, Varick became the first superintendent of the Zion denomination, which quickly attracted congregations on Long Island and in New Haven and Philadelphia.[73]

Some adherents to the new movement still hoped that sympathetic white Methodists would be able to convince the General Conference of 1824 to set up "an annual conference for our coloured preachers." That conference dashed those expectations and continued the exclusive precedent until the Washington and Delaware colored conferences were formed in 1864.[74] Left to go its own way, the African Methodist Episcopal, Zion denomination, which rarely used the appendage "Zion" for much of the antebellum period, completed the institutionalization of racial separation by denomination among Methodists until these were renewed during the era of Reconstruction.[75]

V

Your committee feel well satisfied from good authority, that it is not yet time to set off an annual conference, for our coloured preachers; and that such an act, would not at this time, be useful to them, or us; but dangerous to theirs [*sic*], and our common good.

Report of the committee to whom was referred the affairs of the people of colour, Methodist Episcopal General Conference, 1824

Although there were differences in the situations described in the four case studies in this essay, black Methodists in each city faced a set of common circumstances. Their routes to congregational autonomy required them to resolve conflicts with the denomination over property ownership, church building and maintenance, black trusteeism, access to local preacher, exhorter and diaconal ranks of ministry, control of congregational discipline, and denominational representation. In Philadelphia, where the refusal to grant full ordination was the most blatant, the Bethel congregation took the overwhelming majority of black Methodists into a new separated denomination. In Baltimore, the Bethel secessionists had no separate property claims; these remained with black loyalists, who were in the majority and who constituted the largest black congregations in episcopal Methodism until after the Civil War. Denial of elder's orders and hence of denominational representation lay behind the dissatisfaction of the separatists, who refused to be pacified by the agreement of 1814 seeking more attention from white pastors. In Wilmington, the Baltimore story had been foreshadowed when the loyalists at the Ezion church maintained property for the Methodist Episcopal denomination.

The African Union church was unable to protect any of the resources its founder had possessed when active in the Asbury and Ezion congregations. Once again, conflicts with white elders triggered a schism. In New York the Zion church focused its attention on the issue of ordination, remaining patient beyond any realistic expectation that the Methodist Episcopal Church would budge from its policies of the previous twenty years. When the plan for an African conference within the biracial denomination failed, a third denominational break was inevitable.

Episcopal Methodism's limitation on black ministerial standing— blacks could rise no higher than local deacon—had no comparable precedent in the early African Baptist and African Presbyterian organizations in Boston (1805), New York (1808), and Philadelphia (1809, 1811). Biracial Baptist associations and presbyteries ordained black men to the ministry and accepted them and their congregations into regular status in their judicatories. In contrast, the Methodist Episcopal legislation on the black diaconate was kept private, and all ordinations performed by Asbury were conducted apart from regular conference procedures. Without full ordination, blacks had no chance for direct denominational representation and participation in governance. Episcopal Methodism upheld its ban on full ordination throughout the pre-Civil War period, denying full participation to blacks even as they were denied full participation in civil government at national, state, and local levels. Only the Protestant Episcopal Church practiced a comparable discrimination. It granted priestly orders to its first African candidates, but diocesan leaders, first in Pennsylvania and then in New York, denied congregational representation to black churches and their ministers.[76]

These African Methodisms illustrate an important application of trusteeism, a movement pervasive in both white Protestant and Roman Catholic churches of the same period. If the black membership in the four Methodist societies considered in this study had not been able to have black trustees, the economic basis for owning property and erecting church buildings would have been undermined. Saint Thomas's African Episcopal Church pioneered the trustee movement, and Allen and his Methodist associates were quick to follow its lead. Trustees in the Zion Society in New York did not have as much power as their Philadelphia counterparts, but their presence nonetheless provided grounds for a separate establishment. In Baltimore and Wilmington, where independence meant the loss of property, black trustees loyal to the Methodist Episcopal Church retained their power and forced new options upon those who seceded.

The Bethel congregation in Philadelphia made the most effective use of trusteeism for controlling pastoral assignments and for exercising congregational discipline and authority. In Baltimore and in New York, the thrust for independence came from the ministerial leadership, black deacons, local preachers, and exhorters, whereas in Wilmington the movement was based entirely in lay leadership. Pastoral and disciplinary issues did not hamper the independent developments among black Baptists and Presbyterians, because their pastors had full ordination and equal ministerial standing and because matters of church discipline had not been racially divisive. The trustees and the vestry of Saint Thomas's Episcopal Church had power comparable to that of the trustees of the Bethel church in Philadelphia, but they did not exercise it in ways that provoked controversy or forced decisions about denominational separation and reorganization.

Interpreters of black church history have often claimed that the evangelical fervor of the Second Great Awakening accounts for the fact that blacks gravitated to Methodist and Baptist churches, rather than to more ritualistic or confessional denominations. Following Donald Mathews's revisionist interpretation of early-nineteenth-century revivals, our analysis of the origins of three African Methodisms demonstrates that black Methodists participated in distinctive ways in the organizational revolution of American Protestantism, which is the social meaning of the Second Awakening. They worked with the institutional innovations of the Methodist system to promote local, then connectional, autonomy. They moved into lay roles as trustees and class leaders. They sought ordination and got a partial resolution. They purchased property and built churches. When the logic of their developing autonomy failed to include conference membership for ministers, direct representation in the denomination, and full ordination, the biracial association that had existed for a generation broke down, and complete independence brought black denominationalism.[77]

NOTES

1. Carter G. Woodson, *History of the Negro Church* (Washington, D.C.: Associated Publishers, 1921). Recent examples of the concept occur in Carol V. R. George, *Segregated Sabbaths: Richard Allen and the Rise of Independent Black Churches, 1760–1840* (New York: Oxford University Press, 1973), and Gayraud S. Wilmore, *Black Religion and Black Radicalism* (New York: Anchor, 1973).

2. James W. Hood, *Sketch of the Early History of the African Methodist Episcopal Zion Church with Jubilee Souvenir and an Appendix* (n.p., n.d.), pp. 61–62; *One Hundred Years of the African Methodist Episcopal Zion Church* (New York: AME Zion Book Concern, 1895), pp. 5–7.

3. John H. Bracey, Jr., August Meier, Elliot Rudwick, eds., *Black Nationalism in America* (Indianapolis: Bobbs-Merrill, 1970), pp. xxvi–xxvii, 3–17; Alain Rogers, "The African Methodist Episcopal Church: A Study in Black Nationalism," *The Black Church* (1972): 17–43.

4. For examples of this interpretive perspective, see Theodore Hershberg, "Free Blacks in Antebellum Philadelphia," *Journal of Social History* 5 (1971–72): 183–209; Ira Berlin, "The Structure of the Free Negro Caste in the Antebellum United States," *Journal of Social History* 9 (1975–76): 297–318, and "Time, Space and the Evolution of Afro-American Society on British Mainland North America," *American Historical Review* 85 (February 1980): 44–78. More di-

rectly applicable to the black church are two exceptional essays, George A. Levesque, "Inherent Reformers—Inherited Orthodoxy: Black Baptists in Boston, 1800–1873," *Journal of Negro History* 60 (October 1975): 491–525, and Emma Jones Lapansky, " 'Since They Got Those Separate Churches': Afro-Americans and Racism in Jacksonian Philadelphia," *American Quarterly* 32 (Spring 1980): 54–78. See also Gayraud S. Wilmore, "Reinterpretation in Black Church History," *The Chicago Theological Seminary Register* 73 (Winter 1983): 25–37, with the phrase "nationalist aspirations" quoted on p. 30.

 5. E. Franklin Frazier, *The Negro Church in America* (New York: Schocken, 1974), ch. 3, and W. E. B. Du Bois, *The Souls of Black Folk;* in *Three Negro Classics,* intro. John Hope Franklin (New York: Avon Books, 1965), p. 215.

 6. Floyd J. Miller, *The Search For a Black Nationality: Black Colonization and Emigration* (Urbana: University of Illinois Press, 1975), pp. 6–15; Dorothy Sterling, ed., *Speak Out in Thunder Tones: Letters and Other Writings by Black Northerners, 1787–1865* (Garden City, N.Y.: Doubleday, n.d.), pp. 3–12. The records of the Free African Union Society of Newport show an entry for June 20, 1793, about a contribution by the Rhode Island organization to the African Church building project in Philadelphia. See William H. Robinson, ed., *The Proceedings of The Free African Union Society and The African Benevolent Society. Newport, Rhode Island, 1780–1824* (Providence: The Urban League of Rhode Island, 1976), p. 109.

 7. Daniel Coker, *Dialogue Between a Virginian and an African Minister* (Baltimore: Benjamin Edes for Joseph James, 1810), pp. 37–42. This paper omits consideration of black Methodist churches in Long Island; in Salem, New Jersey; in Annapolis, Maryland; and in West Chester, Pennsylvania, which are on Coker's list. There was also an African Presbyterian church in Philadelphia that he did not include and an African church in Wilmington, North Carolina, in 1807, mentioned in *The Journal and Letters of Francis Asbury,* ed. Elmer T. Clark (Nashville, Tenn.: Abingdon, 1958), vol. 2, pp. 556, n. 117. Coker was also oblivious to African Baptist organizations in Virginia and Georgia, of which the congregation in Savannah whose pastor was Andrew Bryan was the most significant. See Mechal Sobel, *Travelin' On: The Slave Journey of an Afro-Baptist Faith,* (Westport, Conn.: Greenwood Press, 1979).

 8. The historiographical context of blacks within Methodism is ably demonstrated in Harry V. Richardson, *Dark Salvation* (Garden City, N.Y.: Doubleday, 1976).

 9. Russell E. Richey begins to raise the questions about black denominationalism that American church historians have neglected. See his edited volume, *Denominationalism* (Nashville, Tenn.: Abingdon, 1977), pp. 207–209.

 10. Clark, ed., *The Journal and Letters of Francis Asbury,* vol. 3, pp. 366–367.

 11. Allen dated the opening in July 1794 in *The Life Experience and Gospel Labors of the Rt. Rev. Richard Allen* (New York: Abingdon, 1960), p. 31. See also Clark, ed., *The Journal and Letters of Francis Asbury,* vol. 2, p. 18.

 12. Allen, *The Life Experience,* p. 24. See also, *Minutes of the Methodist Conferences, Held Annually in America; From 1773 to 1813* (New York: Daniel Hitt and Thomas Ware, 1813), p. 60.

 13. The first published reference to the incident is in the preface to *The Doctrines and Discipline of the African Methodist Episcopal Church* (Philadelphia: John H. Cunningham, 1817), p. 4. Milton Sernett has refuted the traditional date of 1787 on the basis of records showing that the first gallery at Saint George's

was constructed in 1792–1793. Without denying that the event happened, he proposes a closer chronological connection to the dedication of the first building and the public statement of 1794. See his *Black Religion and American Evangelicalism* (Metuchen, N.J.: Scarecrow Press, 1975), pp. 116–121, 218–220. See also Benjamin Tucker Tanner, *An Outline of Our History and Government for African Methodist Churchmen, Ministerial and Lay* (Philadelphia: AME Book Concern, 1884), pp. 142–148. Allen's account in *The Life Experience* is undated, pp. 25–26, but in 1823 he attested to the veracity of the incident to answer a disaffected church member, Jonathan Tudas. See Trustees of Bethel and Wesley churches, *The Sword of Truth* (Philadelphia: J. H. Cunningham, 1823), p. 13.

14. Allen, *the Life Experience,* p. 24, and *Minutes of the Methodist Conferences, 1773–1813,* pp. 74, 93, 104.

15. William Douglass, *Annals of the First African Church in the United States of America* (Philadelphia: King and Baird, 1862), pp. 10–11, 15–22, 33–40, 45–46; L. H. Butterfield, ed., *The Letters of Benjamin Rush* (Princeton: Princeton University Press, 1951), vol. 1, pp. 599–600, 602–603, 608–609, 716–717; vol. 2, p. 1071. See also George W. Corner, ed., *The Autobiography of Benjamin Rush* (Princeton: Princeton University Press, 1948), pp. 202–203, 221; Allen, *The Life Experience,* pp. 29–30.

16. Tanner, *An Outline,* pp. 142–148, contains this important document.

17. Allen, *The Life Experience,* pp. 26–27, and *Minutes of the Methodist Conferences, 1773–1813,* pp. 116, 161. See also George A. Phoebus, ed., *Beams of Light on Early Methodism in America* (New York: Phillips and Hunt, 1887), pp. 217, 222–223.

18. *Articles of Association of the African Methodist Episcopal Church, of the City of Philadelphia, in the Commonwealth of Pennsylvania* (1799; reprint ed., Philadelphia: Rhistoric Publications, n.d.), pp. 3–4, 8, 10; Douglass, *Annals,* pp. 104–106.

19. Jesse Lee, *A Short History of the Methodists* (Baltimore: Magill and Clime, 1810), pp. 271–272; Reginald Hildebrand, "Methodist Episcopal Policy on the Ordination of Black Ministers, 1784–1864," *Methodist History* 20 (April 1982): 125–126.

20. Hildebrand, "Methodist Episcopal Policy," pp. 126–127.

21. *Minutes of the Methodist Conferences* (1799), pp. 223–226; (1805), pp. 343–347. J. R. Flanigen, *Methodism: Old and New* (Philadelphia: Lippincott & Co., 1880), pp. 51–52, 61–62. The building at Bethel was expanded in 1800. On Allen's secular employment, see George, *Segregated Sabbaths,* pp. 75, 90; Charles H. Wesley, *Richard Allen: Apostle of Freedom* (Washington, D.C.: Associated Publishers, 1935), pp. 99–123; *The Philadelphia Directory for 1798* (n.p., n.d.), p. 15.

22. *A Collection of Spiritual Songs and Hymns Selected From Various Authors by Richard Allen, African Minister* (Philadelphia: John Ormrod, 1801); a second edition issued later the same year added ten additional hymns. See Eileen Southern, *The Music of Black Americans: A History* (New York: W. W. Norton, 1971), pp. 86–93, 517.

23. Phoebus, ed., *Beams of Light,* pp. 252–54; Clark, ed., *The Journal and Letters of Francis Asbury,* vol. 2, pp. 235, 432; Francis H. Tees, *The Ancient Landmark of American Methodism or Historic Old St. George's* (Philadelphia: Message Publishing Co., 1951), p. 94. The unpublished journal of William Colbert at Garrett-Evangelical Theological Seminary has twenty-six references to working with and sometimes boarding with Richard Allen between 1796 and 1811.

24. George, *Segregated Sabbaths,* pp. 66–69; Allen, *The Life Experience,* pp. 32, 37–41 (for text of the African Supplement).

25. Allen, *The Life Experience,* pp. 37–41.

26. Clark, *The Journal and Letters of Francis Asbury,* vol. 3, pp. 366–367.

27. *Minutes of the Methodist Conferences* (1812), p. 562. The reconstruction of these events comes from notes taken in the 1816 legal suit in the Edward Carey Gardiner Collection, Pennsylvania Historical Society. Although there is no record in his *Letters* or *Journal,* at least one conference was held with Asbury according to these notes and to AME *Doctrines and Discipline,* p. 6.

28. J. Emory to "Sir," (6 April 1815), in the Gardiner Collection, articulated the logic of the white elders.

29. Allen, *The Life Experience,* pp. 33–34; AME *Doctrines and Discipline,* pp. 5–6.

30. See my essay "Early Methodism and Slavery: The Roots of Tradition," *The Drew Gateway* 30 (Spring 1964): 150–165. A copy of one of the expurgated versions of the Methodist Episcopal *Discipline* is in the Perkins Library Rare Book Room, Duke University. See also George, *Segregated Sabbaths,* pp. 77–80.

31. See the entry for 5 February 1809 in Clark, ed., *The Journal and Letters of Francis Asbury,* vol. 2, p. 591. Lorenzo Dow first accused Asbury in print in 1816 of being jealous of the rising power of Richard Allen. See *History of Cosmopolite* (Cincinnati: H. M. Rulison, 1856), pp. 545–548.

32. See notes of the legal suit of 1816 in the Gardiner Collection for references to the public letter by Emory, also mentioned in Allen, *The Life Experience,* pp. 33–34. The text, "To the Trustees, Preachers, Exhorters, Leaders, and Members of the African Church, called Bethel Church, in Philadelphia," is in *The Life of the Rev. John Emory, D.D. by his eldest son* (New York: George Lane, 1841), pp. 71–72. For the case of *Green* v. *African Church Called Bethel,* see miscellaneous legal notes in the Yeates Papers, Pennsylvania Historical Society, and Wesley, *Richard Allen,* pp. 147–148.

33. Allen, *The Life Experience,* p. 34, and Robert Burch, 16 December 1815, in notes for the legal suit of 1816 in the Gardiner Collection.

34. *Minutes Taken At Several Conferences of The Methodist Episcopal Church in the United States of America for the Year 1815* (New York: J. C. Totten, 1814), p. 36.

35. See notice of sheriff's sale dated June 12, 1815, and a copy of the certificate of sale, stating that Allen had purchased the "brick meeting house and Lot of ground" for $9,600, plus two-year rent charges amounting to $525. Wesley links the sale to the legal case of 1816, but it clearly belongs to the settlement involving Robert Green, for which see Wesley, *Richard Allen,* p. 146.

36. Allen, *The Life Experience,* pp. 34–35, and Richard Allen to Daniel Coker, 18 February 1816, as reprinted in Tanner, *An Outline,* pp. 152–155. See also legal notes for the case of 1816 and Burch's letter of 16 December 1815 in the Gardiner Collection and Wesley, *Richard Allen,* pp. 140–141.

37. AME *Doctrines and Discipline,* pp. 8–9; Daniel A. Payne, *History of the African Methodist Episcopal Church* (1891; reprint ed., New York: Arno Press, 1969), pp. 13–14. Blacks in Philadelphia Methodism left to join the Bethel movement, as demonstrated by the drop in numbers in the Methodist Episcopal Church from 1371 in 1815 to seventy-five in 1816. See *Minutes of the Methodist Conference,* 1815, pp. 21–29, and 1816 (New York: J. C. Totten, 1816), 27–35.

38. James A. Handy, *Scraps of African Methodist Episcopal History* (Philadelphia: AME Book Concern, n.d.), pp. 13–14.

39. Allen, *Minutes of the Methodist Conferences, 1773–1813,* 60–61, 75, 154–56.

40. Clark, ed., *The Journal and Letters of Francis Asbury,* vol. 2, pp. 51, 65.

41. Ibid., p. 129, and vol. 3, p. 160.

42. Handy, *Scraps,* pp. 14, 24, and James M. Wright, *The Free Negro in Maryland* (New York: Columbia University Press, 1921), p. 216.

43. Bettye C. Thomas, "History of the Sharp Street Memorial Episcopal Church, 1787–1920," pamphlet (n.p., n.d.), unnumbered page 2; Cornelius William Stafford, *The Baltimore Directory, For 1802* (Baltimore: John W. Butler, n.d.), p. 64; A. Hoen & Co., "Baltimore in 1804," and Peale Museum, Baltimore, "Improved Plan of the city of Baltimore" both at the Lovely Lane Museum and Methodist Historical Society, Baltimore; Wright, *The Free Negro,* 213.

44. Thomas, "History," unnumbered page 3; Wright, *The Free Negro,* pp. 213, 217–218, 222–223; Baltimore City Class Records, Lovely Lane Museum; *Biography of Rev. David Smith, of the A.M.E. Church* (Xenia, Oh.: Xenia Gazette Office, 1881), pp. 28–29. Even after the separation of 1815, the loyalists continued to use the name "African Methodist Episcopal."

45. Coker, *Dialogue,* p. 41; Allen, *Minutes of the Methodist Conferences, 1773–1813,* 420–425, 592–599.

46. Baltimore City Station Class Records.

47. Ibid.

48. Glen A. McAninch, "We'll Pray for You: Methodist Ethnocentrism in the Origins of the African Methodist Episcopal Church in Baltimore" (Masters thesis, University of North Carolina at Chapel Hill, 1973), pp. 41, 50.

49. *Biography of Rev. David Smith,* pp. 26–30. The Baltimore City Station Class Records show forty black classes with 1,274 members after Coker's secession. I counted 217 names stricken from the lists.

50. McAninch, "We'll Pray," p. 73; Wright, *The Free Negro,* pp. 217–218, 222–223; *Minutes of Two Conferences of the African Methodist Preachers Held at Baltimore and Philadelphia in April and May, 1818* (Philadelphia: Richard Allen, 1818), pp. 9, 14. There were 1,322 black Methodists remaining with the Methodist Episcopal societies in 1818; see *Minutes Taken at the Several Annual Conferences of the Methodist Episcopal Church . . . 1818* (New York: J.C. Totten, 1818), pp. 22–31, and Bethel AME Church, Baltimore, incorporation papers, dated April 7–8, 1816, July 19, 1819, and April 3, 1820, at the Maryland Hall of Records, Annapolis.

51. The only extant copy, apparently, of Coker's sermon, now in the New York Public Library's main branch, was torn out of a bound volume of collected pamphlets. A summary of the sermon is in Wesley, *Richard Allen,* pp. 141–142, 150, and an extract is in Herbert Aptheker, ed., *A Documentary History of the Negro People of the United States* (1951; reprint ed., New York: The Citadel Press, 1969), vol. 1, pp. 67–69.

52. AME *Doctrines and Discipline,* p. 190. The complete title of Coker's sermon is *Sermon Delivered Extempore In The African Bethel Church In The City of Baltimore, On The 21st of January, 1816, To A Numerous Concourse of People, On Account Of The Coloured People Gaining Their Church (Bethel) In The Supreme Court Of The State Of Pennsylvania, By The Rev. D. Coker, Minister*

Of The Said Church, To Which Is Annexed A List Of The African Preachers In Philadelphia, Baltimore & Who Have Withdrawn From Under The Charge Of The Methodist Bishops And Conference, (BUT ARE STILL METHODISTS), n.p., n.d.

53. *The Discipline of the African Union Church of The United States of America,* 3rd. ed., enl. (Wilmington: Porter & Eckel, 1852), p. iv.

54. John D. C. Hanna, *The Centennial Services of Asbury Methodist Episcopal Church, Wilmington, Delaware, October 13–20, 1889* (Wilmington: Delaware Printing Co., 1889), pp. 146, 160.

55. See notice in the Wilmington *Mirror of the Times and General Advertiser* (6 February 1805).

56. Asbury preached in "the African chapel in Wilmington" on May 2, 1810. See Clark, ed. *The Journal and Letters of of Francis Asbury,* vol. 2, p. 636.

57. Hanna, *Centennial Services,* p. 160, and *the Discipline of the African Union Church,* pp. iii–v.

58. The Articles of Association are recorded in the Division of Historical and Cultural Affairs, Department of State, Dover, Delaware. Typed versions are in the Historical Society of Delaware, Wilmington. *A Directory and Register For the Year 1814 . . . of the Borough of Wilmington and Brandywine* (n.p.: R. Porter, 1814), as a typed copy in the Historical Society of Delaware, pp. 45–52, shows home addresses and vocations for three fourths of the charter members of the African Union Church.

59. *Union Church of Africans* v. *Ellis Sanders,* Court of Errors and Appeals, June term, 1855, typed copy in Historical Society of Delaware, unnumbered page 4; Lewis V. Baldwin, " 'Invisible' Strands of African Methodism" (Ph.D. diss., Northwestern University, 1980), pp. 103–105, 118–122. There were 1,263 members in four states in 1837.

60. Baldwin, " 'Invisible' Strands, pp. 105–108.

61. Ibid., p. 87, and *A Directory and Register For the Year 1814,* pp. 45–52.

62. William J. Walls, *The African Methodist Episcopal Zion Church: Reality of the Black Church* (Charlotte: AME Zion Publishing House, 1974), p. 49, quoting the first *Discipline.*

63. Samuel A. Seaman, *Annals of New York Methodism* (New York: Hunt & Eaton, 1892), p. 465.

64. Walls, *The AME Zion Church,* pp. 47–48; *The Journal and Letters of Francis Asbury,* vol. 2, pp. 55, 95–96.

65. *American Citizen and General Advertizer (New York),* 21 March 1800, as quoted in Walls, *The AME Zion Church,* p. 53; also pp. 56–57, where the General Conference report instructed the Zion Society to model itself after the Bethel Articles of Agreement or to obtain a charter like that of white congregations within the New York Conference. See Allen, *Minutes of the Methodist Conferences, 1773–1813,* p. 247.

66. *Articles of Agreement Between the General Conference of The Methodist Episcopal Church, and the Trustees of the African Methodist Episcopal Church, in the City of New York* (Brooklyn: Thomas Kirk, 1801), pp. 6–7; Walls, *The AME Zion Church,* pp. 56–57.

67. Clark, ed., *The Journal and Letters of Francis Asbury,* vol. 2, pp. 506, 568; Walls, *The AME Zion Church,* pp. 65–69.

68. Dorothy Porter, ed., *Early Negro Writing 1760–1837* (Boston: Beacon Press, 1971), 343–345, 365, 374. for three orations. See also Adam Carman, *Oration Delivered At The Fourth Anniversary Of The Abolition Of Slave Trade,*

In The Methodist Episcopal Church, In The Second-Street, New York, January 1, 1811 (New York: John C. Totten, 1811), and William Miller, *Sermon On The Abolition Of Slave Trade: Delivered In The African Church, New York, On The First Of January, 1810* (New York: John C. Totten, 1810). See my "The Dialectic of Double-Consciousness in Black American Freedom Celebrations, 1808–1863," *Journal of Negro History"* 78 (Winter 1982): 302–317.

69. David Henry Bradley, Sr., *A History of The AME Zion Church* (Nashville: Parthenon Press, 1956), pp. 65–66.

70. There were 963 members of the Zion and the Asbury churches in 1818. *Minutes of the Methodist Conferences, 1818,* pp. 28–37; Christopher Rush, *A Short Account Of The Rise And Progress Of The African ME Church In America* (New York: Christopher Rush et al., 1866), 32ff.

71. John Jamison Moore, *History Of The AME Zion Church In America* (York, Penn.: Teachers' Journal Office, 1884), p. 59.

72. Walls, *The AME Zion Church,* pp. 76–82.

73. Ibid., p. 83.

74. *Journal Of The General Conference Of The Methodist Episcopal Church, 1824,* pp. 244, 246, 254 and Peter Cartwright et al., "Report of the committee to whom was referred the affairs of the people of colour" (May 27, 1824), General Conference Papers, Drew University, Madison, New Jersey.

75. I have examined the beginnings of a fourth black Methodist denomination in "The Social, Political and Religious Significance of the Formation of the Colored Methodist Episcopal Church (1870)," *Methodist History* 18 (October 1979): 3–25.

76. These comparative conclusions come from my continuing research on the origins and development of African-American independent churches and denominations from the late eighteenth century through Reconstruction. They were first formulated in an unpublished paper given at the Society for Historians of the Early American Republic in July 1982 at Memphis under the title "The Exodus: The Emergence of Independent Black Churches in the New Nation, 1787–1821." See also my "The Rise of African Churches in America: Re-examining the Contexts," *Journal of Religious Thought* 41 (1984): 58–73.

77. Donald Mathews, "The Second Great Awakening as an Organizing Process," *American Quarterly* 21 (1969): 23–42.

Presbyterians and the Mystique of Organizational Efficiency, 1870–1936

JAMES H. MOORHEAD

In 1922 William Adams Brown of Union Theological Seminary in New York City published an extensive survey of American Protestantism. The noted educator, Presbyterian minister, and ecumenist wrote *The Church in America* because he believed that Protestant denominations had reached a moment of truth: "We are trying an experiment," noted Brown, "which will have a far-reaching effect upon the future of democracy, an experiment which will show whether it is possible to supply the unifying spiritual influence needed in a democracy by means of a strong, coherent, free Church, and so make possible under the conditions of our modern life the coming of the new social order called by our Maker the Kingdom of God." Protestants could exercise that "unifying spiritual influence" only to the extent that they reordered their institutions for more effective ministry. Brown allowed that the churches needed more than new organizational blueprints. "We may plan as we will, but when all is done, there is always something incalculable about religion. Chief of all the factors in the life of the soul is the free Spirit of God." That Spirit gives to humanity "the refreshing shower. The Church is but the channel through which the water is conveyed." But having made his disclaimer, Brown quickly added: "[W]ater may be wasted for lack of a proper conduit, and those who build the reservoirs and lay the pipes have an essential part in the preparation of the Kingdom of God." In the several hundred pages that followed, Brown occupied himself with a careful analysis of the "reservoirs and pipes" and suggested ways in which they might be more efficiently constructed.[1]

Brown voiced a widespread concern. Even as he wrote, his own Presbyterian Church was designing a major reorganization of its agencies. In the first several decades of this century, Episcopalians, Methodists, Baptists, and the Disciples of Christ did likewise. Protestant churches also federated at local, state, and national levels to promote cooperation across denominational lines. In support of these ventures, religious leaders spoke repeatedly of the churches' need to employ scientific planning, businesslike management, rational organization, professional expertise, and effective promotional techniques. Churches were not, of course, the only groups using this vocabulary. The ideal of efficiency enchanted businesspeople, would-be reformers, politicians, and educators. In the years after 1910, the enthusiasm became what Samuel Haber has called "an efficiency craze—a secular Great Awakening, an outpouring of ideas and emotions in which a gospel of efficiency was preached without embarrassment to businessmen, workers, doctors, housewives, and teachers, and yes, preached even to preachers.... Efficient and good came closer to meaning the same thing in these years than in any other period of American history." Thus, to examine the Presbyterian mystique of efficiency is to study one instance of a phenomenon far transcending the bounds of a single denomination and to illumine broader cultural trends.[2]

I

The rage for efficiency had grown out of the sprawling disorder of the late nineteenth century. Robert Wiebe, in a now classic phrase, has styled the American of that era a "distended society." Large economic conglomerates came into existence because technology made them feasible and because relaxed laws governing the formation of corporations made them possible. Initially, however, many of these giants resembled aggregations of diverse entities more than well-integrated enterprises. The major political parties were a congeries of factions and interests. Governmental power was diffuse and inadequate to its tasks. The major cities groaned under the dislocations imposed by industrialization and by the rapid influx of new immigration. Large numbers of workers and farmers rose to protest their loss of self-mastery to impersonal banks, railroads, and industries; as strikers or populists, they became symbols of disorder to other Americans. Henry Adams provided a classic metaphor for the age: Modern civilization, its energies dissipating, exemplified the principle of entropy.[3]

Yet in these same years, America groped toward a new sense of order. Business led the way. First among railroads and then in other economic areas, what Alfred Chandler has called "a managerial revolution" took place. Subdivisions of corporations, which theoretically might have existed as separate entities, were organized under a hierarchical chain of control. Various phases of production, distribution, and advertising were placed in specialized departments and subjected to coordination by managers. In each department, these managers strove for the most cost-effective means to fulfill their tasks.[4]

Other aspects of American society exhibited a similar consolidation. With the new research universities in the lead, higher education segmented itself into discrete departments, regularized procedures for academic appointments and responsibilities, and sought means to assess the efficiency of its faculties. Out of the new academe came a host of professionals, armed with statistical surveys and eager to use their expertise to reshape America along more rational or efficient lines. Similarly, the chaos of politics was partly alleviated in 1896 when the Democratic party successfully absorbed—and largely tamed—the populist movement and when the victorious Republican candidate, William McKinley, managed to create what would prove to be an enduring political majority.[5]

In the progressive era the streamlining of American life became a self-conscious political goal as many called for an efficient society based on systematic planning and on the use of technical experts and fact finding. Two pivotal events in 1910–1911 epitomized the new mentality. In a celebrated case before the Interstate Commerce Commission in 1910, Louis Brandeis argued against a rate increase for major eastern railroads on the grounds that scientific management of the companies would save a million dollars a day. Then Frederick W. Taylor, long noted for his time efficiency studies in the work place, published in 1911 *The Principles of Scientific Management.* Soon books, conferences, and articles swelled a chorus extolling efficiency as a panacea for the ills of the nation. Efficiency had a seductive appeal because it resonated with many of the commitments of the American people. It invoked their faith in technology, it legitimated the search for profit, and it promised a social harmony, transcending the clash of labor and capital, if only its scientific, class-neutral principles were obeyed. Above all, efficiency had a moral appeal. As Haber has observed, it "promised a moral clean-up. The high wages and low costs provided by the efficiency systems would check the greed of the employer and the laziness of the employee." Efficiency was the Protestant work ethic reborn in modern guise. It is not surprising, then, that many church leaders formed a Church Efficiency Committee and that articles and books in praise of religious efficiency soon rolled from the presses.[6]

Church people climbed on the bandwagon of efficiency in part because their organizations, like other large bodies, faced the problem of disorder. In a process similar to the jerry-built expansion of many businesses in the early Gilded Age, Protestant operations since the 1870s had enlarged and proliferated, often with little thought as to how these new activities would fit into a coherent pattern. With the expanded interest in foreign missions, for example, new interdenominational organizations— numerous women's societies, the Student Volunteer Movement, the World Student Christian Federation, the Foreign Work Department of the YMCAS, the Laymen's Missionary Movement, and the World Missionary

Council—came into existence. Between 1880 and 1900 major denominations dramatically increased the number of workers they deployed in foreign fields and augmented their mission budgets accordingly (sometimes two- and threefold), hiring more people to staff the home office and spawning new agencies and auxiliaries. The growth of organization brought serious problems. Denominational agencies often acted as independent fiefdoms competing with one another for the dollars of the folks in the pews. Pastors resented a chaotic situation that forced them to spend many Sundays each year dunning their congregations in behalf of various agencies and causes. Moreover, many Protestants lamented that the lack of coordination within individual denominations was matched, if not superseded, by the wasteful duplication and diffusion of energies among the communions. In 1893 Josiah Strong noted the vast problems facing the Protestant churches—the breakdown of order in the cities, the alienation of the working classes from the churches, and the weakening of Protestant forces in relation to the rising power of the Catholic menace. Protestantism was shattered, he moaned, into "scores of fragments," and he offered as remedy a more scientific, efficient cooperation among Protestants. Planned coordination would, in short, remedy a perceived threat to Protestant hegemony.[7]

The desire for the efficient management of Protestant forces was voiced by the Laymen's Missionary and by the Men and Religion Forward Movement. The formation of the Federal Council of Churches in 1908 was in part a response to this demand, as was the United War Work Campaign of the Churches (1917) and the short-lived Interchurch World Movement (1919). Within the denominations, major reorganizations occurred in the name of efficiency. The churches authorized central agencies to coordinate budgets; to raise these budgets they inundated the local churches with promotional literature extolling the virtue of stewardship, defined as proportionate giving to ecclesiastical causes. By encouraging the every-member canvass, they hoped to rescue denominational finances from the uncertainties of the old haphazard system of special offerings and pew rents. Underlying these endeavors was a dream of what Shailer Mathews, dean of the University of Chicago Divinity School, called in a 1912 book *Scientific Management in the Churches.* Four years later Mathews stated the gist of that outlook when he observed that a minister might "set churches into operation by spiritual preaching" but would fall short of ultimate success without the "grace of committees."[8]

II

Presbyterians would appear to have been well prepared for the grace of committees. As a connectional church composed of ascending governing bodies, Presbyterianism had little aversion to centralized control. The General Assembly of the church in 1797 described "the radical [that is, root] principles" of Presbyterian polity in these terms:

That the several different congregations of believers, taken collectively, constitute one Church of Christ, called emphatically the Church; that a larger part of the Church, or a representation of it, should govern a smaller, or determine matters of controversy which arise therein; that, in like manner, a representation of the whole should govern and determine in regard to every part . . . ; and consequently that appeals may be carried from lower to higher governing bodies, till they be finally decided by the collected wisdom and united voice of the whole Church.

Yet the path from the "radical principles" to a national structure of denominational boards and agencies was neither simple nor direct, for the statement was intended as a prescription for unity in doctrine and discipline, not as a charter for centralized bureaucracy. Its meaning for organizational questions remained unclear.[9]

Early in the nineteenth century, those questions were thrust on the denomination. How were new congregations to be established on the rapidly moving American frontier, and how should the church fulfill its obligation to send the Gospel to foreign lands? Initially the church favored interdenominational cooperation with other communions, chiefly with Congregationalists, through voluntary societies such as the American Board of Commissioners for Foreign Missions (1810) and the American Home Missionary Society (1826). By the 1830s the church was divided into a New School wing supporting these arrangements and an Old School wing opposing them out of fear that distinctive Presbyterian theology and practice were being diluted. Arguing that the church itself—that is, the Presbyterian denomination—was responsible for conducting mission, the Old School demanded that many tasks performed by the voluntary societies be assigned to denominational agencies directly accountable to Presbyterian judicatories. After these two factions broke into separate churches in 1837–1838, the Old School set itself to forming such agencies. For a time, New Schoolers continued to pursue the path of voluntary societies; as that option proved unsuccessful, they, too, turned to the creation of denominational agencies. Yet even when the principle of denominational organization triumphed, the exact form of such agencies remained controversial. Some in the Old School, for example, wanted to devolve missionary responsibilities upon the lower judicatories—synods and presbyteries—while others favored organization at the national level. And if organized nationally, should the agencies be committees of the General Assembly, subject to close scrutiny by that body, or should the agencies be constructed as boards possessing greater administrative leeway? Objectors to the board system complained that it was "an excrescence upon Presbyterianism," a scheme for removing actual control from the church courts and for creating a "disguised power, in a few central hands, at the seat of operations." Although the principle of national boards was firmly established by the time the Old and New Schools reunited in 1870, the antebellum doubts and questions would subsequently return to haunt the church.[10]

In the next half century, the size and number of Presbyterian agencies dramatically increased. The number of missionaries working for the Board of National Missions nearly doubled, and specialized departments were created to supervise rural work, city and industrial ministry, evangelism of Jews, ministry in lumber camps, and work among various immigrant groups. The thriving Board of Foreign Missions found its enterprises so large and far flung that it had to divide itself into two departments, one for the supervision of the missionary enterprise itself and the other to maintain support among the home churches. For promotional purposes, the Board also created regional field representatives in the United States and for a time employed a fund-raiser whose task was to cultivate wealthy donors. From 1868 to 1887 six regional women's boards for foreign missions came into existence, and a seventh was added as a result of the merger with the Cumberland Presbyterian Church in 1907. The Board of Relief for Disabled Ministers, whose original task was to provide, upon application, cash payments to infirm ministers or their survivors, assumed additional responsibilities. In 1883 the Board received the first of several properties that it converted into Ministers' Homes for elderly or disabled clergy. Administration of the homes also embroiled the Board in efforts to secure medical treatment for residents. In 1906 the General Assembly tried yet another way to care for aged ministers by creating, separate from the Board of Relief, a Sustentation Fund paying an annual annuity to all participating ministers after age 70.[11]

As the number and the size of programs grew, Presbyterians experienced the frustrations common to other denominations: lack of coordinated planning, the difficulty of raising money for so many different enterprises, and rivalries among agencies. The poor relationship between the leaders of the Board of Relief and of the Sustentation Fund provides a particularly graphic illustration of bureaucratic strife. In an effort to preempt the work of the Fund, Benjamin Agnew of the Board hired five field agents to canvass the church for $10 million. Agnew's action deeply offended the leader of the Fund, and the two executives struggled to maintain the autonomy of their organizations. The conflict came to a head when both agencies organized conferences—perhaps one should call them pep rallies—prior to the 1911 General Assembly and brought in noted personalities to tout their respective causes. To put an end to such imbroglios, the Assembly federated the two agencies the following year.[12]

Out of disorder gradually emerged the signs of a new organizational style. When fully developed, its marks included specialized departments governed by regularized administrative rules, staffed by "experts," and organized under central coordination. In performing their tasks, these agencies accumulated data in a scientific fashion and employed businesslike sales campaigns to promote support.

Changes in the office of the stated clerk of the General Assembly during the tenure of William Henry Roberts from 1884 to 1920 provided one barometer of the transformation. When Roberts assumed the position, it was a part-time job requiring chiefly that the occupant take the minutes of the annual meeting of the Assembly, preserve denominational statistics, and receive overtures from lower judicatories. It carried minimal compensation and afforded neither office space nor clerical assistance. In his early years in the job, Roberts was also librarian at Princeton Seminary and subsequently professor at Lane Seminary in Cincinnati, but by 1894 the duties of the stated clerk had become sufficiently burdensome that the Assembly made Roberts's position a full-time one and assigned him permanent office space. The Assembly had already authorized secretarial help in 1890 and subsequently provided additional clerical assistance. In 1907 the General Assembly created the post of assistant stated clerk and a year later established an advisory committee to aid Roberts.[13]

Free to devote himself fully to his post, Roberts served as an agent of coordination for Presbyterians, both in their internal life and in their relations with other religious bodies. Despite the fact that the denomination possessed a Permanent Judicial Commission, those who wished clarifications of fine points of Presbyterian polity increasingly turned to Roberts, who had won the nickname "Encyclopedia of Ecclesiastical Law." He wrote for the General Assembly a *Manual for Ruling Elders,* a compendium of *Laws Relating to Religious Corporations,* and articles on the legal status of the church's seminaries. Roberts also represented the church in wider ecumenical contacts. He was a delegate to the Alliance of the Reformed Churches, chaired the committee that negotiated reunion in 1906 with the Cumberland Presbyterians, and assumed various administrative responsibilities in the Federal Council of Churches after its formation in 1908.[14]

Another sign of the "organizational revolution" was the creation in 1903 of the Workingman's Department (later renamed the Department of Church and Labor) under the aegis of the Board of National Missions. Charles Stelzle led the department. A former machinist who had grown up among the immigrant working class of the Bowery, Stelzle combined the passion of a social prophet with the methodical traits of an efficiency expert. He ardently endorsed the Social Gospel and believed that his department had to raise the consciousness of the church regarding the plight of workers. To accomplish this goal, Stelzle relied heavily upon the social survey, that instrument so much beloved in the Progressive era. Creating a Survey Department within the Department of Church and Labor, Stelzle and his associates accumulated statistics on labor crises and on the demographics of particular cities. He inaugurated the Labor Temple in New York City as an open forum for the exchange of views and information between the church and the laboring class. Stelzle also spearheaded the Social Service Division of the efficiency-minded Men and Religion Forward Movement, served as chair of the Church Efficiency Committee of the Efficiency Society, and authored *The Principles of Successful Church Advertising.* In 1912 he ran for the New Jersey legislature on the Progressive ticket headed by Theodore Roosevelt, who called for a

"New Nationalism" that included centralized regulation of American business. Whether playing the role of amateur politician, gathering data about labor crises, setting forth ecclesiastical advertising techniques, or speaking before churches and labor conventions, Stelzle understood himself to be, as he later said, a sociologist, one who would help persons understand the laws "governing social phenomena . . . [and] the progress of civilization." Yet behind Stelzle's search for scientific or systematic order always lay a religious vision of "the larger righteousness of the Kingdom of God, which is 'human society organized according to the Will of God.' "[15]

A comparable ideal animated his colleague Warren H. Wilson. After graduating in 1893 from Union Seminary in New York City, Wilson took an upstate parish in the small village of Quaker Hill. He loved the community but was appalled by the economic and religious divisions within it. To combat this fragmentation, he created a nondenominational congregation that included his own Presbyterians as well as members of four other religious bodies. He wished to revivify the notion of the congregation as a parish, with the church as the community center. After six years, Wilson left Quaker Hill to pursue a Ph.D. in sociology because he had become convinced that rural churches needed scientific guidance. In 1908 he took a position in the Department of Church and Labor, where he conducted programs on the rural church. Playing on rising public interest in the problems of the country, he persuaded the church to create a separate Department of Church and Country Life in 1910. With that organizational base, Wilson and his staff conducted surveys of rural areas, sponsored educational programs for rural ministers, and created "demonstration parishes" in the countryside. He continued to prescribe federation for country churches, maintaining that wasteful sectarian rivalries had to be eliminated if the rural church were to fulfill its mission as community center.[16]

Both Stelzle and Wilson ran afoul of powerful interests within the church, and the backlash came at the 1913 General Assembly. Accused by conservatives of being a socialist, Stelzle resigned his post. The same assembly abolished the Department of Church and Country Life and hived off its various activities to other agencies (although Wilson himself remained). Thereafter, the denomination's rural work accented the development of Presbyterian congregations more than the formation of federated churches. Yet Stelzle and Wilson were far from beaten men. Upon his resignation, Stelzle said he intended to become "a consulting sociologist and efficiency engineer for national church organizations, social service agencies and industrial enterprises." Both he and Wilson achieved this goal, Stelzle as the field secretary for social service of the Federal Council of Churches and Wilson, while remaining with the Board of National Missions, as consultant to various interdenominational research projects. Moreover, the concerns represented by both remained entrenched in the agency structure of Presbyterianism, albeit in truncated form. They were, in short, prototypes of the specialized experts who would become increasingly common in the higher echelons of the church.[17]

As the number of specialized agencies and the scope of their work increased, Presbyterians also slowly groped toward more efficient means of raising money. In the decades after the 1870 reunion, the denomination attempted several major fund-raising campaigns. It also created, abolished, and then reestablished a committee charged with the cultivation of systematic benevolence in the churches—that is, regular weekly giving to Presbyterian causes. To stabilize finances, the General Assembly of 1908 adopted a budget plan providing apportionments for the various boards. Presbyterian authors stressed the need for careful analysis of the problem of money. For example, in 1916 Albert McGarrah, lecturer on church efficiency at McCormack Seminary in Chicago, wrote *Church Finance,* in which he explored practical ways to run every-member canvasses, develop building plans, and wage capital fund campaigns. For McGarrah, systematic fund-raising assumed patriotic as well as eschatological significance. "God," he explained,

> has entrusted present day America with so much of the wealth of the world because American churches are entrusted with most unusual duties and responsibilities in connection with His world program for the perfecting of His Kingdom on earth. As goes America so goes the world.... He has entrusted to American churches the clearest understanding of the intellectual and educational and evangelistic and social methods which are to be used by the churches of the future that we may perfect these as contributions to the ultimate efficiency of all Christendom. If American churches are to perform their magnificent duties, to help perfect ideals of democracy and liberty for the benefit of the world, to develop ideal Christians and an ideal church which shall be object lessons in all lands, and to meet the unprecedented calls for foreign mission workers to enter the world's open doors, American churches must have unprecedented funds at their command. There should be an almost unlimited increase in their incomes.

These paeans to systematic finance and promotion reached their culmination in the New Era movement begun in 1918.[18]

New Era, as its name suggests, offered a grandiose vision, and the time seemed ripe for a great dream. For nearly a decade, books and articles had extolled the power of efficient management and promotion. During the war, the denominations had pooled resources through the General War-Time Commission of the Churches. Presbyterians had occupied prominent positions in the Commission, with Robert E. Speer as chairman and William Adams Brown as general secretary. Moreover, the YMCAs, the Red Cross, and the Liberty Bond campaigns had also set the precedent for successful fund-raising on a grand scale. The sponsors of the New Era movement self-consciously imitated these ventures. They sought, in the words of one blurb, "to put the money of Presbyterians behind all of their great agencies in one unified presentation." To advertise the campaign, the church create a Department of Publicity, and the official missionary journal, *The Assembly Herald,* was renamed *The New Era.* Timed to coincide with the annual every-member canvass in March

1919, the campaign sought a large sum of money. Failure to reach the goal only prompted the sponsors to target an even higher figure in 1920. This goal, too, was not met. Acceding to reality, the movement's leaders ultimately settled for a more modest end: promoting greater acceptance of the unified budget system by the church as a whole.[19]

Even though the New Era movement fell short of its aims, it left an important legacy: Systematic financial contribution had been elevated to a chief mark of Christian discipleship. A little book by David McConaughy, written to promote the movement, illustrates the new mentality. McConaughy designed *Money: The Acid Test* as a study series on stewardship. Although McConaughy acknowledged that money constituted but one part of stewardship, the subject of finance dominated the book. Numerous pages laid down the principles one should use in determining the amount to give to God's work. Money spent for oneself must be geared to *legitimate* needs; contributions must be proportionate, the proportion increasing with one's means. Case studies of sample family budgets made the principles explicit. McConaughy's book manifested what some have called the essence of modern sales techniques: It mystified, as it were, the subject of money. Money became more than a neutral medium of exchange. According to the author, money measured a person's time, skill, and talent. Money had a "magic power" to shape character, for in its proper use (especially in its disposal through charitable giving) one attained a greater nobility of character. Properly used, money had the power to bring in the millennium. McConaughy cited lines from Horace Bushnell: "What we are waiting for is the consecration of the vast money power of the world to the work and cause and kingdom of Jesus Christ; for that day when it comes will be the morning, so to speak, of the new creation. That tide [*sic*] wave in the money power can as little be resisted, when God brings it, as the tides of the sea; and, like these, also, it will flow across the world in a day." Adding his own gloss to Bushnell, McConaughy added: "According as Christians fulfil or fail to fulfil this function they become stepping-stones to higher things or stumbling blocks in the way of those who are waiting to enter into the kingdom of God."[20]

Alongside the New Era movement were other grand enterprises growing out of the war. According to William Adams Brown, the war had taught two basic lessons. It "revealed to American Protestantism its essential unity. . . . But while the war disclosed to the churches their essential unity, it showed them at the same time that they lacked the agencies through which that unity could express itself effectively in action." To some degree disunity had found remedy in the coordinated work of the General War-Time Commission; perhaps a similar, but even larger, endeavor might win the peace. That, at least, was the hope of Brown and of other Protestant leaders who on December 17, 1918, gathered together in an "upper room" in New York City because "they had seen a vision— the vision of a united church in a divided world, and under the spell of what they saw all things seemed possible." What seemed possible was the

Interchurch World Movement. That movement, supported by Presbyterians and most other major denominations, aimed to be a gatherer of and clearinghouse for information about the religious state of America and of the rest of the world. With accurate information in hand, the denominations could then efficiently coordinate their resources. Brown and others wanted a religious analog to an army general staff—an organization looking at the world from a transdenominational perspective and suggesting ways that individual churches could best deploy their forces. Renting a large suite of offices and hiring a staff of more than 2,000 people for the headquarters in New York City, the IWM launched a fund-raising campaign of gargantuan proportions.[21]

Presbyterians in 1918 approved another far-reaching ecumenical proposal. Responding to overtures from thirty-five presbyteries, the General Assembly "unanimously adopted by a rising vote" a resolution affirming "that the time has come for Organic Church Union of the Evangelical Churches of America." The Assembly invited other communions to a conference for the preparation of a tentative plan of union.[22]

Both the IWM and organic union quickly foundered. The Interchurch World Movement succeeded in raising only a fraction of the needed money and soon closed its doors. The Council on Organic Unity, meeting in February 1920 in response to the Presbyterian initiative, drew up a preliminary plan for a federative union of "The United Churches of Christ in America." Although the plan preserved the powers of the respective communions, it also entailed considerable administrative centralization. The General Assembly, after receiving a divided committee report on the plan, sent it to the presbyteries for action. The latter decisively rejected it. Both the IWM and the plan for organic union fell afoul off a resurgent denominational consciousness. Along with other Protestant skeptics, many Presbyterians feared the loss of identity in a centralized superchurch. These failures chagrined William Adams Brown, but he professed to see grounds for hope. Perhaps the turn toward denominationalism might be useful if it prompted the communions to become individually more efficient. As Brown put it: "A chain is only as strong as its weakest link, and if the churches are to co-operate effectively with one another, they must first learn to co-operate effectively within themselves."[23]

In the 1920s Presbyterians did not forsake the search for efficiency, but they directed it toward finding ways to "co-operate effectively" within their own denominational structure. At the beginning of the decade, the General Assembly had ten boards and four permanent committees. To streamline and coordinate these operations, the Assembly created in 1920 a Special Committee on the Reorganization and Consolidation of Boards and Agencies. The Rev. John Timothy Stone, pastor of the Fourth Presbyterian Church of Chicago, chaired the committee. Stone was a moderately conservative individual who was deeply concerned that the church achieve businesslike efficiency. Indeed, as *The Christian Herald* observed, much of the appeal of the widely popular Stone came from the fact that he appeared to be a "business man in religion." "Coming across him in the business world, in Wall Street, in New York, in the grain exchanges in Chicago or in the shipping business in California, you would know that you had encountered a superior businessman who was making a success of his life, who was master of his environment." To master the environment of the Presbyterian Church, Stone and his committee proposed a sweeping reorganization of denominational structures—a reorganization that would give the church many of the features of a large corporation.[24]

In preparing its report, the committee solicited proposals from the officers of existing boards. Robert E. Speer of Foreign Missions wrote privately to his friend Stone urging that all activities be consolidated under four agencies and that an executive committee be created to supervise their work in the interim between General Assemblies. Although the Stone Committee later held public hearings, Speer's early intervention proved decisive in shaping the organization. When the committee made its recommendations to the General Assembly, it proposed four boards to supervise the denomination's work: National Missions, Foreign Missions, Christian Education, and Ministerial Relief and Sustentation. It recommended that the work of other existing committees and agencies be assigned to departments within the appropriate board. Thus, formerly autonomous agencies dealing with missions for freedmen, funds for church erection, evangelism, temperance, and sabbath observance were converted into subunits of the four "superboards"; the Woman's Board of Home Missions and the Woman's Board of Foreign Missions were abolished. Moreover, the Stone Committee altered the basis of membership on the boards. Previously, many agencies had drawn support on a largely regional basis. The Freedmen's Board, for example, had historic ties to Pittsburgh Presbytery. The new structure deliberately suppressed localism in favor of boards drawn from the national constituency. The Stone Committee also proposed the creation of a general Council, to be led by a full-time chairman. This new body would function as an executive committee of the church between meetings of the General Assembly and would advise the various boards, maintain communications with lower governing bodies, and help prepare unified budgets for all the agencies. Furthermore, continuing the trends that had marked the tenure of William Henry Roberts as stated clerk, the committee proposed an expanded role for that office.[25]

Stone's recommendations aroused opposition. Those whose boards would be subsumed under larger agencies objected to the implicit demotion of their work. In the church at large, some echoed antebellum arguments, complaining that centralization would effectively remove power from the judicatories and lodge it in the hands of a small cadre of officials. Many women resented their organization's loss of autonomy. (Indeed, the rage for efficiency, with its overtones from the male-dominated arena of business, may in fact have carried implicitly negative implications for women's role in the church.) Similarly, a number of

African-American Presbyterians protested the sacrifice of their interests. But the recurring phrases the Stone Committee employed to justify its proposals—"simplicity, efficiency, and economy"—had such appeal that opposition was overrun at the 1922 Assembly after only five hours of debate, and reorganization won lopsided approval. (The creation of a General Council demanded action by lower governing bodies—the presbyteries—and during the following year they endorsed the change by a vote of 152 to 100.) The Assembly also charged the Stone Committee with the task of implementing the plan. Choosing to interpret its mandate broadly, the group appointed members of the reconstituted boards and decided to drop many veteran leaders deemed resistant to the new order. By the time the 1923 Assembly convened, the Stone Committee had thus completed an organizational coup.[26]

The restructuring left the Board of Ministerial Relief and Sustentation relatively intact, but Stone underscored the need for the agency to "enlarge the scope of its work." The admonition reflected the crisis into which the Board's activities, especially the Sustentation Fund, had fallen. Despite dramatic increases in its assets, the Fund enrolled no more than a quarter of all Presbyterian ministers, and inflation had rendered the annual annuity grossly inadequate. Faced with these realities and nettled by Stone's criticisms during the hearings on reorganization, the head of the Board, Henry Master, made plans for a more comprehensive pension system and skillfully maneuvered behind the scenes to drum up support. By 1923—the year reorganization went into effect—a number of presbyteries were requesting a new system, and the General Assembly created a special Laymen's Committee to draft a proposal.[27]

Prominent businessmen dominated the committee. Led by Will H. Hays, postmaster general in the Harding administration and later an entrepreneur in the movie industry, the committee prepared a plan that built on the principles of the Sustentation Fund but went far beyond it. The goal of the plan remained an annual annuity for ministers, but unlike the earlier program, the new plan provided an annuity that, while subject to a maximum limit, would be based on both years of service to the church and average salary. Funds for the plan would come from a 10 percent annual payment of participants' salaries (7.5 percent from the church, 2.5 percent from the minister). The plan would go into effect only when 4,000 churches or salary-paying organizations agreed to support it, when 4,000 ministers and other church employees agreed to contribute, and when adequate reserve funds were raised. The committee set this figure at $15 million.[28]

The campaign to raise this amount enlisted businesspeople and methods. Andrew Mellon, secretary of the Treasury, served as the treasurer of the drive. A professional fund-raiser, Arnaud Marts, president of Marts and Lundy of New York, directed the campaign. R. Douglas Brackenridge and Lois Boyd have succinctly summarized the promotional techniques employed:

Marts launched a campaign utilizing slick brochures and catchy phrases ("Religion is the one essential industry of the world. The management of that industry is in the hands of ministers.") He organized a series of nation-wide inspirational rallies that Mellon and others underwrote. Marts formed a "National Committee of 100" (later increased to 200) of laypersons from every presbytery in the denomination. He instigated a competitive pro-gram of benevolence among four regions of the country. Within a year the campaign had reached a successful conclusion.

At the 1927 Assembly, with an American flag prominently displayed and with the commissioners singing the doxology, Hays announced the suc-cess of the financial drive. By 1928 the majority of presbyteries had announced that they would no longer allow a minister to be settled in a church unless he and his congregation agreed to participate in the plan. Now the church's pension plan as well as the structure of the church had been reorganized in accordance with the canons of efficiency.[29]

III

The mystique of efficiency triumphed during the same years that Presbyte-rians were reassessing their theological identity. Fearful that modernism and destructive forms of biblical criticism might infiltrate the church, several General Assemblies beginning in 1892 sought to enumerate sup-posedly essential tenets of the Westminster Confession of Faith—for exam-ple, the inerrancy of Scripture—and thus in theory made assent to these views mandatory for every minister in the denomination. In the first half of the 1920s, during the so-called Fundamentalist controversy, some conser-vatives launched a campaign to enforce this restrictive ideal. J. Gresham Machen, an assistant professor at Princeton Theological Seminary, voiced the sentiments of this group when he declared in 1923 that two irreconcil-able religions—Christianity and liberalism—inhabited the Presbyterian fellowship. Hence, liberals should withdraw or be excluded from a body whose official beliefs they could no longer in honesty profess.[30]

For a moment, the ultraconservatives appeared poised for victory. Yet in the end they were deserted by many who sympathized with their theology but lacked the stomach for a heresy hunt. When these moderate conservatives opted for tolerance, Presbyterianism took a decisive turn toward greater confessional inclusiveness—a turn symbolized by a Spe-cial Commission of Fifteen, named by the moderator of the 1925 General Assembly. In its report, adopted by the two subsequent Assemblies, the Committee denied the power of any General Assembly to define a priori the essential articles of the Westminster Confession and thus, in effect, disavowed attempts of earlier Assemblies to make such pronouncements. In the very years that it centralized administrative functions, the denomi-nation decentralized its control over theological questions. The historian must ask how the two processes were related.[31]

In some instances theological conservatives resisted administrative centralization, and liberal to moderate Presbyterians favored it. For example, at the 1911 General Assembly, Mark Mathews, a leading conservative, defended the Board of Relief against the more centralized efforts of the Sustentation Fund. In 1920 he and a fellow conservative, Maitland Alexander, railed at the administrative pretensions of the Interchurch World Movement. When the Stone Committee was preparing its recommendations, *The Presbyterian,* the denominational newspaper farthest to the right theologically, relentlessly criticized the process. J. Gresham Machen, the undisputed intellectual leader of the archconservatives, despised what he saw as the collectivist tendencies of the age and attacked "the centralization of power which is going on in the modern Church." Two prominent leaders in the Board of Home (later National) Missions exemplify the point from the other end of the theological spectrum. Although Warren Wilson's works were more sociological than theological in nature, he clearly inclined toward liberal views, and Charles Stelzle moved well beyond his training at Moody Bible Institute to favor a more inclusive theological vision.[32]

Yet one must not push these identifications too far. William Henry Roberts espoused traditional views and, while at Lane Seminary, approved the ouster of a fellow professor because of the latter's acceptance of modern biblical criticism. J. Wilbur Chapman, a darling of the church's conservatives, played a prominent role in the New Era movement until his death in 1919. Mark Matthews ultimately supported the pension plan adopted in 1927, and John Timothy Stone had written an article for *The Fundamentals.*[33]

The relationship of theology to the mystique of efficiency was not straightforward. What a person believed generally mattered less than the relative importance he or she attributed to doctrine per se. Thus J. Gresham Machen, for whom correct belief was the fountain of all true Christian activity, hated administrative centralization in part because it relegated theological distinctions to a place of lesser significance. By contrast, Robert E. Speer, secretary of the Board of Foreign Missions for forty-six years, illustrated a different approach to the church's organizational revolution. As a young man Speer fell under the influence of the conservative A. T. Pierson, including the latter's premillennialism. Speer never repudiated his early convictions. He continued to profess belief in the virgin birth and as late as 1937 avowed that he awaited the Second Coming of Christ. Yet years of service at the Foreign Board and wide ecumenical contacts prompted him to view theological differences very differently from Machen. Speer saw a divided world in desperate need of unity in Christ. The task of the church was to embody such unity in its own life and mission. An evangelical centrist, Speer longed for a comprehensive Christianity encompassing the insights of various theological persuasions. That ideal informed his prodigious capacity for attention to the minutiae of restructuring. He was not merely tinkering with administrative flow charts but searching for a way to give efficient expression to a vision of evangelical unity in Christ. As Richard Reifsnyder has written of Speer's role in the reorganization of the 1920s, "Speer had a way of making bureaucratic transformation seem filled with high moral and spiritual purpose." The vision was apparently contagious, for Speer was elected moderator of the denominator by virtual acclamation in 1927.[34]

The triumph of moderation did not mean that theology had ceased to matter or that Presbyterian ministers had acquired a license to teach or preach anything. The vast majority within the denomination continued to adhere to a decidedly evangelical understanding of the faith. Theological boundaries, albeit fuzzier ones, remained. Presbyterian response to the publication of *Rethinking Missions: A Layman's Inquiry after One Hundred Years* (1932) helped to mark those limits. The book, commissioned by laypersons of seven denominations, espoused a view of the missionary enterprise at odds with traditional approaches. The authors urged that missionaries not seek to convert others to Christianity but rather encourage understanding among all faiths and promote universal spiritual principles. Voicing the consensus of the Foreign Board and the church at large, Robert E. Speer emphasized that Presbyterian missionary work rested upon the finality of Christ and the uniqueness of the Christian revelation.[35]

A vaguely postmillennial aura also hovered about the idea of efficiency. To be sure, not all who espoused the idea adhered to that eschatological persuasion, as Robert Speer's affinity for premillennialism attested. But the themes characteristically invoked on behalf of efficiency—for example, Stelzle's vision of promoting a "human society organized according to the Will of God," McGarrah's conception of American churches charged with the perfecting of God's kingdom on earth, McConaughy's belief in the power of sanctified giving to usher in the morning of the new creation—all appeared to fit into a loosely postmillennial scheme. By the 1920s that viewpoint, as a distinct biblically grounded eschatology, was disappearing, but its shadow persisted in the mystique of efficiency and progress.[36]

Despite a persistent theological consensus, the ideology of efficiency gave a new basis for denominational identity. The church increasingly defined itself by its programs, and the measure of Presbyterian unity was loyal support of those activities. Reporting to the 1927 General Assembly, Will Hays said of the campaign to raise money for the new pension plan: "If there were no other evidence of the essential unity of our great denomination than this . . . , this fact alone—that practically every self-supporting church voluntarily cooperated in a united effort for a common cause is overwhelming proof of our desire and ability to work together in the interest of the Kingdom." Hays did allude to "many other" (unspecified) evidences of unity, but significantly he accented the importance of the "common cause"—in this instance, a successful fund-raising drive.

Actions by the General Assembly in the 1930s disclosed how important a mark of Presbyterianism these common causes had become. In

1933 J. Gresham Machen and others organized the Independent Board for Presbyterian Foreign Missions. The following year the General Assembly received from the General Council a study paper affirming the power of the Assembly over its agencies and denying that Presbyterians had the right to create organizations that would work against this authority. Accordingly, the Assembly ordered that the Independent Board cease its operations, that all Presbyterians associated with it renounce the affiliation, and that presbyteries institute disciplinary proceedings against any of their members who failed to comply with the resolution. On the basis of this mandate, J. Gresham Machen was eventually suspended from the ministry; along with a handful of others, he withdrew to form a separate denomination. Lefferts Loetscher has sagely observed that a comparison of the 1934 study paper "with the reports of the Special Commission of 1925 as adopted by the Assemblies of 1926 and 1927 graphically illustrates the way in which the Church was moving simultaneously toward administrative centralization and theological decentralization."[37]

As the mystique of efficiency triumphed, it sometimes tended to undercut its own premises. Those who espoused administrative reshuffling and promotional campaigns argued that they were trying to provide unified, effective expression to the denomination's common mind. In reality, the new denominational organizations could undermine unity as well as advance it. Those who spent their careers working for national agencies of the church often acquired perspectives different from those of the people to whom they were responsible. As the people with the "facts" about their specialized domains or, alternately, as the ones keeping a steady gaze on the entire mission of the church, they often viewed as narrow the outlook of parish ministers and their congregations. Accordingly, board leaders often sought to shape the mind of the denomination. As William Adams Brown observed: "The boards are not simply agents to carry out the will of the churches; they are in a very real sense teachers of the Church as to what ought to be done. Much of their energy is spent in preparing informational literature and in bringing home to the consciences of their constituency facts regarding the needs of their field." One could point to many specific instances of officials functioning as "teachers of the Church": Speer working behind the scenes to shape the Stone Committee's recommendations, Master orchestrating a grass-roots campaign for pension reform, Wilson trying to get country churches to surrender their parochial loyalties in favor of federation, Stelzle seeking to raise the consciousness of Presbyterians regarding the problems of labor. Despite the arguable merits of these various schemes, they sometimes provoked resentment among constituents who preferred to see the boards as servants rather than as masters. Tradition of localism, democratic control, and anti-elitism were sunk deep in American life; they coexisted uneasily with centralized denominational control. Moreover, as centralization proceeded, certain groups unquestionably found themselves and their causes excluded from the seats of power as the experience of African-Americans, women, and some theological conservatives attested during the reorganization of 1923.

But the fundamental problem did not reside in the alienation of particular groups from the national ecclesiastical agencies, for that issue could be adjusted by mutual compromise and concession. The real predicament was a contradiction within the mystique of efficiency itself. John Higham's comments about the "experts" of the Progressive era are equally applicable to the new class of agency leaders in the Presbyterian Church: "Contrary to what the progressives supposed, technical organization is essentially undemocratic. Not equal rights but the hierarchical articulation of differentiated functions is its working principle. The more complex the knowledge required for maintaining a system, the further the professional expert is detached from the common life and the more the centers of power are hidden from public view." Bureaucratic efforts to give the concerns of aggrieved groups representation within the agencies could alleviate the problem but could not address the underlying issue.[38]

Drives for reorganization also manifested an ambivalence about the domain to be rendered more efficient: Was it the denomination or American Protestantism as a whole? (Catholicism, of course, still generally lay outside the pale of consideration.) Presbyterians generally claimed that the two tasks were complementary. Thus, in its first report to the General Assembly, the New Era Committee, after spelling out numerous ways to make the internal workings of Presbyterianism more efficient, quickly added:

> Through the New Era Movement . . . , there should be the fullest co-operation with the Inter-Church World Movement which seeks to federate the evangelical Protestant communions about their common Kingdom task, assigning to each denomination its full and fair share of responsibility as an administrative unit and calling forth the co-operative labors of the whole Christian community in securing adequate resources to meet the whole responsibility. Out of such a co-operative Movement it is believed that there may be placed upon the national and the world the impact of a united Protestantism, which alone can meet the incoming tide of social and economic unrest, as well as religious and moral unbelief and depression.

Yet this beautiful ideal was more readily attainable in theory than in practice. For all their genuine desire to be part of a united Protestant phalanx, Presbyterians were equally zealous to protect their own programs and to expand their own churches. Thus, when money proved difficult to raise for the New Era campaign (and virtually impossible for the IWM) and when Presbyterians appeared ready to rend themselves during the theological strife of the 1920s, the denomination was forced to determine the greater priority. It chose to emphasize the reorganization and the consolidation of its own life. Yet the ecumenical vision would not fade, for ultimately the mystique of efficiency, continuing the historic Protestant quest for a "Christian America," aimed at nothing less than shaping the ethos of the nation itself, and no single denomination alone was up to the task. Committed to Christianizing the republic and yet often forced to settle for reshuffling denominational agencies, the reorganizers found themselves with means woefully inadequate to their aspirations.[39]

The mystique of efficiency was perhaps disproportionate to its goals in a more fundamental sense. The ideal had arisen in the milieu of corporate business where efficiency could be measured by the volume of goods sold and profits earned. Yet churches traded in the intangibles of symbolic rewards less susceptible to precise computation. William Adams Brown had admitted as much when he declared in 1922 that "there is always something incalculable about religion." Yet, aside from periodic grumbling about the church being overrun by its machinery, few persons, if any, systematically explored the implications of this complaint. The failures to do so would have far-reaching consequences. With uncertainties and unresolved questions built into the search for an ill-defined efficiency, Presbyterians could never be sure whether they had completed the quest and thus returned again and again to the pursuit of an elusive goal. Institutional reorganization would become an endemic feature of Presbyterian life.[40]

IV

The story of Presbyterians' organizational revolution raises intriguing issues that call for further investigation. One wonders how deeply notions of efficiency penetrated the local churches and whether congregational worship and work changed significantly. Was the fact that nearly 40 percent of the presbyteries voted against the creation of a General Council in 1922–1923 evidence of a grassroots backlash against an efficiency-minded establishment? In recent decades, various students of the "mainline" denominations have investigated that they perceive as a major gulf separating rank-and-file Protestants from their leadership. Usually these scholars trace the emergence of the divide to the turmoil of the 1960s, but perhaps the first hints of division appeared much earlier in the wake of the organizational revolution.[41]

The Presbyterian experience also demands comparison with that of other denominations. Did Presbyterians, for example, with their system of ascending governing bodies, turn to centralized structure more readily than did Baptists, who emphasized the autonomy of each congregation? Did Presbyterians who believed in the parity of all clergy take a different path to bureaucracy than did more hierarchically minded Episcopalians? Although definitive answers to these questions await considerable research, the similarities among the various Protestant churches appear to have outweighed the differences. In each instance, reorganization pushed questions of distinctive theology and tradition into the background in the name of efficiency. One might tentatively argue that the mystique of efficiency promoted similar aims, rationales, and vocabularies within various churches and thus contributed to what Robert Wuthnow has called "the declining significance of denominationalism." Whatever answers further research yields, it is clear that the Presbyterian organizational revolution provides important clues to religious and cultural trends not limited to one denomination.[42]

NOTES

1. William Adams Brown, *The Church in America: A Study of the Present Condition and Future Prospects of American Protestantism* (New York: Macmillan, 1922), pp. ix, 11.

2. Samuel Haber, *Efficiency and Uplift: Scientific Management in the Progressive Era* (1964; reprint, ed., Chicago: University of Chicago Press, 1973), p. ix; Ben Primer, *Protestants and American Business Methods* (Ann Arbor: University of Michigan Research Press, 1979); and Paul M. Harrison, *Authority and Power in the Free Church Tradition: A Social Case Study of the American Baptist Convention* (Princeton: Princeton University Press, 1959) provide ample illustrations of the preoccupation with efficiency and administrative restructuring in numerous denominations. On Presbyterians, see Richard W. Reifsnyder, "The Reorganizational Impulse in American Protestantism: The Presbyterian Church (U.S.A.) as a Case Study, 1788–1983" (Ph.D. diss., Princeton Theological Seminary, 1984), and Louis Weeks, "The Incorporation of American Religion: The Case of the Presbyterians," *Religion and American Culture* 1 (Winter 1991): 100–118. Also very helpful is Milton J Coalter, John M. Mulder, and Louis Weeks, eds., *The Organizational Revolution: Presbyterians and American Denominationalism* (Louisville, Ky.: Westminster/John Knox, 1992), which Milton Coalter graciously made available to me in galley form. Although Presbyterian churches other than the Presbyterian Church in the U.S.A. were affected by the organizational revolution, my study is confined to that body.

3. Robert H. Wiebe, *The Search for Order, 1877–1920* (New York: Hill and Wang, 1967), pp. 11–110, 142; Alan Trachtenberg, *The Incorporation of American: Culture and Society in the Gilded Age* (New York: Hill and Wang, 1982), pp. 3–10.

4. Alfred D. Chandler, Jr., *The Visible Hand: The Managerial Revolution in American Business* (Cambridge, Mass.: Harvard University Press, Belknap Press, 1977).

5. Clyde W. Barrow, *Universities and the Capitalist State: Corporate Liberalism and the Reconstruction of American Higher Education, 1894–1928* (Madison: University of Wisconsin Press, 1990); Burton J. Bledstein, *The Culture of Professionalism: The Middle Class and the Development of Higher Education in America* (New York: W. W. Norton and Company, 1976); Laurence R. Veysey, *The Emergence of the American University* (Chicago: University of Chicago Press, 1965); H. Wayne Morgan, *From Hayes to McKinley: National Party Politics, 1877–1896* (Syracuse: Syracuse University Press, 1969).

6. Quotation from Haber, *Efficiency and Uplift*, p. 59; see also pp. ix–x,

18–74. On progressivism, consult also David W. Noble, *The Progressive Mind, 1890–1917,* rev. ed. (Minneapolis: Burgess Publishing Company, 1981); Wiebe, *Search for Order,* pp. 164–223; Robert M. Crunden, *Ministers of Reform: The Progressives' Achievement in American Civilization, 1889–1920* (New York: Basic Books, 1982). Subsequent to the writing of *Search for Order,* Wiebe has in *The Segmented Society: An Introduction to the Meaning of America* (New York: Oxford University Press, 1975) qualified his earlier argument. In the latter work he stressed that many of the America's "island communities" and regional variations have continued to resist consolidation.

7. Patricia R. Hill, *The World Their Household: The American Woman's Foreign Mission Movement and Cultural Transformation, 1870–1920* (Ann Arbor: University of Michigan Press, 1985), pp. 1–7; Valentin H. Rabe, *The Home Base of American China Missions, 1880–1920* (Cambridge, Mass.: Harvard University Press, 1978), pp. 9–48; Primer, *Protestants,* pp. 27–63; Josiah Strong, *The New Era; or the Coming Kingdom* (New York: Baker and Taylor, 1893), p. 30. Strong's call for effective coordination of Protestant forces in the face of religious diversity appears to lend at least partial credence to the judgment of Kevin J. Christiano, *Religious Diversity and Social Change: American Cities, 1890–1906* (Cambridge: Cambridge University Press, 1987), p. 135: "Unity did not arrive when ideological boundaries separating the denominations crumbled. . . . Protestant consolidation appeared, rather, as social boundaries stiffened—that is, when evangelical Christianity coalesced to confront foreign religions, the implications of whose presence in American society were unacceptable to Protestants."

8. Rabe, *Home Base,* pp. 49–171; Primer, *Protestants,* pp. 65–154; Shailer Mathews, *Scientific Management in the Churches* (Chicago: University of Chicago Press, 1912) and "Theological Seminaries as Schools of Religious Efficiency," *Biblical World* 47 (1916): 84.

9. *The Constitution of the Presbyterian Church (U.S.A.): Part II: Book of Order* (Louisville, Ky.: Office of the General Assembly, 1989), p. G-1.0400.

10. Quotation in Earl R. MacCormac, "The Development of Presbyterian Missionary Organizations: 1790–1870," *Journal of Presbyterian History* 43 (September 1965): 149–73; George M. Marsden, *The Evangelical Mind and the New School Presbyterian Experience: A Case Study of Thought and Theology in Nineteenth-Century America* (New Haven: Yale University Press, 1970), pp. 7–30, 59–87, 104–127; Ernest Trice Thompson, *Presbyterians in the South,* 3 vols. (Richmond, Va.: John Knox Press, 1963–72), 1: 510–516.

11. Clifford M. Drury, *Presbyterian Panorama: One Hundred and Fifty Years of National Missions History* (Philadelphia: Board of Christian Education, Presbyterian Church in the U.S.A., 1952), pp. 171–210; Arthur Judson Brown, *One Hundred Years: A History of the Foreign Missionary Work of the Presbyterian Church in the U.S.A.* (New York: Fleming H. Revell, 1936), pp. 59–60; R. Douglas Brackenridge and Lois A. Boyd, *Presbyterians and Pensions: The Roots and Growth of Pensions in the Presbyterian Church (U.S.A.)* (Atlanta: John Knox Press, 1988), pp. 56–62, 64–68.

12. Boyd and Brackenridge, *Presbyterian and Pensions,* pp. 66–67; Reifsnyder, "The Reorganizational Impulse," pp. 218–260.

13. Bruce David Forbes, "William Henry Roberts: Resistance to Change and Bureaucratic Adaptation," *Journal of Presbyterian History* 54 (Winter 1976): 405–421.

14. Ibid.

15. Charles Stelzle, *A Son of the Bowery: The Life Story of an East Side American* (New York: George H. Doran Company, 1926), p. 96; George H. Nash III, "Charles Stelzle: Social Gospel Pioneer," *Journal of Presbyterian History* 50 (Fall 1972): 206–228; Haber, *Efficiency and Uplift,* p. 63.

16. Warren H. Wilson, *The Church of the Open Country* (New York: Missionary Education Movement, 1911) and *The Church at the Center* (New York: Missionary Education Movement, 1914); Merwin Swanson, "The Country Life Movement and the Churches," *Church History* 46 (September 1977): 358–373; James H. Madison, "Reformers and the Rural Church, 1900–1950," *Journal of American History* 73 (December 1986): 645–668.

17. Swanson, "Country Life Movement," p. 370; Nash, "Charles Stelzle," pp. 224–226. For a general survey of the manner in which specialized social ministries acquired a niche in the emerging bureaucratic structure of Protestantism, see Donald K. Gorrell, *The Age of Social Responsiblility: The Social Gospel in the Progressive Era* (Macon, Ga.: Mercer University Press, 1988).

18. Reifsnyder, "The Reorganizational Impulse," pp. 249, 252, 253, 284, 300–301; Albert F. McGarrah, *Modern Church Finance: Its Principles and Practice* (New York: Fleming H. Revell, 1916), pp. 26–27.

19. John E. Lankford, "The Impact of the New Era Movement on the Presbyterian Church in the United States of America, 1918–1925," *Journal of Presbyterian History* 40 (December 1962): 213–224. "Practical Points for Promoting Publicity," *New Era Magazine* 26 (February 1920): 113, gives examples of the promotional tactics favored by the movement. For an analysis placing the movement within a larger context, see John E. Lankford, "Protestant Stewardship and Benevolence, 1900–1941: A Study in Religious Philanthropy" (Ph.D. diss., University of Wisconsin, 1961). John F. Piper, Jr., *The American Churches in World War I* (Athens: Ohio University Press, 1985), esp. pp. 8–68, surveys Protestants activities during the conflict.

20. David McConaughy, *Money the Acid Test* (Philadelphia: Westminster Press, 1918), 185; Brown, *One Hundred Years,* p. 60. Trachtenberg, *Incorporation of America,* p. 135, argues, for example, of modern advertising that it serves "not only to instill desires for goods but also to disguise the character of consumption, to make it seem an act different from a merely functional, life-enhancing use of an object . . . it also aimed to make habitual the identification of products with something else, with ideas, feelings, status."

21. Brown, *Church in America,* pp. 101, 119, 340–345; Eldon Ernst, *Moment of Truth for Protestant America: Interchurch Campaigns Following World War I* (Missoula, Mont.: Scholars' Press, 1974), pp. 51–114, and "Presbyterians and the Interchurch World Movement—A Chapter in the Development of Protestant Unity in Twentieth Century America," *Journal of Presbyterian History* 48 (Winter 1970): 231–248.

22. Lefferts A. Loetscher, *The Broadening Church: A Study of Theological Issues in the Presbyterian Church since 1869* (Philadelphia: University of Pennsylvania Press, 1954), p. 100.

23. Ibid., p. 101; Ernst, *Moment of Truth,* pp. 137–174, and "Presbyterians and the Interchurch World Movement"; Brown, *Church in America,* pp. 123–124.

24. Reifsnyder, "The Reorganizational Impulse," pp. 327–329; *Christian Herald* 46 (27 January 1923), quoted in Rolf Lunden, *Business and Religion in the American 1920s* (Westport, Conn.: Greenwood Press, 1988), p. 66.

25. Reifsnyder, "The Reorganizational Impulse," pp. 329–355.

26. Ibid., 327–355; Lois Boyd and R. Douglas Brackenridge, *Presbyterian Women in America: Two Centuries of a Quest for Status* (Westport, Conn.: Greenwood Press, 1983), pp. 59–75. Gail Bederman, " 'The Women Have Had Charge of the Church Work Long Enough' ": The Men and Religion Forward Movement of 1911–1912 and the Masculinization of Middle-Class Protestantism," *American Quarterly* 41 (September 1989): 432–465, makes the case that the drive for efficiency had as one of its goals male control of religious life. Kathy Ferguson, *The Feminist Case Against Bureaucracy* (Philadelphia: Temple University Press, 1984), offers a similar analysis from a broader theoretical perspective.

27. Brackenridge and Boyd, *Presbyterians and Pensions,* p. 72.

28. Ibid., pp. 72–74.

29. Ibid., pp. 74–76. A further observation on the part played by the mystique of efficiency in the creation of pension plans is in order. William Graebner, *A History of Retirement: The Meaning and Function of an American Institution. 1885–1978* (New Haven: Yale University Press, 1980), notes that after 1900 the burgeoning number of pension plans—and accompanying mandatory retirement—reflected the effort of corporate capitalism to organize the workforce in a more efficient fashion. "Organized systems of mandatory retirement now seemed possible (because the working class was organized into more manageable units) as well as more necessary. For leaders in business, labor, and the professions, retirement became a panacea for the ills that beset their particular fields. For business, retirement meant reduced unemployment, lower rates of turnover, a younger, more efficient, and more conservative work force; for labor, it was in part a way of transferring work from one generation to another in industries with a surplus of workers; for many religious denominations, it promised the recruitment of a young clergy capable of invigorating a moribund church; for educators . . . , it held out hopes of developing university settings fully as committed to efficiency as their counterparts in industry" (p. 13). These observations provide only a partially accurate description of the Presbyterian pension plan. Bowing to the old conviction that God's call to preach had no age limit, the plan did not mandate retirement. In fact, the promoters of the system emphasized that it was designed to prevent retirement. "The board," observe Brackenridge and Boyd, "based this feature on studies of ministerial salaries which indicated that incomes peaked about age forty-nine and then dramatically declined. Larger churches wanted younger ministers, so older ministers were faced with taking smaller churches that offered reduced salaries. The pension, therefore, was designed to provide supplementary income for active clergy when their resources became inadequate" (p. 74). Thus, in its own way the Presbyterian plan represented an effort to provide for an efficient allocation of ministers in accordance with the prevailing preferences of congregations. Also, the ideal of efficiency was evident in that the pension plan, unlike the old system of ministerial relief, which relied on a case-by-case analysis of the merits of needy clergy, imposed a uniform standard for rendering financial assistance.

30. Loetscher, *The Broadening Church,* 116–17; George M. Marsden, *Fundamentalism and American Culture: The Shaping of Twentieth-Century Evangelicalism, 1870–1925* (New York: Oxford University Press, 1980), pp. 109–118, 164–184; J. Gresham Machen, *Christianity and Liberalism* (New York: Macmillan, 1923).

31. Loetscher, *The Broadening Church,* pp. 125–36; Bradley J. Longfield,

The Presbyterian Controversy: Fundamentalists, Modernists, and Moderates (New York: Oxford University Press, 1991), esp. pp. 128–161.

32. Brackenridge and Boyd, *Presbyterians and Pensions,* p. 66; Ernst, *Moment of Truth,* p. 148; Reifsnyder, "The Reorganizational Impulse," p. 349; Machen, *Christianity,* p. 171; Warren H. Wilson, *The Second Missionary Adventure* (New York: Fleming H. Revell, 1915); Stelzle, *Son of the Bowery,* pp. 328–335.

33. Forbes, *William Henry Roberts,* pp. 411–412; Lankford, "Impact of the New Era Movement," p. 219; John Timothy Stone, "Pastoral and Personal Evangelism, or Winning Men to Christ One by One," in *The Fundamentals,* ed. R. A. Torrey et al. (reprint ed., Grand Rapids, Mich.: Kregel Publications, 1990), pp. 467–476.

34. Longfield, *Presbyterian Controversy,* pp. 28–53, 181–208; Loetscher, *The Broadening Church,* p. 133; Reifsnyder, "The Reorganizational Impulse," p. 333.

35. James A. Patterson, "Robert E. Speer and the Crisis of the American Protestant Missionary Movement," (Ph.D. diss., Princeton Theological Seminary, 1980); Loetscher, *The Broadening Church,* pp. 149–150.

36. James H. Moorhead, "The Erosion of Postmillennialism in American Religious Thought," *Church History* 53 (March 1984): 61–77. Jean Quandt, "Religion and Social Thought: The Secularization of Postmillennialism," *American Quarterly* 25 (October 1973): 390–409, argues that much of the social thought of the Progressive era, from which the mystique of efficiency emerged, was a secularized version of postmillennialism.

37. "Seventy-Second Annual Report of the Presbyterian Board of Ministerial Relief and Sustentation," in *Minutes of the General Assembly of the Presbyterian Church in the U.S.A.: Part II: The Reports of the Boards* (Philadelphia: Office of the General Assembly, 1927), p. vii; Longfield, *Presbyterian Controversy,* pp. 209–212; Loetscher, *The Broadening Church,* p. 151.

38. Brown, *Church in America,* p. 234; John Higham, "Hanging Together: Divergent Unities in American History," *Journal of American History* 61 (June 1974): 26. For an account of the power of anti-elitism in American religion, see Nathan O. Hatch, *The Democratization of American Christianity* (New Haven: Yale University Press, 1989).

39. "First Annual Report of the Committee on the New Era Expansion Program," in *Minutes of the General Assembly of the Presbyterian Church in the U.S.A.: Part II: Reports of the Boards* (Philadelphia: Office of the General Assembly, 1919), p. 27; Robert T. Handy, *A Christian America: Protestant Hopes and Historical Realities,* 2nd ed. (New York: Oxford University Press, 1984), 101ff.

40. For information on reorganizations since the 1920s, see Richard W. Reifsnyder, "Managing the Mission: Church Restructuring in the Twentieth Century," in Coalter, Mulder, and Weeks, eds., The Organizational Revolution.

41. See, for example, Jeffrey K. Hadden, *The Gathering Storm in the Churches* (Garden City, N.Y.: Doubleday, 1969); and Robert Wuthnow, *The Restructuring of American Religion* (Princeton: Princeton University Press, 1988), pp. 133–72.

42. Wuthnow, *Restructuring,* pp. 71–99; Primer, *Protestants,* p. 79; Harrison, *Authority and Power,* pp. 47, 51.

"Denominational" Colleges
in Antebellum America?:
A Case Study of Presbyterians
and Methodists in the South

BRADLEY J. LONGFIELD

Since the early settlement of Massachusetts Bay by English Puritans, Christians in America have sought to unite religion and learning through the founding of academies of higher education. The relationship between these schools and Protestant denominations in the years before the Civil War has become a matter of some debate among historians of higher education. For years, Donald Tewksbury's claim that "the 'denominational college' was the prevailing American college of the middle period of our history"[1] held sway and was widely echoed in general surveys. More recently, however, numerous scholars have been challenging the portrayal of antebellum colleges as "denominational" institutions. In an influential essay, David Potts, for example, claims that "there is good reason to anticipate that the traditional generalization concerning a basic trend from sectarianism toward secularism, when applied to American collegiate history during the nineteenth century, will have to be inverted." James McLachlan has described the college-founding movement as "pan-Protestant," and Natalie Naylor has claimed that "relatively few colleges ... had actually been founded by the initiative of official church bodies, received financial support from denominations, or were truly under ecclesiastical control."[2] Such scholars, seeming to understand a "denominational college" to be one primarily administratively connected to and funded by a church judicatory and emphasizing the "local" rather than the "denominational" aspects of these schools, have argued that "actual denominational colleges were few or in only an embryonic state in the first half of the nineteenth century."[3] "This was the age not of the denominational college," Natalie Naylor concludes, "but of the Christian college."[4]

Historians such as Potts and Naylor raise important questions about the use of the term *denominational* to describe colleges in the nineteenth century and rightly stress local influences on these schools. Tewksbury, as Naylor claims, might well be criticized for trying "to impose upon the ante-bellum institutions later nineteenth and twentieth century models," and the use of the label "denominational college" might well be more nuanced.[5]

On the other hand, perhaps the older historiography can point in a fruitful direction for understanding antebellum colleges and denominations. Rather than assuming some normative "denominational" relationship by which to measure a school's "denominationalism"—as it appears Potts and Naylor do—perhaps these schools reflect a way or ways of being denominational in the antebellum period. That is, instead of asking the question, "How denominational were these colleges?" it might be helpful to ask, "How were these schools denominational, and what might this tell us about the denominations in this era?" The way the schools and their leadership envisioned their missions and the types of relationships that the schools maintained with their religious constituency might well help us to understand similarities and differences between the denominations in the antebellum United States and the development of denominationalism in this nation.[6]

In order to illumine the denominationalism of schools in different religious traditions, this essay explores selected Presbyterian and Methodist colleges that were founded in the antebellum South during what was traditionally considered the heyday of the denominational college movement.[7] Maryville, Davidson, and Oglethorpe serve as exemplars in the Presbyterian stream, and Randolph-Macon, Emory, and Wofford exemplify Methodist-related schools.

The use of southern schools in this study could prove helpful for two reasons. First, in the historiography of higher education, southern schools tend to be slighted in favor of institutions in the Northeast and in the Midwest, which often reflected the Puritan/Whig spirit manifest in the Society for the Promotion of Collegiate and Theological Education at the West.[8] While southern schools were indebted to New England for providing much of the leadership, southern colleges, reflecting the growing regional distinctiveness of this era, might offer a somewhat different story than that of their northern counterparts, thereby providing an alternate perspective on antebellum education.[9]

Second, limiting the study to a particular geographic region minimizes the impact of regional differences between colleges and denominations that might obscure important tendencies. Given the predominantly local and regional emphases of denominations in this period, a focus on a particular region might also help to illumine regional tendencies within denominations and their respective colleges.

Of the Presbyterian schools here considered, Maryville College in Tennessee is the oldest, having been founded by the Synod of Tennessee in 1819 as the Southern and Western Theological Seminary.[10] While the immediate intent of the synod was to provide a training facility for Presbyterian ministers for the frontier, Maryville's founders did not limit their vision to the immediate future. Imbued with the millennial zeal of the age, these Presbyterians looked to the day when the school would result in "the church increased, millions made happy on earth, heaven peopled with multitudes . . . and the inhabitants of both rising up to call its founders and patrons blessed."[11]

Isaac Anderson, a Presbyterian minister and the chief proponent of this venture, oversaw the institution from its founding until his death in 1857. The constitution of the college specified that all professors—of which there were eight in the years before the Civil War—were to be ordained Presbyterian ministers.[12]

Given the lack of educational opportunity on the frontier, the seminary had to offer not simply a theological curriculum but also the preparatory and college instruction necessary to prepare students for theological study. Within a few years of the seminary's founding, students in the preparatory and college divisions outnumbered those in the religious program, and the school came to be known as the College at Maryville.[13]

Fear among state legislators that the Presbyterians were, under the guise of education, attempting to grab political power and to establish their faith, held up approval of a charter for the school until 1842. In the first twenty-three years of the institution's existence, therefore, the Synod of Tennessee elected both the directors and the faculty of the school and approved all the directors' decisions. According to the constitution, two thirds of the directors were to be Presbyterian clergy and one third, Presbyterian laymen.[14]

The legislature, when it finally approved a charter, responded to fears of sectarian domination by lodging ownership of the college in the board of directors and by stipulating that the first board would be elected by the county court, then to become self-perpetuating. Fears about the school's purposes subsided enough in the following years for the legislature to amend the charter in 1845, returning the authority to elect the school's directors to the Synod.[15]

Maryville, like all denominational schools of the antebellum era, professed an openness to young men of all evangelical denominations "of good moral and religious character." The constitution insisted that students were free to believe what they wished within the bounds of evangelical Christianity. Seeking to be tolerant, the founders nonetheless required the disciplining of any student who denied the Trinity, total depravity, or the need for spiritual regeneration. These rules, though originally conceived for the theological seminary, apparently applied to all students and helped to foster an orthodox and pious student body. An estimated 250 individuals graduated from Maryville in the antebellum years, some 150 of them becoming ministers.[16]

Maryville was connected to the town and to the Prebyterian community by its president, who was also pastor of the local Presbyterian church. In addition to his responsibilities in Maryville, Isaac Anderson organized and pastored the Second Presbyterian Church in Knoxville for ten years, was seven times moderator of the Synod, and sat on the American Board of Commissioners for Foreign Missions.[17]

The dominance of Anderson, Maryville College, and Presbyterianism in Maryville is suggested by the fact that Anderson was bold enough to run a series of catechetical questions and answers for his congregation in the town paper, the *Maryville Intelligencer,* in 1836. This, combined with a series of sermons on doctrinal matters, inspired a devout and educated Presbyterian clientele.[18] Local Presbyterians volunteered their sanctuary for college commencements and supported the college by making contributions and offering free board to the students.[19]

Further to the east, Presbyterians in North Carolina in 1835 took the first steps in founding Davidson College, a manual-labor school intended to prepare young men for the ministry and to extend "the means of education more generally among all classes of the community."[20] The institution, which was to be under the control of Concord Presbytery and guided by the Scriptures of the Old and New Testaments, was—in nonsectarian fashion—open to all young men of "good moral character."[21] As with Maryville, this openness was not simply an effort to appeal to a denominationally diverse regional constituency and to appease legislators wary of denominational control but also manifested the Presbyterian desire to influence the culture, Christianize the nation, and bring as many as possible under the denomination's purview. In this sense the state legislators were correct in fearing that education would be a source of increased denominational influence. These schools were indeed, in the eyes of their founders, ways of extending the influence of Christianity over the culture.

Local Presbyterian congregations enthusiastically embraced the venture and camped out at the college site to help clear land and haul bricks for the buildings. Before the college opened its doors in 1837, Bethel Presbytery in South Carolina joined in the undertaking; in 1844 Fayetteville Presbytery in North Carolina followed suit. The three judicatories, in the years before the Civil War, not only elected the trustees and faculty of the fledgling institution but approved the curriculum as well.[22]

When the school sought a charter in 1838, it ran into the same kind of difficulty that Presbyterians had encountered in Tennessee. Many members of the state senate challenged the school "on the ground of its conflict with the University, its *religious character,* [and] its *sectarian tendency.*" Such opposition notwithstanding, Robert Morrison, the young president of Davidson, held his ground, and the charter he won granted the supporting presbyteries the power to appoint the president, professors, tutors, and trustees of the college.[23]

The constitution of the college, adopted by Concord Presbytery in 1839, stated that all trustees and faculty were to be members of the Presbyterian Church. Moreover, in a move reflecting the confessional concerns of most southern Presbyterians, the presbytery required that all faculty had to affirm the Scriptures as the Word of God, accept the Westminster Confession, and promise "not to teach anything that is opposed to any doctrines contained in the Confession of Faith, nor to oppose any of the fundamental principles of the Presbyterian Church government."[24] Six of the first seven faculty at Davidson were Presbyterian clergy.[25]

In the course of the 1840s the presbyteries connected to Davidson worked fervently to fund the college. While numerous small donations helped the school, large donations from wealthy local patrons—revealing important local support for such schools—made the difference. Most important was the legacy of $300,000 left to the college in 1855 by Maxwell Chambers, a member of the Salisbury Presbyterian Church. Legal complications prevented Davidson from realizing the full benefit of this gift, but the college profited immensely from this unprecedented generosity in the years before the war.[26]

The original board of trustees of Davidson was composed of six clergy and eighteen elders. In the antebellum years, the constituency of the board remained completely Presbyterian. Indeed, contrary to David Potts's claim that colleges became more "denominational" in the years after the war, the trustees in 1869 requested the presbyteries to elect some non-Presbyterians to the board "in order to strengthen the hold of Davidson College upon the country by connecting with its government men of wisdom and influence not of our denomination."[27] It was in the years before the Civil War that Calvinists had full sway at Davidson.

Inasmuch as Davidson was a college town throughout the antebellum period (the name of the town was Davidson College), the community reflected the same religious spirit as the college. In those years Presbyterians were the only communion in town with a sanctuary, and the pastor of the church was the president of the college.[28] While there were other religious options in the vicinity, Presbyterianism was the most visible and the most potent religious force in town.

The distinctively Presbyterian tenor found at Davidson was also apparent at Oglethorpe University in Georgia. In the same year that Concord Presbytery founded Davidson, Hopewell Presbytery in Georgia inherited a failing seminary and set out to convert it into a college to nurture ministerial candidates.[29] The resulting school, Oglethorpe University, opened its doors in Midway, Georgia, in January 1838 but quickly found itself in dire financial straits. The trustees, all of whom were Presbyterian, appealed to denominational pride and interdenominational rivalry for assistance from their Presbyterian brothers and sisters. Inasmuch as the school was a child of the Presbyterian Church, the trustees argued, "it is the high duty of that church, in view of what sister denominations are doing, and of the deep and lasting blot which a failure of this enterprise would fix upon it, to come forward cordially and promptly, to the utmost of its ability, to its support." In response, the presbytery, upon the recommendation of the trustees, transferred care of the college to the Synod of South Carolina and Georgia, and three local friends of the college, two of whom were devout Presbyterians, came to the assistance of the college.[30]

Financial difficulties were not the only cause of trouble for the young school in the late 1830s. Oglethorpe had been born just as the Presbyterian Church was embroiled in a controversy between a "New School" prorevivalist faction that stressed evangelism over fine points of doctrine and "Old School" supporters who, while not antirevivalist, believed the church needed to hew close to the mark on subscription to the Westminster Confession.[31] In 1837 the Old School supporters at the General Assembly excised those synods dominated by the New School, essentially splitting the church and, coincidentally, throwing Oglethorpe into disarray.

Charles Howard, chaplain and lecturer at Oglethorpe, was a commissioner from Hopewell Presbytery to the 1837 Assembly. Sympathetic to the New School, he disapproved of the exscinding acts. In protest, Howard and two other members of Hopewell Presbytery withdrew from the presbytery and formed an independent judicatory. Carlisle Beman, president of Oglethorpe, whose brother Nathan was a leader in the New School, was also sympathetic to New School forces, although he chose not to follow Howard out of the presbytery.[32]

These tensions within the denomination did not affect only the peace of the presbytery. They had significant repercussions at Oglethorpe, as well. Howard and Beman, now seriously alienated from important constituencies of the school because of their ecclesiastical and theological convictions, decided that it would be best to resign their positions and pursue their ministries in different fields.[33] To these two individuals Oglethorpe was not simply a Presbyterian school, let alone a "pan-Protestant" institution. Rather, it had become, in important ways, an Old School Presbyterian college, in many ways inhospitable to those with New School connections. Although the school was open to students of all evangelical denominations, Oglethorpe's leadership was staunchly Presbyterian and catered especially to Presbyterians of an Old School stripe.[34]

The claims of Presbyterian schools to be nonsectarian notwithstanding, William G. Brownlow, a Methodist minister, telling in 1848 of a sermon he preached near Maryville College, wrote that he could see the school "where Calvinism, in its multifareous [sic] forms, propels its poisons through its diversified channels."[35] What the Presbyterians thought was broadly evangelical did not sound broad to everyone, at least to every Methodist, within earshot. In time, Methodists decided that they too had a role to play in the educational arena of the nation.

The General Conference of the Methodist Episcopal Church in 1820, in response to a perceived need for Methodist-sponsored higher education, "recommended to all the annual conferences to establish, as soon as practicable, literary institutions, under their own control."[36] In the following three decades the General Conferences of the church reiterated this concern, authorizing the appointment of Methodist preachers to schools and colleges and granting to Annual Conferences the authority to conduct fund-raising for Methodist schools.[37] Randolph-Macon, Emory, and Wofford were all born as a result of this increasing Methodist concern with education.

Virginia Methodists took up the challenge of the General Conference in 1825 when they began the process of establishing a seminary of learning that came to be known as Randolph-Macon College.[38] By 1829 the Conference had decided to locate the school near Boydton, Virginia, and had authorized a committee to apply to the Virginia legislature for a charter.[39] Like Maryville and Davidson, Randolph-Macon ran into trouble with Virginia legislators who feared the school would lead to the establishment of religion. The legislature, acting cautiously, prohibited the college from establishing a chair in theology and created a self-perpetuating board of trustees.[40] Nonetheless, of the thirty trustees appointed in the charter, twenty-six were either Methodist clergy or laity.[41] Stephen Olin, the first president, was perhaps overstating the case when he argued in 1835 that the Methodist Conferences of Georgia, South Carolina, and Virginia were "the *owners* of Randolph-Macon College," but for all intents and purposes he was right.[42] Evangelical Christianity of a Methodist stamp was at the heart of the school.

Money from local citizens of Boydton and from area Methodists helped get the college off the ground. Additionally, the South Carolina and the Georgia Conferences were invited to support the school in return for representation on the board of trustees, and both accepted.[43] The board would later agree to educate ten students each year from each of these conferences tuition-free.[44]

The trustees, in hiring faculty, operated on the assumption that all professors should be Methodist. Given the dearth of college-educated Methodists in the antebellum period, this proved to be a difficult requirement to satisfy. After some initial disappointment, the trustees succeeded in building a faculty, including, most notably, Stephen Olin as president.[45]

Olin was a graduate of Middlebury College. At the time of his appointment, he was on the faculty of Franklin College in Georgia. Although he served as an itinerant preacher for a short time, his health could not withstand the rigors of itinerancy, and he turned to the academic life. In accepting the presidency of Randolph-Macon, Olin saw himself solidly engaged in the mission of Methodism. "I was never so convinced that we must educate our own youth in our own schools," he wrote to Bishop J. O. Andrew, "and there is no work to which I so desire to consecrate myself."[46] Even taking into account the fact that Olin was writing to his ecclesiastical superior, his insistence on the denominational identity of the college is striking.

In 1835 Olin claimed that about half the student body were members of the Methodist Church. The fact that students traveled past William and Mary or Hampden-Sydney to study at Randolph-Macon, and that many were from out of state, suggests that significantly more than half had Methodist roots and saw the college as providing a distinctively Methodist college education.[47]

In the years before the Civil War, approximately 25 percent of Randolph-Macon's graduates pursued a career in teaching, and ministry and law each claimed about 20 percent.[48] This fact suggests that Methodist schools and Methodists perceived the mission of these colleges in a slightly different manner than did Presbyterians. First, unlike Presbyterians, who had a tradition of a college-educated clergy, Methodist schools seemingly attracted fewer students interested in preparing for the ministry and found themselves nurturing young men devoted to other callings.[49] Moreover, while Presbyterians not planning on a clerical career might, as cultural and religious insiders, feel secure in attending a non-Presbyterian school, Methodists of all occupational aspirations, as relative newcomers to the American religious scene, were perhaps more likely to seek the safe confines of a Methodist institution.[50]

William Smith, one of Olin's successors as president of the college, mirrored Olin's concern about the need to nurture the ties between school and church. "Perhaps the leading minister in the Virginia Conference," Smith was a delegate to the General Conference of the Methodist Episcopal Church for every session from 1832 to 1844, played a major role in the founding of the Methodist Episcopal Church, South, and was a delegate to every General Conference of the southern church from its founding in 1844 until 1866. In 1846 he was called from his pastorate to the presidency of the college and, determined to establish the college on a firm financial footing, raised $100,000 and oversaw the enrollment of the largest student body in the young school's history.[51]

The ties to the Methodist Church were not an unmitigated blessing to the college. In 1855 long-simmering tensions between President Young, a Virginian, and Charles Deems, a professor of chemistry and a North Carolinian, led to an ecclesial trial of Smith on charges of "falsehood," "immorality," and "slander." Smith was acquitted by the Conference, but a number of trustees of Randolph-Macon from North Carolina resigned over this event, and North Carolina Methodists began to support Normal College in North Carolina, which would become Trinity College in 1859.[52] While the colleges provided a forum for nurturing interconference ties, they also reflected the regional denominational loyalties and tensions that permeated denominations of the era.

Regional intradenominational competition came not only from Normal College but from other Methodist schools founded hard after Randolph-Macon, such as Emory College in Georgia. Emory was established in 1836 on the foundations of the Georgia Conference Manual Labor School.[53] Methodists, as members of a fledgling denomination in-

tent on establishing its place on the cultural and denominational landscape, were more overt in appealing to interdenominational rivalry as a
motive to establish schools than were Presbyterians. While Presbyterians
in Kentucky, for example, were wary of colleges, such as Transylvania,
that they believed were slipping into deism, Georgia Methodists warned
their children against schools in the traditions of even their sister evangelical denominations.[54] The committee on education of the Georgia
Conference warned:

> A sound and saving piety is probably consistent enough with the creed of
> nearly all other denominations, but to those who have been piously
> trained, religion and their fathers' church are identical things. We fear not
> the charge of bigotry or vanity when we acknowledge that to us and to the
> children whom God has given us Methodism is Christianity. The youth who
> has grown up under our ministry and institutions in exact proportion as in
> his principles and feelings he ceases to be a Methodist will usually be found
> to become an infidel and a profligate.[55]

Despite such fervent concern among Georgia Methodists for denominational identity, the Georgia legislature, uncomfortable with allowing a
church judicatory to have complete authority over a publicly chartered
school, did not give the Georgia Conference the power to elect all the
school's trustees. Rather, the Conference could elect nine of the board's
seventeen trustees, with the remaining eight to be elected by the board
itself.[56]

The college was set on a large piece of land the trustees named
Oxford, after the alma mater of John and Charles Wesley. So the students
could not avoid the Methodist foundations of the school, Oxford's streets
were named after Methodist saints, such as the Wesleys, Francis Asbury,
and Richard Whatcoat.[57] Indeed, in time Oxford seems to become something of a Methodist ghetto. The residents were, by in large, families of
faculty or those who had moved to Oxford to educate their sons; by the
1840s fifteen clergy lived in the hamlet.[58]

At Emory's opening all the professors were Methodist ministers, and
the students, who studied English Bible and the Greek New Testament
and Septuagint for four years, were predominantly from Methodist backgrounds.[59] The Methodist flavor of the school was enhanced by its policy
of educating, free of charge, the sons of Methodist preachers of the Georgia and Florida conferences.[60]

Like its sister Presbyterian schools, Emory stood close to denominational politics. The president of the board of trustees of the college,
Bishop James Andrew, proved to be the flash point for the division of the
Methodist Church into southern and northern factions in 1844. Andrew
had inherited two slaves and could not, in good conscience, release them
because of the laws in Georgia. Those who opposed slaveholding pressed
the issue at the 1844 General Conference, and the church divided over
the issue. Other leaders of Emory—most notably Lovick Pierce, George

Pierce, Augustus Longstreet, and Ignatius Few—were all prominent churchmen who played an active role in the founding conference of the Methodist Episcopal Church, South, in 1845.[61] Emory became a bastion of Southern Methodism.

Despite the obviously Methodist character of the institution, it too portrayed itself as broadly Christian. George Pierce, president from 1848 through 1854, in an effort to allay the fears of those agitated about sectarian education and to demonstrate Methodism's tolerance, downplayed the distinctively denominational motivations for Emory's founding in order to emphasize its simple evangelical nature.[62] At the laying of a cornerstone for a new chapel in 1852, he declared that "Emory College ... was not a sectarian scheme to promote a denominational interest, though justified by the mission of the church and imperiously necessary to the discharge of her high obligation." He continued, "The friends of the State College were alarmed lest these rival [denominational] institutions should drain its patronage and alienate the confidence of the country. Sectarianism, priestly intrigue, church bigotry were dreaded and denounced. Mistaken men! we but meant to do our duty and bless our country."[63]

On the other hand, Pierce was dedicated to providing an education with a distinctly Methodist flavor. A decade earlier, in a commencement address at Emory, he had insisted that Methodist doctrine had a rightful place at the college. "If a Methodist interpretation of the Bible be adopted in a Methodist college," he allowed, "who ought to be surprised? There is no deception; the charter, the board of trust, the name, all proclaim the character of the institution. ... We neither impress nor proselyte, and if the officers can make abiding friends of the passengers by courtesy and usefulness who dare reproach us with being selfish intriguants."[64]

Pierce's attitude, while potentially lending support to those who would question the denominational distinctiveness of these institutions, in fact reflects precisely what the Methodists and other evangelical communions thought denominationalism was all about. In the United States, as Sidney Mead pointed out, the developing denominations in the antebellum era lived in tension between denominational cooperation and denominational rivalry. Freedom of religion in the United States led to competition between Christian groups, but it was an intrafamily rivalry among groups that agreed on the basic tenets of evangelical Christianity.[65]

As a result, leaders of these schools could at once claim that they were denominational and in the same breath maintain that they were nonsectarian. As Winthrop Hudson has argued, "[D]enominationalism is the opposite of sectarianism. The word 'denomination' implies that the group referred to is but one member of a larger group, called or denominated by a particular name."[66] In his dual understanding of Emory's mission, Pierce reflected the precise denominational sense of the evangelical denominations: they were at once broadly Christian and yet distinctively different. The colleges thus were paradigmatically denominational. Pierce's dual view of the mission of Methodism in education was given explicit endorsement when, in

1854, after serving at Emory for four years, he was elected a bishop of the church.[67]

This understanding of the nature of Methodism and Methodist higher education guided not simply only Emory but also Wofford College, founded by South Carolina Methodists in the 1850s. Upon the death of the Rev. Benjamin Wofford in 1850, South Carolina Methodists found themselves the beneficiaries of a $100,000 bequest in Wofford's will to be used to establish a college "to be under the control and management" of the Conference.[68] A temporary board of trustees, named in Wofford's will, was to purchase land and buildings for the college and then to turn the school over to a board of thirteen trustees elected by the South Carolina Annual Conference. In order to safeguard the control of the church, the trustees were to serve terms of only two years and were to report to the Conference every year. The South Carolina legislature granted the school a charter in December 1851, and the Conference elected a board of eight ministers and five laymen.[69]

At the laying of the cornerstone, a festive event attended by an estimated four thousand persons, William M. Wightman, president of the board of trustees, editor of the *Southern Christian Advocate,* and soon to be president of Wofford, set out the aims of the school. "It is impossible to conceive of greater benefits, to the individual or society," he declared, "than those embraced in the gift of a liberal Education, combining the moral principle which grows out of a knowledge of christian truth, with the enlightened and cultivated understanding which is the product of thorough scholarship." He continued:

> Wofford College, I need hardly remind you, will be a *denominational* college. . . . Its chief patrons will be found among the members and friends of the Methodist Episcopal Church. Its Faculty of Instruction will represent that powerful denomination. Its religious service will be adapted to the formularies of that church. It will be known throughout the United States as a Methodist institution of learning. It will thus sail under no doubtful flag and will doubtless be ready to show that flag in the smoke of battle, as well as in the summer of prosperity.[70]

Echoing the tension in Pierce's earlier statements, Wightman neverthe-less insisted that Methodism's embrace of "catholic liberty" would pre-clude Wofford from "sectarian bigotry" and lead it to seek "universal good will."[71]

All of this, of course, would benefit not only the church but the nation. Wofford's faculty, intent on prosecuting the Methodist mission to create a Christian America, would strive to promote Christian education in service to both the church and the republic.[72]

To return then to the presenting question: How were these schools denominational? Most obviously, and contrary to the claims of Potts, Naylor, and McLachlan, they were largely founded and controlled by denominational judicatories. Despite the efforts of some state legislatures opposed to vesting any authority in presbyteries or conferences, the boards of trustees of Maryville, Davidson, Oglethorpe, and Wofford were elected by church courts. Even the boards of Randolph-Macon and Emory, which were, to different degrees, self-perpetuating, were strongly Methodist, forming something of an interlocking directorate with the regional Methodist conferences.

The struggle of some denominational judicatories to procure charters from state legislatures demonstrates how slowly the notion of a denomination as a voluntary association took hold in at least the southern part of the United States. Some state legislators, still operating on a model of established religion, obviously had a difficult time conceiving that a publicly chartered degree-granting institution affiliated with a denomination need not necessarily entail the establishment of religion. Not until after the Civil War, it appears, did the understanding of the denomination as a voluntary institution take firm enough hold of the public mind to alleviate thoroughly the fear of the establishment of religion through the chartering of denominational colleges.[73]

The greater success of Presbyterians in overcoming legislative opposition to oversight of the colleges by church judicatories suggests a difference between the denominations. Presbyterians, far more culturally prominent than Methodists, were apparently able to leverage more influence in state legislatures than were their Methodist counterparts. The schools, as such, not only reflect the similarity between these denominations in their efforts to control the colleges but also reveal the different political authority vested by the culture in each church.

These church judicatories and the boards of trustees oversaw the hiring of administrators and faculty allied with the respective denominations. Again, similarities and differences between the denominations appear. While both Methodists and Presbyterians were intent on hiring their own, Presbyterians, more confessionally oriented than Methodists, were unabashed in their efforts to guarantee doctrinal orthodoxy. Davidson, which insisted that its faculty accept the Westminster Confession, is probably the best example of this, but the resignations of Charles Howard and Carlisle Beman from Oglethorpe, largely over theological differences with Oglethorpe's constituency, also reveal the confessional distinctiveness of these schools.

Although perhaps less important than the boards of trustees, administrators, and faculty in determining the character of a school, students, nonetheless, contributed to the ambiance of these institutions. While all of these colleges insisted that they were nonsectarian and open to young men of all evangelical denominations, the patterns suggest that students viewed the colleges as denominational organs and frequently matriculated with these differences in mind. The renowned southern poet Sidney Lanier, weaned on Presbyterian doctrine by his devout mother, thus avoided Randolph-Macon, the alma mater of his father a former Methodist, in order to attend Oglethorpe.[74] Similarly, Methodist schools, especially given the incentives offered to sons of Methodist clergy, appear to have attracted student bodies that were predominantly, although not exclusively, from Methodist backgrounds.

Methodists and Presbyterians in the communities in which these colleges were lodged accentuated the denominational ties of the schools. Most notable in this respect were Davidson and Oxford, the homes, respectively, of Davidson College and Emory College. Each of these towns grew up around its respective college and became largely a denominational ghetto. The residents in both of these communities were predominantly faculty or families who had moved to the town to educate their sons. While other religious options were available, the religion of the college was the favored faith in town.

The colleges, in conjunction with their towns, could act as transmitters of a denominational culture. Even if distinctively Presbyterian or Methodist doctrine was not taught (and this was not always the case), the young men who studied and lived in these schools and towns for four years absorbed the ethos of what it meant to be a Presbyterian or a Methodist. This seems to be what Georgia Methodists had in mind when they sought to inculcate the "principles and feelings" of Methodism in the students of Emory.

As was noted earlier, the claim of these schools to be at once denominational and at the same time nonsectarian points to another important manner in which the schools reflected the denominational self-understanding of their respective constituencies. Denominations grew up in the new American environment as a means of expressing various divisions within a broader evangelical unity. The churches lived in a tension between their desire to maintain their distinctiveness and their wish to testify to the unity of the evangelical faith.

The colleges here examined manifest this same tension. Methodists especially, as outsiders to the educational venture, clearly enunciated the conflict in their descriptions of their schools. Wanting to build schools to nourish the Methodist heritage, they at the same time held that Methodism, by its nature, was nonsectarian. Living in this tension, they were paradigmatically denominational.

The nonsectarian nature of these schools, inspired in part by the desire to appeal to a diverse regional student constituency, also reflects the broader mission to the culture that was embraced by both the denominations and the colleges. Russell Richey has characterized the evangelical denomination in the early nineteenth century as "a purposive voluntary association, possessed of a vision of its place in a wider Christian unity and structured as an instrument for bringing in the kingdom of God and Christianizing society."[75] Colleges aptly reflected this underlying purposive nature of the denominations—to build a Christian America, to, as George Pierce said, "do our duty, and bless our country."[76] This mission, in fact, gave the colleges one more reason for their nonsectarian character. If they were to cultivate Christian citizens, they could not neglect young men from traditions outside their own. To have the greatest impact on the culture, the schools had to open their nets wide and to disseminate their influence as broadly as possible.

The full scope of the denominational character of these schools, however, cannot be appreciated if the only question asked is how the schools mirrored the ecclesiastical, theological, and cultural views of their respective churches. For in significant ways these schools not only reflected the personalities of their denominations but played an important role within the denomination.

In this era, when denominational bureaucracy was still in its infancy compared to later developments, denominational colleges provided the glue to help hold the churches together.[77] This reality is hinted at in the concern of Georgia Methodists to found schools in order to keep their children in their church.[78] But the ways in which these schools functioned to bind the denominations were much more numerous than simply keeping children under the wing of the church.

Both Methodist and Presbyterian schools provided a focus for the churches that transcended local judicatory lines. Davidson, for example, was supported by Concord and Fayetteville Presbyteries in North Carolina and Bethel Presbytery in South Carolina, and Randolph-Macon was endorsed by the Virginia, South Carolina, and Georgia Conferences. The trustees elected from these various presbyteries and conferences sometimes divided on regional grounds, revealing the local influences on denominational loyalty in this period, but the schools nonetheless created a forum for the cultivation of wider bonds within the church in support of a particular cause.[79]

These colleges further strengthened links within the denominations by creating an intradenominational alumni network that bound church members, and thereby churches, together. Emory and Wofford, for example, provided free education for sons of clergy in the supporting conferences, creating allegiance not only to the school but to the wider denomination. Whether or not these individuals became clergy, their ties to the academy strengthened their ties to their church.

Likewise, these colleges provided a forum for the development and exercise of denominational leadership. The Methodist colleges provide an especially striking example of this. Emory's leadership reads like a directory of Southern Methodism of the era: J. O. Andrew, Lovick Pierce, Augustus Longstreet, Ignatius Few. Moreover, the college presidency was apparently viewed by the Church as valuable preparation for the role of bishop. George Pierce, president of Emory from 1848 to 1854, and W. O. Wightman, president of Wofford from 1854 to 1859, were both eventually elected bishops of the church.[80] No doubt clergy who had studied under these men provided significant support for their candidacies.

The various ways in which these schools were denominational suggest the need to reassess the current tendency to denigrate the denominationalism of antebellum church-related colleges. While scholars such as

Potts and Naylor have rightfully challenged the usefulness and the accuracy of describing all antebellum Christian colleges as denominational and have correctly emphasized the important local support for these schools, the colleges examined here suggest that Presbyterian- and Methodist-related schools in the antebellum South were, in significant ways, denominational institutions. At the very least, more study of specific institutions in diverse regions of the nation might provide a richer and more helpful picture of the denominationalism of antebellum schools than the current historiography suggests.

Just as important, the cases here examined suggest the need to reevaluate the usual tendency to understand denominationalism solely in terms of bureaucratic or theological imagery. While bureaucracy and theology were critical in the development of denominations in the United States, they do not exhaust the ways in which denominationalism in the antebellum United States can be understood. The schools here did manifest bureaucratic and theological distinctives, but they also reveal that influential individuals, ties of friendship and kinship, regional and institutional allegiances, and variations in cultural status all played critical roles in forming and cultivating denominational identity in this era. If these schools are any indication, our understanding of denominational history and of the history of higher education would benefit from a far more textured understanding of denominationalism than that which currently dominates discussions of religion and higher education.

NOTES

I am grateful for the comments of D. G. Hart, George Marsden, R. Bruce Mullin, and Russell Richey on an earlier version of this essay.

1. Donald G. Tewksbury, *The Founding of American Colleges and Universities Before the Civil War* (1832; reprint ed., New York: Arno Press and the New York Times, 1969), pp. 55–56.

2. David B. Potts, "American Colleges in the Nineteenth Century: From Localism to Denominationalism," *History of Education Quarterly* 11 (Winter 1971): 363; James McLachlan, "The American College in the Nineteenth Century: toward a Reappraisal," *Teachers College Record* 80 (December 1978): 302; Natalie A. Naylor, "The Ante-Bellum College Movement: A Reappraisal of Tewskbury's Founding of American Colleges and Universities," *History of Education Quarterly* 13 (Fall 1973): 267. These sentiments are echoed in Robert L. Church and Michael W. Sedlak, *Education in the United States: An Interpretive History* (New York: Free Press, 1976), pp. 44–45; David B. Potts, *Wesleyan University, 1831–1910: Collegiate Enterprise in New England* (New Haven: Yale University Press, 1992); and William C. Ringenberg, *The Christian College: A History of Protestant Higher Education in America* (Grand Rapids, Mich.: Christian University Press, 1984), pp. 58–59.

3. Naylor, "Ante-Bellum College Movement," p. 269; David B. Potts, *Baptist*

Colleges in the Development of American Society: 1812–1861 (New York: Garland Publishing, 1988), pp. 12, 317.

4. Naylor, "Ante-Bellum College Movement," p. 270.

5. Ibid., p. 269.

6. On the development of denominationalism in the United States, see Russell E. Richey, "Denominations and Denominationalism: An American Morphology," in this volume; see also Sidney E. Mead, "Denominationalism: The Shape of Protestantism in America," pp. 70–105, and Winthrop S. Hudson, "Denominationalism as a Basis for Ecumenicity: A Seventeenth Century Conception," pp. 21–42, both in Russell E. Richey, ed. *Denominationalism* (Nashville, Tenn.: Abingdon, 1977).

7. See Tewksbury, *American Colleges,* pp. 70–74.

8. For an excellent study of this organization, see Ruth E. Ratliff, "The Society for the Promotion of Collegiate and Theological Education at the West: A Congregational Education Society," (Ph.D. diss., University of Iowa, 1988).

9. On the growing religious differences between North and South in this period, see Samuel S. Hill, Jr., *The South and the North in American Religion* (Athens: University of Georgia Press, 1980), esp. pp. 36–89.

10. Ralph W. Lloyd, *Maryville College, A History of 150 Years: 1819–1969* (Maryville, Tenn.: Maryville College Press, 1969), p. 5.

11. Quoted in ibid., p. 110.

12. Ibid., pp. 8–9, 99.

13. Ibid., pp. 7, 33, 34.

14. Ibid., pp. 34–35, 59–62, 275.

15. Ibid., pp. 61–62; J. E. Alexander, *A Brief History of the Synod of Tennessee from 1817 to 1887* (Philadelphia: MacCalla & Co., 1890), p. 19. The original charter had given the Blount County Court the authority to elect directors, but this was amended only three weeks later to make the board self-perpetuating. Whether the first provision was a legislative mistake or an effort by some to ensure the school would not be under church control is unclear.

16. Lloyd, *Maryville,* pp. 277, 8, 186.

17. Ibid., pp. 76, 78, 100; Samuel T. Wilson, *Isaac Anderson: Founder and First President of Maryville College* (Maryville, Tenn.: Kindred of Dr. Anderson, 1932), p. 39.

18. Wilson, *Anderson,* p. 47. Darius Hoyt, a professor at Maryville, happened to be the editor of the paper.

19. Lloyd, *Maryville,* pp. 100, 236. See also Alexander, *Synod of Tennessee,* p. 81.

20. Mary D. Beaty, *A History of Davidson College* (Davidson, N.C.: Briarpatch Press, 1988), pp. 3, 4. Quote from Records of Concord Presbytery, April 29, 1835, Historical Foundation of the Presbyterian and Reformed Churches, Montreat, N.C.

21. Cornelia R. Shaw, *Davidson College* (New York: Fleming H. Revell, 1923), p. 14.

22. Beaty, *Davidson,* pp. 13–14, 16, 20, 22; Shaw, *Davidson,* p. 15, 18–19, 49.

23. Quoted in Beaty, *Davidson,* p. 24; Shaw, *Davidson,* pp. 279–280. In 1852 the charter was altered to give the trustees the authority to elect the president and professors (Shaw, *Davidson,* pp. 67–68).

24. Shaw, *Davidson,* pp. 44–45; Beaty, *Davidson,* p. 25.

25. Beaty, *Davidson,* p. 102.

26. Ibid., pp. 36, 60–63.

27. Ibid., pp. 15, 93–94.

28. Mary D. Beaty, *Davidson: A History of the Town from 1835 until 1937* (Davidson, N.C.: Briarpatch Press, 1979), pp. 53, 18–19, 24–25.

29. Allen P. Tankersley, *College Life at Old Oglethorpe* (Athens: University of Georgia Press, 1951), pp. 1, 5.

30. James Stacy, *A History of the Presbyterian Church in Georgia* (n.p., n.d.), pp. 109, 112–15; Tankersley, *Oglethorpe,* pp. 18–21; Charles E. Jones, *Education in Georgia* (Washington, D.C.: Government Printing Office, 1889), p. 82.

31. See George M. Marsden, *The Evangelical Mind and the New School Presbyterian Experience* (New Haven: Yale University Press, 1970).

32. Ernest T. Thompson, *Presbyterians in the South,* vol. 1, *1607–1861* (Richmond, Va.: John Knox Press, 1963), pp. 400–401; Stacy, *Georgia,* pp. 184–186; Tankersley, *Oglethorpe,* p. 7.

33. Tankersley, *Oglethorpe,* pp. 10, 23–24; Stacy, *Georgia,* pp. 185–186; Thompson, *Presbyterians,* p. 401. A contributing factor to Beman's departure was also the trustees' decision that he could not flog upper-class students.

34. Aubre H. Starke, *Sidney Lanier: A Biographical and Critical Study* (Chapel Hill: University of North Carolina Press, 1933), pp. 20–21. Starke notes that when Lanier attended Oglethorpe in the late 1850s, the students at Oglethorpe were "almost without exception of Presbyterian families."

35. William G. Brownlow, "Our Late Tour of the South," in *Jonesborough Monthly Review* 2, new ser., (1848): 92, quoted in George J. Stevenson, *Increase in Excellence: A History of Emory and Henry College* (New York: Appleton-Century-Crofts, 1963), p. 15.

36. *General Conference Journals,* vol. I, p. 208, quoted in Sylvanus M. DuVall, *The Methodist Episcopal Church and Education up to 1869* (New York: Teachers College, Columbia University, 1928), p. 63.

37. Duvall, *Methodist Education,* pp. 63–64.

38. James E. Scanlon, *Randolph-Macon College: A Southern History, 1825–1967* (Charlottesville: University Press of Virginia, 1983), p. 23.

39. Richard Irby, *History of Randolph-Macon College, Virginia* (Richmond: Whittet & Shepperson, n.d.), pp. 13–14.

40. Scanlon, *Randolph-Macon,* pp. 29–32.

41. Irby, *Randolph-Macon,* p. 16.

42. Stephen Olin, *The Life and Letters of Stephen Olin,* vol. I (New York: Harper and Brothers, 1853), p. 185.

43. Scanlon, *Randolph-Macon,* pp. 27, 35, 38.

44. Irby, *Randolph-Macon,* p. 56.

45. Scanlon, *Randolph-Macon,* p. 49–55; Irby, *Randolph-Macon,* p. 35.

46. Irby, *Randolph-Macon,* pp. 35–36; quote on p. 54.

47. Olin, *Life and Letters,* p. 186; Irby, *Randolph-Macon,* pp. 65–67; Scanlon, *Randolph-Macon,* pp. 39, 86, 93.

48. Scanlon, *Randolph-Macon,* p. 59.

49. William W. Sweet, noting the difference between Presbyterian and Methodist schools in their concern for training clergy, claimed the Methodists did not look "upon their early colleges as primarily training schools for preachers." William W. Sweet, *Religion in the Development of American Culture, 1765–1840* (New York: Charles Scribner's Sons, 1952), p. 168.

50. My thanks to R. Bruce Mullin for suggesting this line of thought.

51. William W. Sweet, *Virginia Methodism* (Richmond: Whittet and Shepperson, 1945), pp. 234, 321–23; Irby, *Randolph-Macon,* pp. 105–107

52. Scanlon, *Randolph-Macon,* pp. 105–107; Irby, *Randolph-Macon,* p. 133. See also Nora C. Chaffin, *Trinity College, 1839–1892: The Beginnings of Duke University* (Durham: Duke University Press, 1950), pp. 163–167.

53. Henry M. Bullock, *A History of Emory University* (Nashville, Tenn.: Parthenon Press, 1936), pp. 42–43, 52–56, 62.

54. On Kentucky Presbyterians and the founding of Centre College in opposition to Transylvania University see Hardin Craig, *Centre College of Kentucky* (Louisville, Ky.: Centre College, 1967), pp. 7–13, and Robert Davidson, *History of the Presbyterian Church in the State of Kentucky* (Pittsburgh: Robert Carter, 1847), pp. 288–323.

55. *Georgia Conference Minutes,* Jan. 13, 1834, quoted in Bullock, *Emory,* p. 51.

56. *Acts of the General Assembly of the State of Georgia . . . November and December 1836* (Milledgeville, Ga.: P. L. Robinson, 1837), pp. 99–101. On opposition to the college because of its sectarian nature, see George G. Smith, *The Life and Times of George F. Pierce* (Sparta, Ga.: Hancock Publishing Co., 1888), pp. 169–170.

57. Bullock, *Emory,* pp. 57–58; John D. Wade, *Augustus Baldwin Longstreet: A Study of the Development of Culture in the South* (New York: Macmillan, 1924), p. 241.

58. Bullock, *Emory,* pp. 128, 139, 142; Wade, *Longstreet,* pp. 241, 249; Smith, *Pierce,* p. 160.

59. Bullock, *Emory,* 62, 64, 129, 141.

60. Atticus G. Haygood, ed., *Bishop Pierce's Sermons and Addresses* (Nashville, Tenn.: Southern Methodist Publishing House, 1886), p. 61.

61. Bullock, *Emory,* pp. 86–87; John N. Norwood, *The Schism in the Methodist Episcopal Church, 1844: A Study of Slavery and Ecclesiastical Politics* (Alfred, N.Y.: Alfred Press, 1923).

62. Bullock, *Emory,* p. 89; Smith, *Pierce,* pp. 169–171.

63. Quoted in Smith, *Pierce,* pp. 169–170.

64. Haygood, ed., *Pierce,* p. 33. This address was republished in 1852, lending credence to the belief that Pierce's attitudes had not changed.

65. Mead, "Denominationalism," in Richey, ed., *Denominationalism,* pp. 102–105.

66. Hudson, "Denominationalism," in Richey, ed., *Denominationalism,* p. 22.

67. Smith, *Pierce,* pp. 186–190.

68. Colyer Meriwether, *History of Higher Education in South Carolina* (Washington, D.C.: Government Printing Office, 1889), p. 99; David D. Wallace, *History of Wofford College, 1854–1949* (Nashville, Tenn.: Vanderbilt University Press, 1951), p. 32; "Extracts from the Will of the Reverend Benjamin Wofford," in *A Documentary History of Education in the South Before 1860,* ed. Edgar W. Knight, vol. IV, *Private and Denominational Efforts* (Chapel Hill: University of North Carolina, 1953), p. 361.

69. Wallace, *Wofford,* pp. 41–42.

70. Wallace, *Wofford,* pp. 44–45, 50; "Address of the Reverend William M. Wightman at the Laying of the Cornerstone of Wofford College, South Carolina, 1851," in Knight, *Documentary History,* pp. 370–371.

71. "Address of Wightman," in Knight, *Documentary,* p. 371; Wallace, *Wofford,* pp. 45–46.

72. *Spartan,* July 17, 1851, quoted in Wallace, *Wofford,* pp. 45–46.

73. My thanks to R. Bruce Mullin for suggesting this line of thought.

74. Starke, *Lanier,* 8, 20.

75. Russell E. Richey, "The Social Sources of Denominationalism: Methodism," in Richey, ed., *Denominationalism,* p. 171.

76. Quoted in Smith, *Pierce,* p. 170.

77. Timothy Smith, "Congregation, State, and Denomination: The Forming of the American Religious Structure," pp. 47–67, in Richey, ed., *Denominationalism,* offers insights on the local nature of the denominations in this era.

78. Bullock, *Emory,* p. 51.

79. Beaty, *Davidson,* pp. 14, 32–33; Scanlon, *Randolph-Macon,* pp. 38, 106–107.

80. Bullock, *Emory,* pp. 88–92; Wallace, *Wofford,* p. 53.

Denominational History
as Public History:
The Lutheran Case

CHRISTA R. KLEIN

Lutherans are burdened with expectations. In 1961 Winthrop Hudson wrote in the last paragraph of his bold *American Protestantism* that Lutherans might play an increasing role in the renewal of American Protestantism. Having been "insulated from American life for a long time," Lutherans still had access to the resources of the Christian past through their confessional tradition, liturgical practice, and communal life.[1] The question at hand—is there a difference in doing denominational history when the group under study bears certain ethnic and confessional traditions—probes more than historiography. It fingers unresolved expectations about a peculiarly Lutheran vocation in American culture.

In *First Things* Mark Noll moved Hudson's simmering pot from the back to the front burner for Lutherans when he called on them to make a distinctively Lutheran contribution to Christianity in America by promoting "in an American accent" their sensibilities about history, political structures, and dogma.[2] Then, in *The Christian Century,* he invoked a Lutheran perspective as an alternative to the predominant Reformed spirit in constructing a narrative for American Christianity in the twentieth century. A Lutheran tack might stress "the dissonance between public success and religious faithfulness," thereby honoring Luther's theology of the cross, which assumes that grace abounds in suffering. Such an alternative plot might elevate "questions of integrity over questions of power."[3]

While occasional and lone sentiments such as those voiced by Hudson and Noll dare not be taken as evidence of a groundswell of interest in what Lutheranism might have to offer, they do echo cadences of the Protestant Reformation that carry implications for doing denominational history. First, they register the judgment that the Protestant influence in American Christianity becomes distorted without certain emphases from the conservative wing of the Reformation. Noll even suggests that the dominant interpretive framework still employed by the leading historians in the second half of the twentieth century has been implicitly Reformed, and therefore denominational, in its conception of the public church, including its presumption to define doctrine for all Americans. Other denominational traditions that have never fit the narrative well may have suggestions to make through the writing of their own histories and their perspectives on the larger picture.

Second, these voices remind us that the purposes of denominational history are more than scholarly. Such history may also provoke the self-understanding necessary for those who bear denominational traditions to attend to the renewal of the churches.

These expectations, while flattering, inflict Lutheranism's historians with a call to public discourse and responsibility that is unfamiliar and uncomfortable. Our historians work privately for the most part, thank you. Let Noll and anyone else mine our tradition as they will, Luther is accessible to everyone, and no one needs a Lutheran gloss to interpret him.

My flippancy cradles some hunches I have about historians' dilemmas in doing Lutheran history. In this chapter I will consider the Lutheran absence from public scholarly efforts in denominational history and then explore the element of isolation in the Lutheran experience as it affects historians. The word *private* will refer to denominational history done for a Lutheran audience of those with historical interests or training, and *public* will refer to the audience of professional historians, with or without any denominational ties. Denominational history as a private practice tells a great deal about this history's current state and its future possibilities. Next, I will consider the institutional character of Lutheranism, particularly in light of the current discussion of institutions and the good society. Finally, I will explore the possibilities for a renovated form of institutional history as denominational history. In so doing, I hope to respond to Noll's suggestion that there is a peculiarly Lutheran slant that can counterbalance other interpretations of American Christianity.

The Antecedent Denominational Narrative

The last significant public treatment of denominational history for Lutherans will serve as a backdrop for this discussion. In the late 1960s half a dozen historians set out to create the narrative history *The Lutherans in North America,* which was published in 1975 as the first joint effort among historians representing the several major strands of Lutheranism.[4] These professors had distinguished themselves for their historical research on various organizational, regional, ethnic, and theological pieces of the Lutheran narrative. Each was well positioned at a church-related school: the editor, E. Clifford Nelson, at a college, and five others at theological seminaries.[5] Fortress Press, then expanding its inventory of academic books, hosted the discussions that led to the publication.

The volume aimed to acknowledge the changing character of Lutheranism, particularly the belief that all those many Lutherans of various church backgrounds and ethnic groups needed a sense of one narrative that would, in the words of the cover note, point "beyond family memories to an ongoing and continuing life of which we and our children are a living part." Increased printing costs compressed an ambitious project, begun in 1965 with a plan to produce a book of documents, a scholarly interpretive history, and a popular abridgment, into a single volume. In his preface Nelson emphasizes the addition of sociological analysis to the more familiar history of theological debates and institutional proliferation to make the story "a natural outgrowth of the immigrant's cargo of European influence and his acculturation to the new North American environment."[6]

Sadly, the beachhead established in contemporary scholarship by the 1975 volume was not expanded to include widespread discussion about Lutheranism's North American narrative either among Lutheran historians or in the larger historical guild.[7] *The Lutherans in North America* ended an era of denominational history without beginning another. No collection of documents embracing all the Lutheran traditions has yet appeared.[8] A fine popular history, written at the time of the merger of three church bodies to form the Evangelical Lutheran Church in America, has been allowed to go out of print.[9]

Perhaps the scope of *The Lutherans in North America* was too daunting.[10] The particular in Lutheranism always threatens to sabotage generalizations about the whole. Students using the book easily become overwhelmed by the many pieces and viewpoints present. Moreover, the multiple subplots within the volume invite notice of all that is missing, especially the stories of lay Lutherans, women, and the smaller Lutheran ethnic populations, including Latinos and African-Americans.[11] Subsequent research is demonstrating that the various Lutheran communities or movements had different aptitudes for absorbing German and Scandinavian neopietism and confessionalism, as well as American evangelical revivalism. Regional variations are proving especially crucial and invite historians to consider cultural geography and politics when examining theological debates.[12] Ultimately, Lutheranism is a house divided, even about its Protestant and Catholic origins and proclivities.

The 1975 history illustrates another problem. Some or all of the authors may have hoped that immigrant history would provide a plane above Lutheran infighting upon which to build a narrative structure. Unfortunately, a story line of acculturation posits more stability and uniformity in American culture than exists and anticipates a preemptory telos: Americanization becomes an end in itself. Such a narrative represses further interpretive leads. Nevertheless, at the same time, immigration studies put the narrative in touch with the discussion of cultural studies in religious research.

The Lutherans in North America could have provided a bridge into the university world of both religious studies and church history, but instead the path looped back in upon itself. Instead of invoking a conversation outside Lutheran circles, the book provided the framework for a flourishing local Lutheran historical industry that continues to mine the rich lodes of Lutheran peoples' and pastors' experiences. Coincidental with the Fortress project, regional and national historical societies have grown up.[13] Local markets for parish and regional histories and workshops are strong and are encouraged through grants from two nonprofit Lutheran fraternal insurance societies. Archival collections continue to grow and to gain professional oversight under the impetus of reorganization in the two largest Lutheran church bodies, the Evangelical Lutheran Church in America and the Lutheran Church–Missouri Synod. Independent Lutheran journals pursue scholarly articles on the historical experience of American Lutheranism.

But Lutheran denominational history rarely breaches the walls of the academy as a subject for discussion, nor does it appear to be missed. This is a judgment about narrative history, not about the occasional remarkable monograph. Yet the Lutheran absence is noteworthy. Through size, drama, and personalities, twentieth-century Lutheranism gets its share of media attention. Nevertheless, other Protestant stories have yielded far more public historical scholarship. For example, the troubles wracking the Southern Baptist Convention are provoking a degree of academic analysis that was never equaled during or following the battle in the Missouri Synod in the 1970s. The same can be said when comparing the responses of Presbyterian and Lutheran scholars to uncertain theological or organizational malaise within their respective denominations.[14] In what has become a self-perpetuating cycle, one major Lutheran publishing house, Augsburg Fortress, selectively pursues the academic market in religion and judges that market insufficient to support an aggressive program of publication in denominational history.[15] The other, Concordia Publishing House, publishes denominational history but since the crisis in the Missouri Synod has relinquished its reputation for critical scholarship in this field.

Nowhere is the Lutheran absence in contemporary scholarship on American religious history more evident than in the traditional center for historical studies, the Lutheran theological school. The study of American church history at most Lutheran seminaries remains a makeshift effort with its own internal standards. A 1989 survey of the curricula in church history followed at fourteen Lutheran theological schools revealed that standards of scholarship, choices of subject matter, and the relative standing of both the history of Lutheranism and American church history appeared to be determined on comparatively narrow institutional grounds, chiefly the school's own heritage and the interests of particular faculty members. Such internal standards would never be applied to two staples of Lutheran theological education: historical studies of the sixteenth-century Protestant Reformation and biblical studies.

The questionnaire produced little evidence that Lutheran seminary faculties are engaged in any thoroughgoing discussion of the place of American church history, not to mention denominational studies, within theological education.[16] The apparent isolation of most seminary professors and students from current debates over the narrative of American religious history is an unfortunate commentary on the state of denominational history and its uses in the education of future clergy and lay leaders.

The Problem of Denominational History as Private Practice

This relative indifference to the narrative of the Lutheran experience in America merits some soul searching, especially when contrasted with the continuing interest of and the public contributions made by Lutheran scholars in Reformation history and biblical studies. If a lively tradition of historical scholarship reflects only Lutheranism's biblical and confessional commitments and refuses to incorporate the study of Lutheranism on this side of the Atlantic or in the centuries since the sixteenth, then maybe American Lutheranism suffers from its own form of "Protestant primitivism."[17]

Perhaps Garrison Keillor's depiction of the shy Midwesterner applies to some denominational historians, but Lutherans have also had their share of public historians, such as Jaroslav Pelikan, Sydney Ahlstrom, Martin E. Marty, and Arthur Carl Piepkorn, who have made their mark as narrators. One might even speculate that, like the mythical town of Lake Wobegon, Lutheranism provides a significant perch from which to view the rest of Christianity. Lutheran eyes are likely to be attentive to differences in doctrine and in practice, faith, and order.

But we seem to become less confident, or perhaps we become bored, when we survey our own American array of practices and experiences. Russell Richey's project on the several languages of early American Methodism may provide some clues for sorting out the mix.[18] While contemporary religious research labels us as blending in with the rest of moderate Protestantism, within Lutheranism we have trouble fathoming each other's gut pieties, and it's politically incorrect even to try to name them. Treading in such forbidden territory might locate examples such as the following. A hard-drinking bellicose Slovak who loves to debate theology violates the sensibilities of a temperate and circumspect Swede who prefers finding means for accommodation, while both frustrate a straight-speaking and self-conscious African-American when they fail to get immediately to the ethical heart of the matter. Lutherans raised in ethno-cultural pieties are pained by any expectation that they embrace each other's histories, with their diverse liturgical and political manifestations, as part of the same denominational narrative. Differences of tone and priority, vision and historical loyalties are rooted deeply in American Lutheranism's experience.

But I believe that the root challenge for Lutheran denominational history is even more basic than the problem of contending with heterogeneity, as difficult as that is. Historians of all types would have to make their peace with the institutional character of Lutheranism to find sufficient motivation for engaging in or being engaged by its study. While such a proposal hardly seems radical in the first instance, it would require weaning denominational history from a larger Protestant narrative that favors participation in particular social reform movements as the mark of an American church. The fact that Lutheranism's history is hardly coterminous with the history of reform has always been a source of comment by outsiders and, since the mid-twentieth century, a regular topic of self-consciousness and embarrassment among Lutherans; it is likely the most popular dissertation topic among Lutheran denominational historians.[19]

I would argue that the ordering of society through the creation, modification, and sustenance of religious institutions is also a characteristically American activity, one necessarily a priori to social reform. As a team of authors headed by Robert N. Bellah suggests in *The Good Society,* Americans have not only come to take that task for granted, they have chosen increasingly to honor the needs and wants of individuals over institutions to the point that our institutional ecology is in disarray and our citizens malformed.[20]

Lutherans, like many other immigrant religious populations, reveled in the opportunity to embody their understanding of their religious heritage in institutions that were legalized and shaped by American cultural practices. The evolution among Lutherans of the family, parish, school, fraternal aid society, women's aid and missionary society, college, seminary, hospital, homes for the orphaned, elderly, retarded, and convalescing, and regional and national denominational organizations testify to Lutherans' willingness to engage with American culture to achieve their religious purposes.

This characteristically Lutheran focus on human community at a time when most immigrants were strangers to each other found little appreciation among those engaged in religious and political movements such as the Social Gospel and Progressivism. Now, in the late twentieth century, African-Americans and recent immigrants, including Hispanic and Asian-Americans, crave the same economic and social conditions that gave German, Slovak, and Scandinavian Lutherans the liberty to build and to connect religious and other communities that embodied their traditions.

The shaping of the mindset of Lutheran historians in graduate schools may exacerbate a bias against exploring the institutional life of American Lutherans. The university, after all, is the bastion of the best and the worst of Lockean individualism. While honoring open inquiry, it tends to breed dogmatic anti- or at least a-institutionalism in its clients. In graduate school, many of us who now are either private or public historians of religion first learned how to distance ourselves intellectually from the grasp of the denominational institutions that had spawned us. Some of us liked that and some of us did not. And I suspect that, like others, Lutheran historians live with considerable ambivalence.

I recall that those colleagues of mine in the department of American civilization at the University of Pennsylvania in the late 1960s who were interested in religion were a motley bunch. Many of us were desperate to make sense of our own pasts or at least to tame through social analysis the confining cultures that seemed not to have prepared us for the times. Our professors, whatever their religious biographies, often flaunted their own liberation within the hard-cussing genteel life of academic freedom.

The academic study of religion teases historians into thinking of their own experiences and traditions as a private cache. Knowing the cost of living with a religious subculture, we enjoy the intellectual distance to choose from this reserve what works for us. Moreover, the academic autonomy and the student culture in which we are trained to be independent scholars often devalue the very institution that is protecting our academic freedom. In the university we are privileged to etch out personal domains with little regard for the larger institutional ones in which our own narratives are embedded.

This process may be even more wrenching for students from traditions that are not well mirrored in the scholarship of American religion. The graduate study of religion is no easy place in which to learn about the denominational history of Lutherans. The Lutheran narrative is not part of the discourse, does not fit the standard chronologies or measures or power, demands more than the usual facility in foreign languages, and only rarely finds its way—and usually as example or exception—into creative monographs. A student of denominational history must seek self-education, which has its limitations, since professors will have had scant exposure to the primary sources or the dogmatic and cultural complexity of Lutheranism. Such experience is likely to fan the suspicion either that specialization in denominational history holds few possibilities for publishing or employment or that it consigns one to being a major player in a smaller, more parochial world. Thus the cycle of Lutheran absence in the public study of American religion gets perpetuated.

Institutional History as Moral History

The study of denominational Lutheranism could be a more valuable asset for Lutherans and for the narrative of American Christianity if historians were to mine Lutheranism's theological insights about institutions while also examining its institutional experience. Nancy Ammerman's description of the shifting terrain of denominations categorizes the current denominational conditions along three dimensions—faith and practice, organization, and cultural reality. Those same dimensions can also be explored by describing a denomination as a constellation of institutions, that is, a historical network of forms of human community in which certain traditions of Christian practice are housed. Such a constellation has historical density, since it comprises various individual, social, and religious stories embedded within one another. The historian's job is to unearth and to explore those interrelated narratives and thereby to learn how in the past people have made sense of themselves in their surroundings as they pursued their purposes.

Alasdair MacIntyre suggests in *After Virtue* that traditions are in good order when they embody "continuities of conflict." One might think that MacIntyre had read an account of the confessional arguments and their institutional manifestations in nineteenth-century American Lutheranism before he developed the idea, although Lutherans may have been weak on virtue in their rabid defense of tradition. MacIntyre describes such conflicts as institutional: central to the common life of a university, a farm, or a hospital, bearing as it does a tradition of practices, is an argument over what those institutions ought to be.[21]

His analysis of institutions has the value of introducing ethical categories into the study of their structures. Institutions are the social settings necessary to sustain certain practices; they attend to the "external goods" of allocating and gathering resources and assigning roles, status, and influence that sustain the pursuit of goods internal to practices. Denominational constellations of institutions embody traditional practices. By MacIntyre's analysis, both the quality and the corruptibility of those institutions depend upon the exercise, by those charged with pursuing institutional purposes, of virtues such as courage, justice, truthfulness, integrity, and constancy and upon the leaders' "having an adequate sense of the traditions to which one belongs or which confront one."[22]

In good Aristotelian fashion, MacIntyre recalls the quest for the good as a personal and a social quest shaped by the traditions of which we are a part. The history of any quest explores its purposes along with the self-knowledge revealed along the way. MacIntyre's remedy for the excesses of individualism depends heavily on both the implicitly narrative form of human self-understanding and the explicit task of telling about that narrative through history. Such an analysis bestows a moral role on the historian that may hardly be welcomed.

Asking a scholar to tend to moral history is like sending Jonah to Ninevah. Who wants it? MacIntyre is not alone in imagining (and playing) this role. The authors of *The Good Society* have underscored the same need when they argue that the process of creating and recreating institutions is never morally neutral because institutions "live and die by ideas of right and wrong and conceptions of the good." Furthermore, institutions create us by shaping the metaphorical way in which we norm institutions and actions.[23]

To conceive of denominational history as the moral history of institutions would enable historians to explore a basic insight from the

Reformation—that God's work of ordering the world differs from this work of saving it. When that distinction is maintained, the human task is necessarily provisional. As Mark Noll has pointed out in *One Nation Under God?*, American Lutherans have a potential contribution in their theology of government, since they do not expect social reform to be salvific and therefore may be less tempted than other religious and secular types to pursue social reform to extremes that confuse the work of God with human efforts.[24]

If historians of denominational Lutheranism pursue the study of Lutheran institutions as moral history, then the quality and character of Lutheranism's ordering of human communities in America will become a matter of public record. Such a history would remind Lutherans that their privacy is a false privacy. Lutheran stories are embedded in a larger religious and cultural conversation about how to be faithful under American conditions, which necessarily include regional, ethnic, class, and gender variations. The narrative of Lutheranism cannot be understood apart from accounts of its various institutions, nor are those accounts separate from the experience of other religious communities in America.[25]

Denominational history as the public history of institutions and their morality treats a tradition as a conversation not only within itself but also, and sometimes by proxy, with other traditions. The private practice of denominational history among Lutherans suggests that Lutheranism is a tradition that does not take its American embodiment seriously and thus tends to make Lutheranism invisible to others. Denominational Lutheranism does not need history to press on for a fresh and more American start, as some would argue, but instead to live more self-consciously and critically with its own institutional past.[26] That past is an integral part of the American Christian narrative, and its recovery is critical to American religious history.

NOTES

1. Winthrop Hudson, *American Protestantism* (Chicago: University of Chicago Press, 1961), p. 176.

2. Mark A. Noll, "The Lutheran Difference," *First Things* 20 (February 1992): 36–40; an earlier version with references appears as "Ethnic, American or Lutheran? Dilemmas for a Historic Confession in the New World," *Lutheran Theological Seminary Bulletin* 71 (Winter 1991): 17–43.

3. Mark A. Noll, "The Public Church in the Years of Conflict," *The Christian Century* (May 15–22, 1991): 557.

4. E. Clifford Nelson, ed., *The Lutherans in North America* (Philadelphia: Fortress Press, 1975).

5. Clifford Nelson, the editor, taught at St. Olaf College (American Lutheran Church). The others were leading seminary figures: Theodore G. Tappert at Lutheran Theological Seminary in Philadelphia (Lutheran Church in America), H.

George Anderson at Lutheran Southern Seminary (Lutheran Church in America), August R. Suelflow at Concordia Historical Institute, St. Louis (Lutheran Church–Missouri Synod), Eugene Fevold at Luther Theological Seminary, St. Paul (American Lutheran Church), and Fred W. Meuser at Evangelical Lutheran Theological Seminary, Columbus (American Lutheran Church).

6. *Ibid.,* pp. vii–viii.

7. For earlier reflections on this observation, see Klein, "Lutherans, Merger and the Loss of History," *The Christian Century* (January 2–9, 1985): 18–20. Greenwood Press and Augsburg Fortress have each contracted with single authors for narrative histories. L. DeAne Lagerquist and Todd W. Nichol are currently at work on them.

8. One is currently projected at Augsburg Fortress Publishers. Correspondence to the author from Omar Bonderud, vice president/publishing, Augsburg Fortress Publishers, 26 November 1990.

9. Todd W. Nichol, *All These Lutherans: Three Paths toward a New Lutheran Church* (Minneapolis: Augsburg Publishing House, 1986).

10. I wrestled with the narrative in "Lutheranism," in *Encyclopedia of the American Religious Experience,* ed. Charles H. Lippy and Peter W. Williams, 3 vols. (New York: Charles Scribner's Sons, 1988), 1:431–450.

11. For example, see L. DeAne Lagerquist, *From Our Mother's Arms: A History of Women in the American Lutheran Church* (Minneapolis: Augsburg Publishing House, 1987). Another interpretive theme, ever-widening Lutheran inclusiveness, provided the framework for a history of the Lutheran Church in America before it merged into the Evangelical Lutheran Church in America. See W. Kent Gilbert, *Commitment to Unity: A History of the Lutheran Church in America* (Philadelphia: Fortress Press, 1988).

12. For a remarkable example of the power of regional approaches to Lutheranism, see Richard W. Dishno's insightful article "American Lutheran Historiography: A Regionalist Approach," in "American Lutheranism: Crisis in Historical Consciousness?," ed. August R. Suelflow, *Essays and Reports 1988* 13 (The Lutheran Historical Conference, St. Louis, Missouri, 1990): 29–49.

13. A national organization, the Lutheran Historical Conference, was founded in 1962 to promote research, documentation, and the preservation of resources on the experience of Lutherans from all sectors of the denominational family in North America. Its membership ranges from 100 to 150 annually and includes archivists, librarians, historians, both with advanced degrees and self-educated, and Lutheran institutions of higher education. An example of a regional society is the Lutheran Historical Society, founded in 1843 and refounded in 1989, which emphasizes the historical Lutheran experience in the middle colonies and states.

14. See papers on denominational historical self-consciousness and scholarship by James H. Smylie, James Hennesey, Winthrop Hudson, Bill Leonard, Frederick A Norwood, and Albert N. Keim in "American Lutheranism: Crisis in Historical Consciousness?," pp. 98–202. See also *The Presbyterian Presence,* ed. Milton J Coalter, John M. Mulder, and Louis B. Weeks (Louisville, Ky.: Westminster/John Knox, (1990–92).

15. "We need to plan with the full knowledge that books in some areas, like American Lutheran history, have a potential audience much more narrow than that of so much of our book publishing." Bonderud to Klein, 26 November 1990.

16. Richard W. Dishno, ed., "American Lutheran History in Theological Edu-

cation: Fourteen Seminary Profiles and a Report," (Chicago: The Lutheran Historical Conference, 1990). Available through Concordia Historical Institute, 801 De Mun Avenue, St. Louis, Missouri 63105.

17. See Richard T. Hughes and C. Leonard Allen, *Illusions of Innocence: Protestant Primitivism in America, 1630–1875* (Chicago: University of Chicago Press, 1988).

18. Russell E. Richey, *Early American Methodism* (Bloomington: Indiana University Press, 1991).

19. See, for example, references to Lutherans in Walter Rauschenbusch, *Christianity and the Social Crisis* (New York: Macmillan, 1907) and *Christianizing the Social Order* (New York: Macmillan, 1913); Andre Siegfried, *America Comes to Age: A French Analysis* (1927); Mark A. Noll, *One Nation Under God? Christian Faith and Political Action in America* (San Francisco: Harper & Row, 1988). Notable examples of these dissertations include Lloyd Svendsbye, "The History of a Developing Social Responsibility among Lutherans in America from 1930 to 1960" (Th.D. diss., Union Theological Seminary, 1967), and Paul P. Kuenning, *The Rise and Fall of American Lutheran Pietism* (Macon, Ga.: Mercer University Press, 1988), based on his 1985 Ph.D. dissertation at Marquette University.

20. Robert N. Bellah et al., *The Good Society* (New York: Knopf, 1991).

21. Alasdair MacIntyre, *After Virtue* (Notre Dame, Ind.: University of Notre Dame Press, 1991), p. 206.

22. Ibid., p. 207.

23. Bellah, *The Good Society,* pp. 11–12.

24. Noll, *One Nation Under God?,* pp. 17–22.

25. One example may illustrate the possibilities for such history. In the two-volume work *Pastors and People: German Lutheran and Reformed Churches in the Pennsylvania Field, 1717–1793* (Breinigville, Pa.: The Pennsylvania German Society, 1981), Charles Glatfelter examines the side-by-side history of German Lutheran and Reformed congregations in colonial Pennsylvania. Narratives of these two bodies and stories of each of their pastors and congregations render both the Lutheran and the Reformed experience more intelligible. These church Germans had come from the same states along the Rhine, their families were regularly joined by marriage, and at least half their congregations at one time shared church buildings with the other. Neither the German Lutheran nor the Reformed institutions or practices make sense without consideration of those of the other, and yet each tradition's boundaries were quite strong.

26. See, for example, Todd W. Nichol, "The Lutheran Venture and the American Experiment," *The Lutheran Quarterly* (Spring 1992): 154–164. For a thoughtful examination of one church-related university's struggle over its purposes, see James Nuechterlein, "Athens and Jerusalem in Indiana," *The American Scholar* (Summer 1988).

Index

Abbott, Benjamin, 209
African-Americans, 9, 39, 53, 100, 179;
    Baptist churches, 61, 68, 69, 81,
    256, 258n.7; Methodist churches,
    61, 62, 66, 68, 81; Presbyterian
    churches, 256, 258n.7, 276
African Methodist Episcopal Church,
    60, 65, 66–67, 68–69, 72n.32,
    210–11; *AME Church Review,* 66
African Methodist Episcopal Zion
    Church, 60, 67, 68, 69
Ahlstrom, Sydney E., 3, 37–38, 40,
    175n.14, 180, 311
Albanese, Catherine L., 40
Alexander, June Granatir, 49
Allen, James B., 194n.7
Allen, Richard, 65, 66, 68, 72n.27,
    211, 241–48, 250, 251, 256
American Academy of Religion, 142
American Board of Commissioners for
    Foreign Missions, 268, 291
American Catholic Historical
    Association, 43, 53
American Church History Series, 7,
    19–20, 21, 24
American Convention for Promoting
    the Abolition of Slavery, 248–49
American Home Missionary Society,
    268
American Society of Church History,
    181
Americanization, 48, 52, 53, 309
Ammerman, Nancy Tatom, 98n.62,
    313

Anderson, H. George, 316n.5
Anderson, William, 251–52
Andrew, James O., 294, 296, 301
Andrews, Doris, 208, 210
Anglicans, 78–81, 93n.13, 165, 177
Anti-Catholic sentiment, 139
Appleby, R. Scott, 51
Asbury, Francis, 209, 241, 244–48,
    253, 256, 296
Augsburg Fortress, 310, 316n.7
Ave Maria, 139, 140
Avery, Valeen T., 194n.7

Backus, Isaac, 10n.10
Bainbridge, William Sims, 128n.5
Bainton, Roland H., 23
Baird, Robert, 6, 10n.15, 82
Baker, Robert A., 118
Baldwin, James, 160n.25
Baptists, 10n.10, 28n.12, 72n.29, 76–
    79 passim, 99, 112, 113, 123, 124,
    127, 149, 204, 241, 257, 265, 282;
    Abyssinian, 68; colleges, 84; and
    denominational identity, 119–21
    passim; against establishments, 80;
    and evangelism, 19, 81; and
    feminism, 125; First Great
    Awakening, 91; as missionary
    association, 77; as popular
    movement, 82; predenominational
    existence of, 92; Second Great
    Awakening, 81, 91; and slavery, 83;
    and the UNIA, 69; white clergy in
    black churches, 68; World